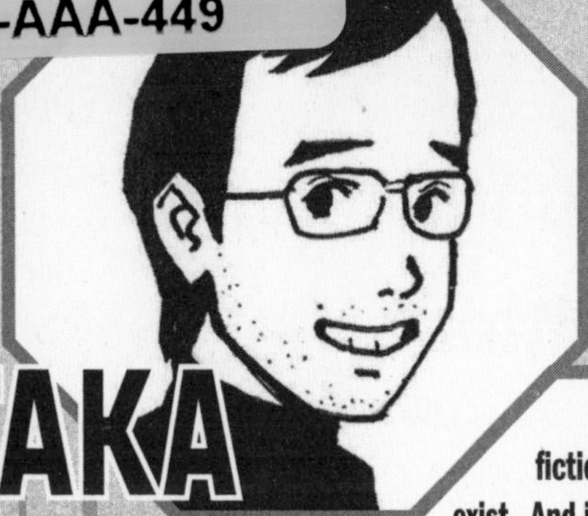

YUTAKA IZUBUCHI

"Nirai-Kanai" is a fictional island. It doesn't exist. And it's not meant to be Okinawa. It's closer to Yakushima or Tanegashima. An island you want to go to but can't. But Nirai-Kanai was taken from an old Okinawan tale of Utopia.

Profile

Born 12/8/58 in Tokyo.
Mech-Designer, Illustrator, Comic Artist. Script, Direction of TV Animation, *RAHXEPHON*. Notable work: *MOBILE POLICE PATLABOR, MOBILE SUIT GUNDAM: CHAR'S COUNTERATTACK* (Mecha Designer).

"Nirai-Kanai," appearing in this issue, is located in the tropical region of Japan, but I've never gone farther south than the Kanto area. I wanna go to the tropics!

Profile

Born 11/8/76.
Debuted in *WEEKLY SHONEN SUNDAY*.
Notable work: *MIAMI GUNS* (Kodansha).

TAKEAKI MOMOSE

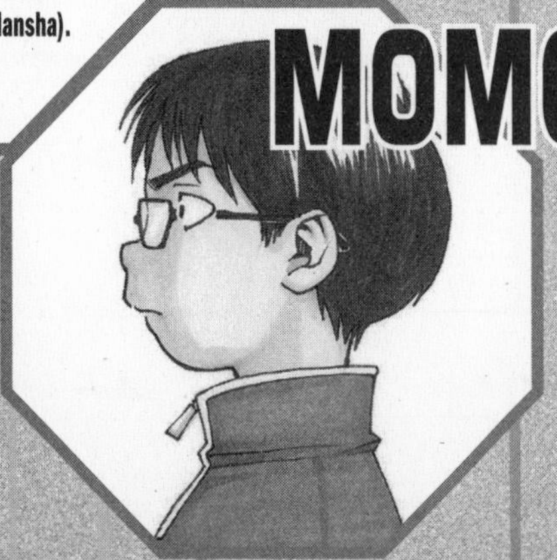

RahXephon
Vol. 2

Action Edition

CREATED BY
YUTAKA IZUBUCHI & BONES
ART BY
TAKEAKI MOMOSE

English Adaptation/Gerard Jones
Translation/Joe Yamazaki
Touch-Up Art & Lettering/Kathryn Renta
Cover, Graphics & Design/Mark Schumann
Editor/Kit Fox

Managing Editor/Annette Roman
Editor in Chief/Alvin Lu
Production Manager/Noboru Watanabe
Sr. Director of Licensing & Acquisitions/Rika Inouye
V.P. of Marketing/Liza Coppola
Executive Vice President/Hyoe Narita
Publisher/Seiji Horibuchi

Printed in the U.S.A.

Published by VIZ, LLC
P.O. Box 77010
San Francisco, CA 94107

Action Edition
10 9 8 7 6 5 4 3 2 1
First printing, June 2004

www.viz.com   store.viz.com   www.animerica-mag.com

CREATED BY **YUTAKA IZUBUCHI**
& **BONES**
ART BY **TAKEAKI MOMOSE**

2
CONTENTS

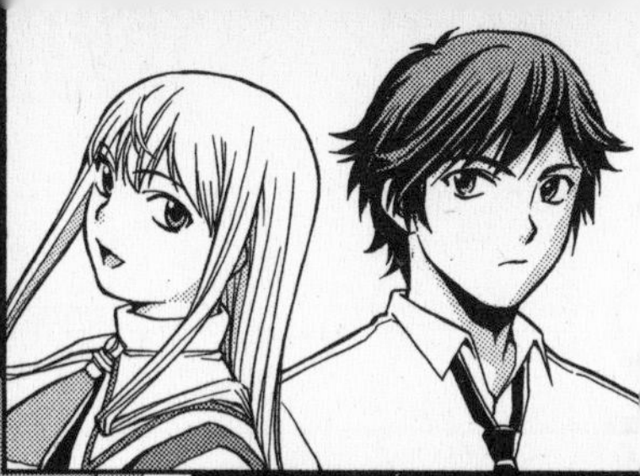

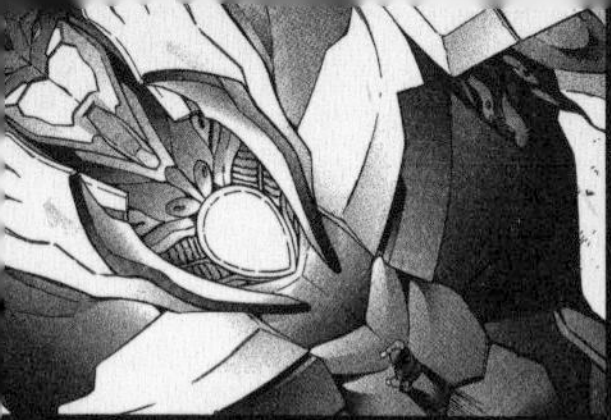

O FAR:

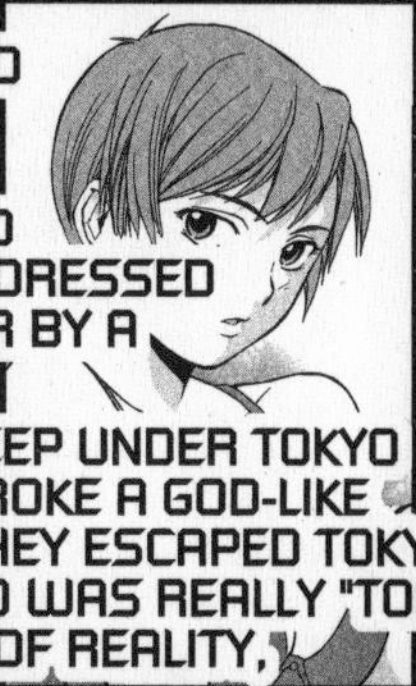

2015 A.D.
SUMMER, TOKYO.
HIGH-SCHOOL STUDENT AYATO KAMINA AND HIS FEMALE ROOMMATE, REIKA MISHIMA, STARTED OUT THEIR DAY LIKE ANY OTHER.

SUDDENLY, A WAR BROKE OUT. AYATO AND REIKA WERE ATTACKED BY STRANGE MEN DRESSED IN BLACK, BUT WERE SAVED FROM DANGER BY A BEAUTIFUL GIRL NAMED HARUKA SHITOW.

LED BY HARUKA, THE TWO WERE TAKEN DEEP UNDER TOKYO BAY TO A GIANT "EGG." FROM THAT EGG BROKE A GOD-LIKE ENTITY CALLED "RAHXEPHON," AND IN IT THEY ESCAPED TOKY THEY LEARNED THAT THE PLACE THEY LIVED WAS REALLY "TOK JUPITER," A CITY CUT OFF FROM THE REST OF REALITY, WHERE EVEN TIME WAS MANIPULATED.

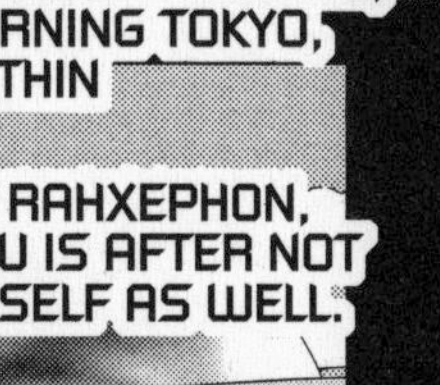

2033 A.D.
THE TRUE YEAR IN THE WORLD BEYOND TOKYO JUPITER.

IT SEEMS THAT HUMANS, IN ORDER TO DEFEAT THE MU, THE MYSTERIOUS ORGANIZATION GOVERNING TOKYO, ESTABLISHED AN ANTI-MU DIVISION WITHIN THE UNITED NATIONS CALLED TERRA.

AYATO, NOW CHOSEN AS THE PILOT OF RAHXEPHON, JOINS TERRA AFTER LEARNING THAT MU IS AFTER NOT ONLY RAHXEPHON, BUT REIKA AND HIMSELF AS WELL.

STILL, NEITHER AYATO NOR REIKA KNOW THEIR TRUE FATE...

mission 6
ALONE

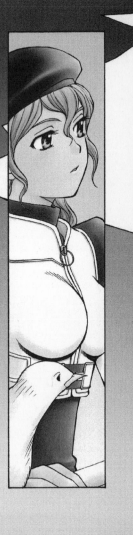

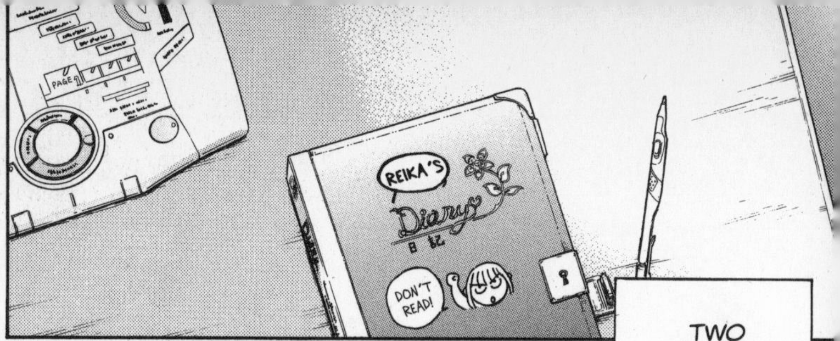
PAGE
REIKA'S
Diary
DON'T READ!

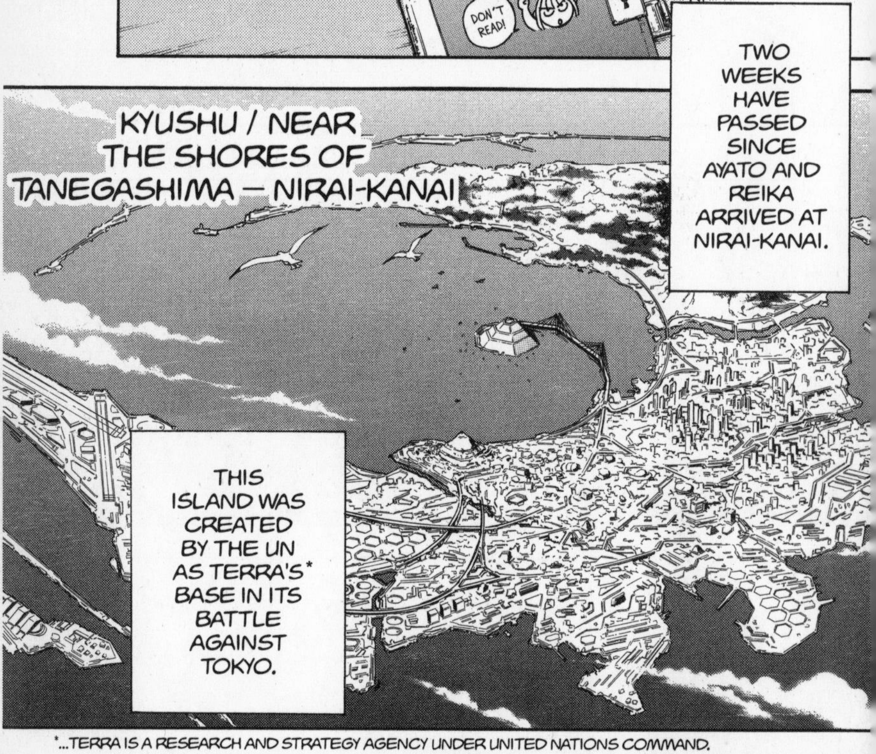
TWO WEEKS HAVE PASSED SINCE AYATO AND REIKA ARRIVED AT NIRAI-KANAI.
KYUSHU / NEAR THE SHORES OF TANEGASHIMA – NIRAI-KANAI
THIS ISLAND WAS CREATED BY THE UN AS TERRA'S* BASE IN ITS BATTLE AGAINST TOKYO.

*...TERRA IS A RESEARCH AND STRATEGY AGENCY UNDER UNITED NATIONS COMMAND.

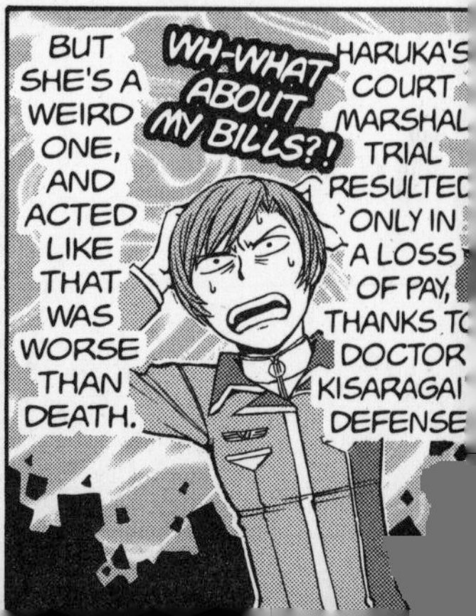
HARUKA'S COURT MARSHAL TRIAL RESULTED ONLY IN A LOSS OF PAY, THANKS TO DOCTOR KISARAGAI DEFENSE
WH-WHAT ABOUT MY BILLS?!
BUT SHE'S A WEIRD ONE, AND ACTED LIKE THAT WAS WORSE THAN DEATH.

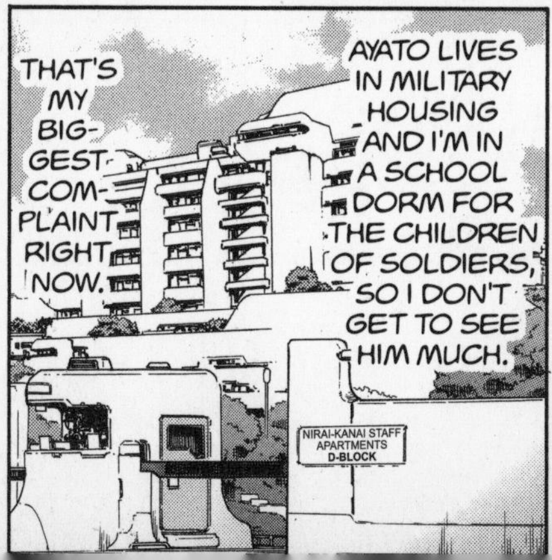
AYATO LIVES IN MILITARY HOUSING AND I'M IN A SCHOOL DORM FOR THE CHILDREN OF SOLDIERS, SO I DON'T GET TO SEE HIM MUCH.
THAT'S MY BIG-GEST COM-PLAINT RIGHT NOW.
NIRAI-KANAI STAFF APARTMENTS D-BLOCK

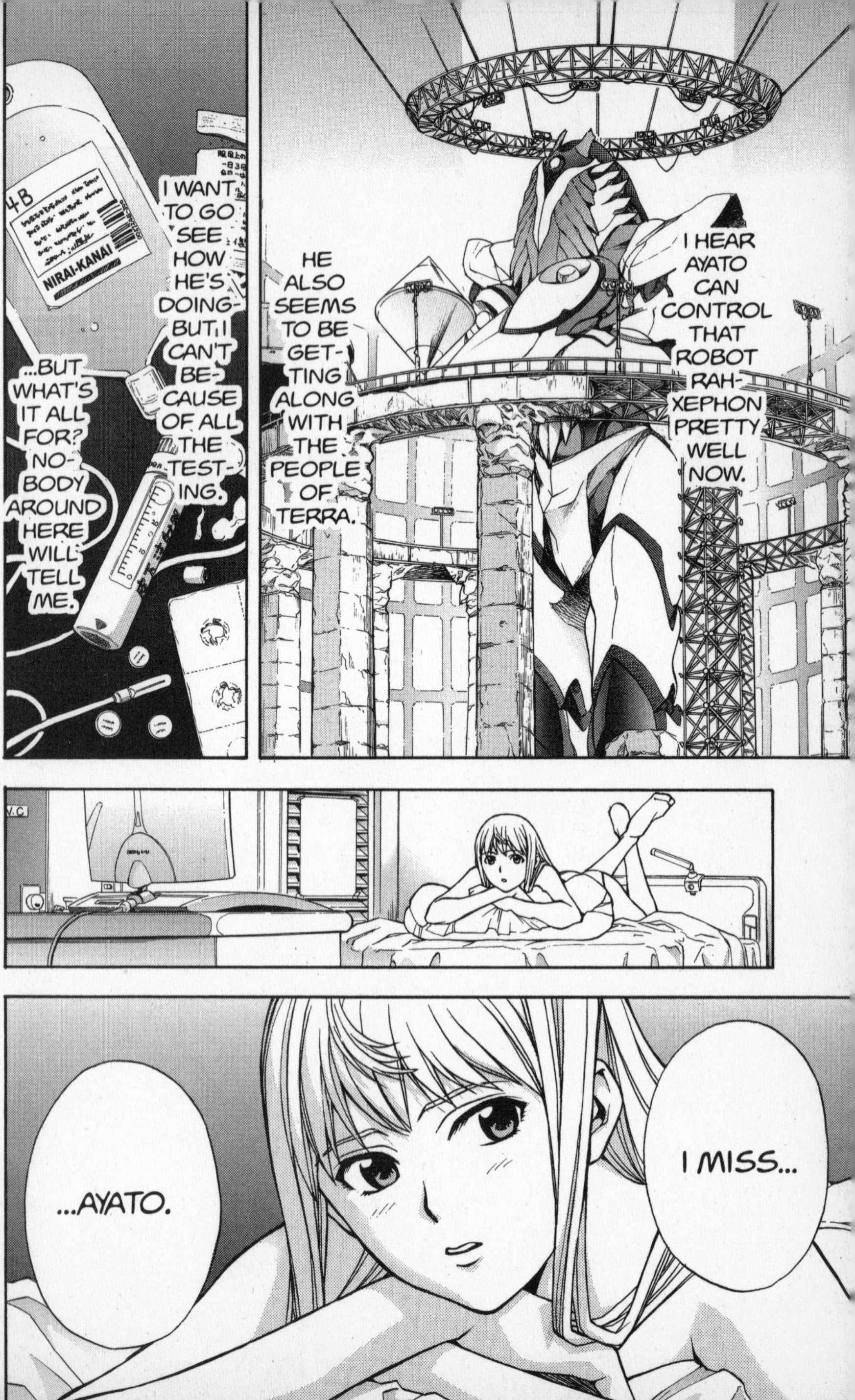
I HEAR AYATO CAN CONTROL THAT ROBOT RAHXEPHON PRETTY WELL NOW.
HE ALSO SEEMS TO BE GETTING ALONG WITH THE PEOPLE OF TERRA.
I WANT TO GO SEE HOW HE'S DOING-BUT I CAN'T BECAUSE OF ALL THE TESTING.
...BUT WHAT'S IT ALL FOR? NOBODY AROUND HERE WILL TELL ME.
4B
NIRAI-KANAI
I MISS...
...AYATO.

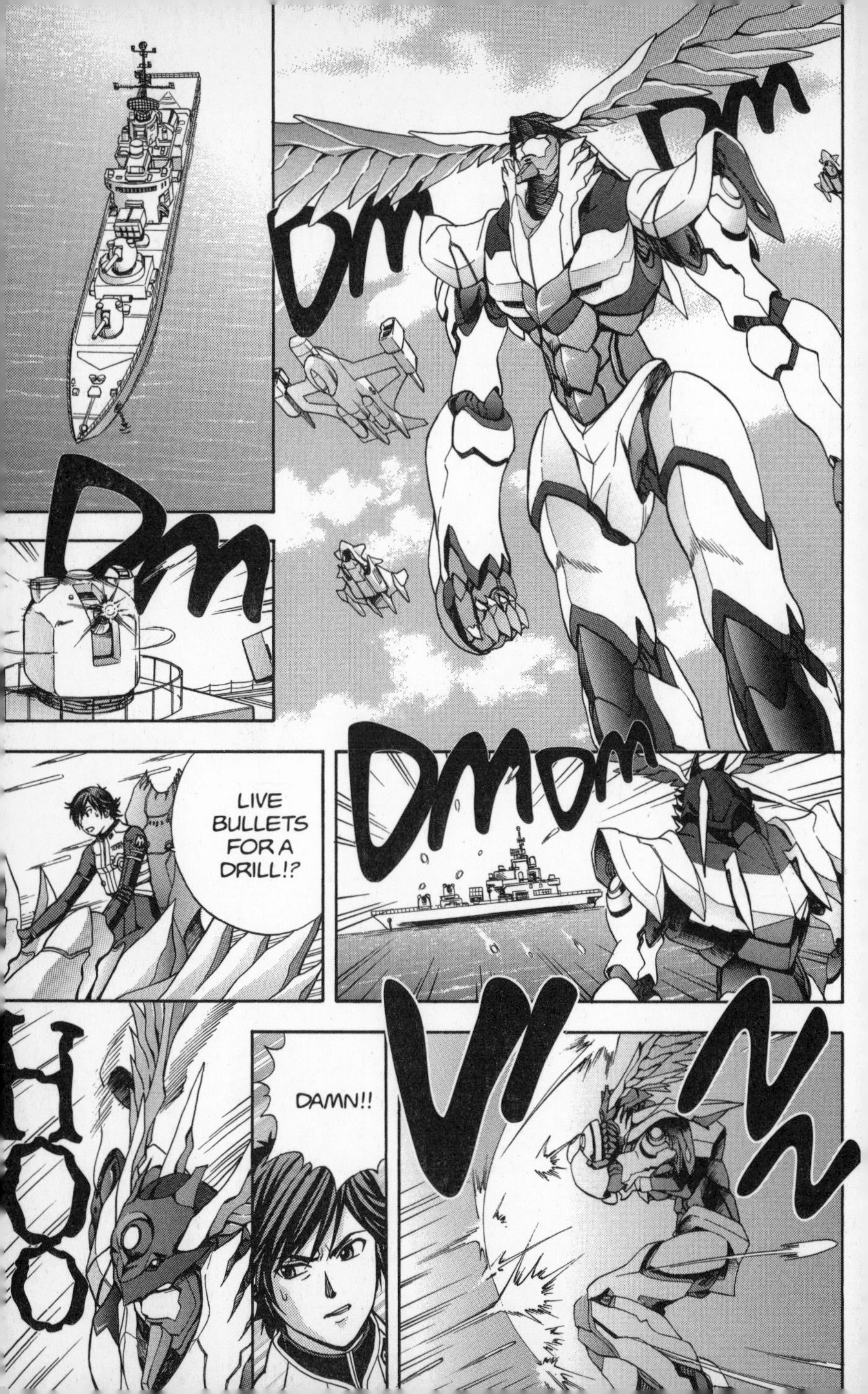
Dm
Dm
Dm
Dm
DmDm
LIVE BULLETS FOR A DRILL!?
DAMN!!
HOO

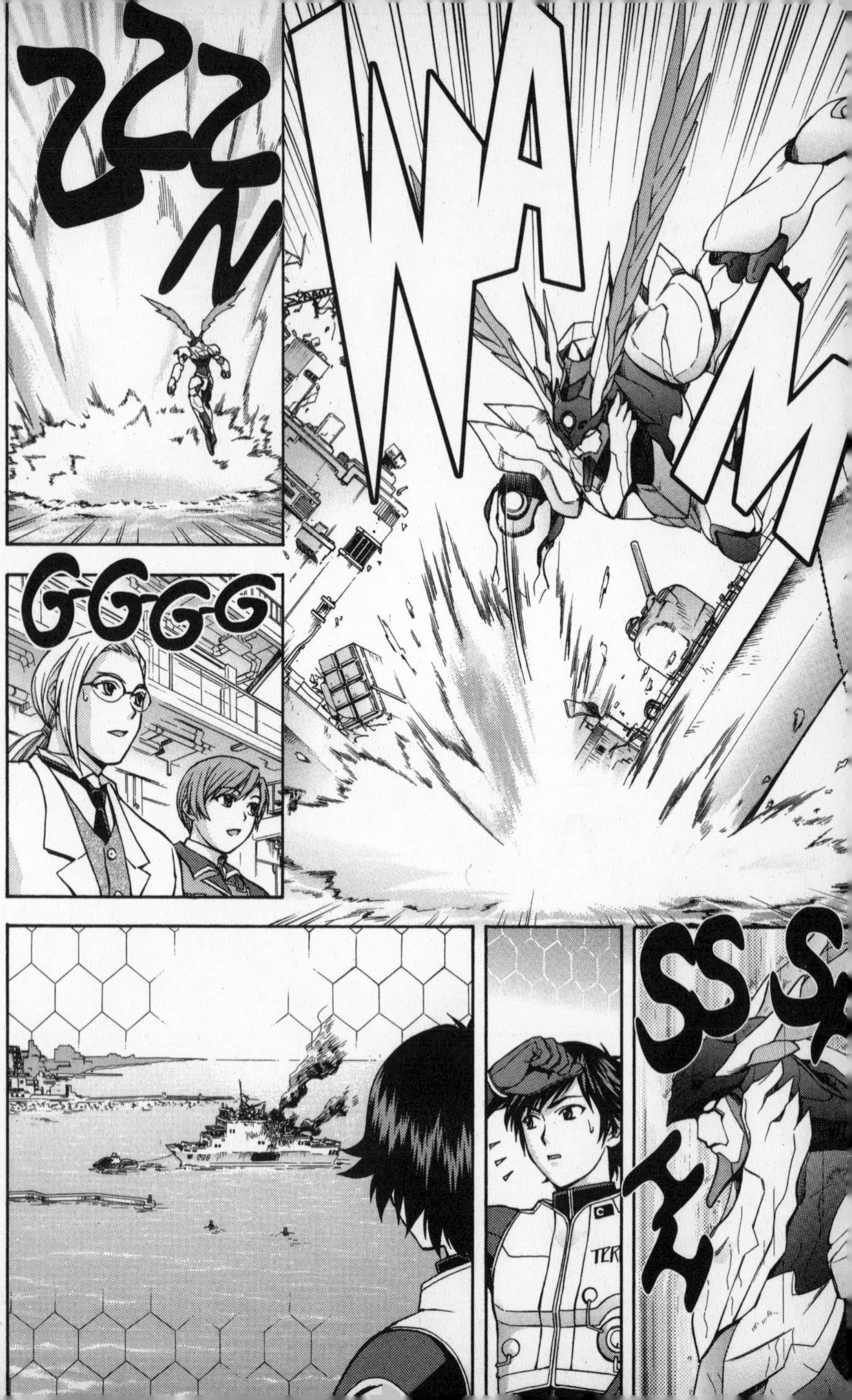
WAMM
ZZZN
GGGG
SSS

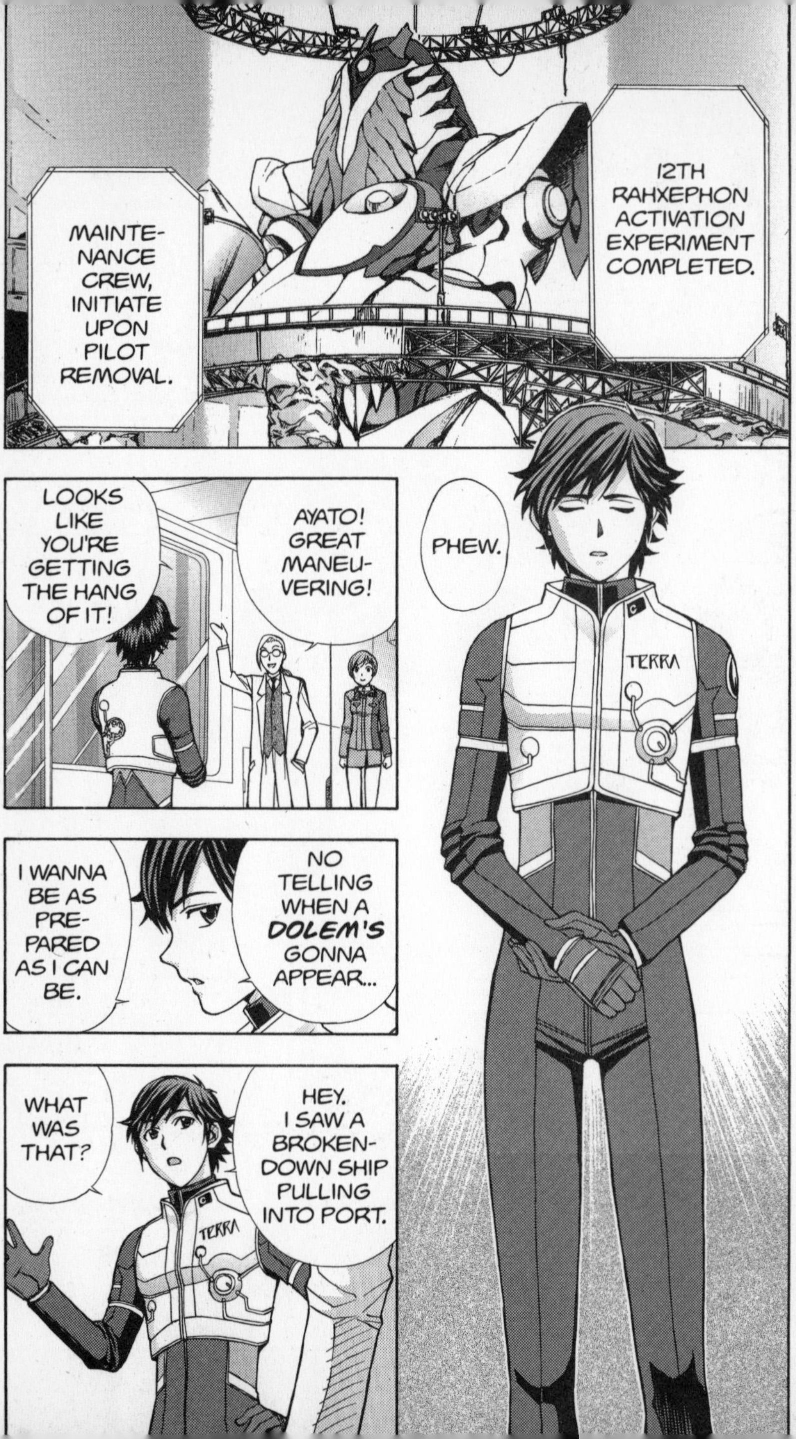
12TH RAHXEPHON ACTIVATION EXPERIMENT COMPLETED.
MAINTENANCE CREW, INITIATE UPON PILOT REMOVAL.
PHEW.
TERRA
AYATO! GREAT MANEUVERING!
LOOKS LIKE YOU'RE GETTING THE HANG OF IT!
NO TELLING WHEN A DOLEM'S GONNA APPEAR...
I WANNA BE AS PREPARED AS I CAN BE.
HEY. I SAW A BROKEN-DOWN SHIP PULLING INTO PORT.
WHAT WAS THAT?
TERRA

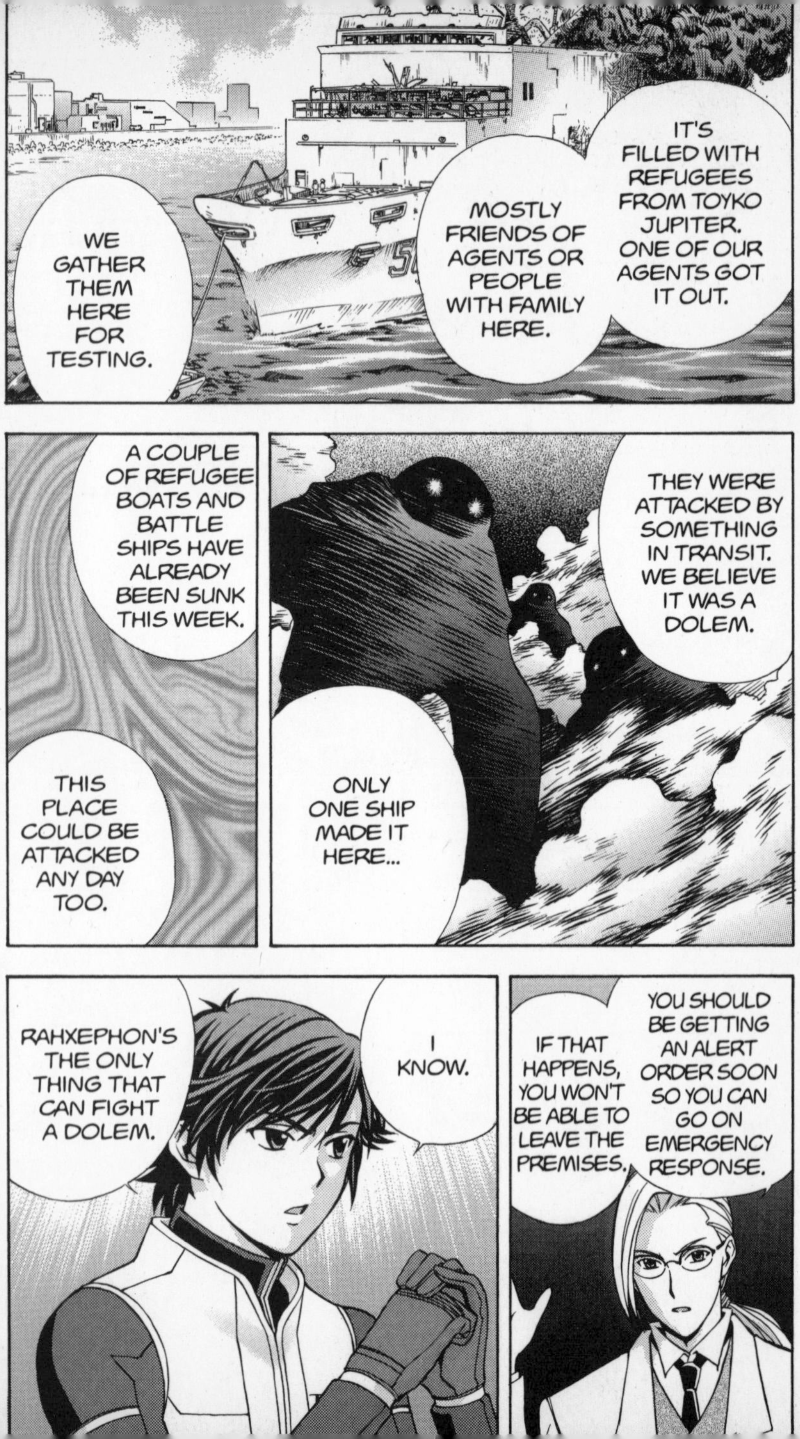
IT'S FILLED WITH REFUGEES FROM TOYKO JUPITER. ONE OF OUR AGENTS GOT IT OUT.
MOSTLY FRIENDS OF AGENTS OR PEOPLE WITH FAMILY HERE.
WE GATHER THEM HERE FOR TESTING.
THEY WERE ATTACKED BY SOMETHING IN TRANSIT. WE BELIEVE IT WAS A DOLEM.
ONLY ONE SHIP MADE IT HERE...
A COUPLE OF REFUGEE BOATS AND BATTLE SHIPS HAVE ALREADY BEEN SUNK THIS WEEK.
THIS PLACE COULD BE ATTACKED ANY DAY TOO.
YOU SHOULD BE GETTING AN ALERT ORDER SOON SO YOU CAN GO ON EMERGENCY RESPONSE.
IF THAT HAPPENS, YOU WON'T BE ABLE TO LEAVE THE PREMISES.
I KNOW.
RAHXEPHON'S THE ONLY THING THAT CAN FIGHT A DOLEM.

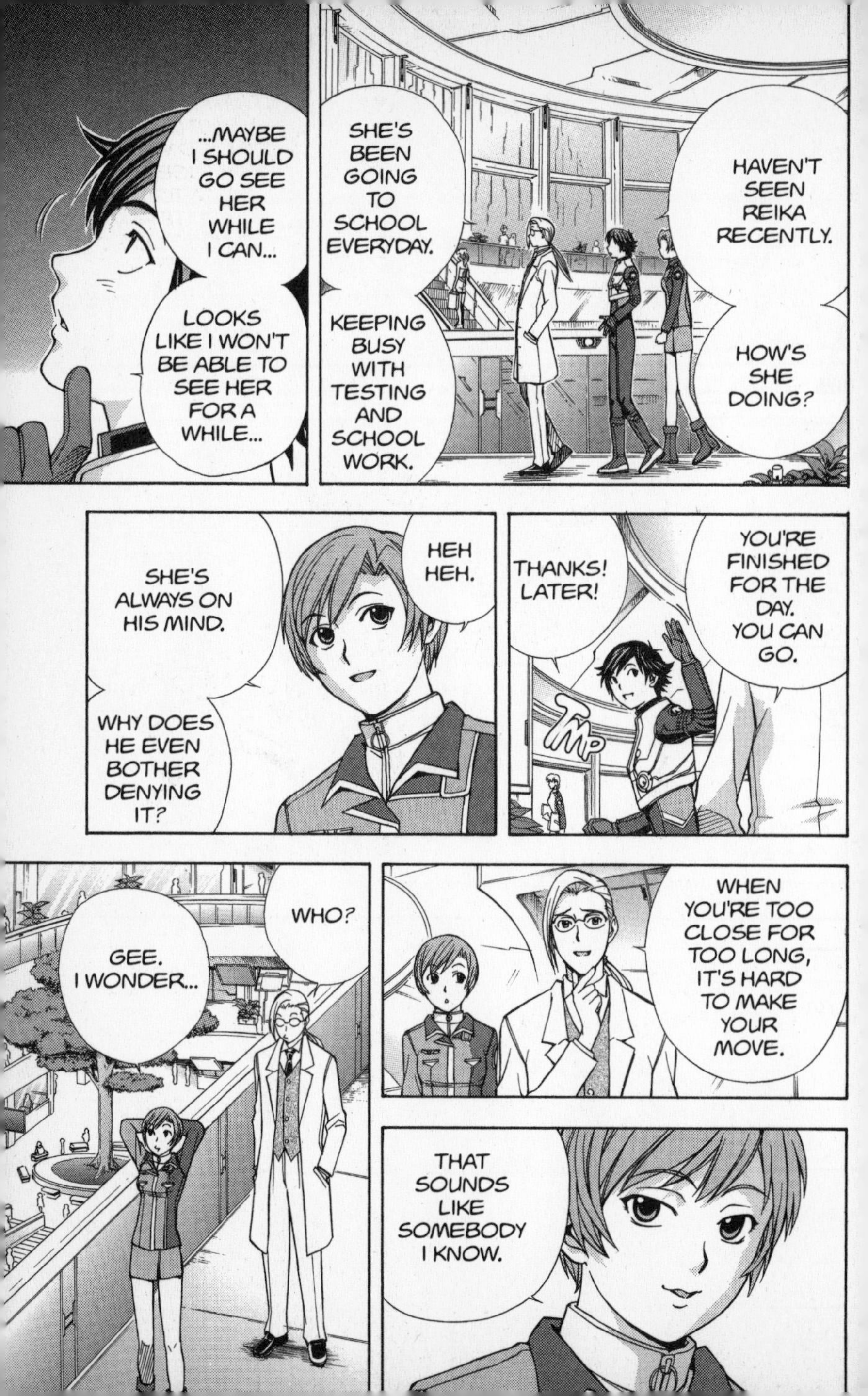
HAVEN'T SEEN REIKA RECENTLY.
HOW'S SHE DOING?
SHE'S BEEN GOING TO SCHOOL EVERYDAY.
KEEPING BUSY WITH TESTING AND SCHOOL WORK.
...MAYBE I SHOULD GO SEE HER WHILE I CAN...
LOOKS LIKE I WON'T BE ABLE TO SEE HER FOR A WHILE...
YOU'RE FINISHED FOR THE DAY. YOU CAN GO.
THANKS! LATER!
TMP
HEH HEH.
SHE'S ALWAYS ON HIS MIND.
WHY DOES HE EVEN BOTHER DENYING IT?
WHEN YOU'RE TOO CLOSE FOR TOO LONG, IT'S HARD TO MAKE YOUR MOVE.
THAT SOUNDS LIKE SOMEBODY I KNOW.
WHO?
GEE. I WONDER...

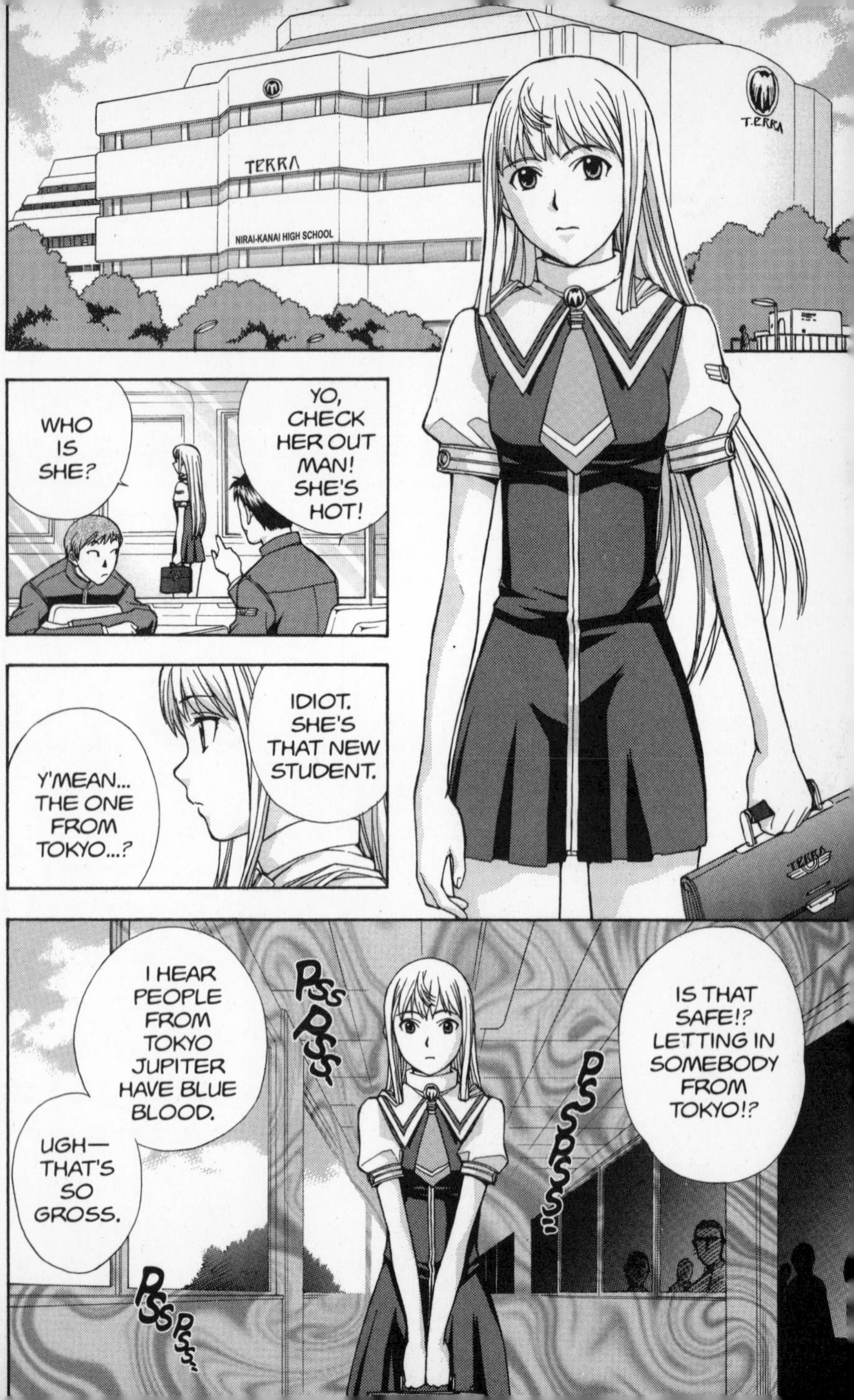
TERRA
NIRAI-KANAI HIGH SCHOOL
TERRA
YO, CHECK HER OUT MAN! SHE'S HOT!
WHO IS SHE?
IDIOT. SHE'S THAT NEW STUDENT.
Y'MEAN... THE ONE FROM TOKYO...?
IS THAT SAFE!? LETTING IN SOMEBODY FROM TOKYO!?
PSSSPSSS!
PSS PSS
I HEAR PEOPLE FROM TOKYO JUPITER HAVE BLUE BLOOD.
UGH— THAT'S SO GROSS.
PSS PSS

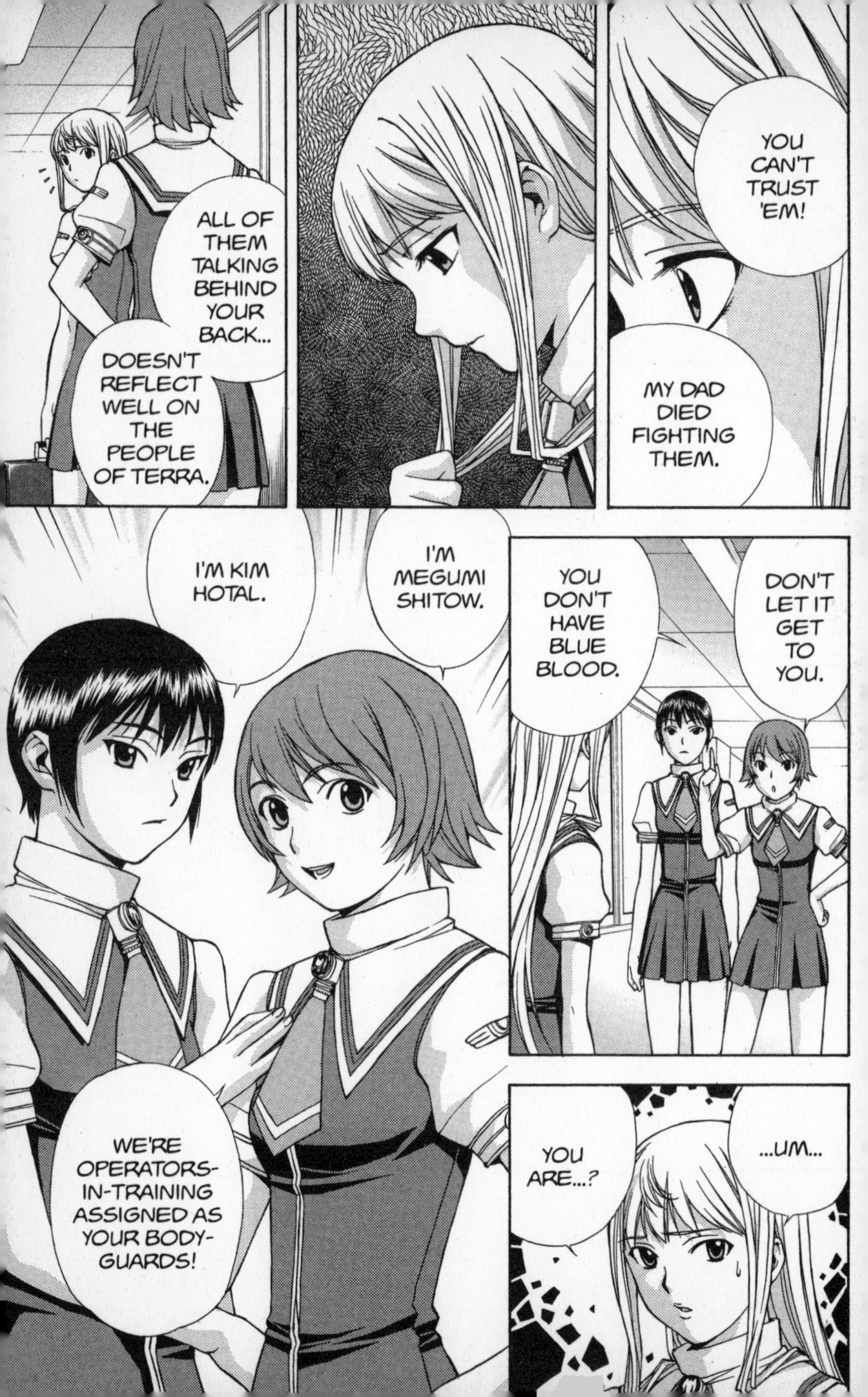
YOU CAN'T TRUST 'EM!
MY DAD DIED FIGHTING THEM.
ALL OF THEM TALKING BEHIND YOUR BACK...
DOESN'T REFLECT WELL ON THE PEOPLE OF TERRA.
DON'T LET IT GET TO YOU.
YOU DON'T HAVE BLUE BLOOD.
...UM...
YOU ARE...?
I'M MEGUMI SHITOW.
I'M KIM HOTAL.
WE'RE OPERATORS-IN-TRAINING ASSIGNED AS YOUR BODY-GUARDS!

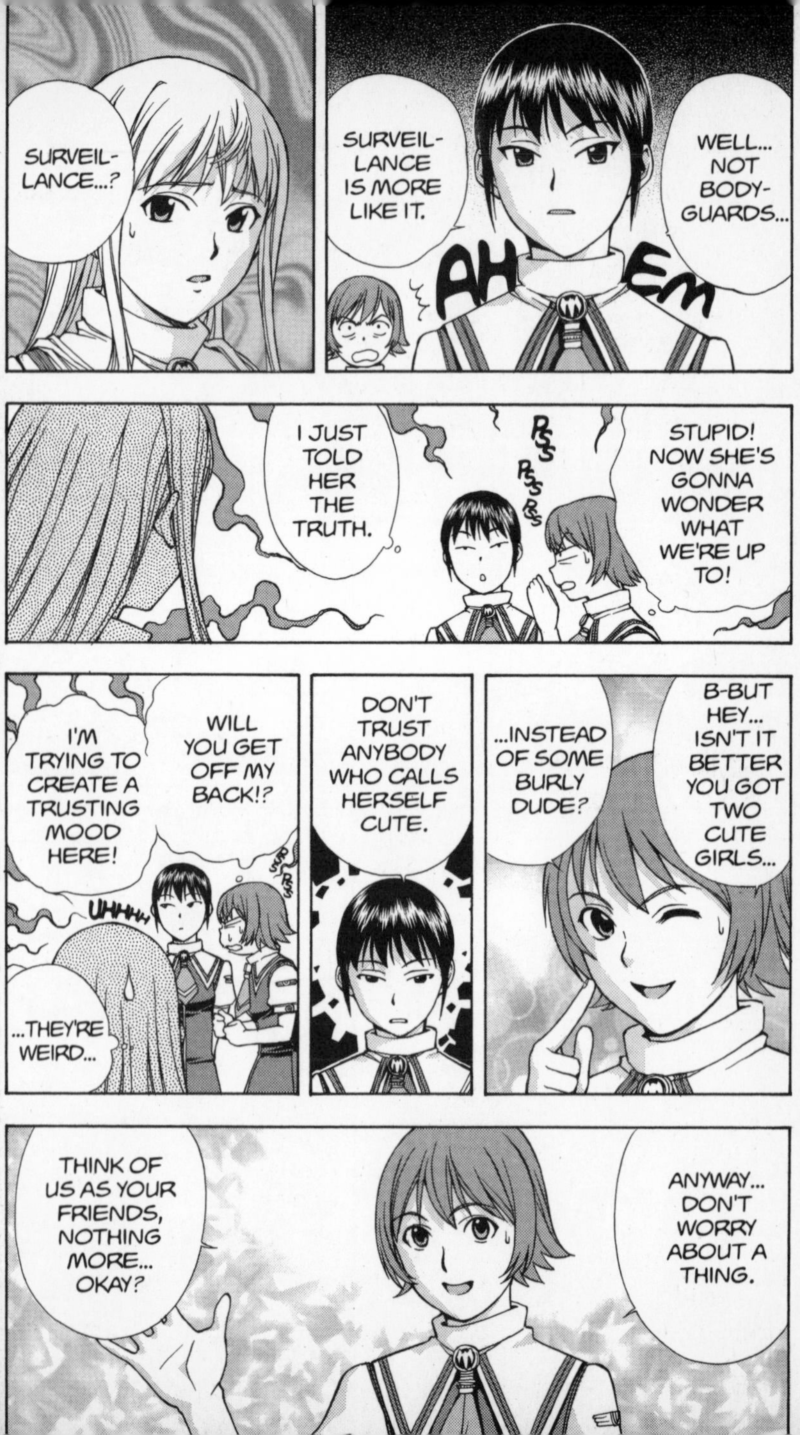
WELL... NOT BODY-GUARDS...
SURVEIL-LANCE IS MORE LIKE IT.
AHEM
SURVEIL-LANCE...?
STUPID! NOW SHE'S GONNA WONDER WHAT WE'RE UP TO!
PSS PSS PSS
I JUST TOLD HER THE TRUTH.
B-BUT HEY... ISN'T IT BETTER YOU GOT TWO CUTE GIRLS...
...INSTEAD OF SOME BURLY DUDE?
DON'T TRUST ANYBODY WHO CALLS HERSELF CUTE.
WILL YOU GET OFF MY BACK!?
I'M TRYING TO CREATE A TRUSTING MOOD HERE!
UHHHH
...THEY'RE WEIRD...
ANYWAY... DON'T WORRY ABOUT A THING.
THINK OF US AS YOUR FRIENDS, NOTHING MORE... OKAY?

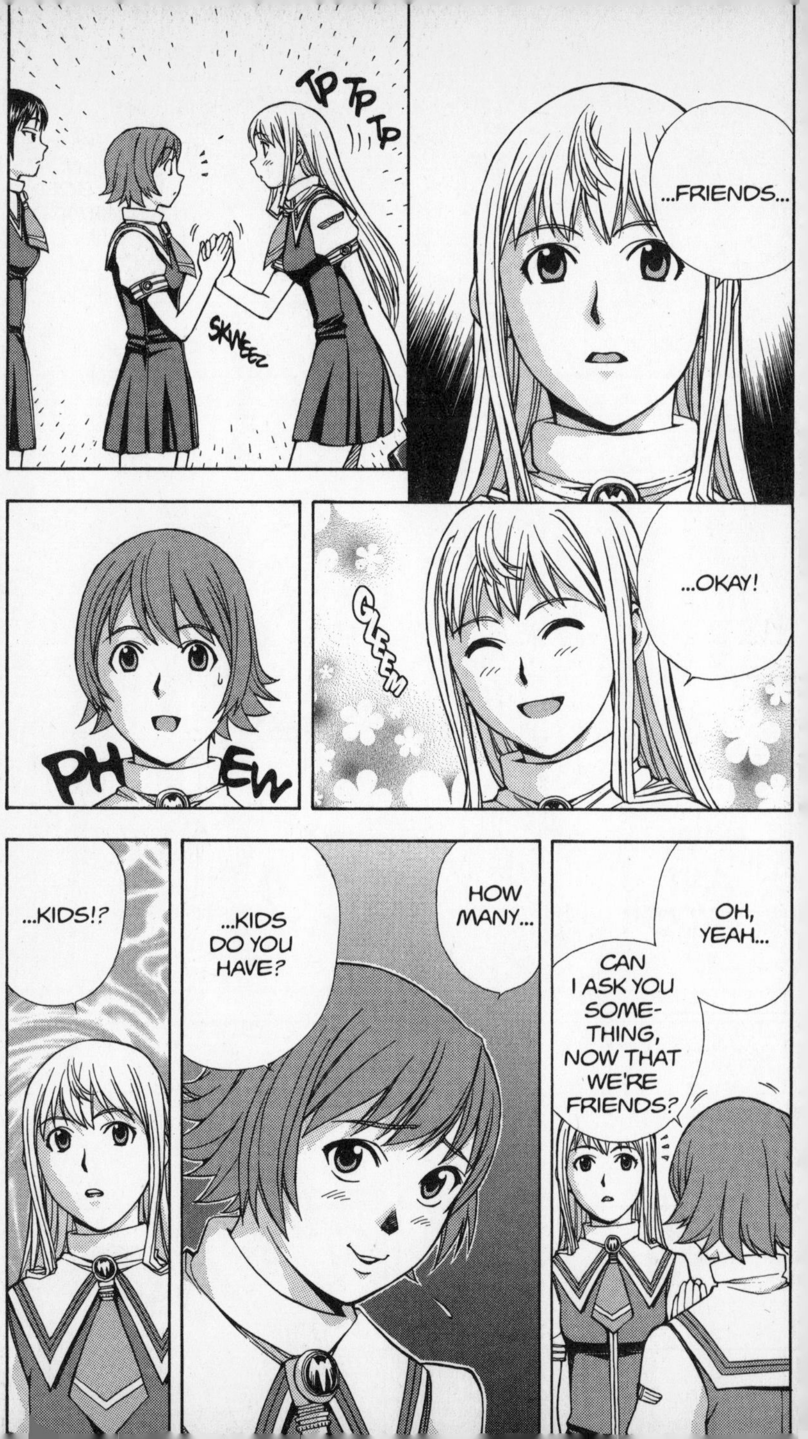
...FRIENDS...
TP TP TP
SKWEEZ
...OKAY!
GLEEM
PHEW
OH, YEAH...
CAN I ASK YOU SOME-THING, NOW THAT WE'RE FRIENDS?
HOW MANY...
...KIDS DO YOU HAVE?
...KIDS!?

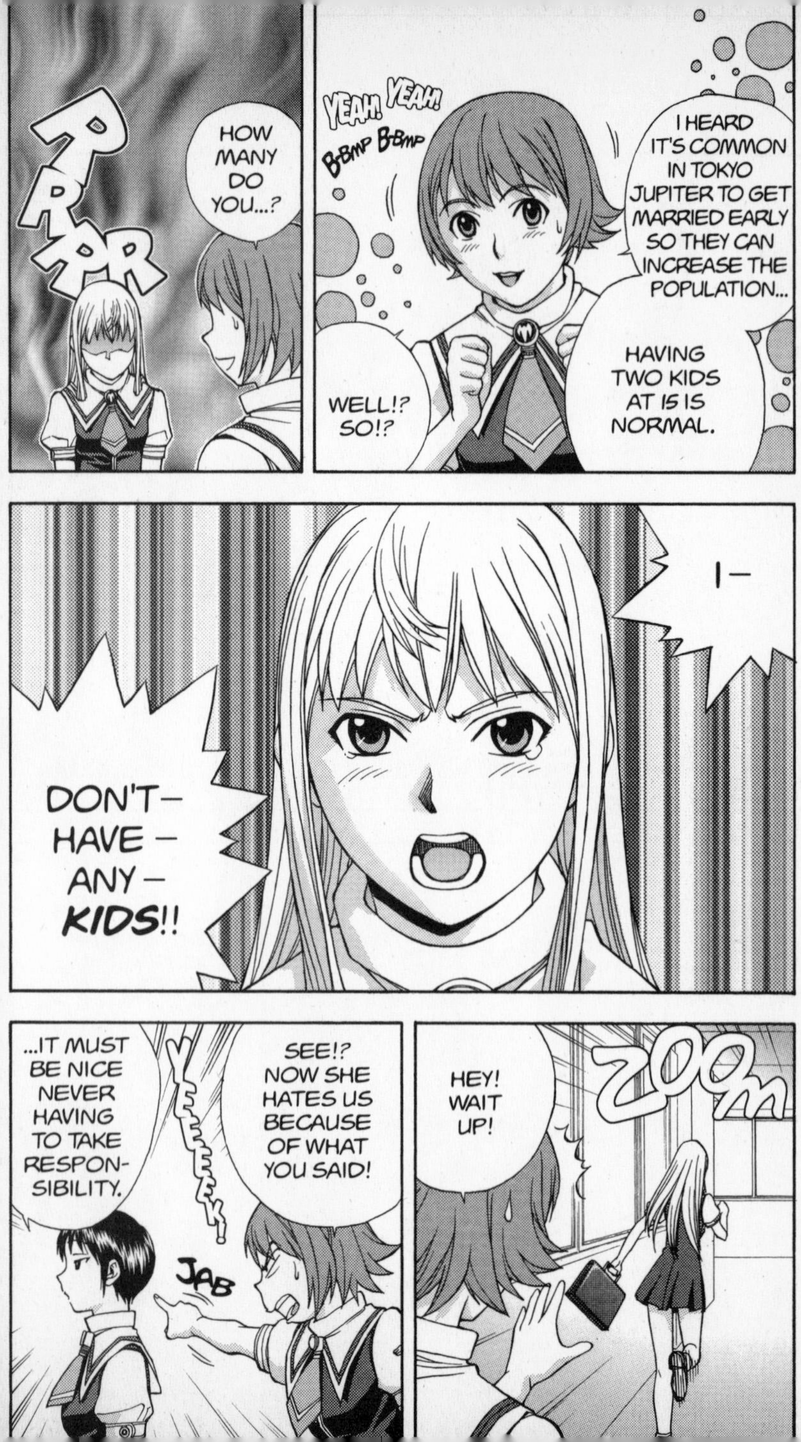
YEAH! YEAH!
B-BMP B-BMP
I HEARD IT'S COMMON IN TOKYO JUPITER TO GET MARRIED EARLY SO THEY CAN INCREASE THE POPULATION...
HAVING TWO KIDS AT 15 IS NORMAL.
WELL!? SO!?
HOW MANY DO YOU...?
PRRR
I—
DON'T— HAVE — ANY — KIDS!!
ZOOM
HEY! WAIT UP!
SEE!? NOW SHE HATES US BECAUSE OF WHAT YOU SAID!
YEEEEK!
JAB
...IT MUST BE NICE NEVER HAVING TO TAKE RESPON-SIBILITY.

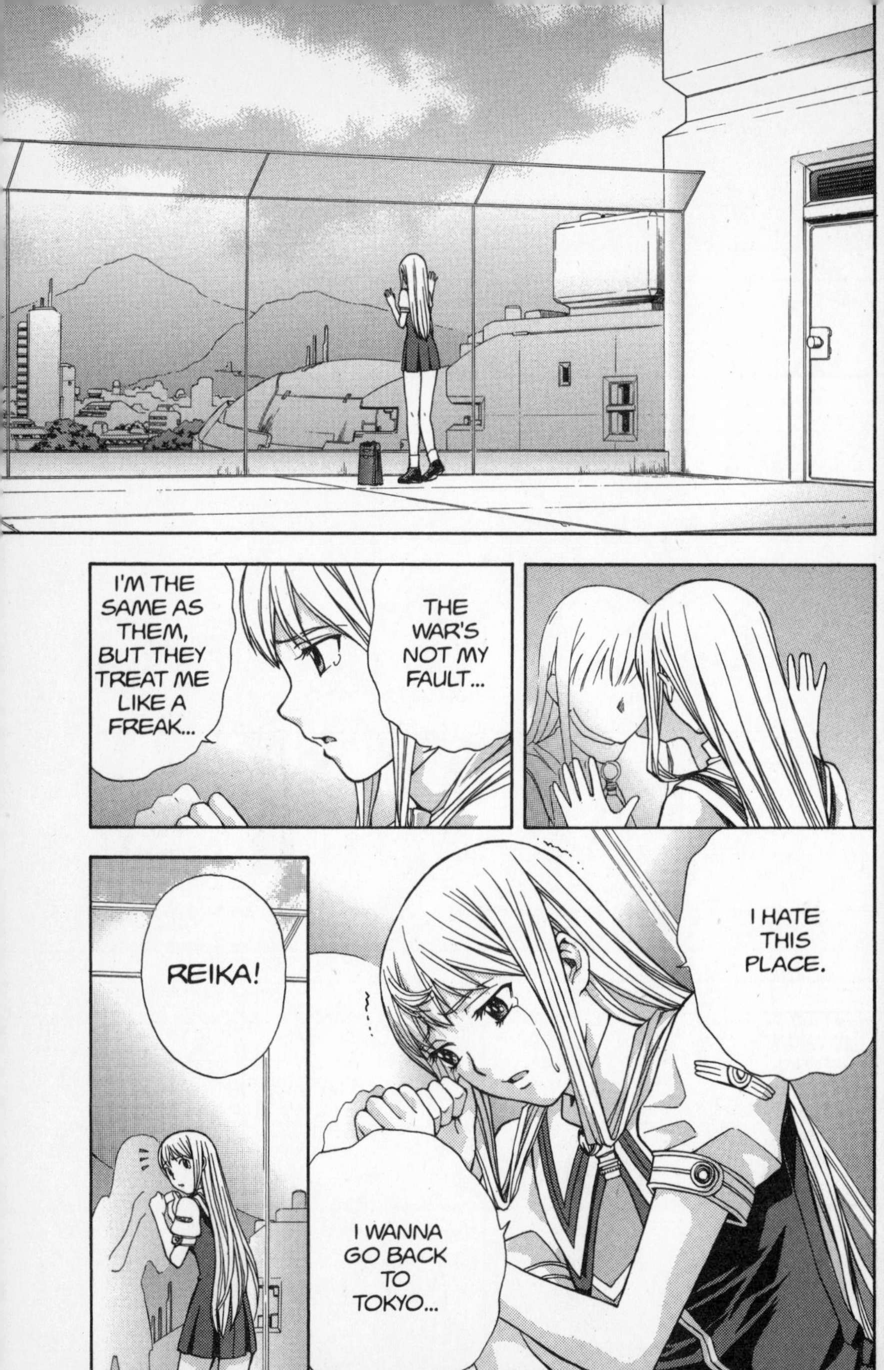
THE WAR'S NOT MY FAULT...
I'M THE SAME AS THEM, BUT THEY TREAT ME LIKE A FREAK...
I HATE THIS PLACE.
I WANNA GO BACK TO TOKYO...
REIKA!

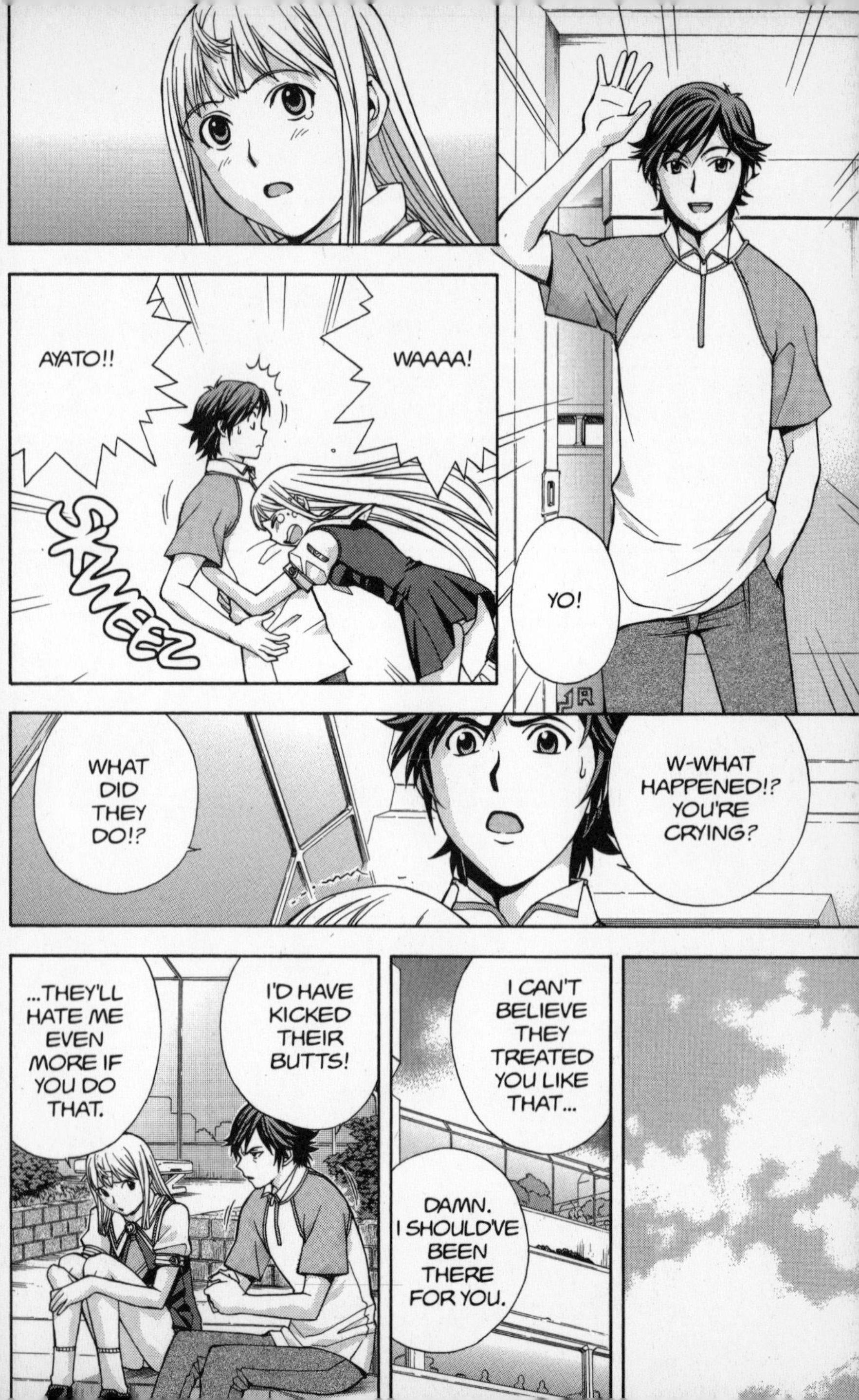
YO!
WAAAA!
AYATO!!
SKWEEZ
W-WHAT HAPPENED!? YOU'RE CRYING?
WHAT DID THEY DO!?
I CAN'T BELIEVE THEY TREATED YOU LIKE THAT...
DAMN. I SHOULD'VE BEEN THERE FOR YOU.
I'D HAVE KICKED THEIR BUTTS!
...THEY'LL HATE ME EVEN MORE IF YOU DO THAT.

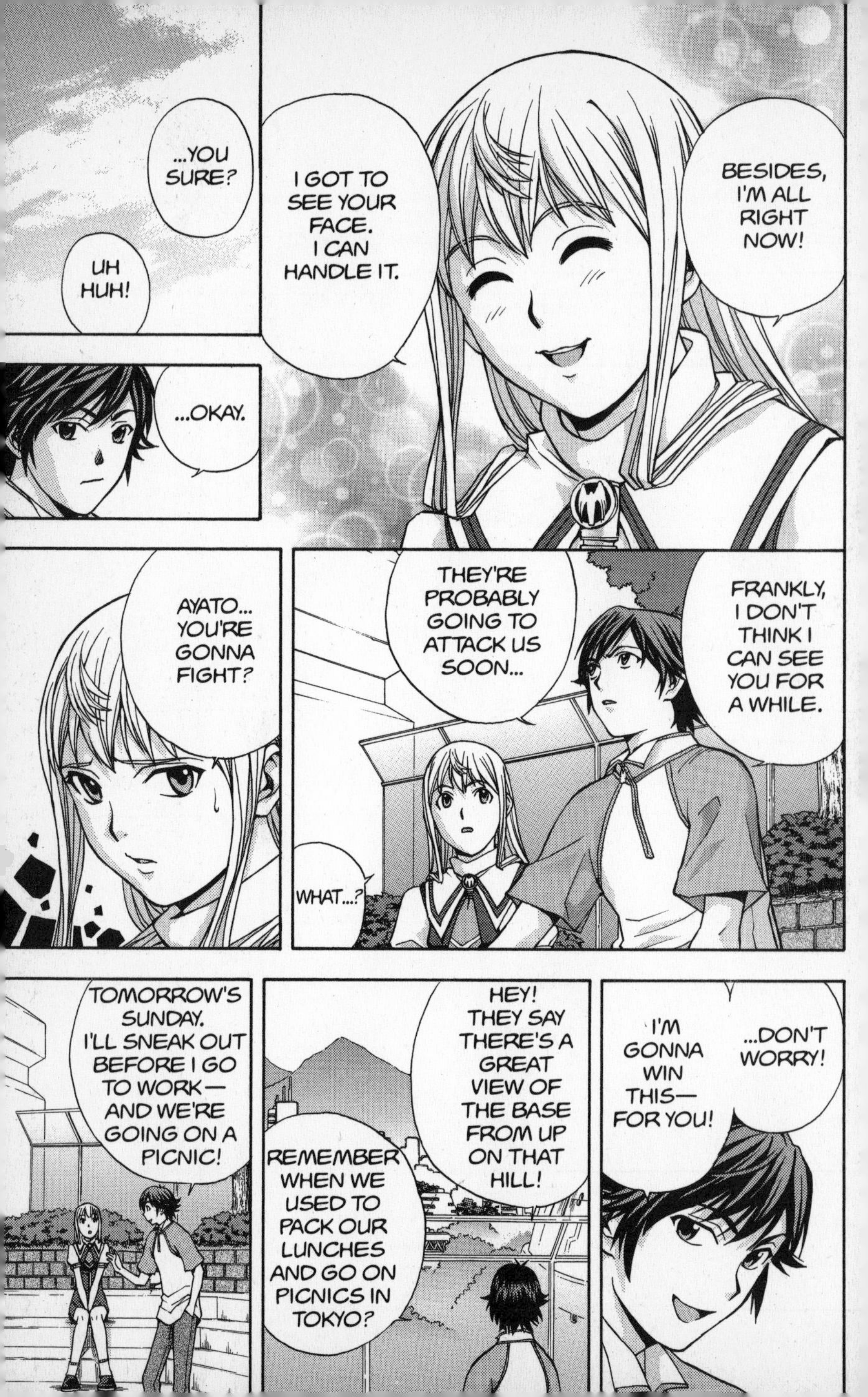
BESIDES, I'M ALL RIGHT NOW!
I GOT TO SEE YOUR FACE. I CAN HANDLE IT.
...YOU SURE?
UH HUH!
...OKAY.
FRANKLY, I DON'T THINK I CAN SEE YOU FOR A WHILE.
THEY'RE PROBABLY GOING TO ATTACK US SOON...
WHAT...?
AYATO... YOU'RE GONNA FIGHT?
...DON'T WORRY!
I'M GONNA WIN THIS— FOR YOU!
HEY! THEY SAY THERE'S A GREAT VIEW OF THE BASE FROM UP ON THAT HILL!
REMEMBER WHEN WE USED TO PACK OUR LUNCHES AND GO ON PICNICS IN TOKYO?
TOMORROW'S SUNDAY. I'LL SNEAK OUT BEFORE I GO TO WORK— AND WE'RE GOING ON A PICNIC!

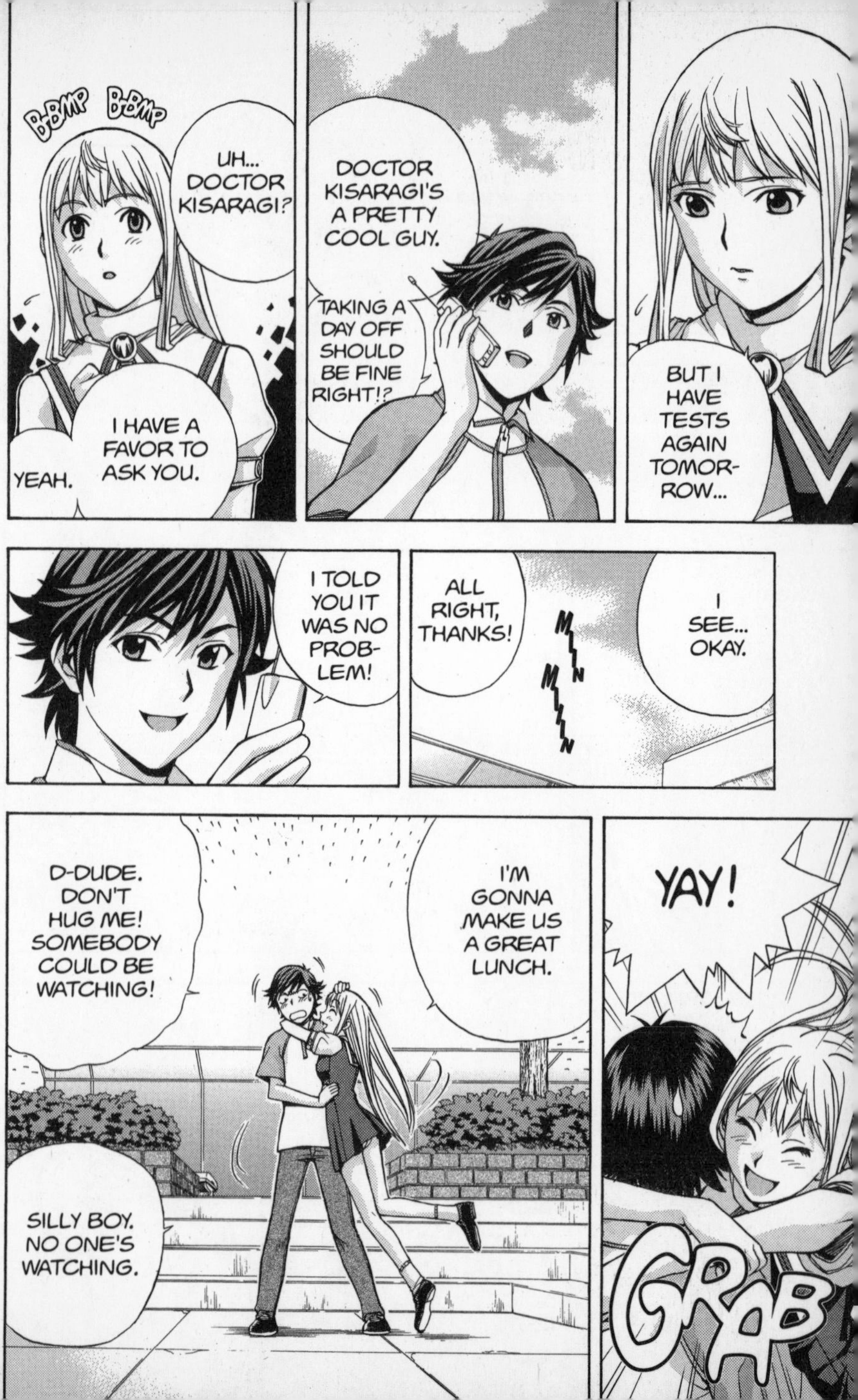
BUT I HAVE TESTS AGAIN TOMORROW...
DOCTOR KISARAGI'S A PRETTY COOL GUY.
TAKING A DAY OFF SHOULD BE FINE RIGHT!?
B-BMP B-BMP
UH... DOCTOR KISARAGI!?
I HAVE A FAVOR TO ASK YOU.
YEAH.
I SEE... OKAY.
ALL RIGHT, THANKS!
I TOLD YOU IT WAS NO PROBLEM!
YAY!
GRAB
I'M GONNA MAKE US A GREAT LUNCH.
D-DUDE. DON'T HUG ME! SOMEBODY COULD BE WATCHING!
SILLY BOY. NO ONE'S WATCHING.

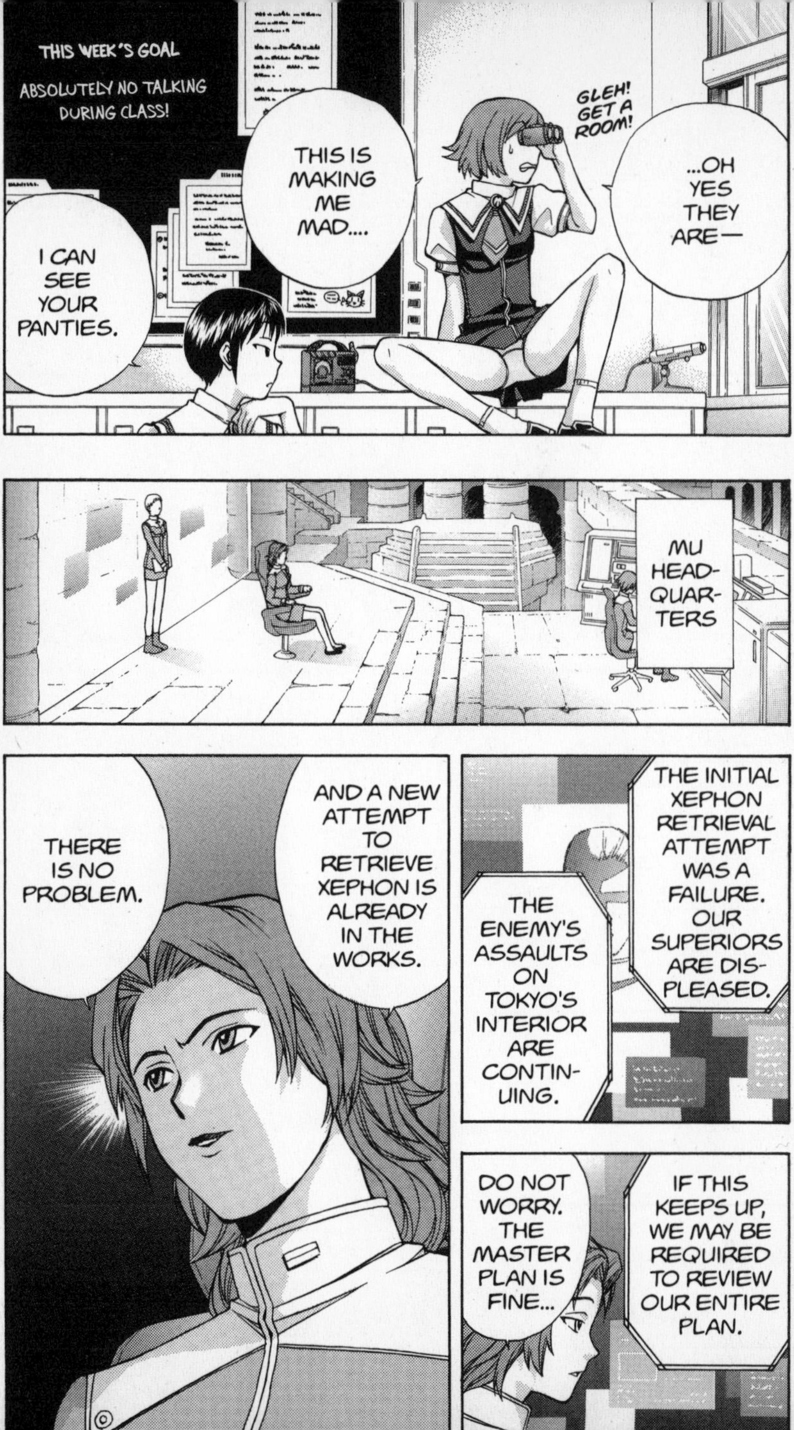
...OH YES THEY ARE—
GLEH! GET A ROOM!
THIS IS MAKING ME MAD....
THIS WEEK'S GOAL
ABSOLUTELY NO TALKING DURING CLASS!
I CAN SEE YOUR PANTIES.
MU HEADQUARTERS
THE INITIAL XEPHON RETRIEVAL ATTEMPT WAS A FAILURE. OUR SUPERIORS ARE DISPLEASED.
THE ENEMY'S ASSAULTS ON TOKYO'S INTERIOR ARE CONTINUING.
IF THIS KEEPS UP, WE MAY BE REQUIRED TO REVIEW OUR ENTIRE PLAN.
DO NOT WORRY. THE MASTER PLAN IS FINE...
AND A NEW ATTEMPT TO RETRIEVE XEPHON IS ALREADY IN THE WORKS.
THERE IS NO PROBLEM.

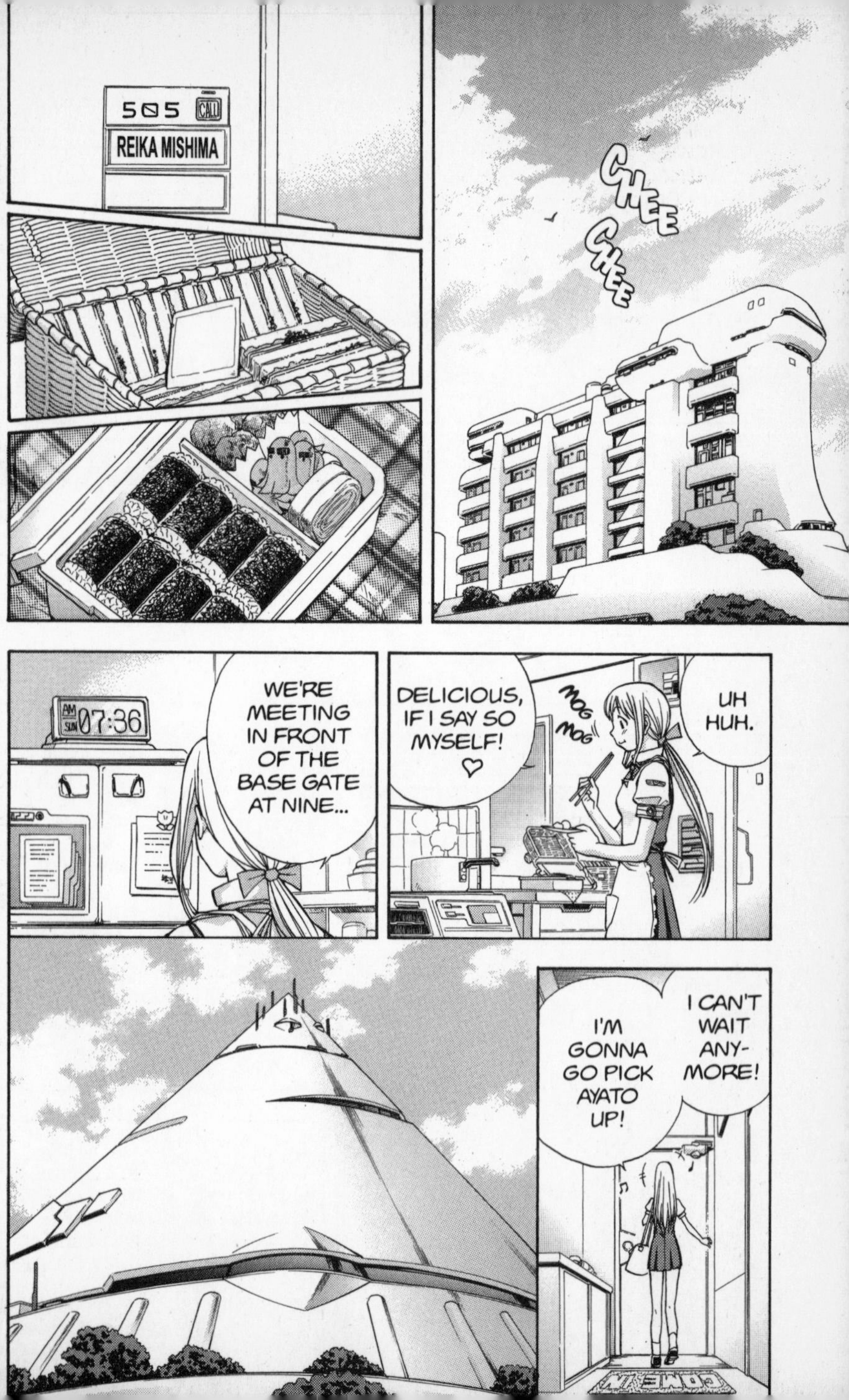
CHEE CHEE
505 CALL
REIKA MISHIMA
UH HUH.
MOG MOG
DELICIOUS, IF I SAY SO MYSELF! ♡
AM SUN 07:36
WE'RE MEETING IN FRONT OF THE BASE GATE AT NINE...
I CAN'T WAIT ANY-MORE!
I'M GONNA GO PICK AYATO UP!
COME IN

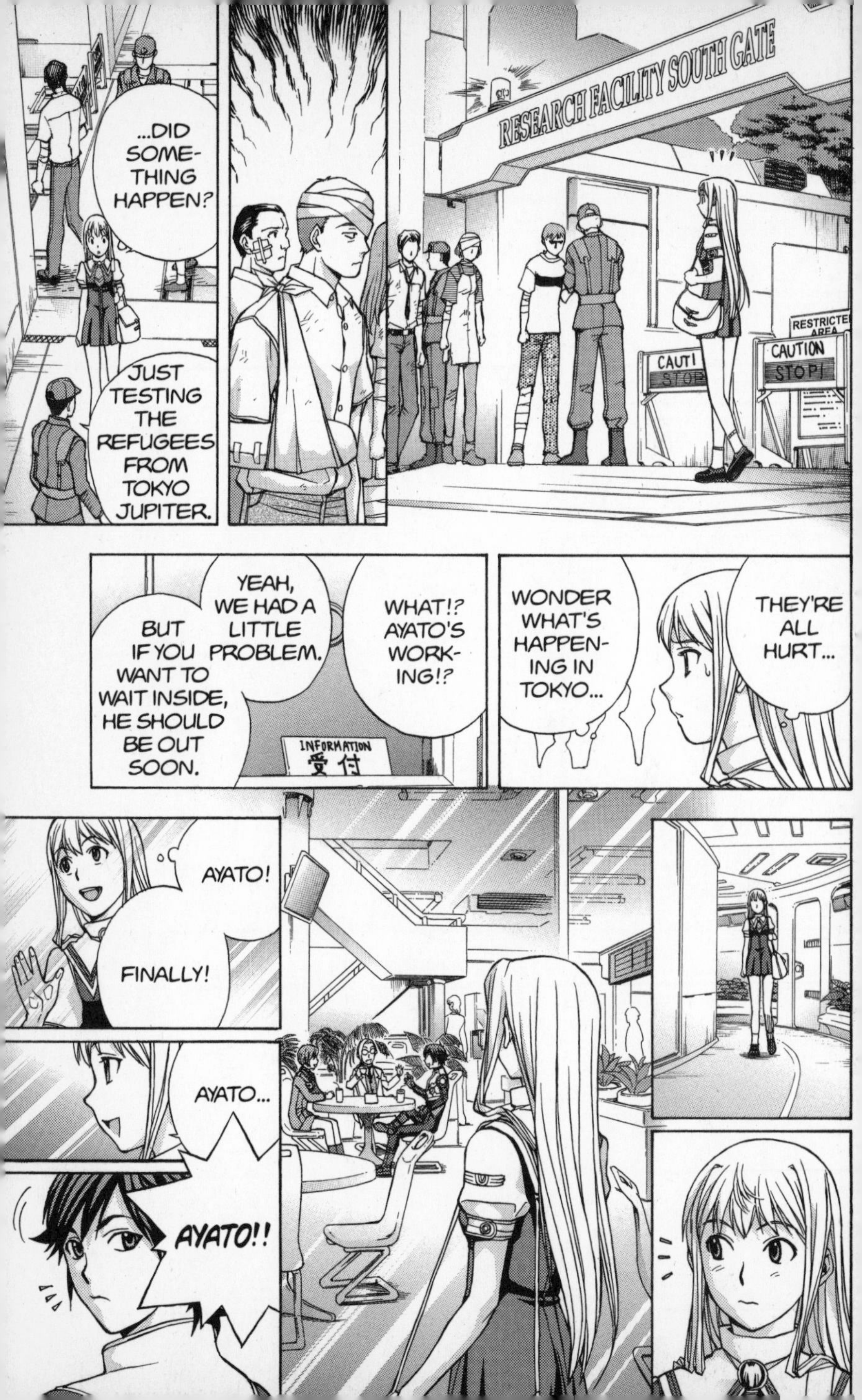
RESEARCH FACILITY SOUTH GATE
CAUTI STOP
CAUTION STOP!
...DID SOMETHING HAPPEN?
JUST TESTING THE REFUGEES FROM TOKYO JUPITER.
THEY'RE ALL HURT...
WONDER WHAT'S HAPPENING IN TOKYO...
WHAT!? AYATO'S WORKING!?
YEAH, WE HAD A LITTLE PROBLEM.
BUT IF YOU WANT TO WAIT INSIDE, HE SHOULD BE OUT SOON.
INFORMATION 受付
AYATO!
FINALLY!
AYATO...
AYATO!!

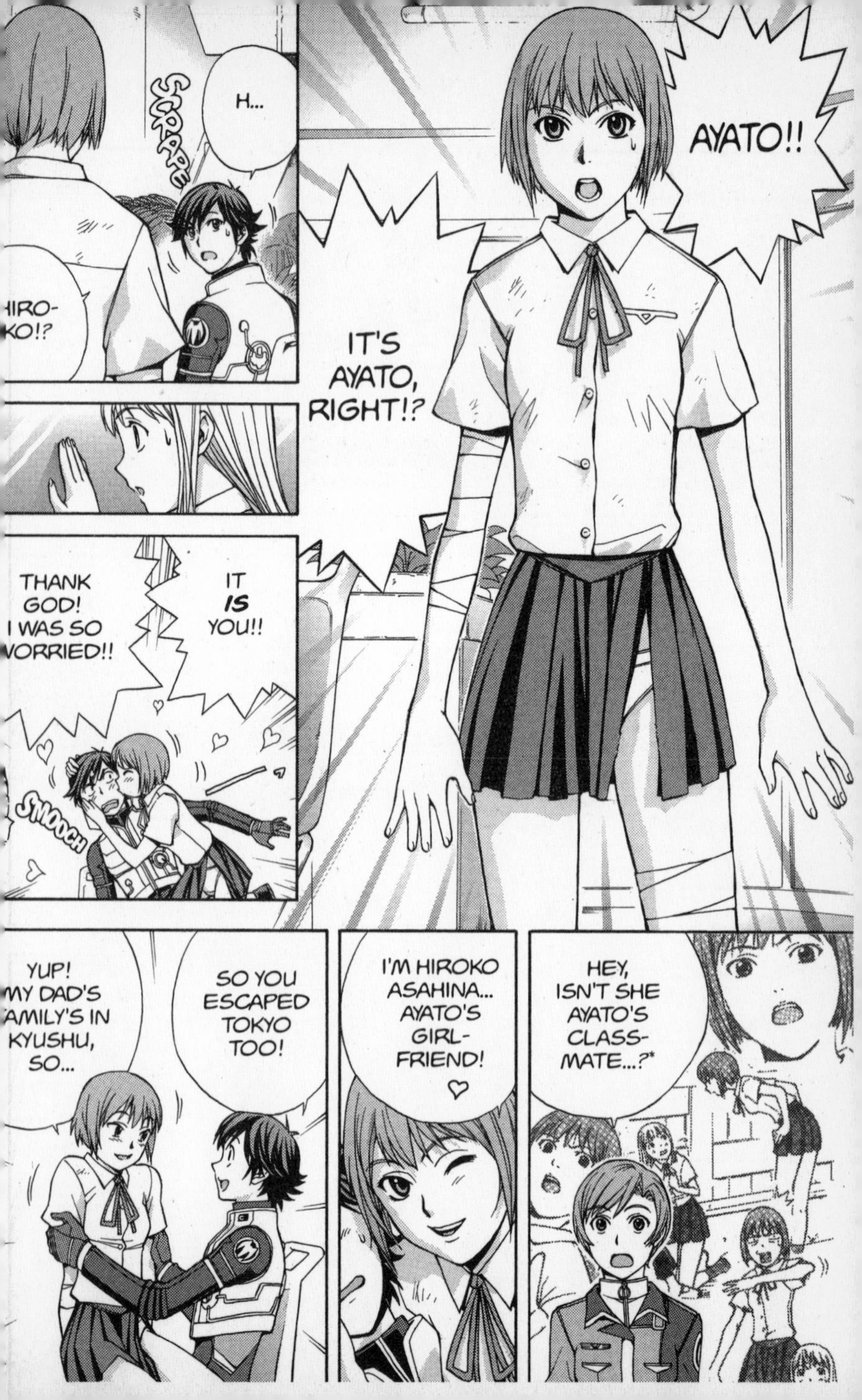
AYATO!!
IT'S AYATO, RIGHT!?
SCRAPE
H...
IRO-KO!?
IT IS YOU!!
THANK GOD! I WAS SO ORRIED!!
SMOOCH
HEY, ISN'T SHE AYATO'S CLASSMATE...?*
I'M HIROKO ASAHINA... AYATO'S GIRLFRIEND! ♡
SO YOU ESCAPED TOKYO TOO!
YUP! MY DAD'S AMILY'S IN KYUSHU, SO...

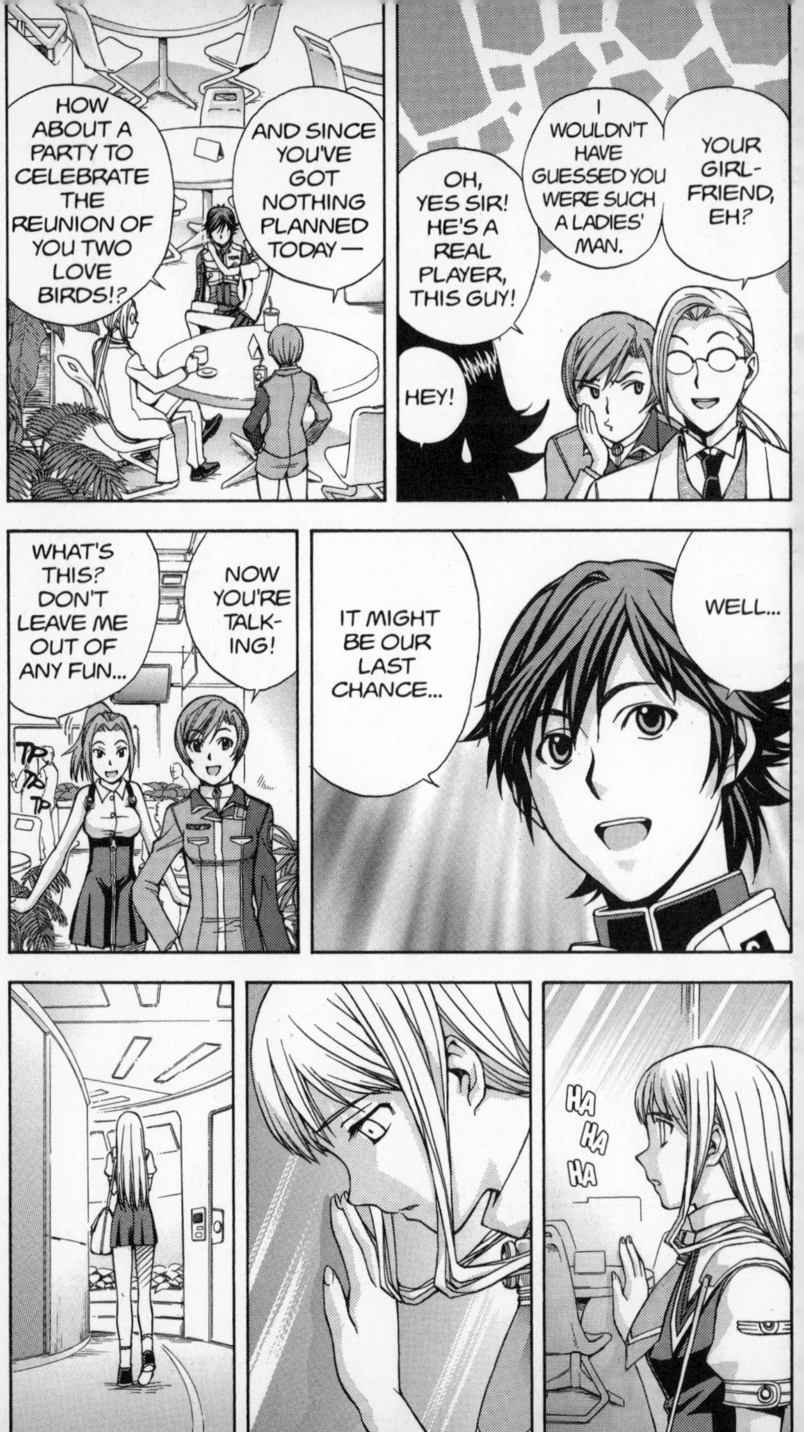
YOUR GIRL-FRIEND, EH?
I WOULDN'T HAVE GUESSED YOU WERE SUCH A LADIES' MAN.
OH, YES SIR! HE'S A REAL PLAYER, THIS GUY!
HEY!
AND SINCE YOU'VE GOT NOTHING PLANNED TODAY—
HOW ABOUT A PARTY TO CELEBRATE THE REUNION OF YOU TWO LOVE BIRDS!?
WELL...
IT MIGHT BE OUR LAST CHANCE...
NOW YOU'RE TALK-ING!
WHAT'S THIS? DON'T LEAVE ME OUT OF ANY FUN...
TP TP TP
HA HA HA

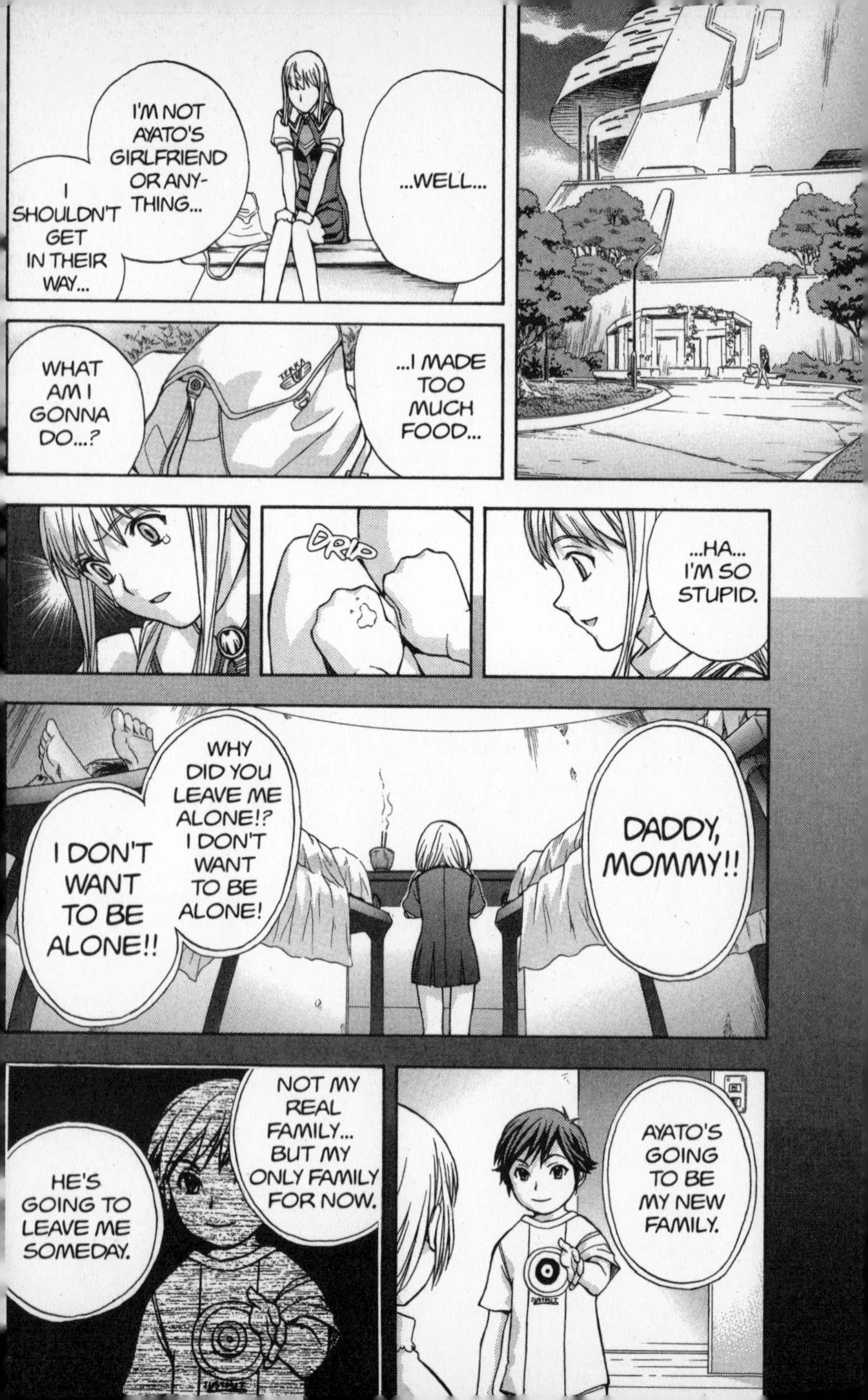
...WELL...
I'M NOT AYATO'S GIRLFRIEND OR ANYTHING...
I SHOULDN'T GET IN THEIR WAY...
...I MADE TOO MUCH FOOD...
TERRA
WHAT AM I GONNA DO...?
...HA... I'M SO STUPID.
DRIP
DADDY, MOMMY!!
WHY DID YOU LEAVE ME ALONE!? I DON'T WANT TO BE ALONE!
I DON'T WANT TO BE ALONE!!
AYATO'S GOING TO BE MY NEW FAMILY.
NOT MY REAL FAMILY... BUT MY ONLY FAMILY FOR NOW.
HE'S GOING TO LEAVE ME SOMEDAY.

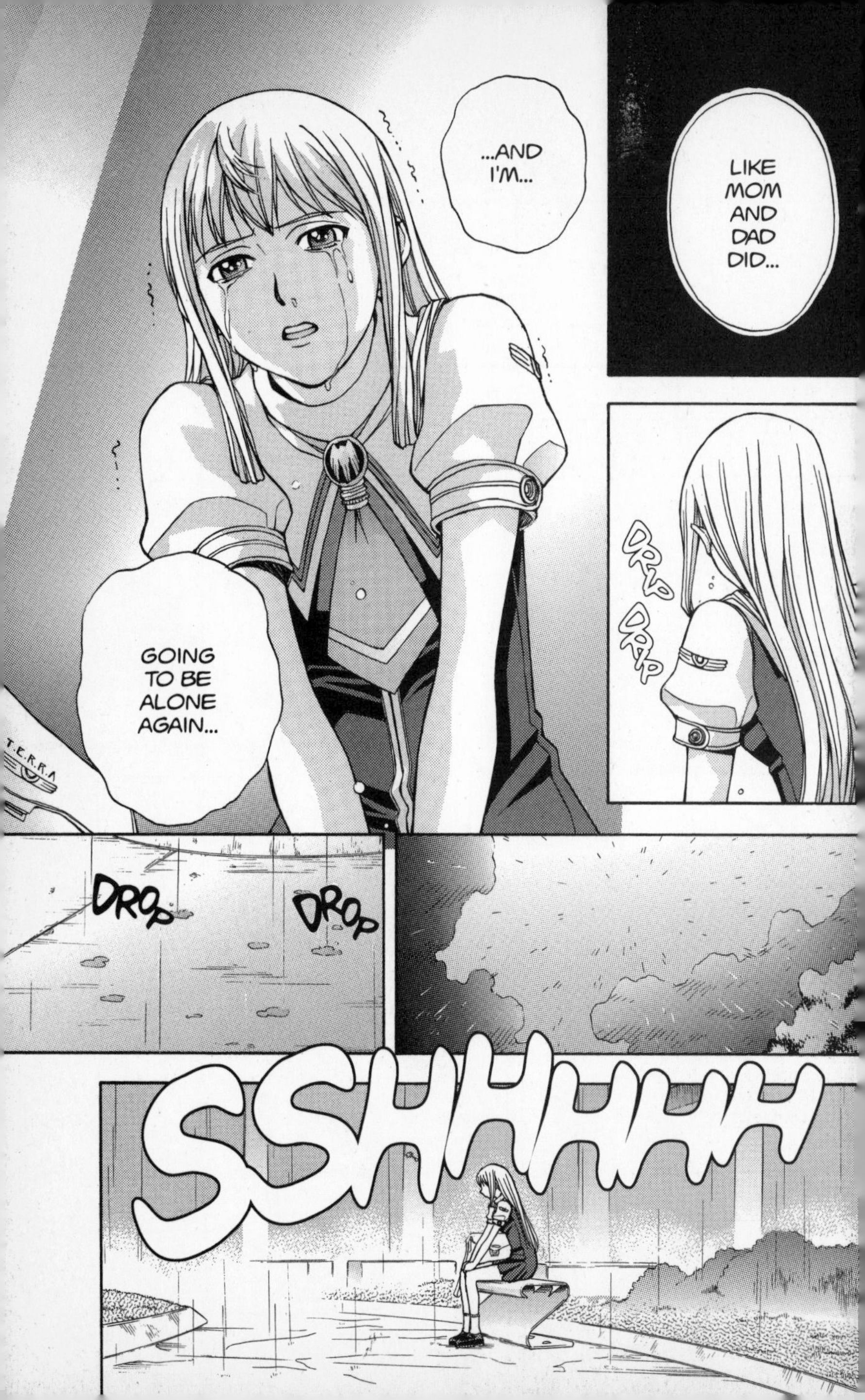
LIKE MOM AND DAD DID...
DRIP DRIP
...AND I'M...
GOING TO BE ALONE AGAIN...
T.E.R.R.A
DROP DROP
SSHHHHH

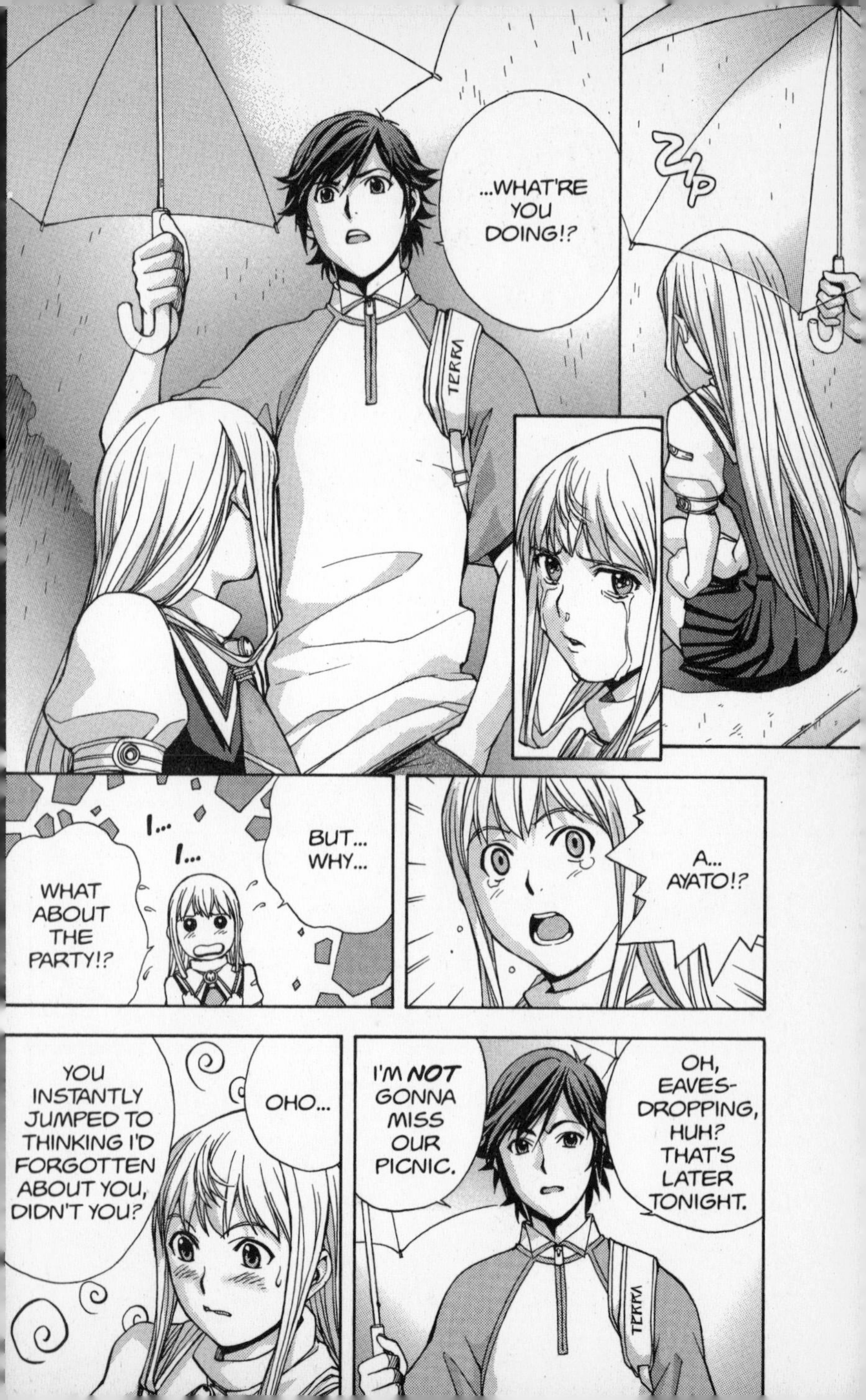
Zip
...WHAT'RE YOU DOING!?
TERRA
A... AYATO!?
BUT... WHY...
I...
I...
WHAT ABOUT THE PARTY!?
OH, EAVES-DROPPING, HUH? THAT'S LATER TONIGHT.
I'M ***NOT*** GONNA MISS OUR PICNIC.
OHO...
YOU INSTANTLY JUMPED TO THINKING I'D FORGOTTEN ABOUT YOU, DIDN'T YOU?

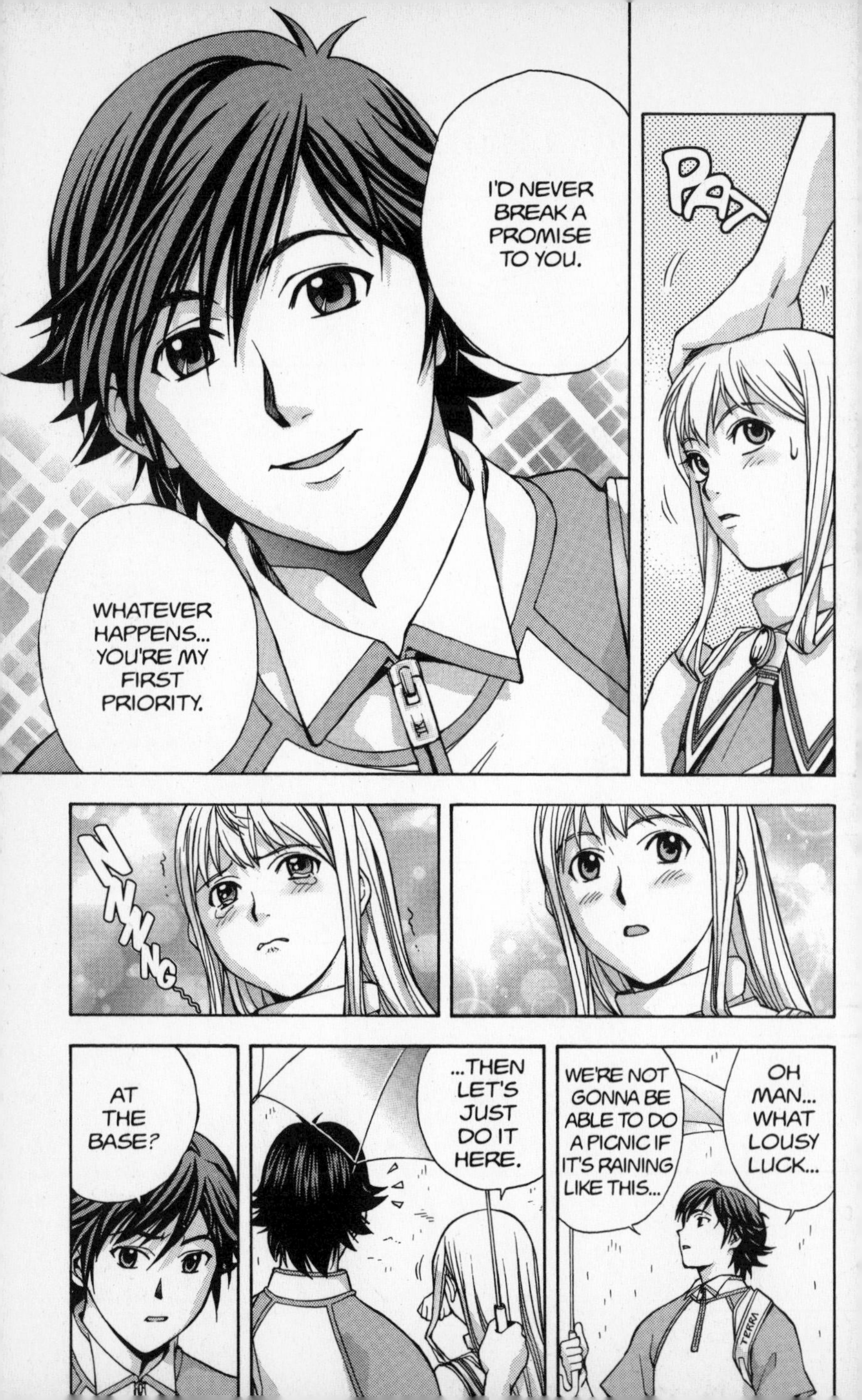
PAT
I'D NEVER BREAK A PROMISE TO YOU.
WHATEVER HAPPENS... YOU'RE MY FIRST PRIORITY.
ZNNNG
OH MAN... WHAT LOUSY LUCK...
WE'RE NOT GONNA BE ABLE TO DO A PICNIC IF IT'S RAINING LIKE THIS...
...THEN LET'S JUST DO IT HERE.
AT THE BASE?

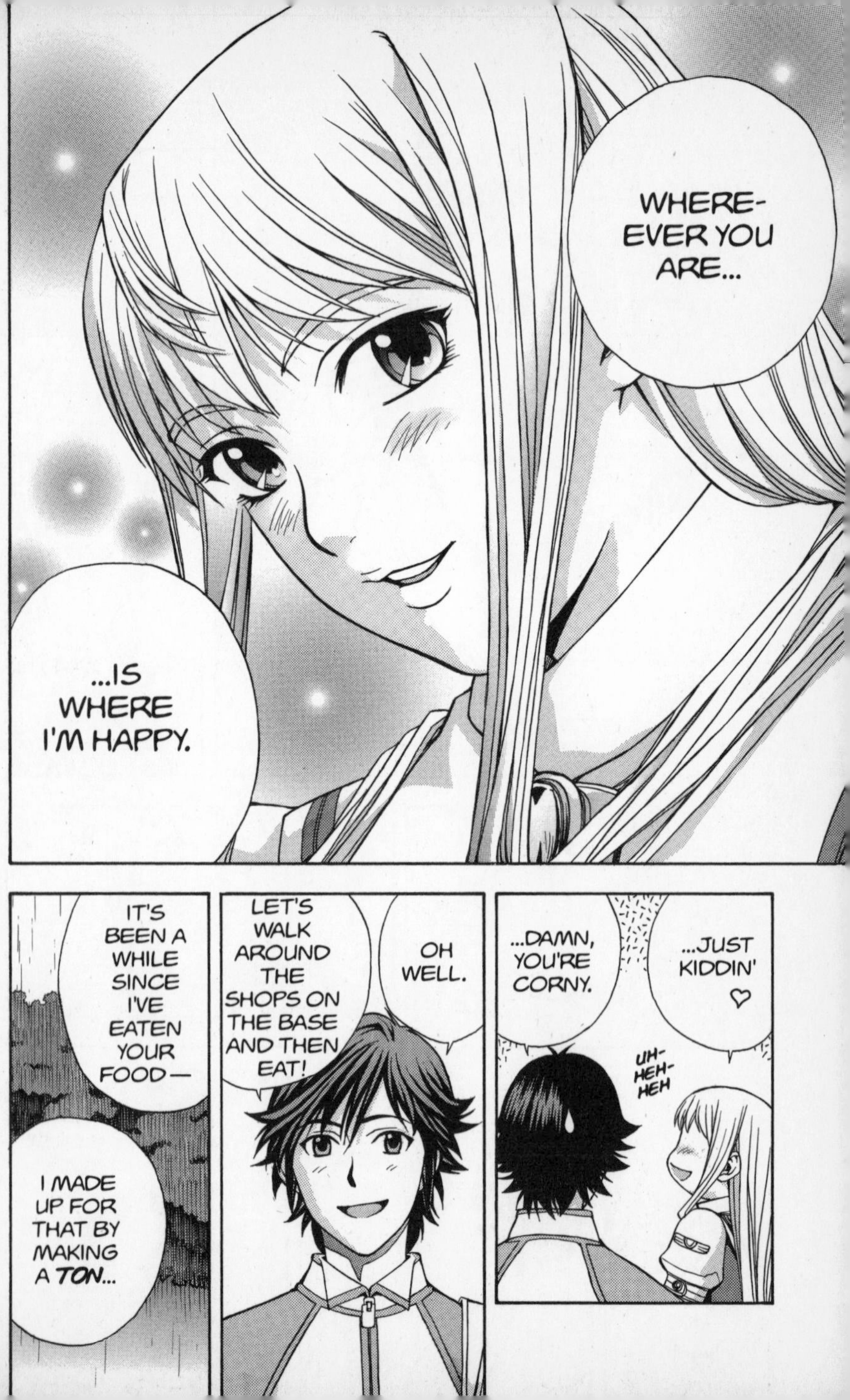
WHERE-EVER YOU ARE...
...IS WHERE I'M HAPPY.
...JUST KIDDIN' ♡
...DAMN, YOU'RE CORNY.
UH-HEH-HEH
OH WELL.
LET'S WALK AROUND THE SHOPS ON THE BASE AND THEN EAT!
IT'S BEEN A WHILE SINCE I'VE EATEN YOUR FOOD—
I MADE UP FOR THAT BY MAKING A **TON**...

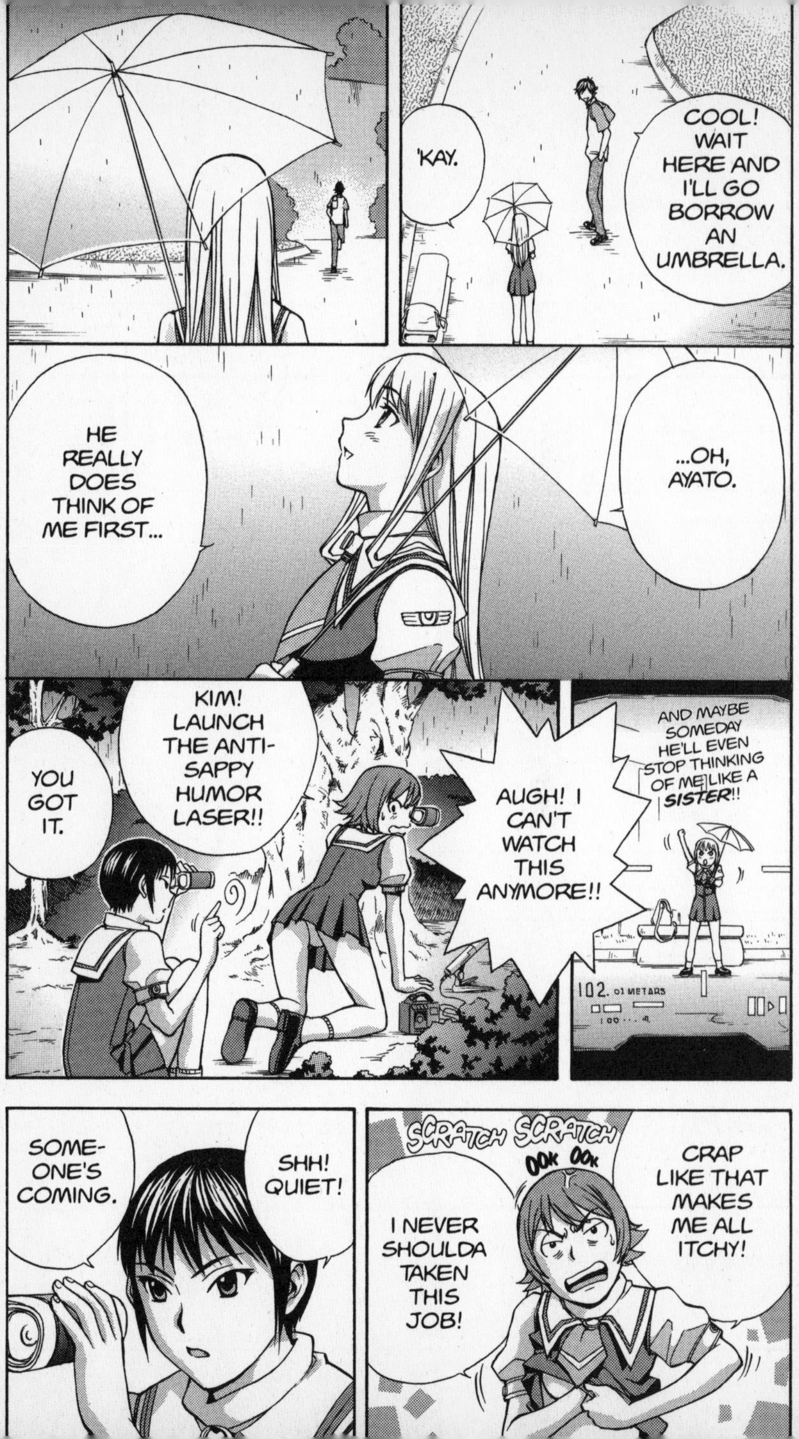
COOL! WAIT HERE AND I'LL GO BORROW AN UMBRELLA.
'KAY.
...OH, AYATO.
HE REALLY DOES THINK OF ME FIRST...
AND MAYBE SOMEDAY HE'LL EVEN STOP THINKING OF ME LIKE A SISTER!!
AUGH! I CAN'T WATCH THIS ANYMORE!!
KIM! LAUNCH THE ANTI-SAPPY HUMOR LASER!!
YOU GOT IT.
SCRATCH SCRATCH
OOK OOK
CRAP LIKE THAT MAKES ME ALL ITCHY!
I NEVER SHOULDA TAKEN THIS JOB!
SHH! QUIET!
SOME-ONE'S COMING.

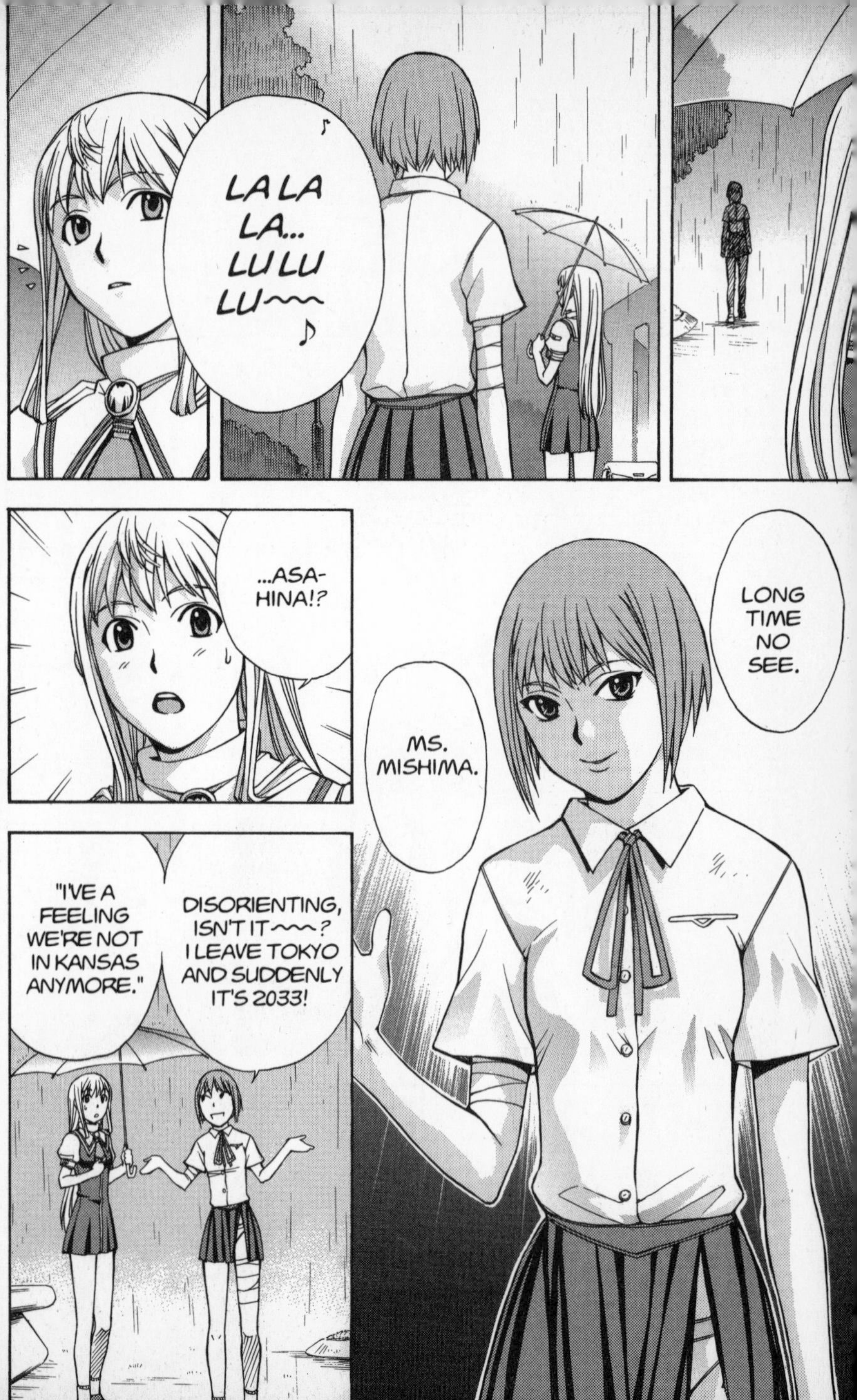
LA LA LA... LU LU LU~~ ♪
LONG TIME NO SEE.
MS. MISHIMA.
...ASA-HINA!?
DISORIENTING, ISN'T IT~~? I LEAVE TOKYO AND SUDDENLY IT'S 2033!
"I'VE A FEELING WE'RE NOT IN KANSAS ANYMORE."

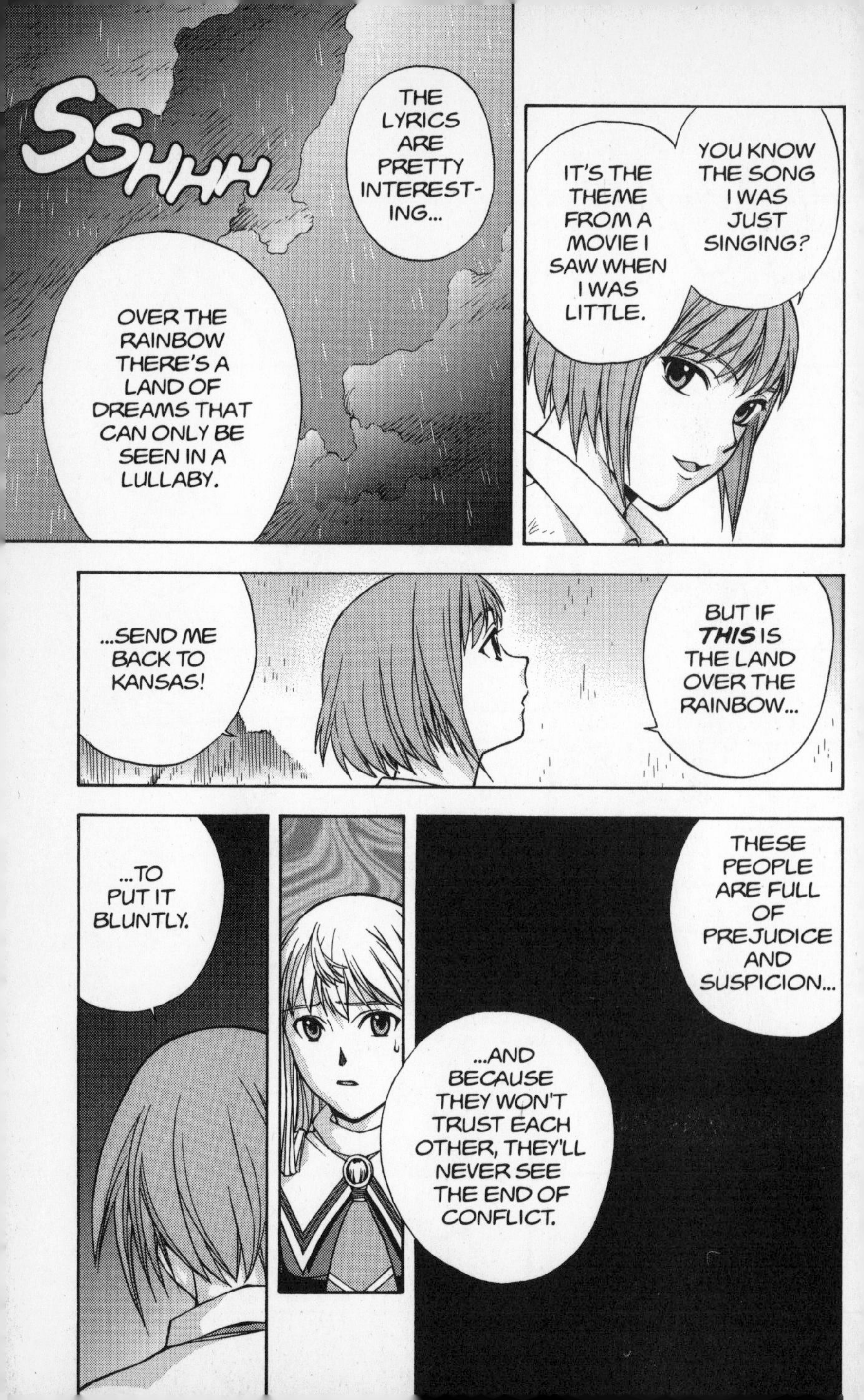
YOU KNOW THE SONG I WAS JUST SINGING?
IT'S THE THEME FROM A MOVIE I SAW WHEN I WAS LITTLE.
SSHHH
THE LYRICS ARE PRETTY INTEREST-ING...
OVER THE RAINBOW THERE'S A LAND OF DREAMS THAT CAN ONLY BE SEEN IN A LULLABY.
BUT IF *THIS* IS THE LAND OVER THE RAINBOW...
...SEND ME BACK TO KANSAS!
THESE PEOPLE ARE FULL OF PREJUDICE AND SUSPICION...
...AND BECAUSE THEY WON'T TRUST EACH OTHER, THEY'LL NEVER SEE THE END OF CONFLICT.
...TO PUT IT BLUNTLY.

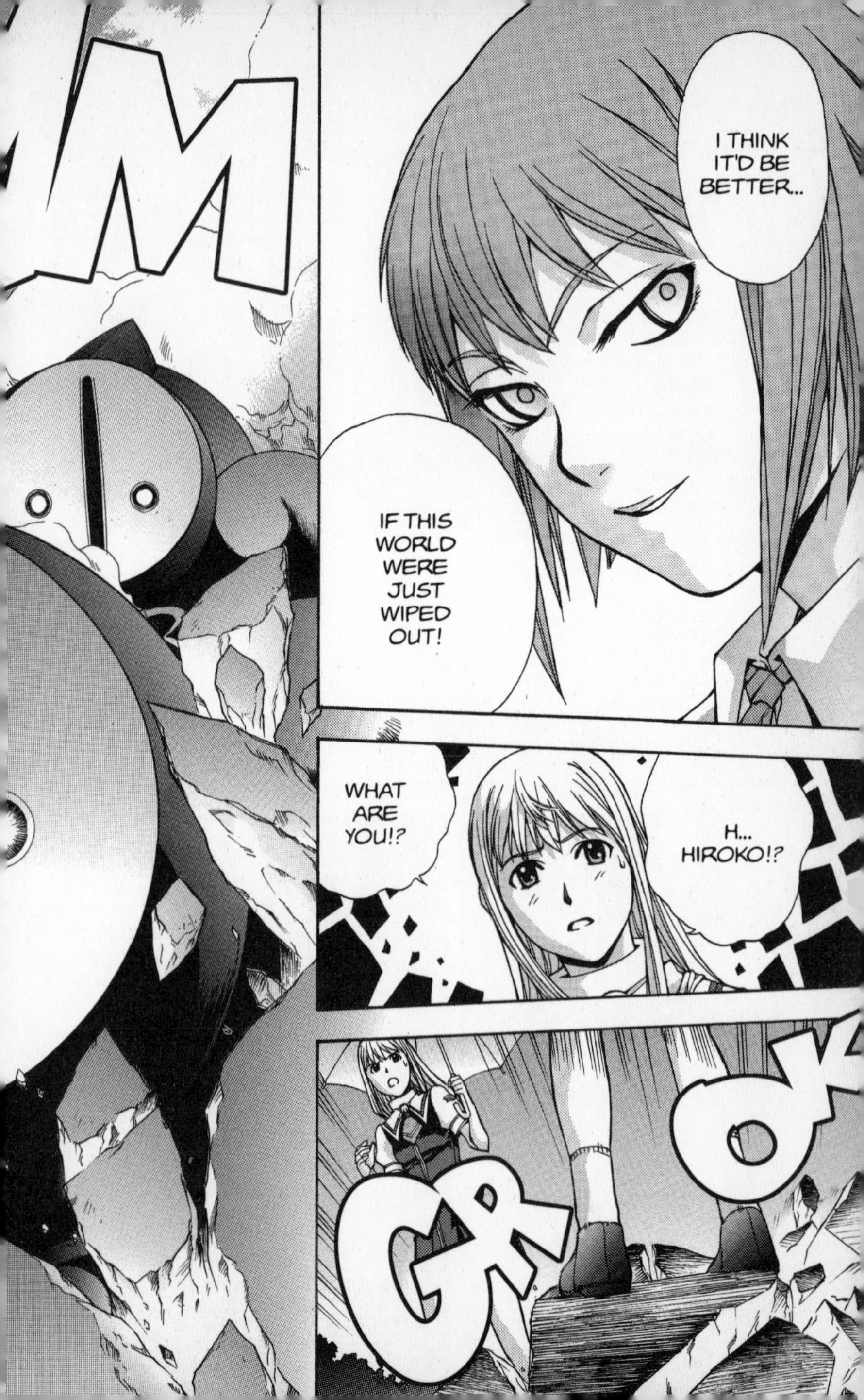
I THINK IT'D BE BETTER...
IF THIS WORLD WERE JUST WIPED OUT!
H... HIROKO!?
WHAT ARE YOU!?
GR
OK
M

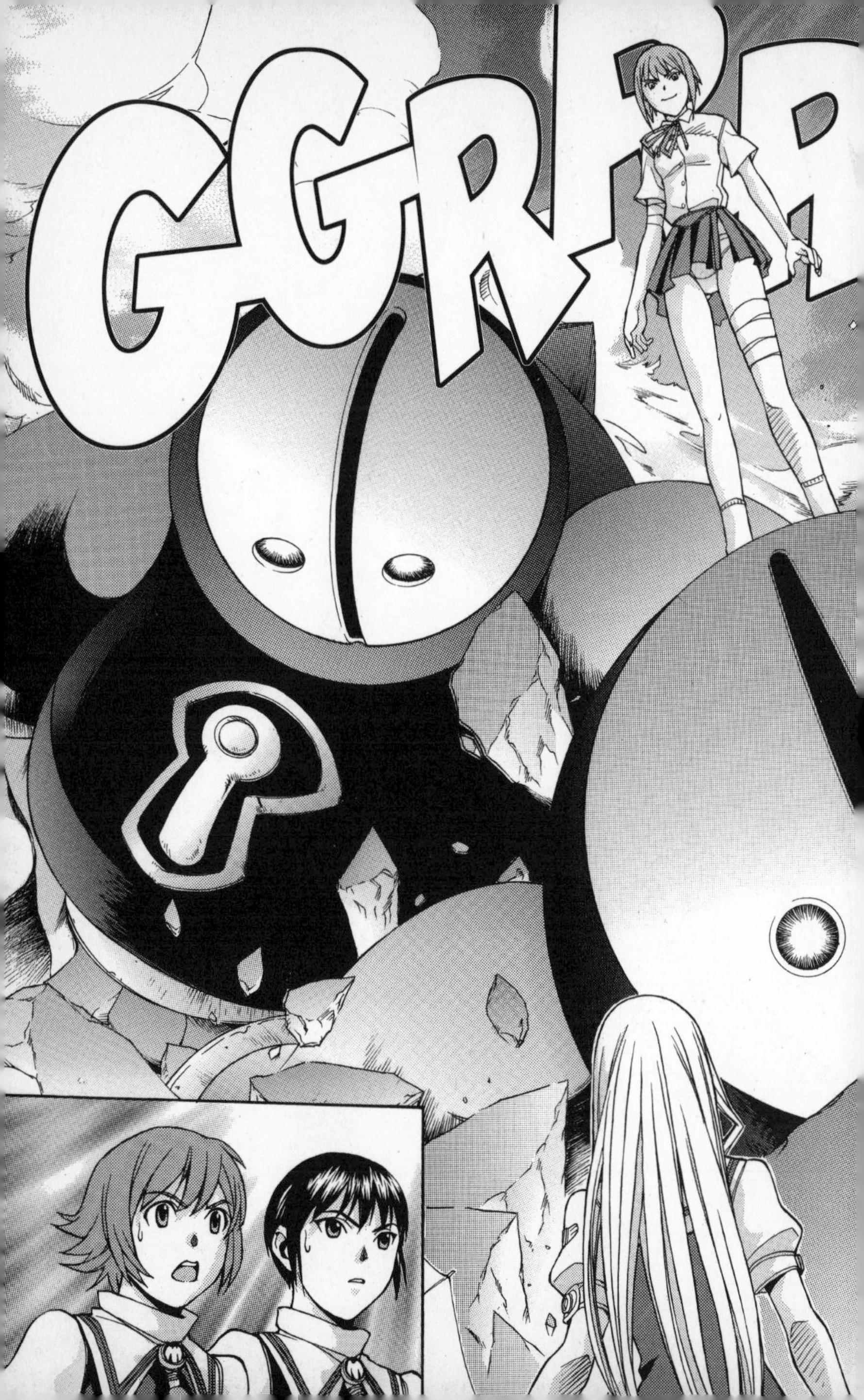
GGRRR

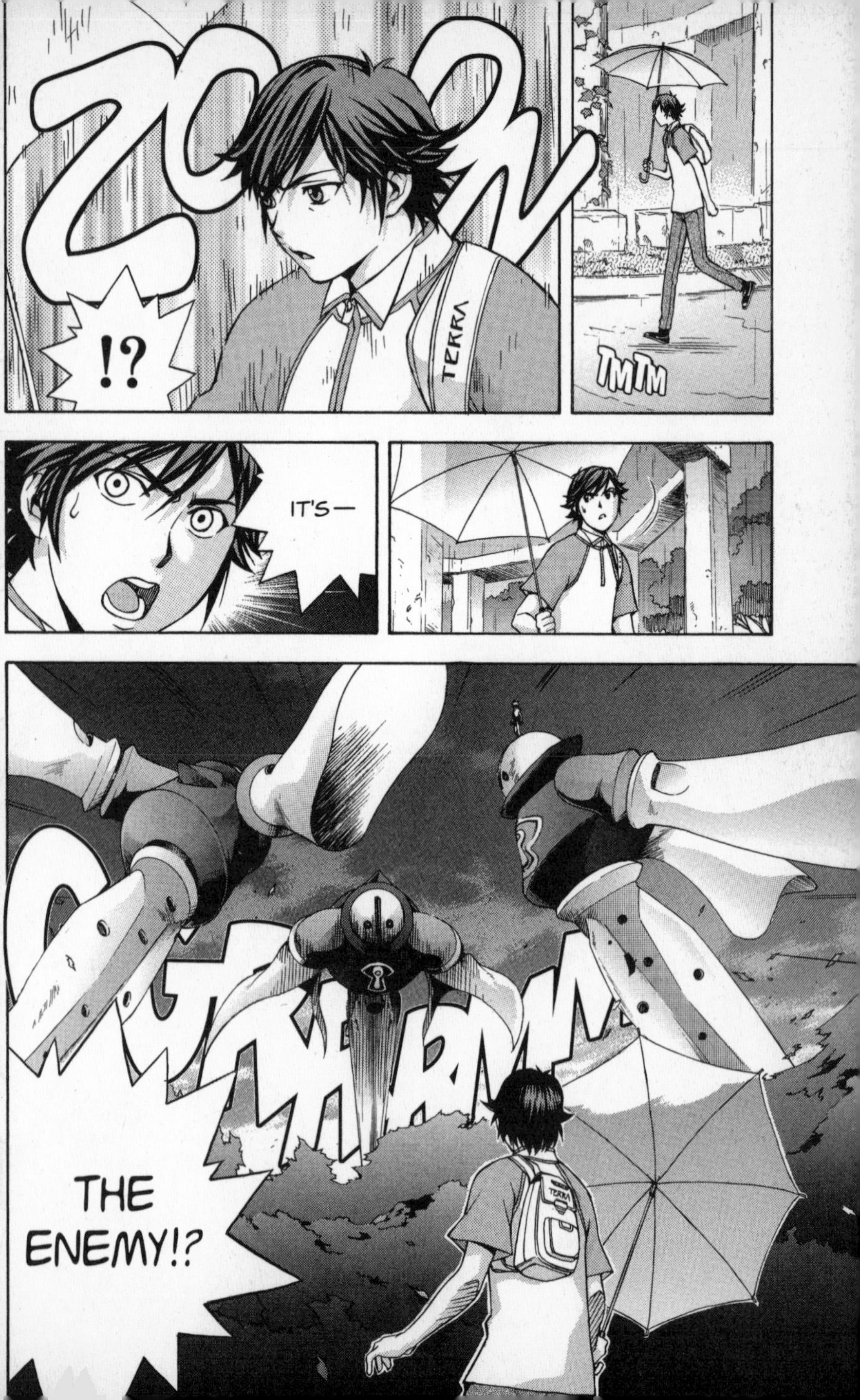
TMTM
ZOOM
!?
IT'S—
THE ENEMY!?

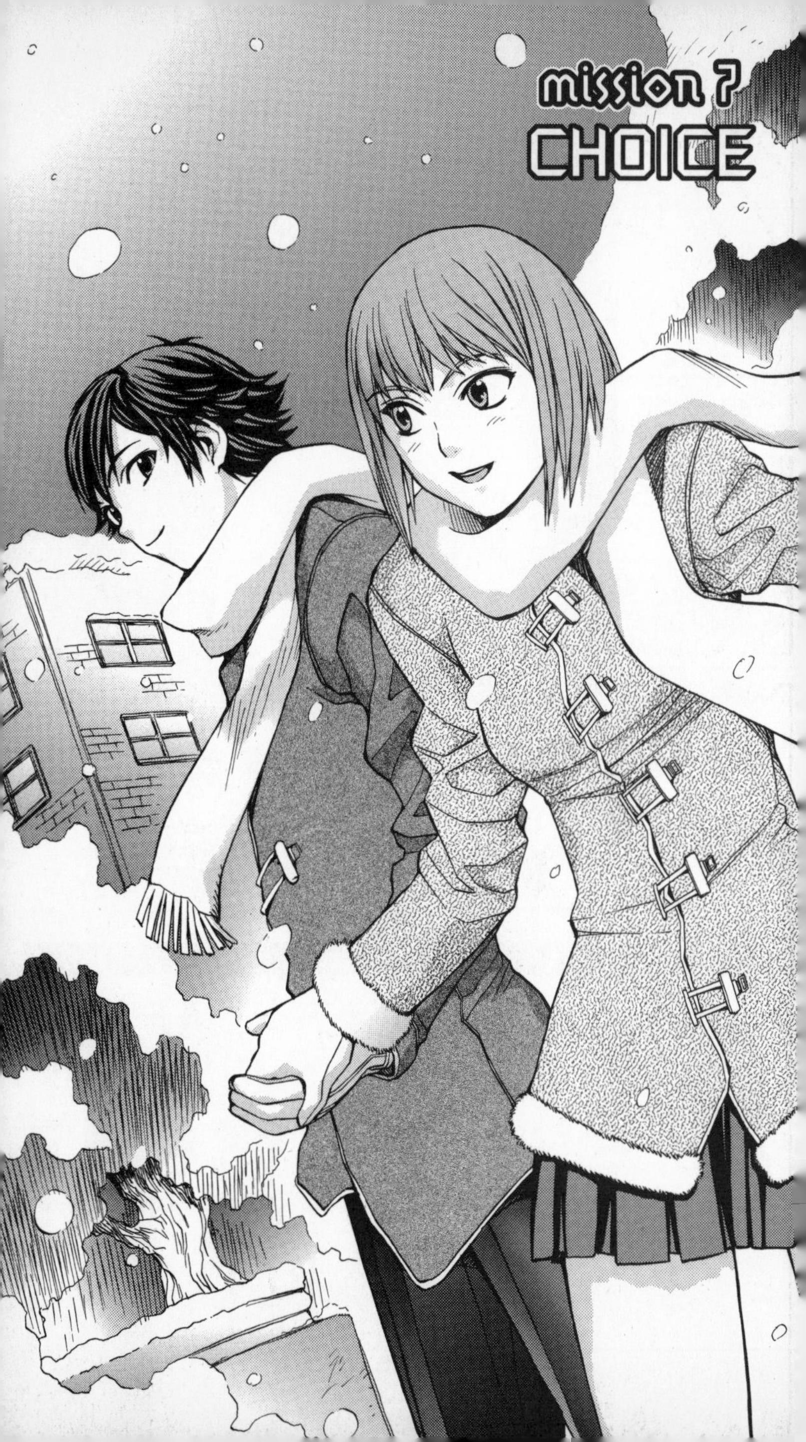
mission 7
CHOICE

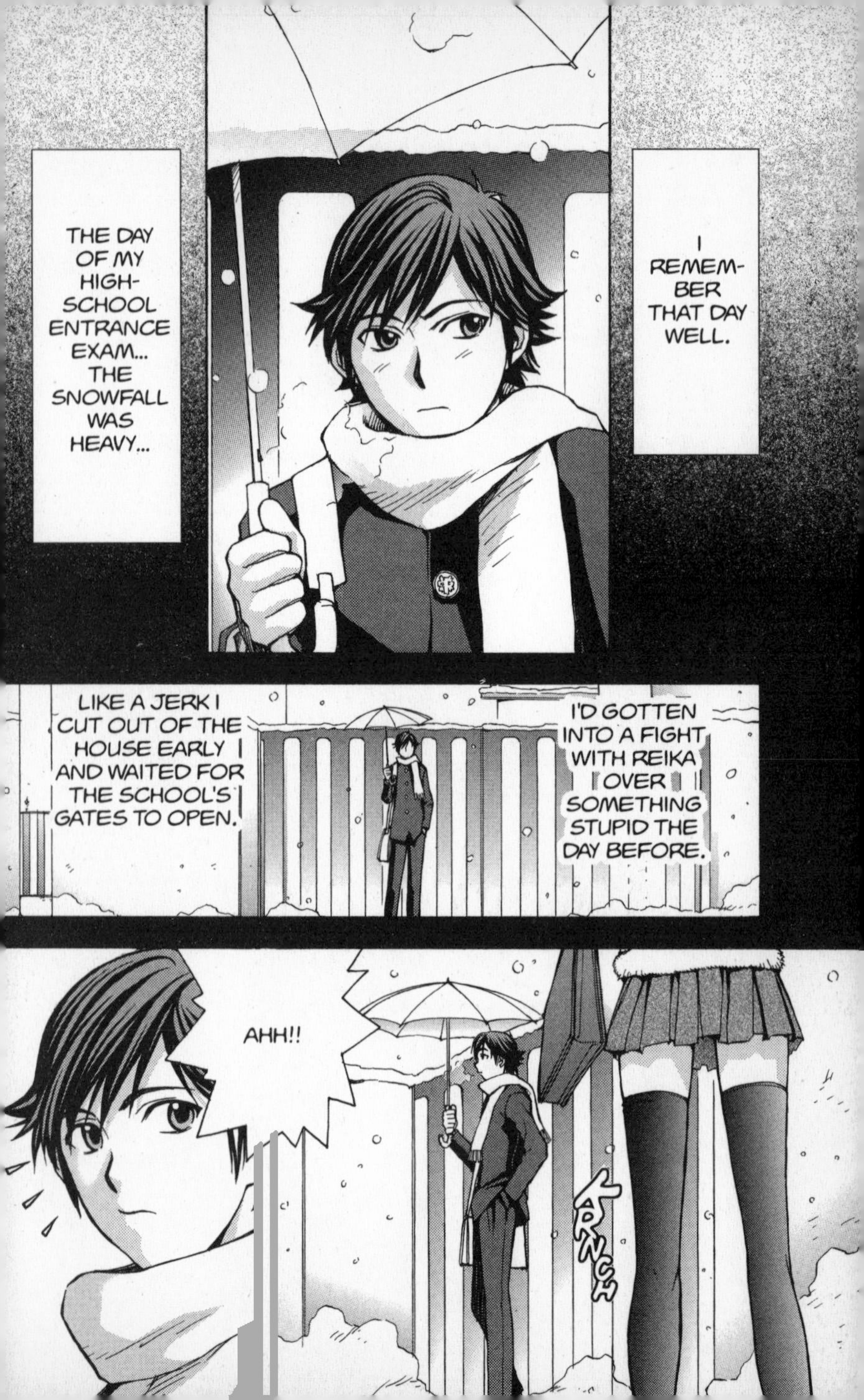
I REMEMBER THAT DAY WELL.
THE DAY OF MY HIGH-SCHOOL ENTRANCE EXAM... THE SNOWFALL WAS HEAVY...
I'D GOTTEN INTO A FIGHT WITH REIKA OVER SOMETHING STUPID THE DAY BEFORE.
LIKE A JERK I CUT OUT OF THE HOUSE EARLY AND WAITED FOR THE SCHOOL'S GATES TO OPEN.
KRNCH
AHH!!

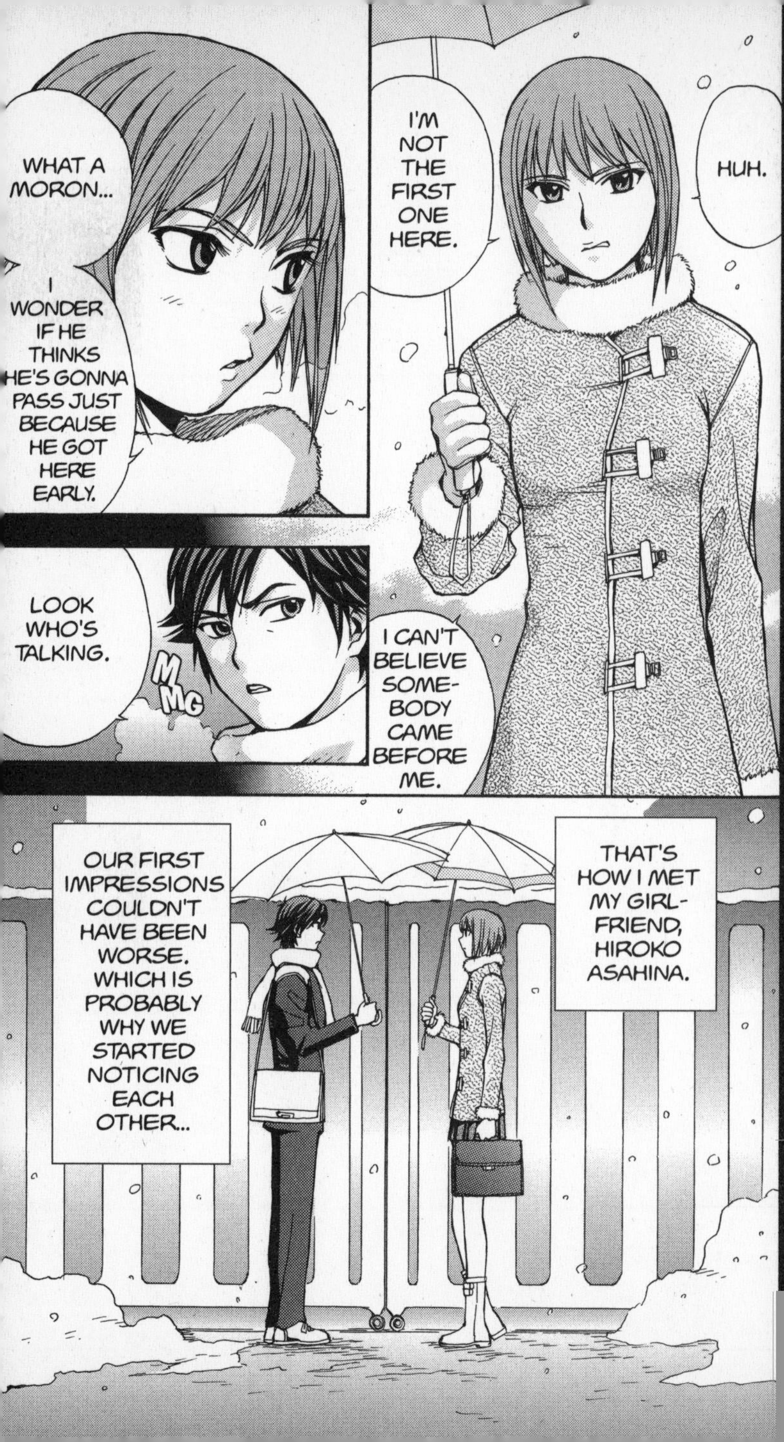
HUH.
I'M NOT THE FIRST ONE HERE.
I CAN'T BELIEVE SOME-BODY CAME BEFORE ME.
WHAT A MORON...
I WONDER IF HE THINKS HE'S GONNA PASS JUST BECAUSE HE GOT HERE EARLY.
LOOK WHO'S TALKING.
MMG
THAT'S HOW I MET MY GIRL-FRIEND, HIROKO ASAHINA.
OUR FIRST IMPRESSIONS COULDN'T HAVE BEEN WORSE. WHICH IS PROBABLY WHY WE STARTED NOTICING EACH OTHER...

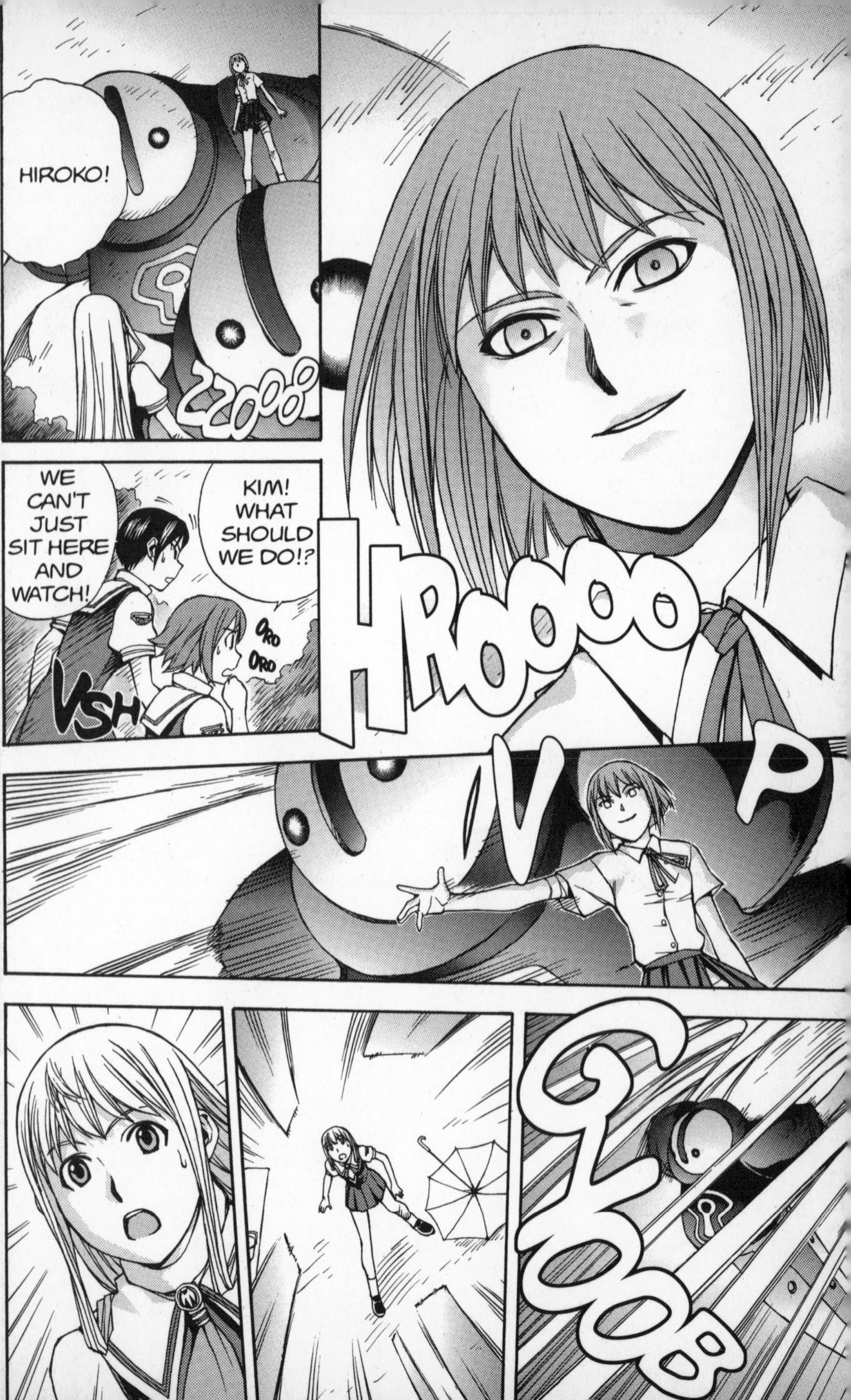
HROOOOVP
HIROKO!
ZZOooo
KIM! WHAT SHOULD WE DO!?
WE CAN'T JUST SIT HERE AND WATCH!
ORO ORO
VSH
GYOOB

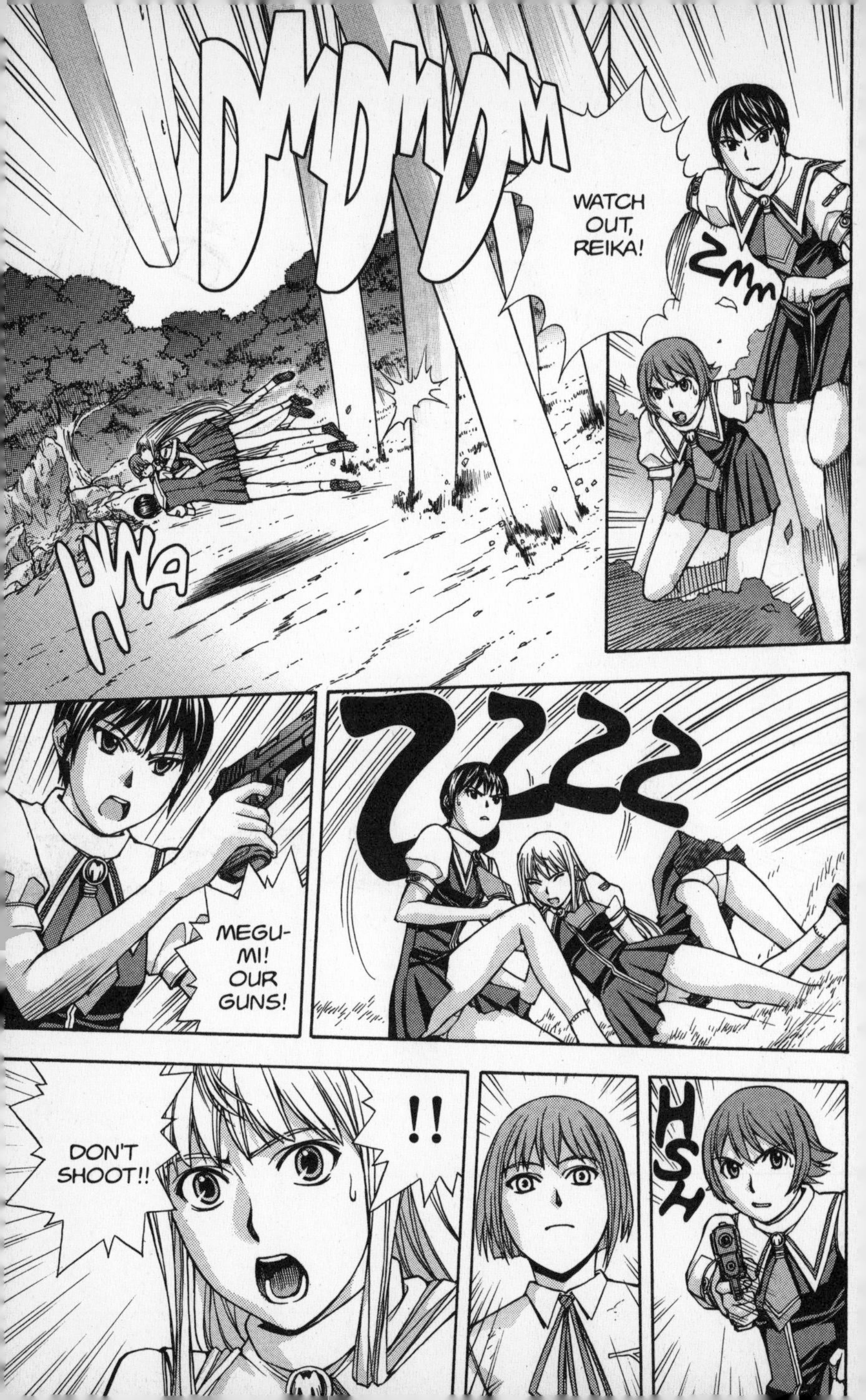
WATCH OUT, REIKA!
ZMM
DMDMDM
HWA
ZZZZ
MEGUMI! OUR GUNS!
HSH
!!
DON'T SHOOT!!

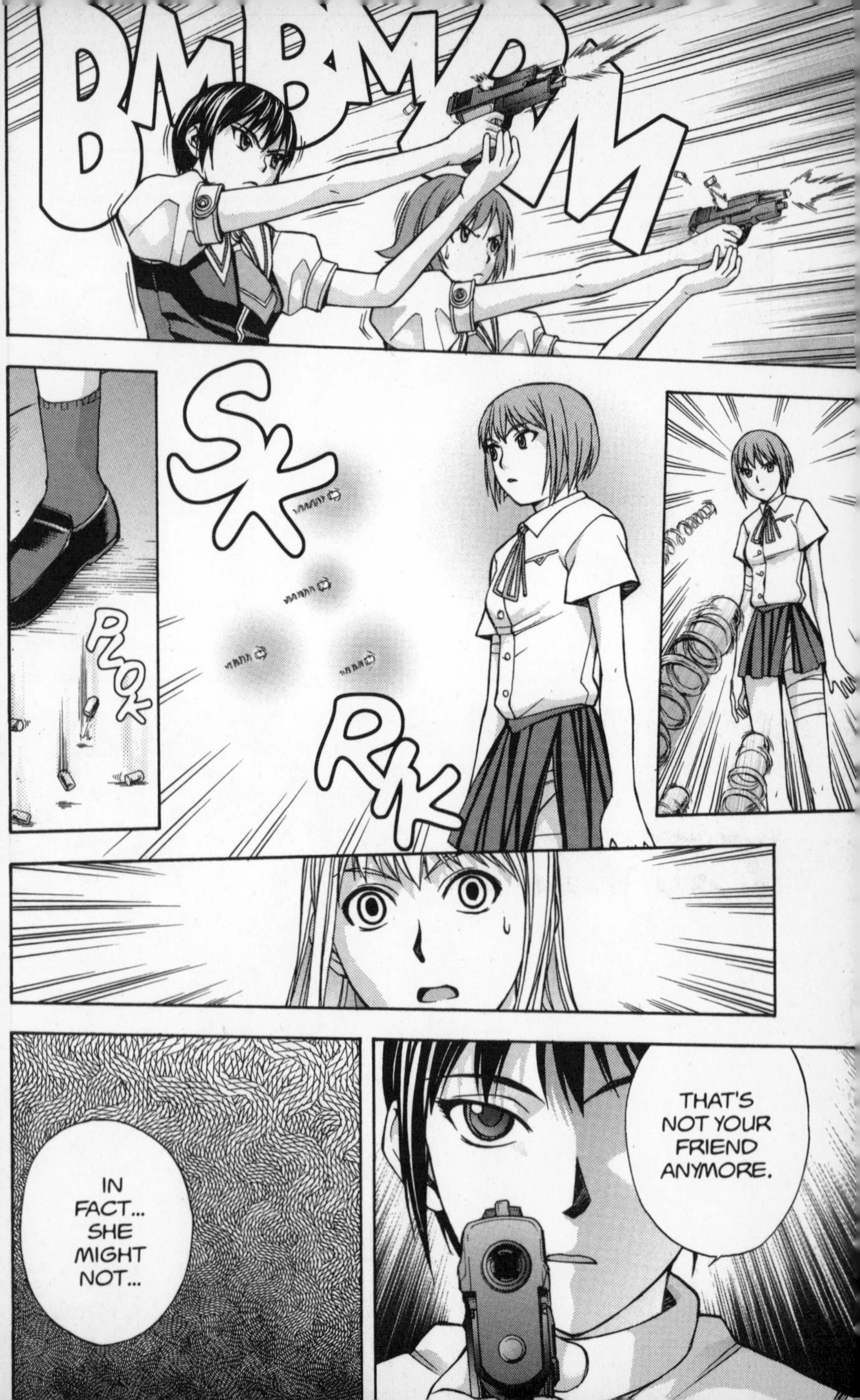
BMBMBM
SK
PLOK
RK
THAT'S NOT YOUR FRIEND ANYMORE.
IN FACT... SHE MIGHT NOT...

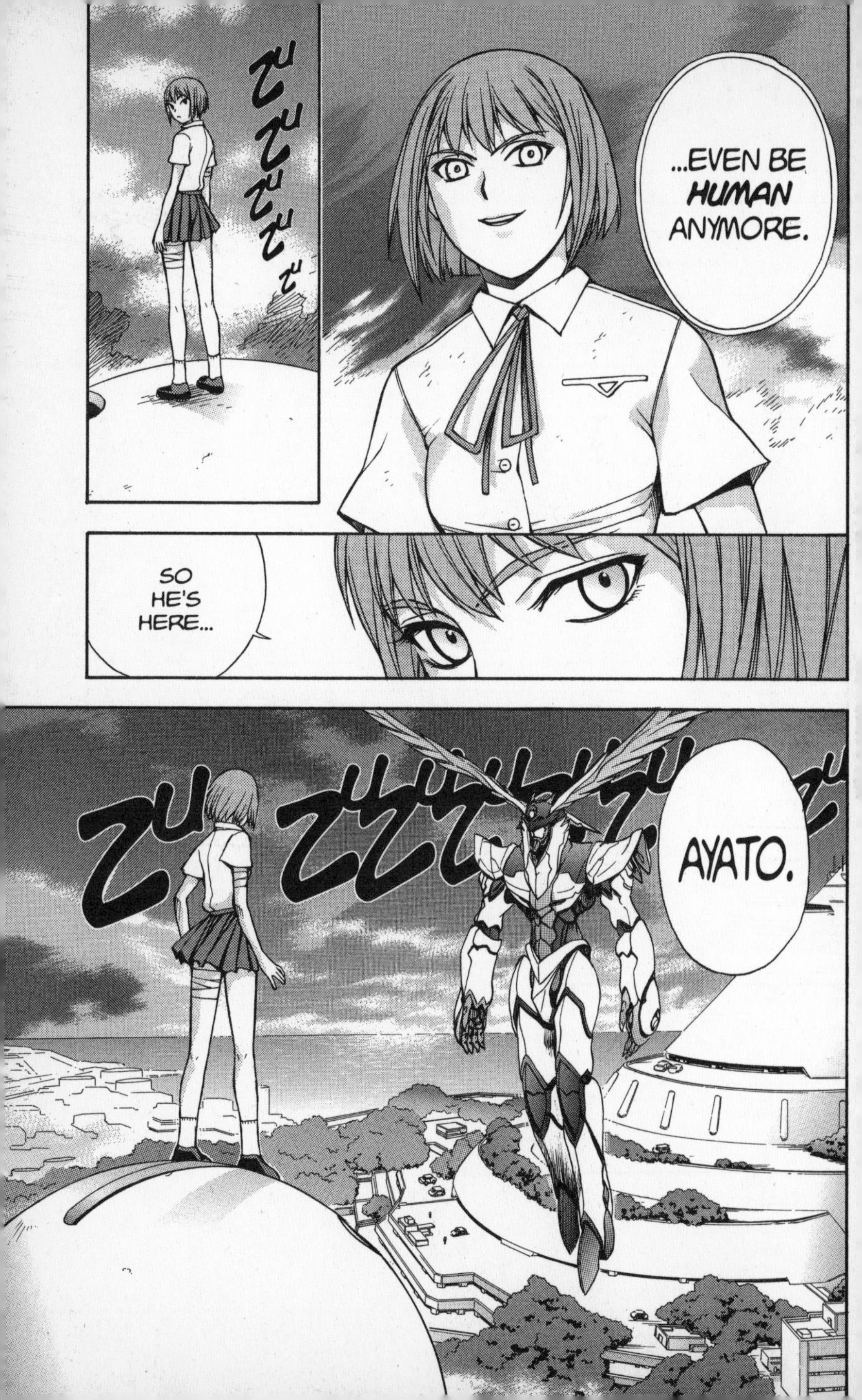
...EVEN BE *HUMAN* ANYMORE.
SO HE'S HERE...
AYATO.

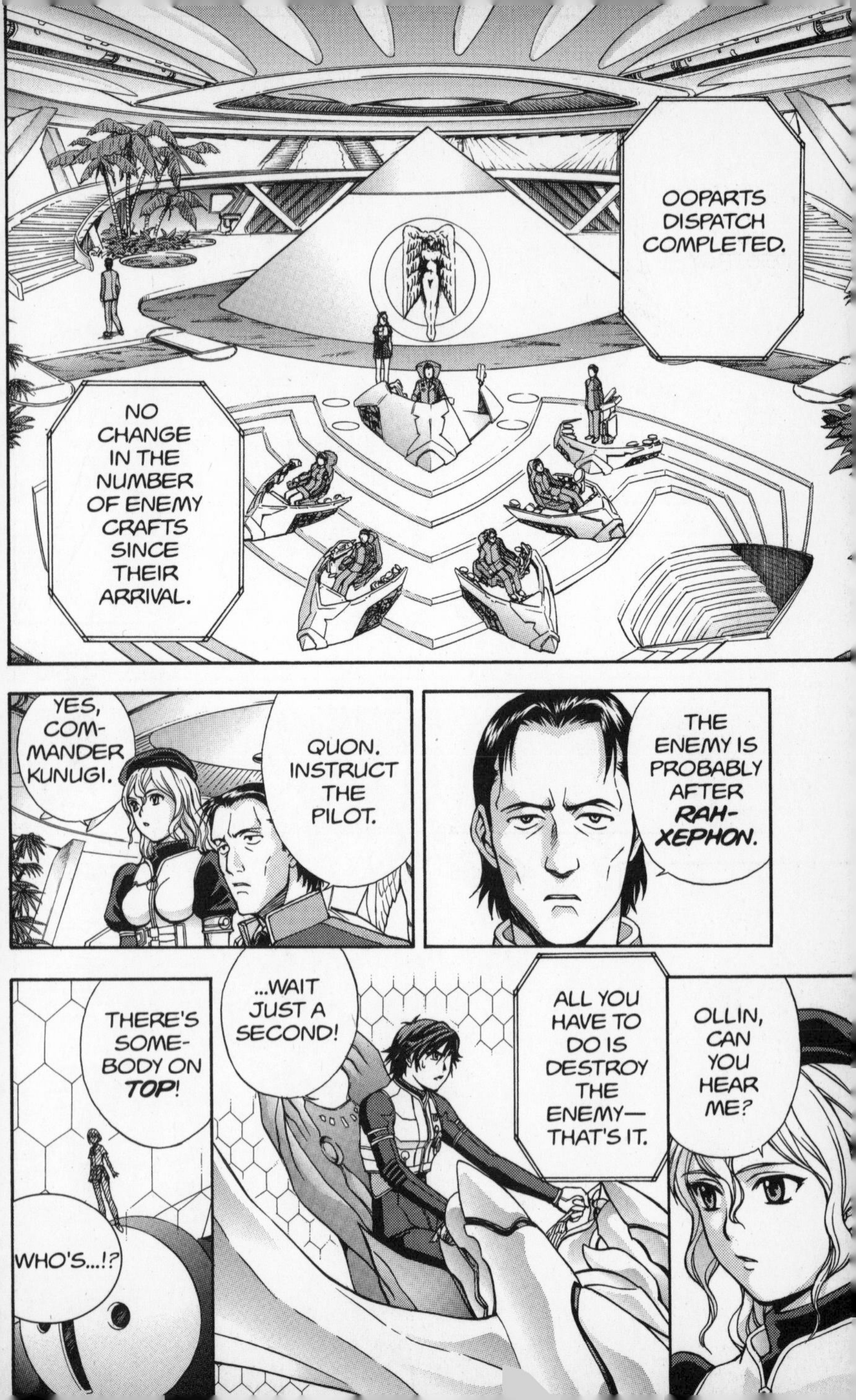

OOPARTS DISPATCH COMPLETED.
NO CHANGE IN THE NUMBER OF ENEMY CRAFTS SINCE THEIR ARRIVAL.
THE ENEMY IS PROBABLY AFTER *RAH-XEPHON*.
QUON. INSTRUCT THE PILOT.
YES, COMMANDER KUNUGI.
OLLIN, CAN YOU HEAR ME?
ALL YOU HAVE TO DO IS DESTROY THE ENEMY—THAT'S IT.
...WAIT JUST A SECOND!
THERE'S SOMEBODY ON *TOP*!
WHO'S...!?

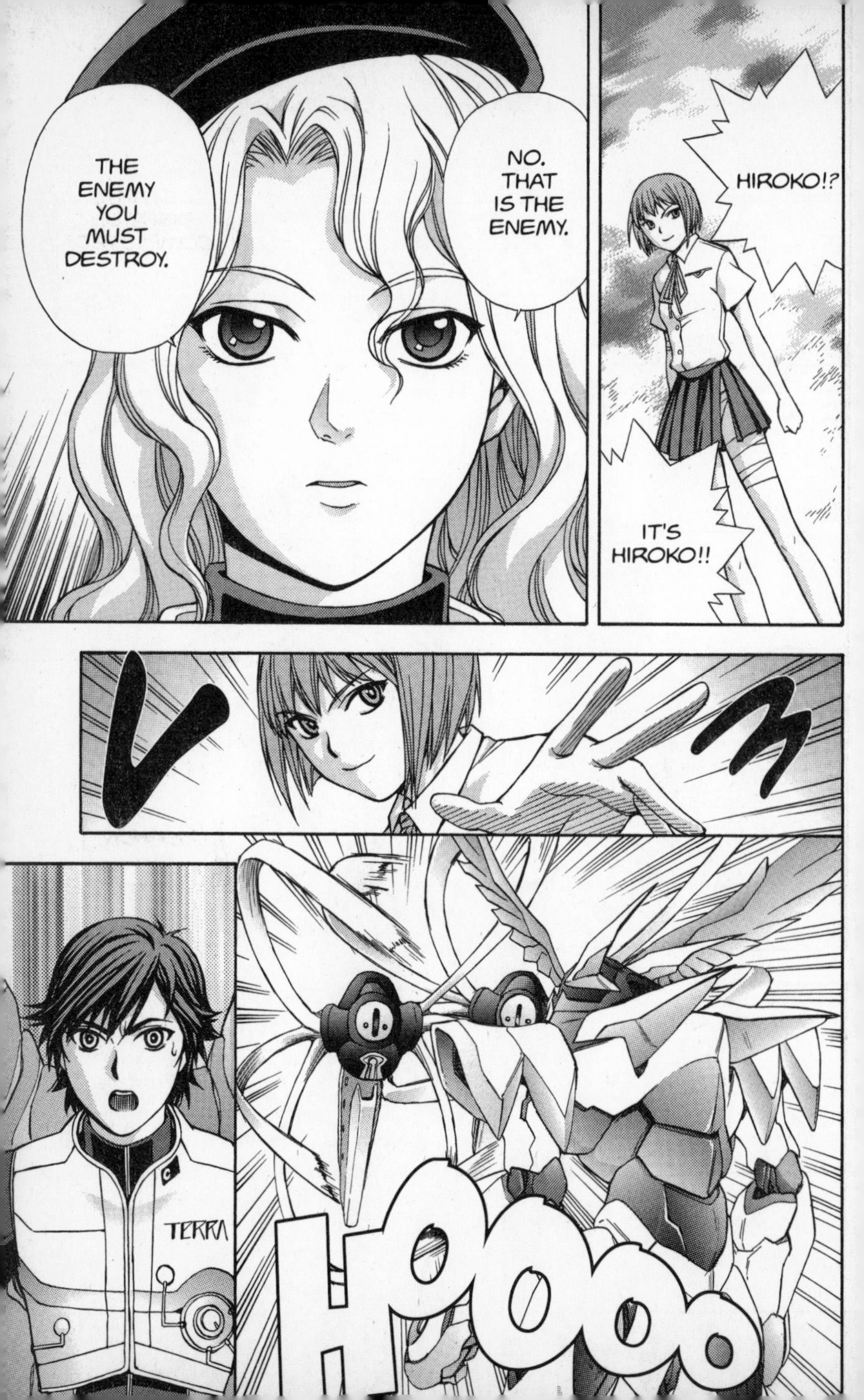
HIROKO!?
IT'S HIROKO!!
NO. THAT IS THE ENEMY.
THE ENEMY YOU MUST DESTROY.
VM
HOOOO
TERRA

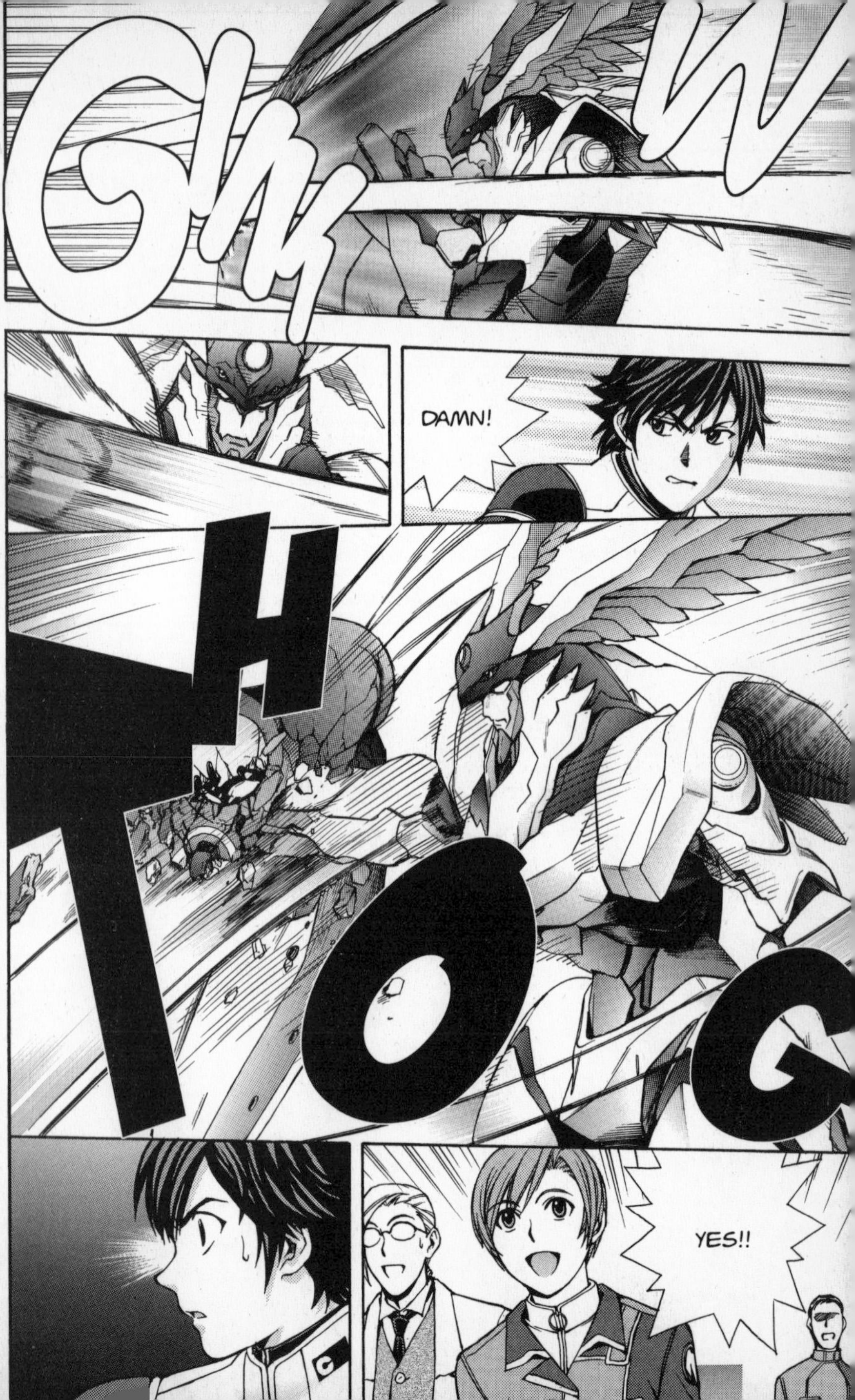
Ghyw
DAMN!
THOG
YES!!

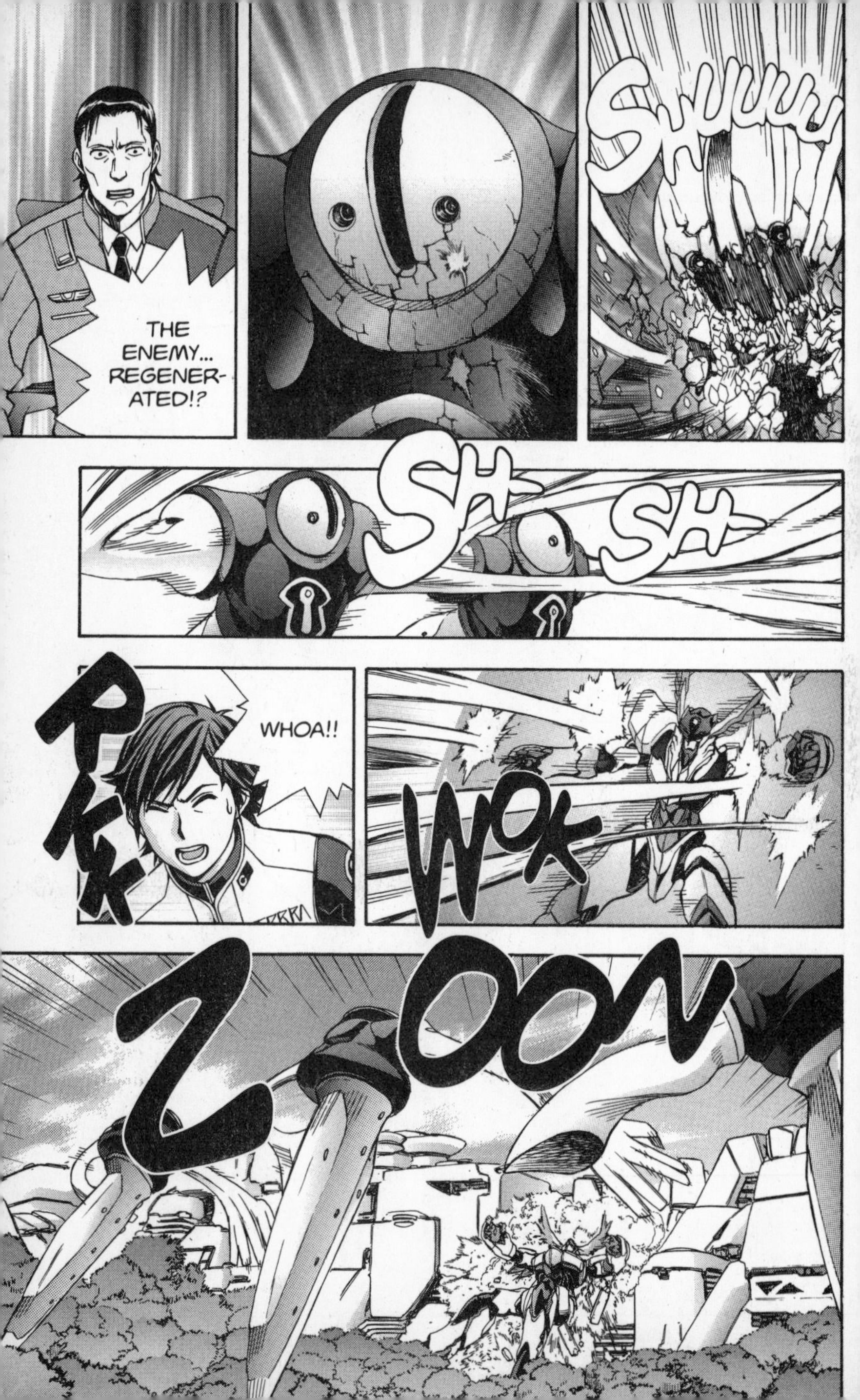
SHUUUU
THE ENEMY... REGENERATED!?
SH
SH
WHOA!!

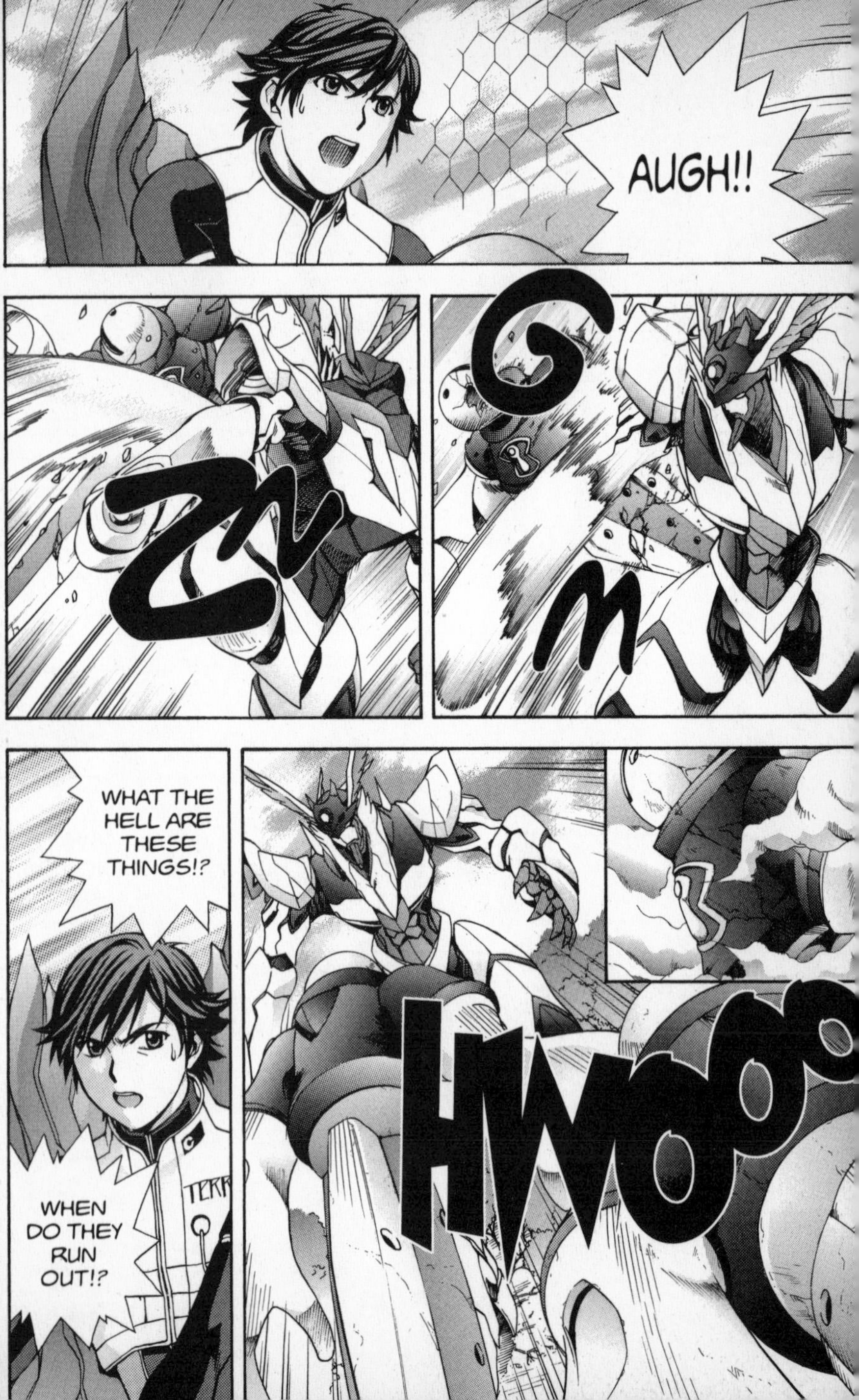
AUGH!!
HWOOO
WHAT THE HELL ARE THESE THINGS!?
WHEN DO THEY RUN OUT!?

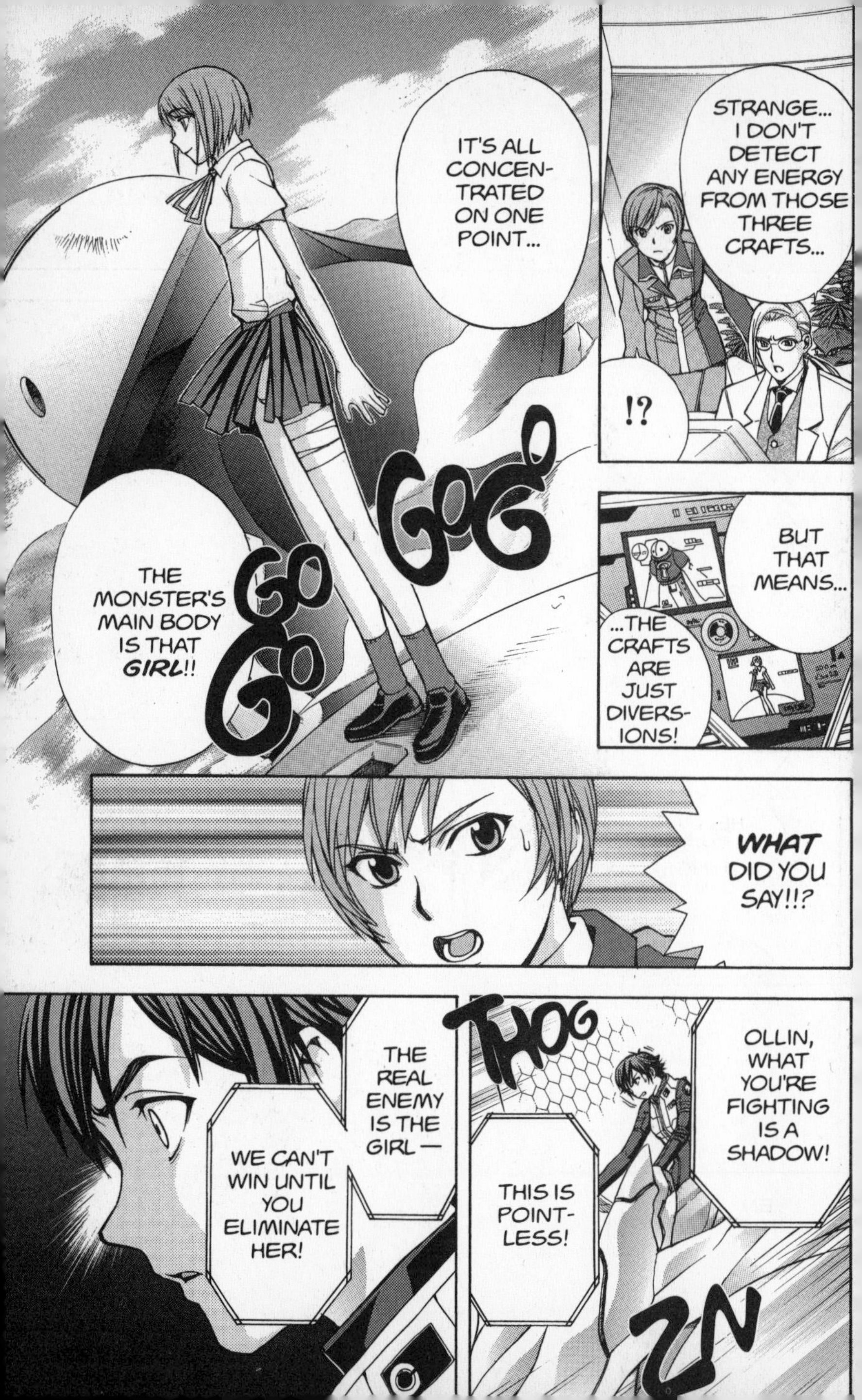
STRANGE... I DON'T DETECT ANY ENERGY FROM THOSE THREE CRAFTS...
!?
BUT THAT MEANS...
...THE CRAFTS ARE JUST DIVERSIONS!
IT'S ALL CONCENTRATED ON ONE POINT...
GOGO
GOGO
THE MONSTER'S MAIN BODY IS THAT **GIRL**!!
WHAT DID YOU SAY!!?
OLLIN, WHAT YOU'RE FIGHTING IS A SHADOW!
THOG
THIS IS POINTLESS!
ZN
THE REAL ENEMY IS THE GIRL —
WE CAN'T WIN UNTIL YOU ELIMINATE HER!

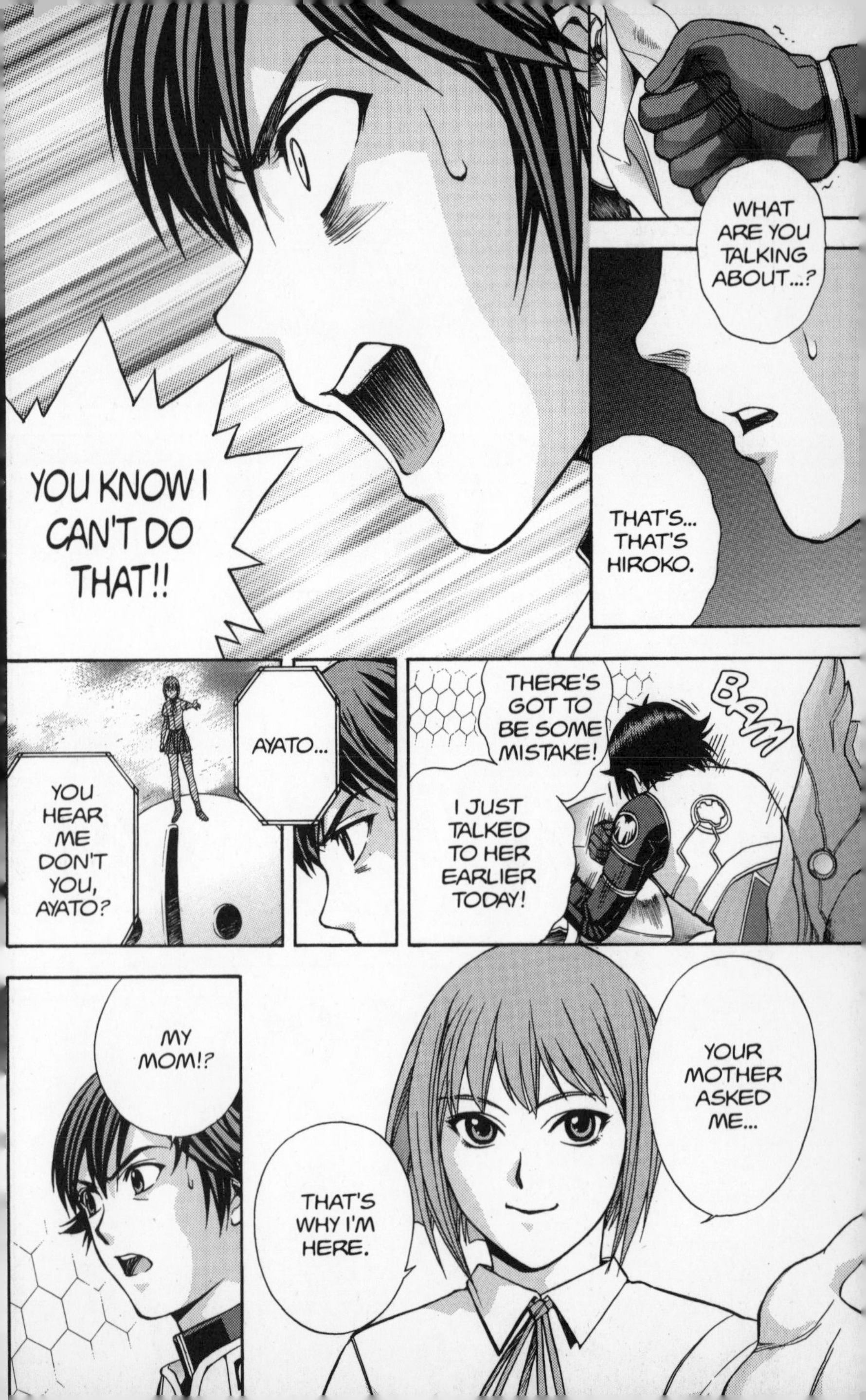

WHAT ARE YOU TALKING ABOUT...?
THAT'S... THAT'S HIROKO.
YOU KNOW I CAN'T DO THAT!!
BAM
THERE'S GOT TO BE SOME MISTAKE!
I JUST TALKED TO HER EARLIER TODAY!
AYATO...
YOU HEAR ME DON'T YOU, AYATO?
YOUR MOTHER ASKED ME...
THAT'S WHY I'M HERE.
MY MOM!?

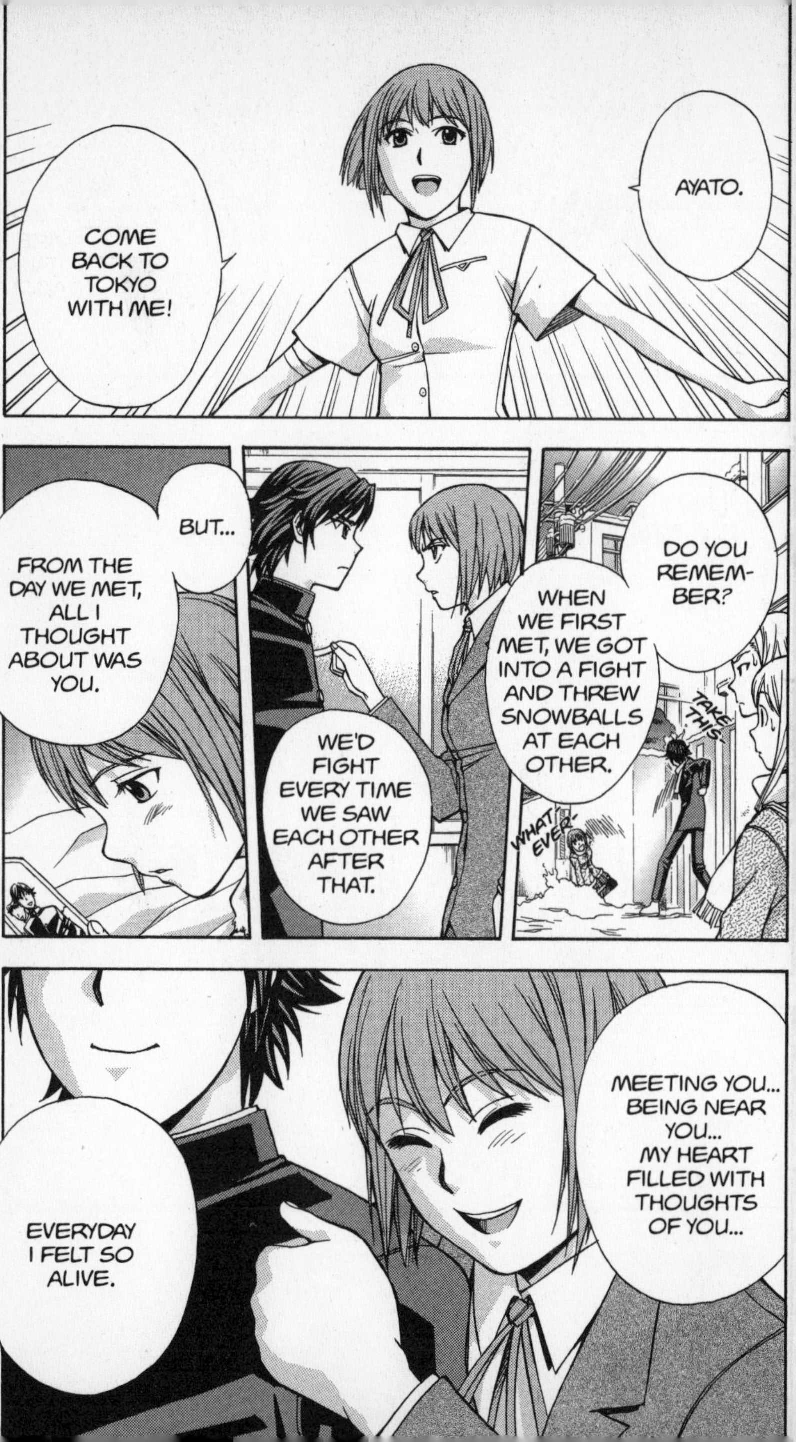

AYATO.
COME BACK TO TOKYO WITH ME!
DO YOU REMEMBER?
WHEN WE FIRST MET, WE GOT INTO A FIGHT AND THREW SNOWBALLS AT EACH OTHER.
TAKE THIS!
WHATEVER!
WE'D FIGHT EVERY TIME WE SAW EACH OTHER AFTER THAT.
BUT...
FROM THE DAY WE MET, ALL I THOUGHT ABOUT WAS YOU.
MEETING YOU... BEING NEAR YOU... MY HEART FILLED WITH THOUGHTS OF YOU...
EVERYDAY I FELT SO ALIVE.

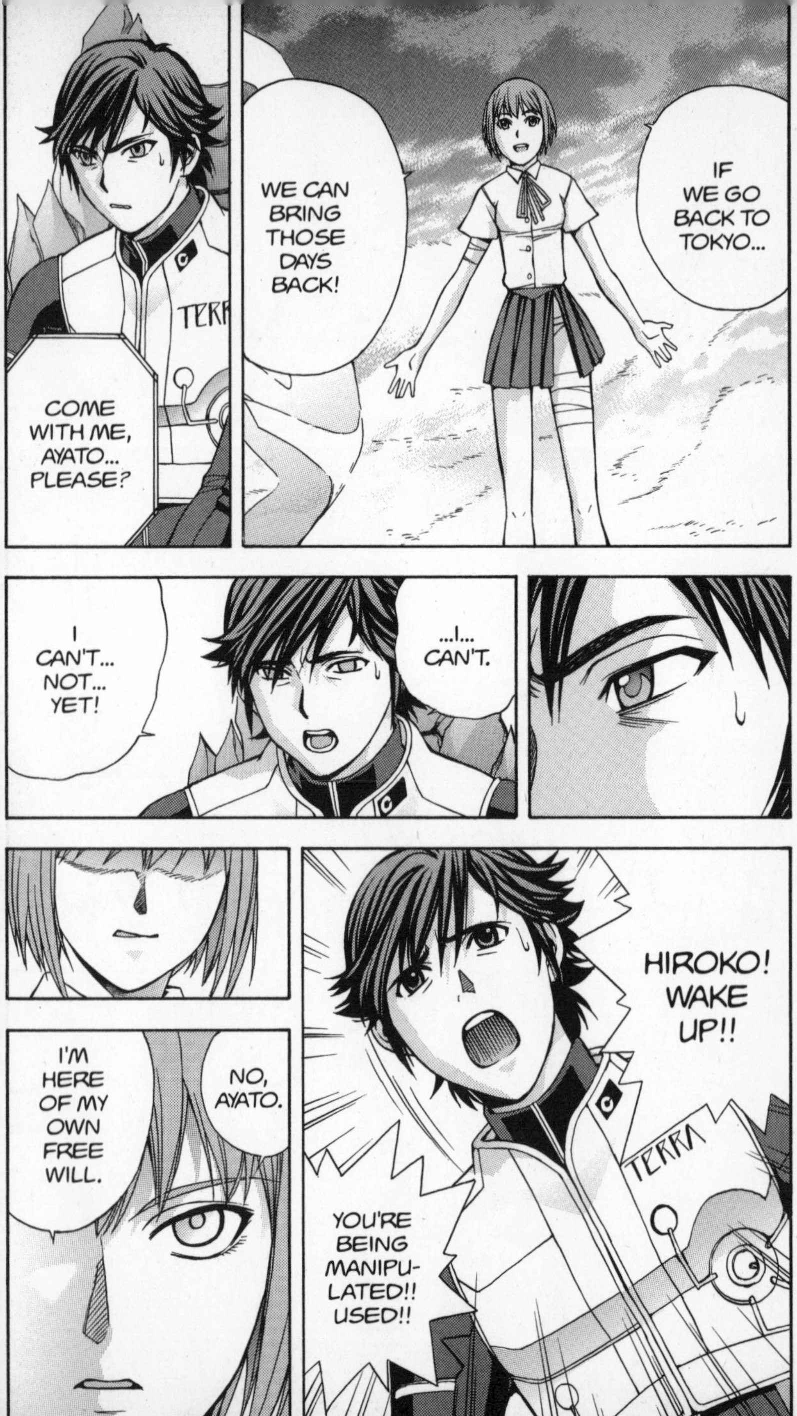
IF WE GO BACK TO TOKYO...
WE CAN BRING THOSE DAYS BACK!
COME WITH ME, AYATO... PLEASE?
...I... CAN'T.
I CAN'T... NOT... YET!
HIROKO! WAKE UP!!
YOU'RE BEING MANIPU-LATED!! USED!!
NO, AYATO.
I'M HERE OF MY OWN FREE WILL.

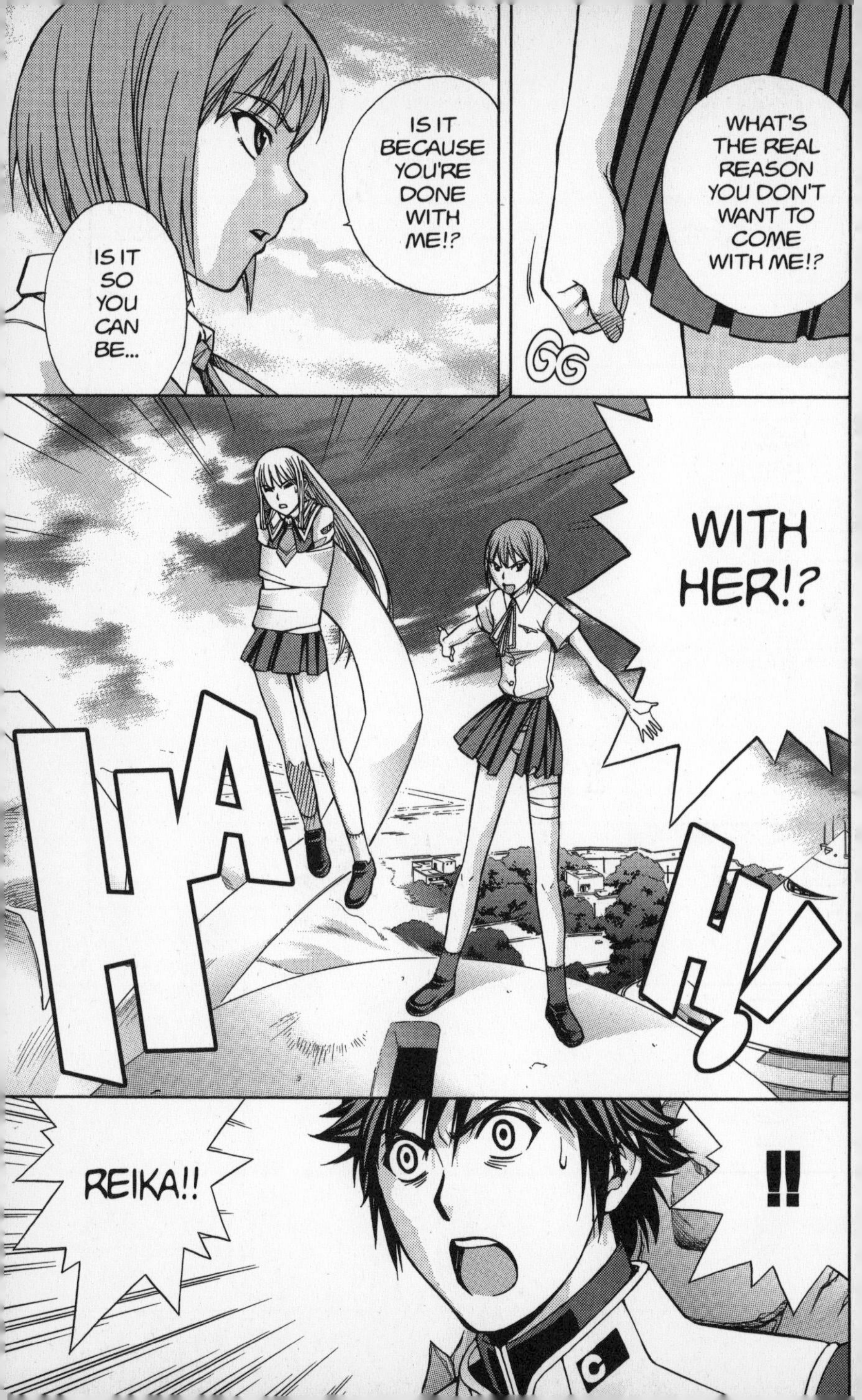
WHAT'S THE REAL REASON YOU DON'T WANT TO COME WITH ME!?
GG
IS IT BECAUSE YOU'RE DONE WITH ME!?
IS IT SO YOU CAN BE...
WITH HER!?
HAH!
!!
REIKA!!

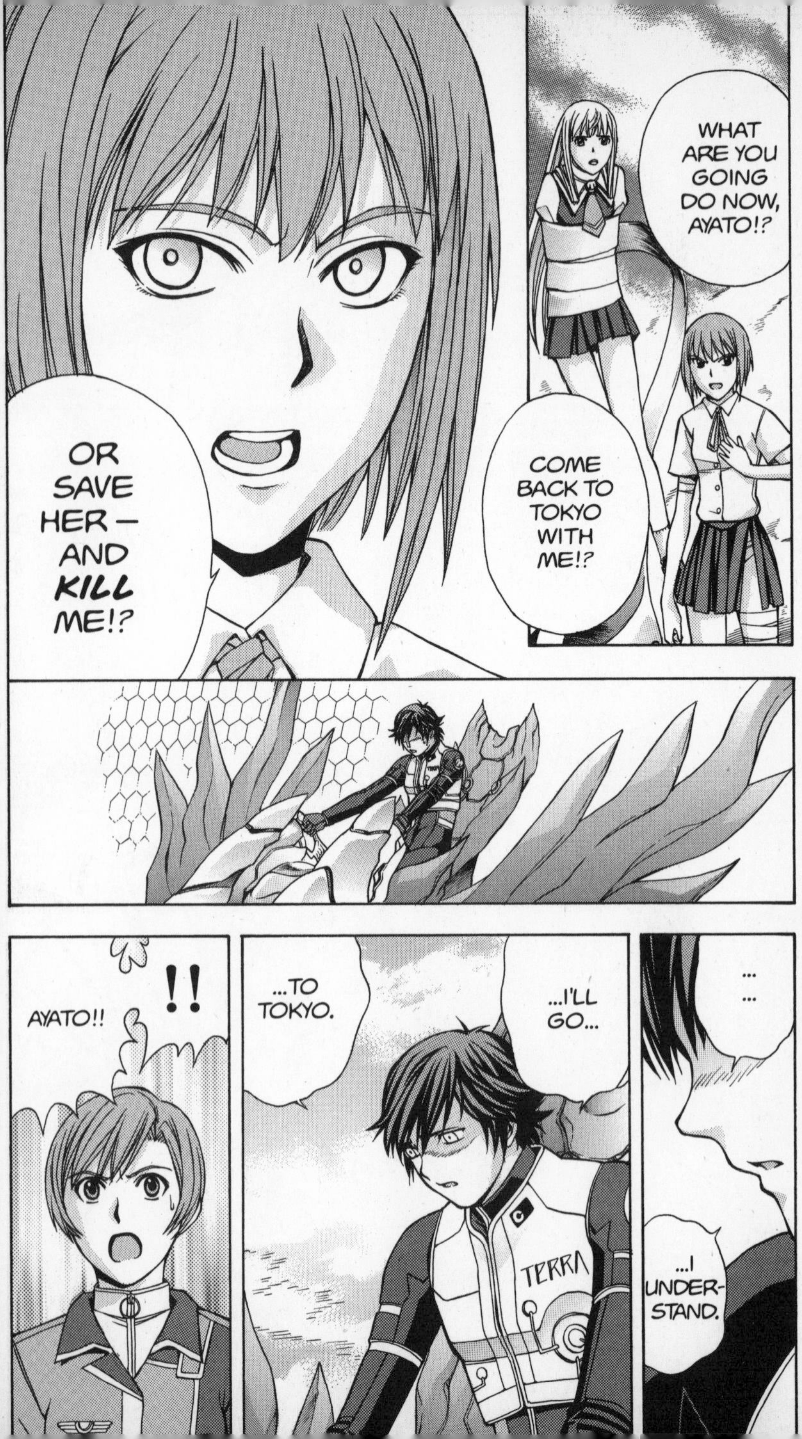
WHAT ARE YOU GOING DO NOW, AYATO!?
COME BACK TO TOKYO WITH ME!?
OR SAVE HER— AND **KILL** ME!?
... ...
...I UNDER-STAND.
...I'LL GO...
...TO TOKYO.
!!
AYATO!!

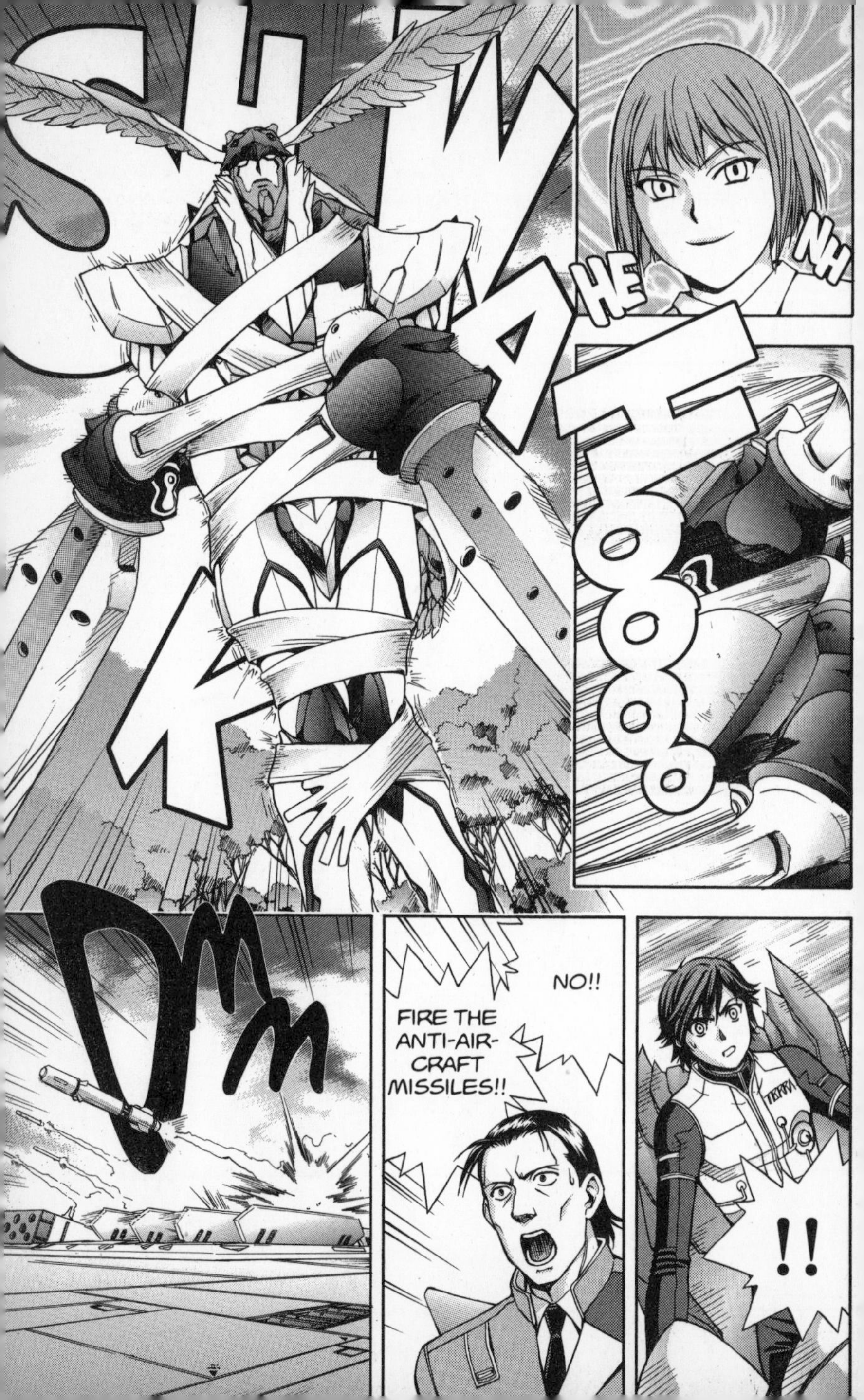

HE NH
FOOOOO
SHWAK
!!
NO!!
FIRE THE ANTI-AIR-CRAFT MISSILES!!
DMm

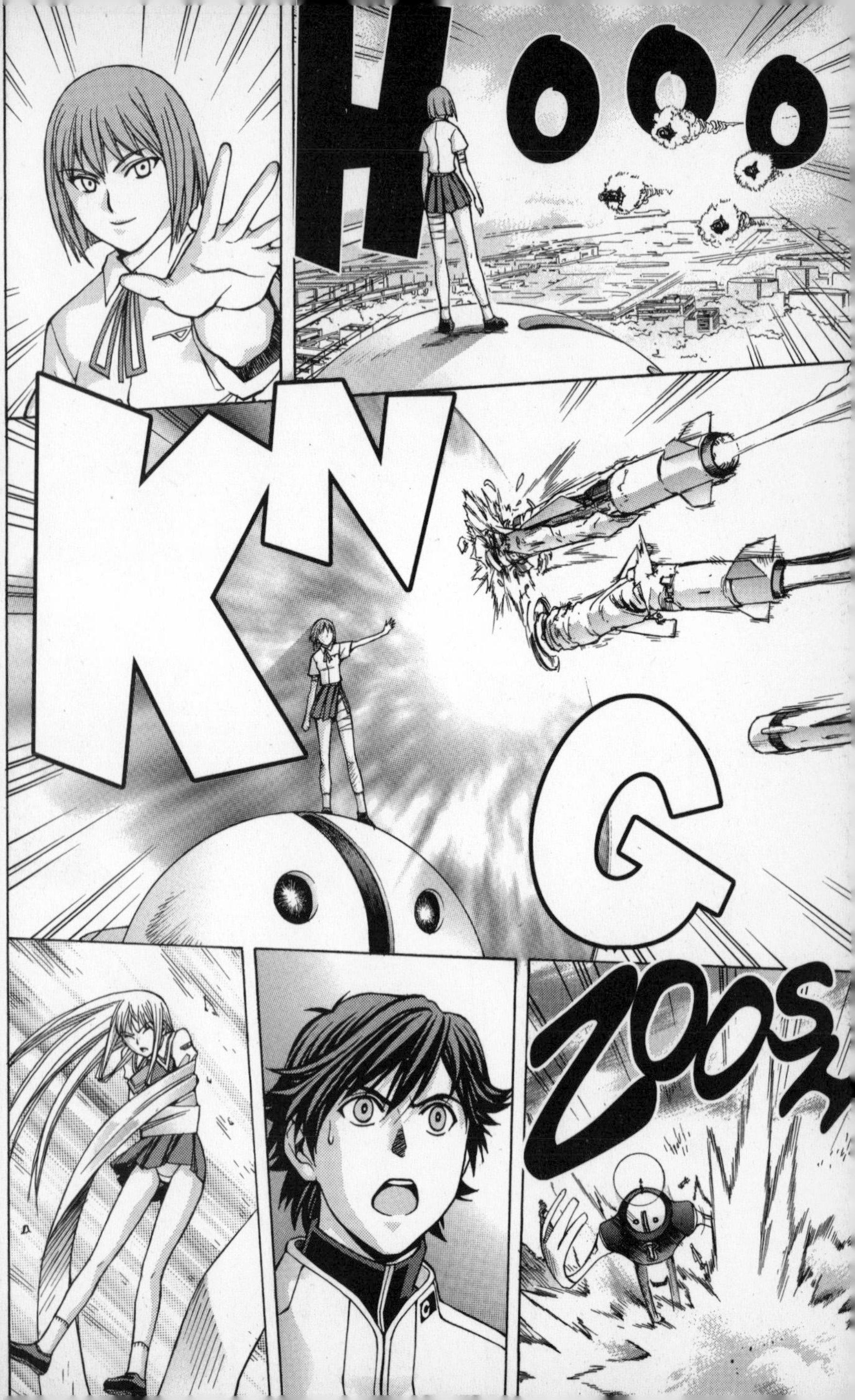
HOOO
KNG
ZOOS

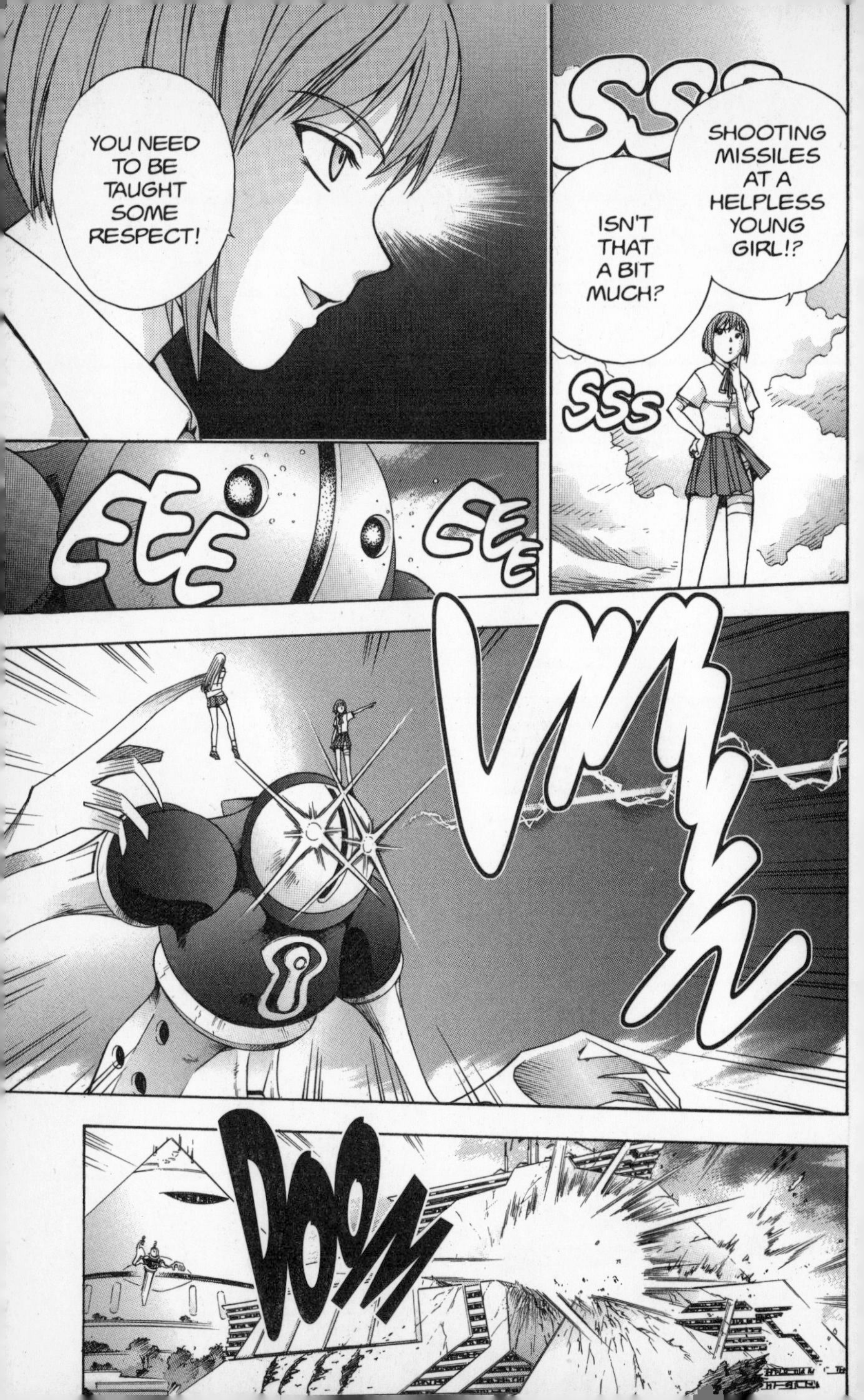
SSS
SHOOTING MISSILES AT A HELPLESS YOUNG GIRL!?
ISN'T THAT A BIT MUCH?
SSS
YOU NEED TO BE TAUGHT SOME RESPECT!
EEE
EEE
DOOM

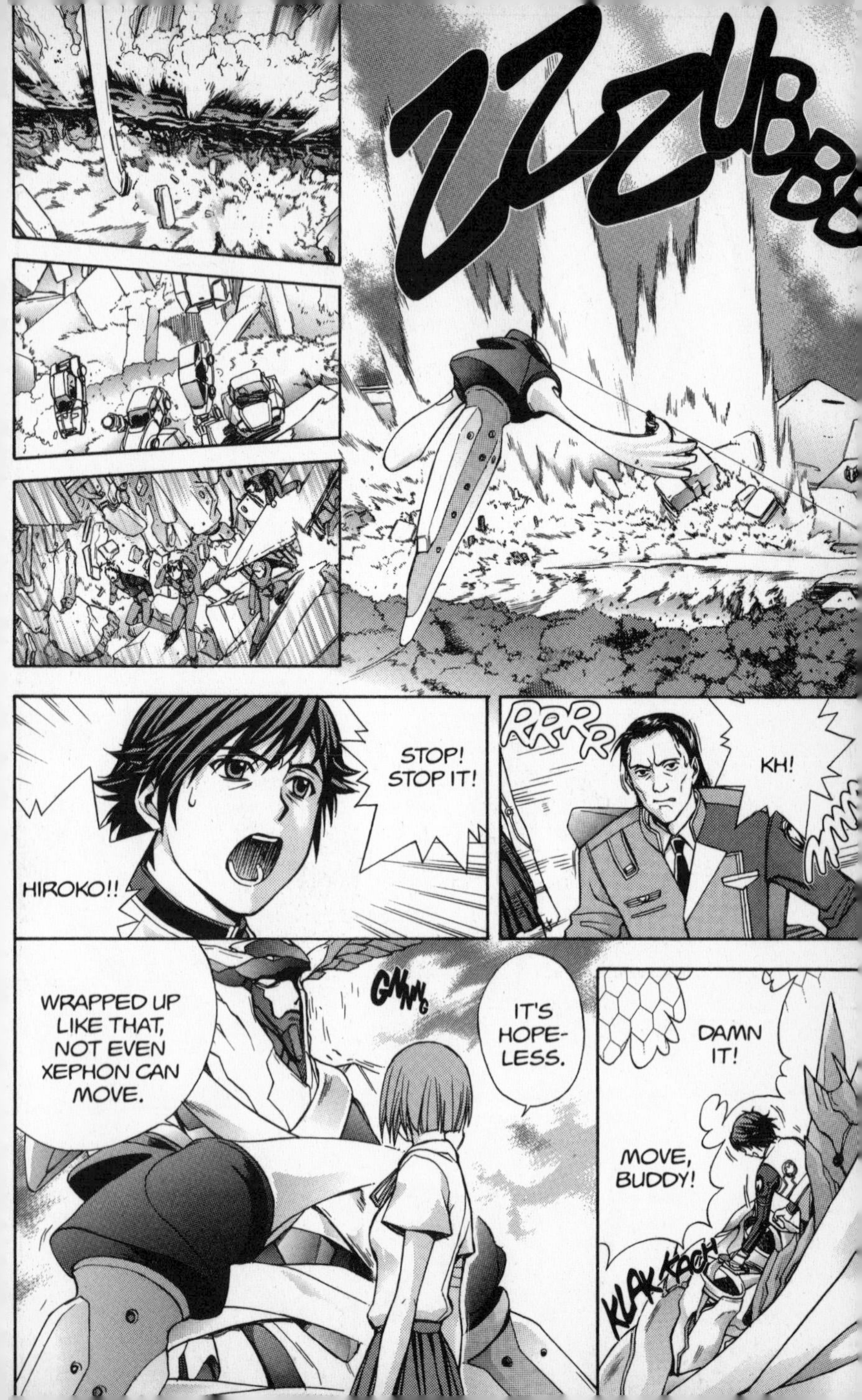
ZZZUBBB
KH!
STOP! STOP IT!
HIROKO!!
DAMN IT!
MOVE, BUDDY!
KLAK KACH
IT'S HOPE-LESS.
GNNNG
WRAPPED UP LIKE THAT, NOT EVEN XEPHON CAN MOVE.

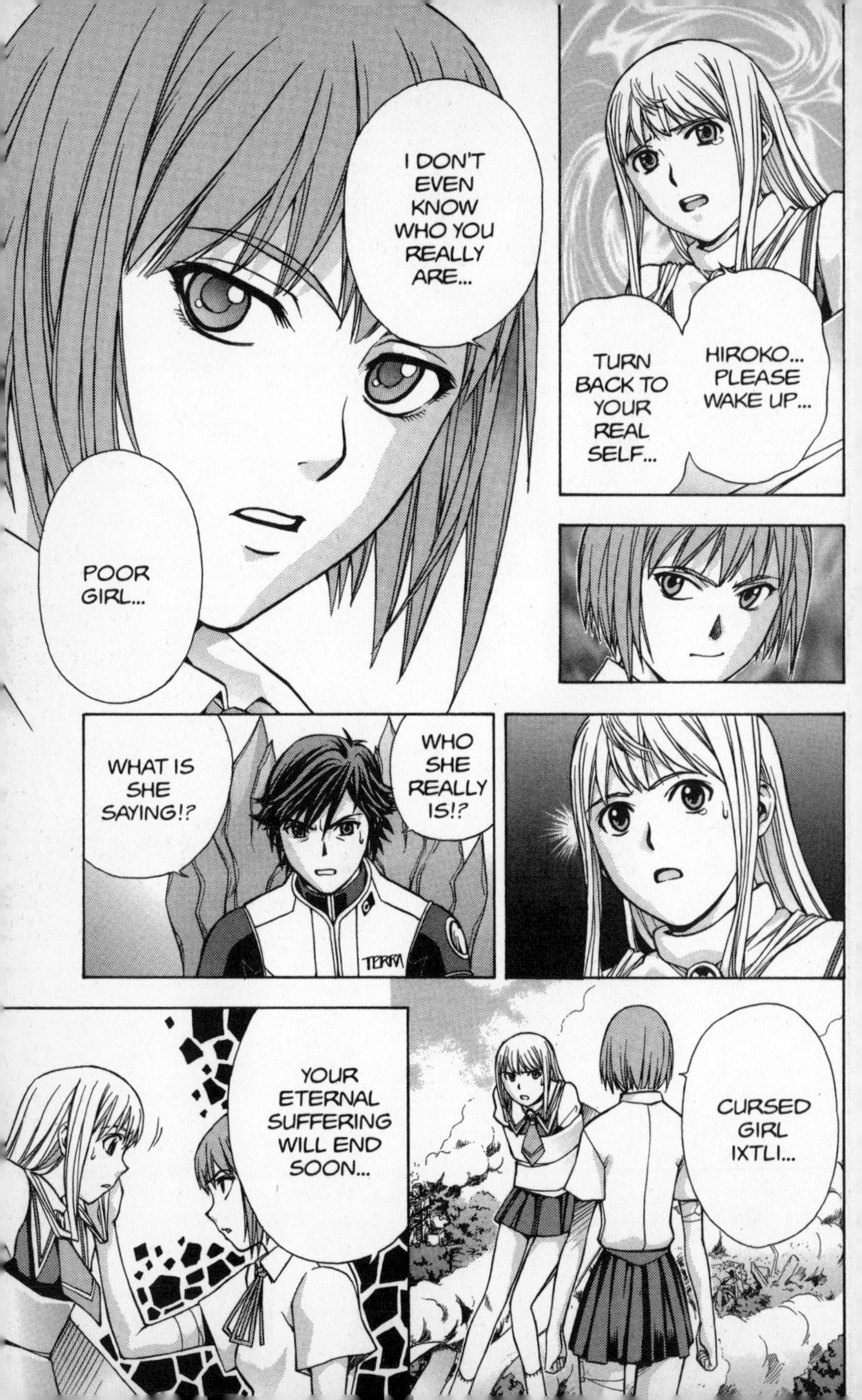
HIROKO... PLEASE WAKE UP...
TURN BACK TO YOUR REAL SELF...
I DON'T EVEN KNOW WHO YOU REALLY ARE...
POOR GIRL...
WHO SHE REALLY IS!?
WHAT IS SHE SAYING!?
CURSED GIRL IXTLI...
YOUR ETERNAL SUFFERING WILL END SOON...

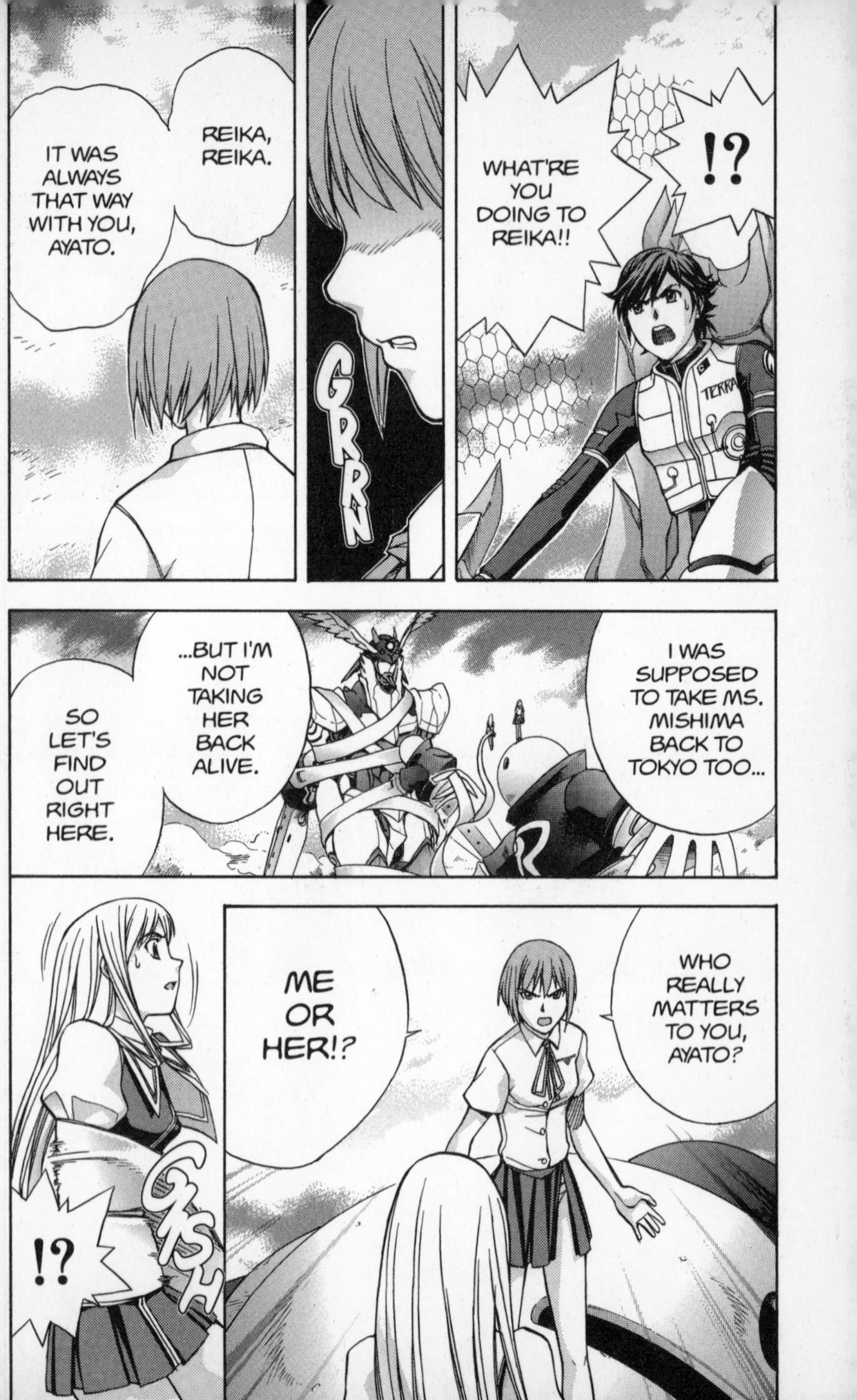
!?
WHAT'RE YOU DOING TO REIKA!!
GRRN
REIKA, REIKA.
IT WAS ALWAYS THAT WAY WITH YOU, AYATO.
I WAS SUPPOSED TO TAKE MS. MISHIMA BACK TO TOKYO TOO...
...BUT I'M NOT TAKING HER BACK ALIVE.
SO LET'S FIND OUT RIGHT HERE.
WHO REALLY MATTERS TO YOU, AYATO?
ME OR HER!?
GASH
!?

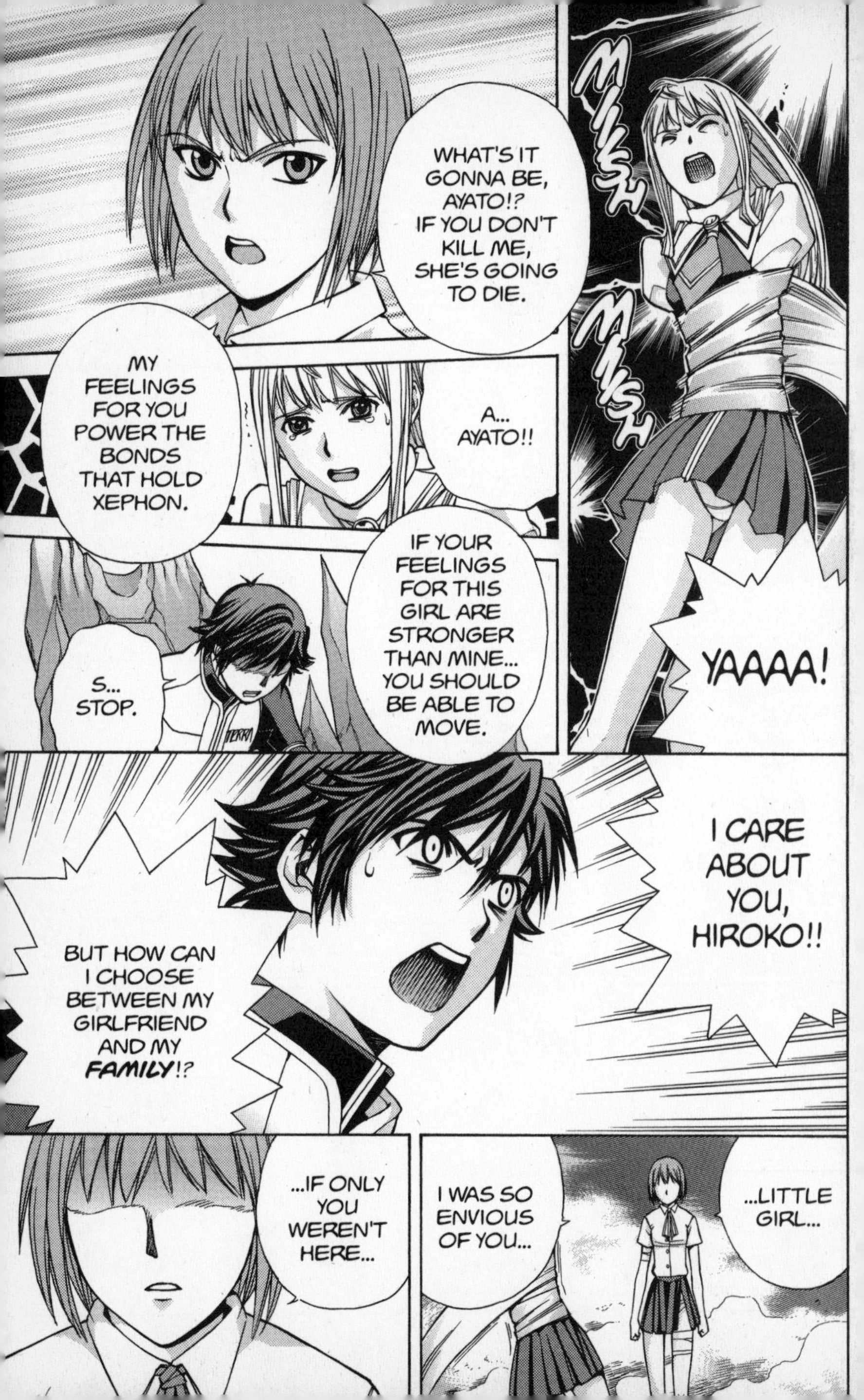
MIIISH
MIIISH
YAAAA!
WHAT'S IT GONNA BE, AYATO!? IF YOU DON'T KILL ME, SHE'S GOING TO DIE.
A... AYATO!!
MY FEELINGS FOR YOU POWER THE BONDS THAT HOLD XEPHON.
IF YOUR FEELINGS FOR THIS GIRL ARE STRONGER THAN MINE... YOU SHOULD BE ABLE TO MOVE.
S... STOP.
I CARE ABOUT YOU, HIROKO!!
BUT HOW CAN I CHOOSE BETWEEN MY GIRLFRIEND AND MY FAMILY!?
...LITTLE GIRL...
I WAS SO ENVIOUS OF YOU...
...IF ONLY YOU WEREN'T HERE...

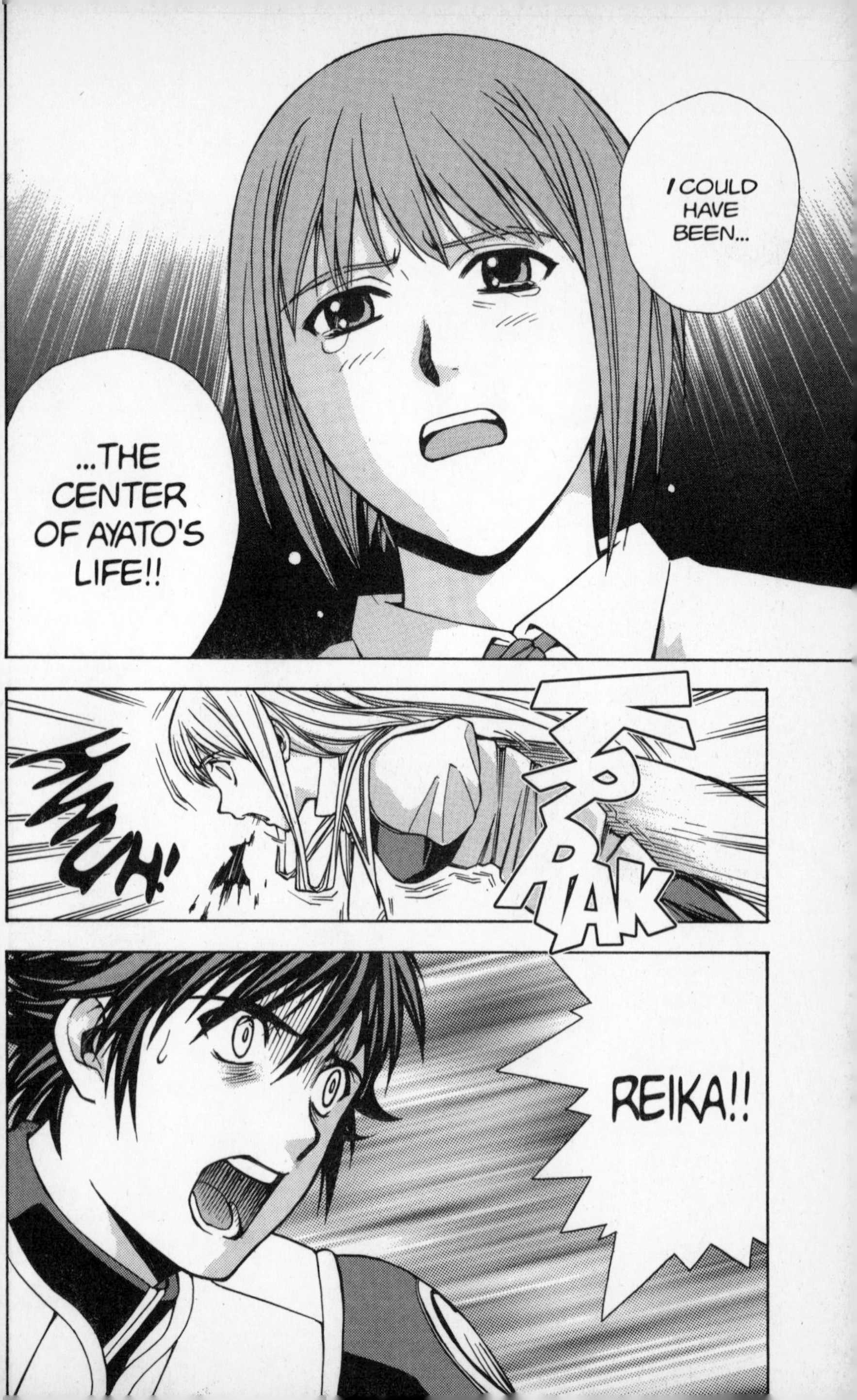
I COULD HAVE BEEN...
...THE CENTER OF AYATO'S LIFE!!
HWUH!
REIKA!!

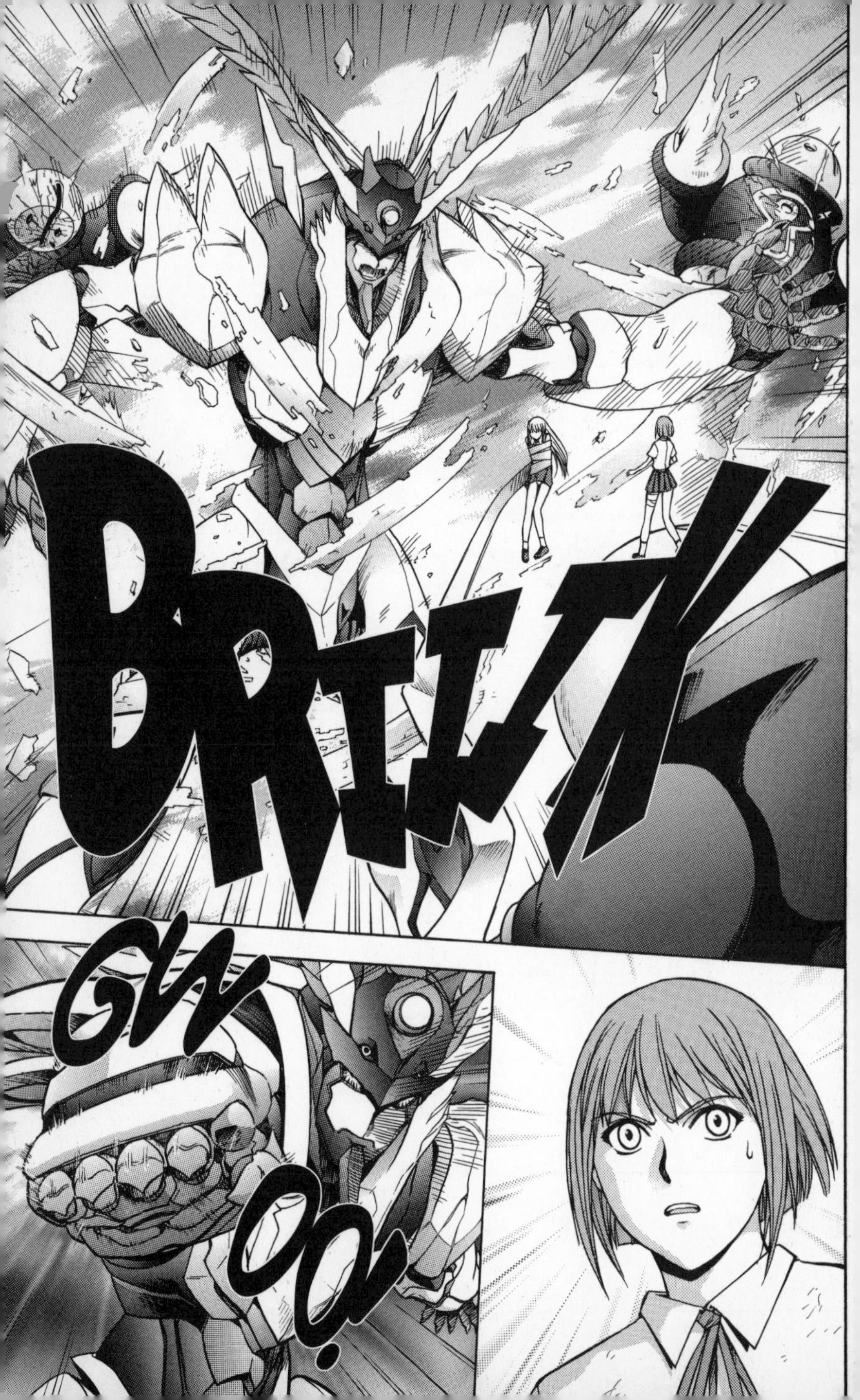
BRIIIK
GWOOO

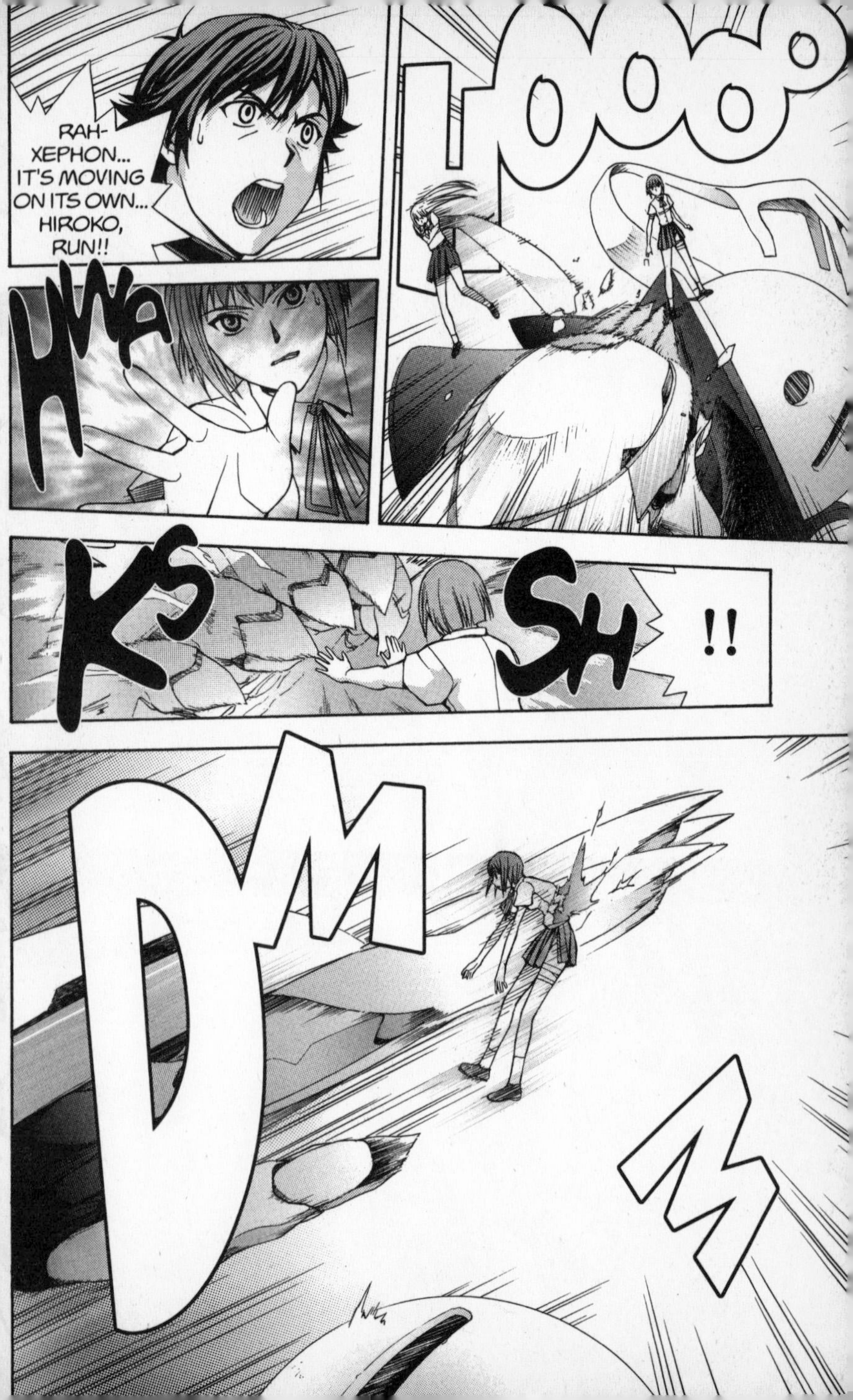
TOOOP
RAH-XEPHON... IT'S MOVING ON ITS OWN... HIROKO, RUN!!
HWA
KSSH!!
DMM

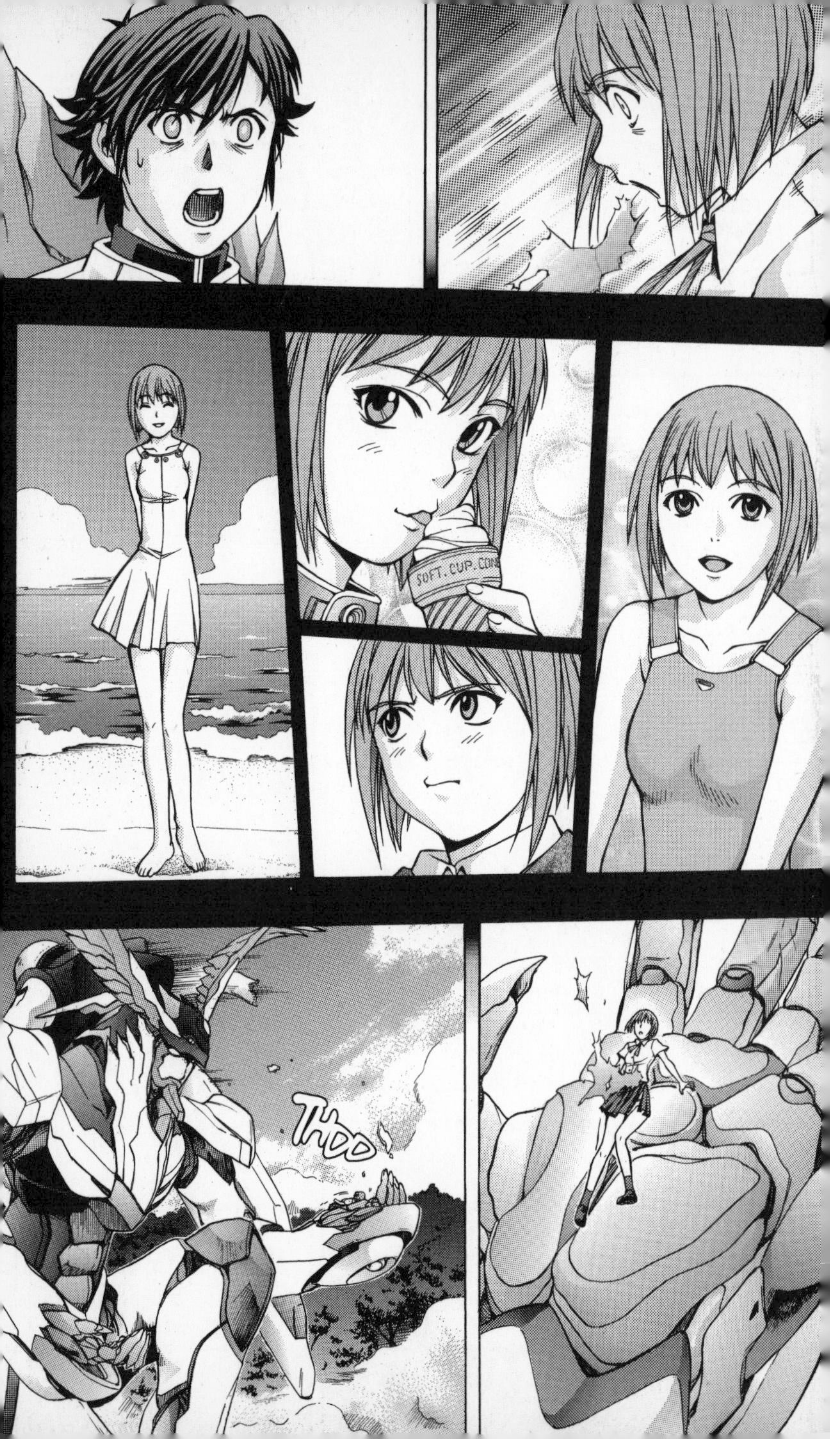
SOFT.CUP.CON
THOO

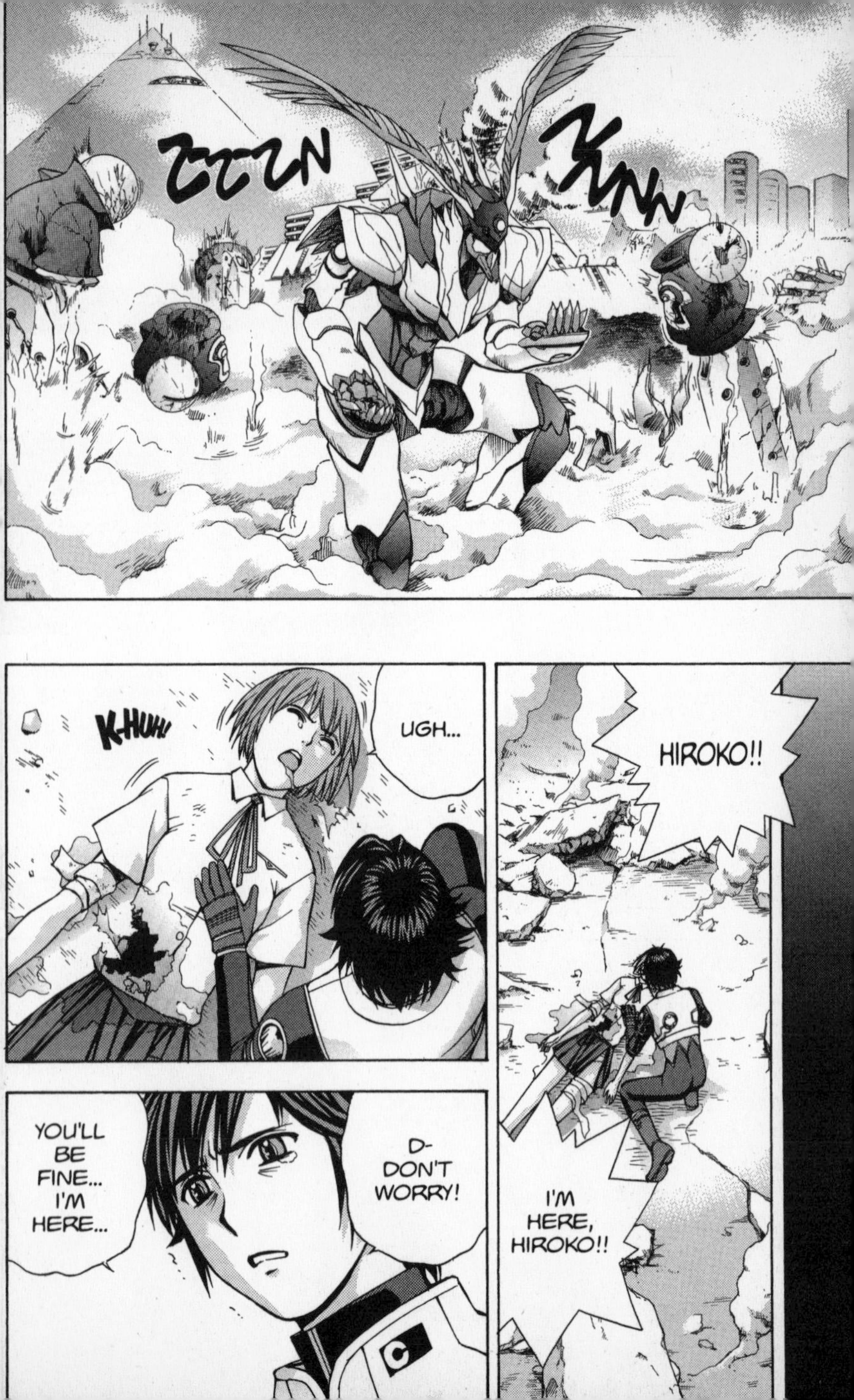
HIROKO!!
I'M HERE, HIROKO!!
UGH...
K-HUH!
D-DON'T WORRY!
YOU'LL BE FINE... I'M HERE...

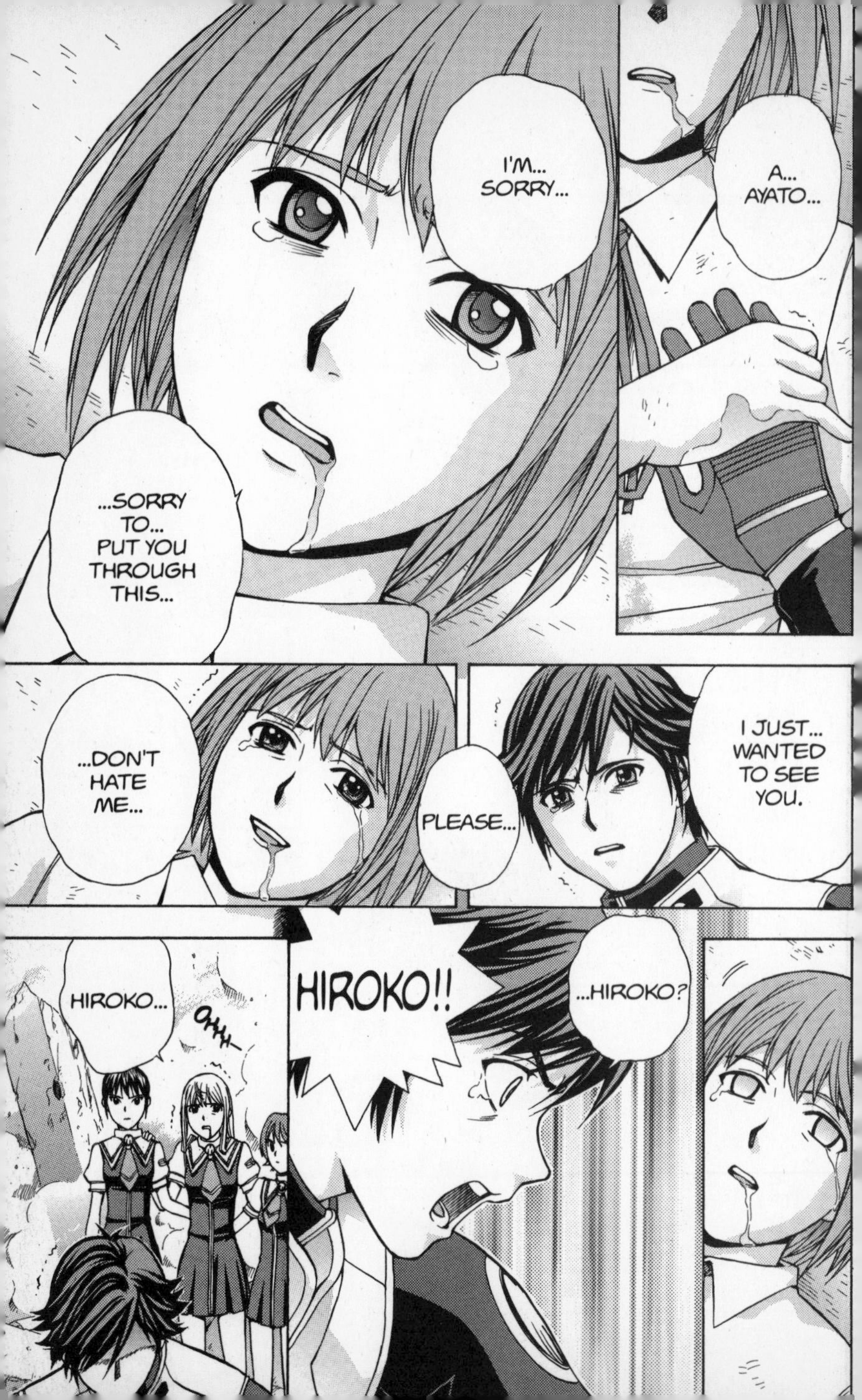
A... AYATO...
I'M... SORRY...
...SORRY TO... PUT YOU THROUGH THIS...
I JUST... WANTED TO SEE YOU.
PLEASE...
...DON'T HATE ME...
...HIROKO?
HIROKO!!
HIROKO...
OHHH-

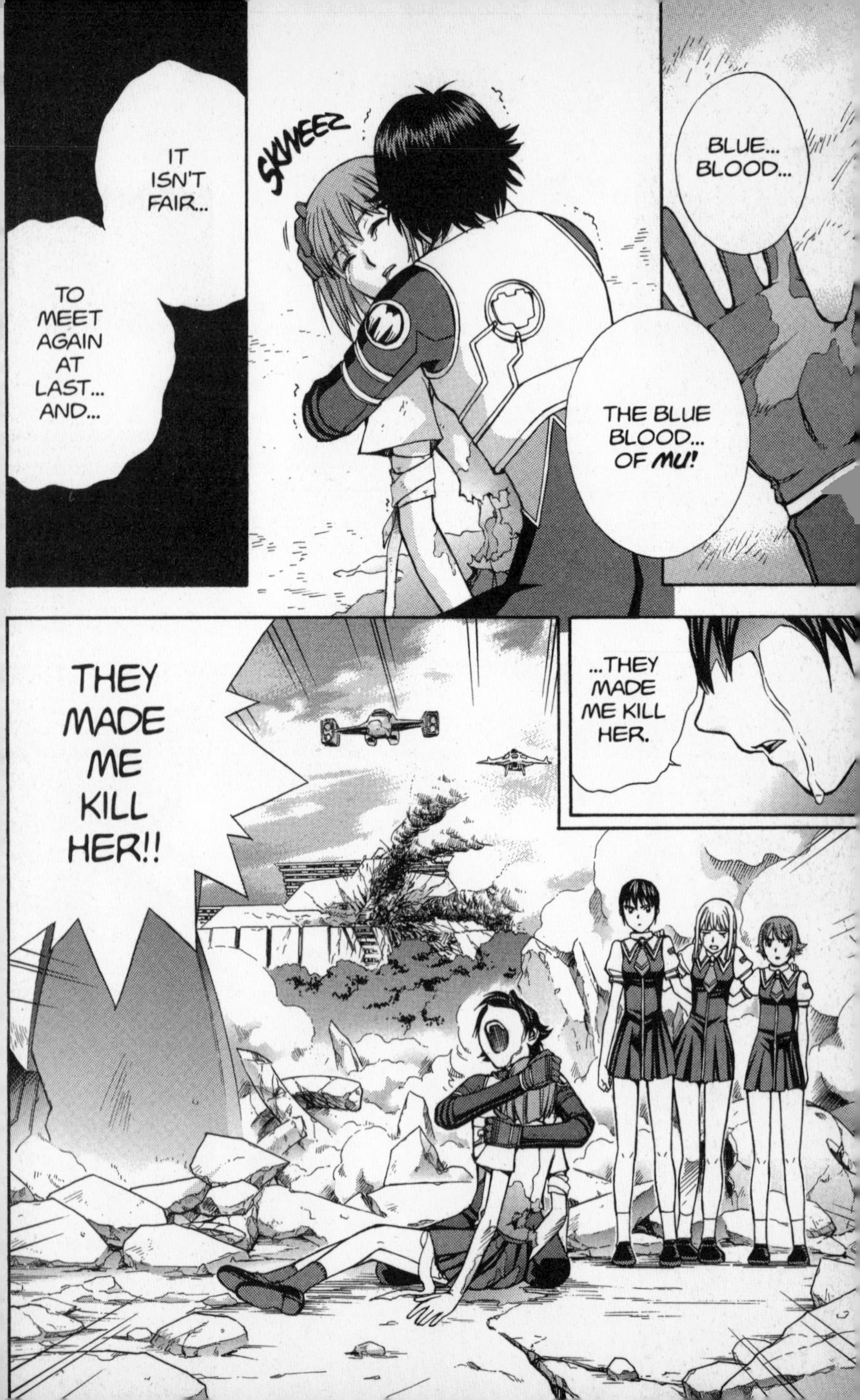
BLUE... BLOOD...
THE BLUE BLOOD... OF MU!
SKWEEZ
IT ISN'T FAIR...
TO MEET AGAIN AT LAST... AND...
...THEY MADE ME KILL HER.
THEY MADE ME KILL HER!!

mission 8
DECISION

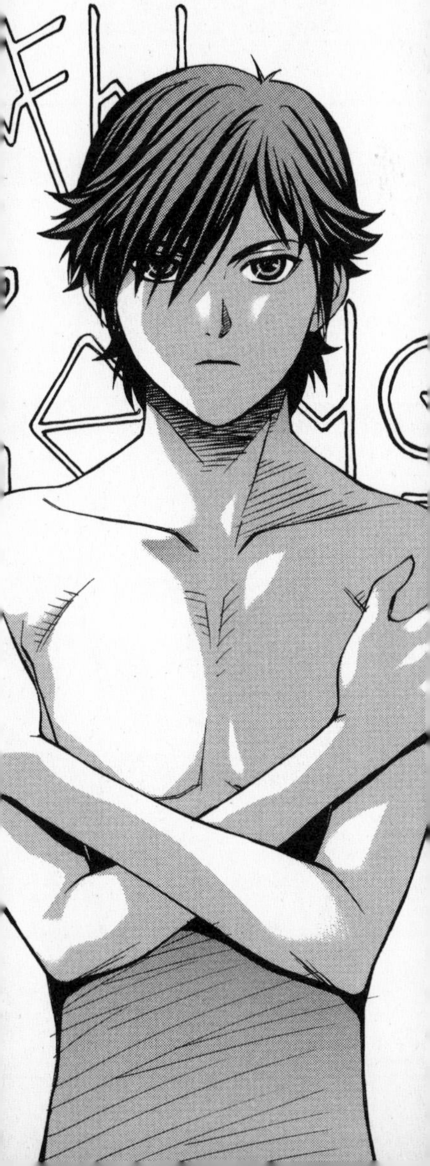

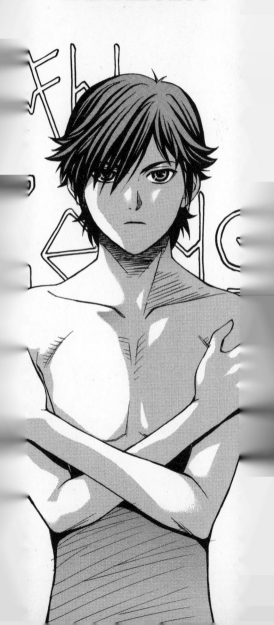

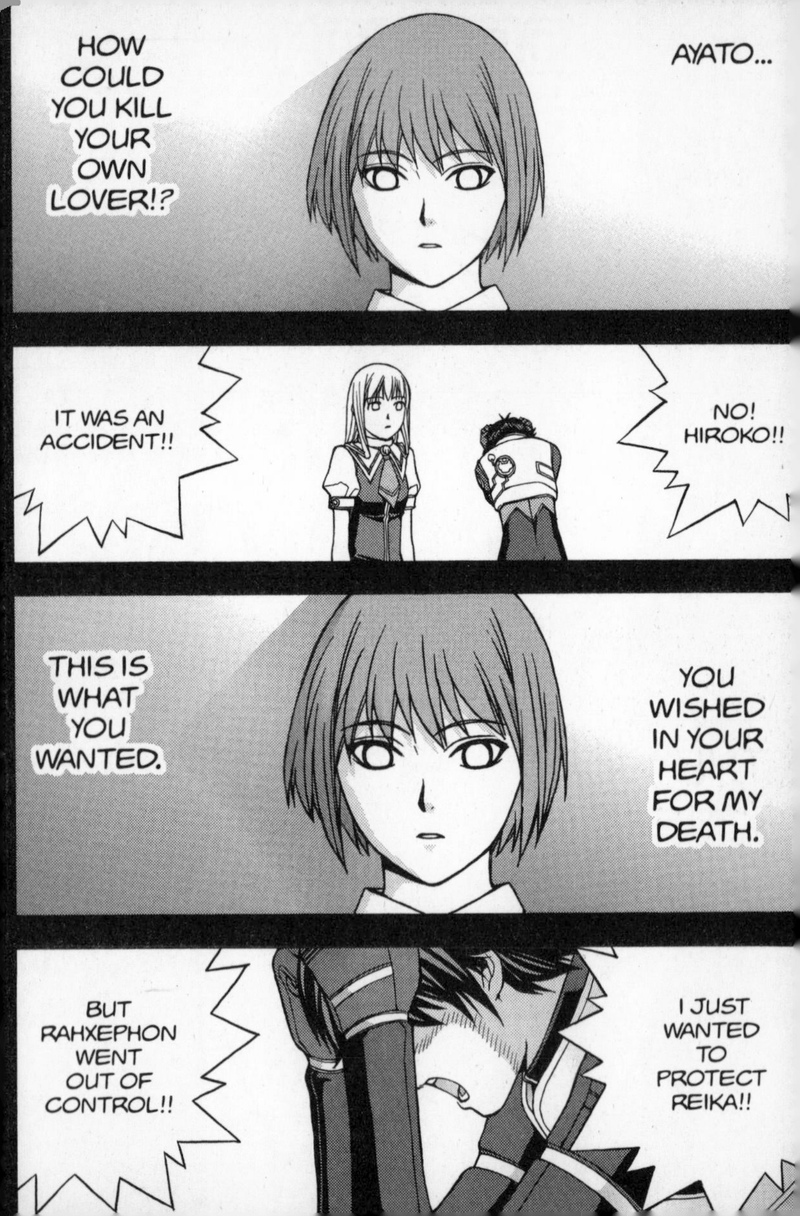
AYATO...
HOW COULD YOU KILL YOUR OWN LOVER!?
NO! HIROKO!!
IT WAS AN ACCIDENT!!
YOU WISHED IN YOUR HEART FOR MY DEATH.
THIS IS WHAT YOU WANTED.
I JUST WANTED TO PROTECT REIKA!!
BUT RAHXEPHON WENT OUT OF CONTROL!!

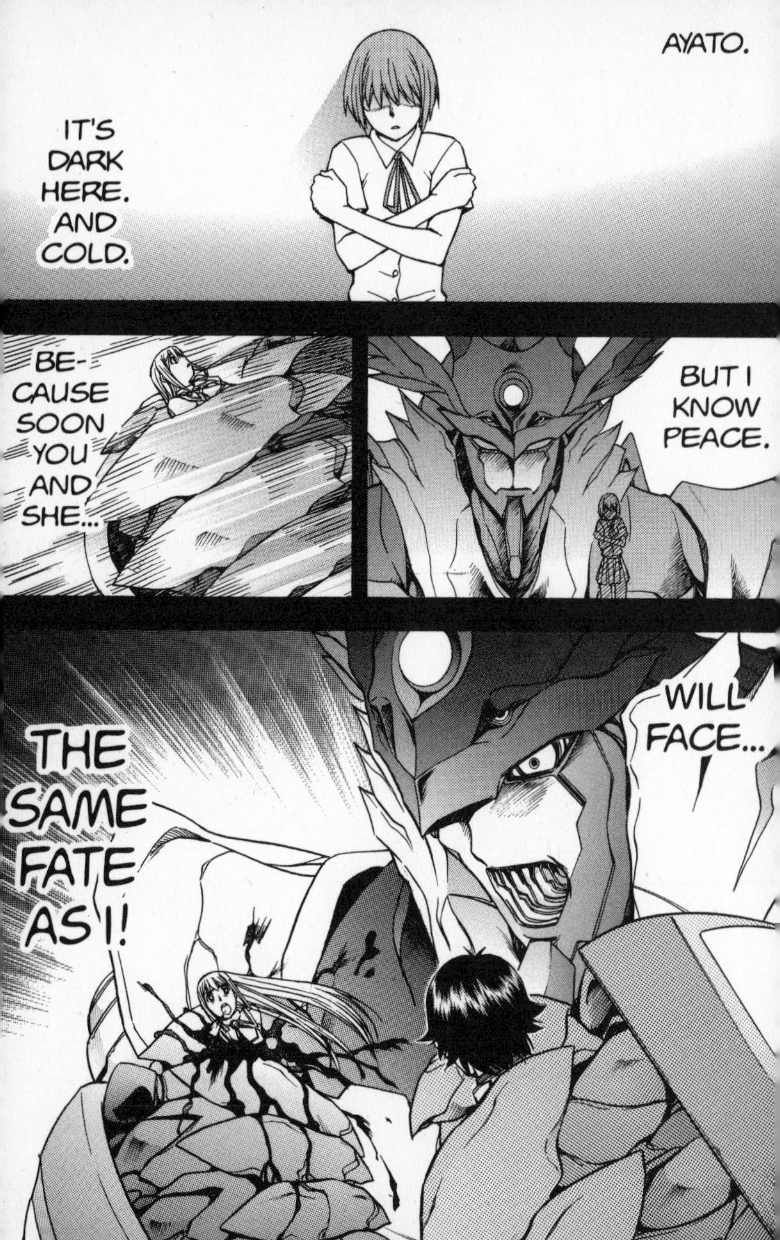
AYATO.
IT'S DARK HERE. AND COLD.
BUT I KNOW PEACE.
BE-CAUSE SOON YOU AND SHE...
WILL FACE...
THE SAME FATE AS I!

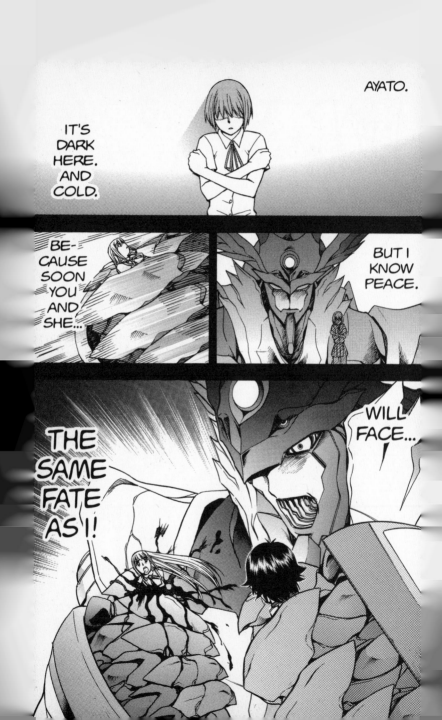

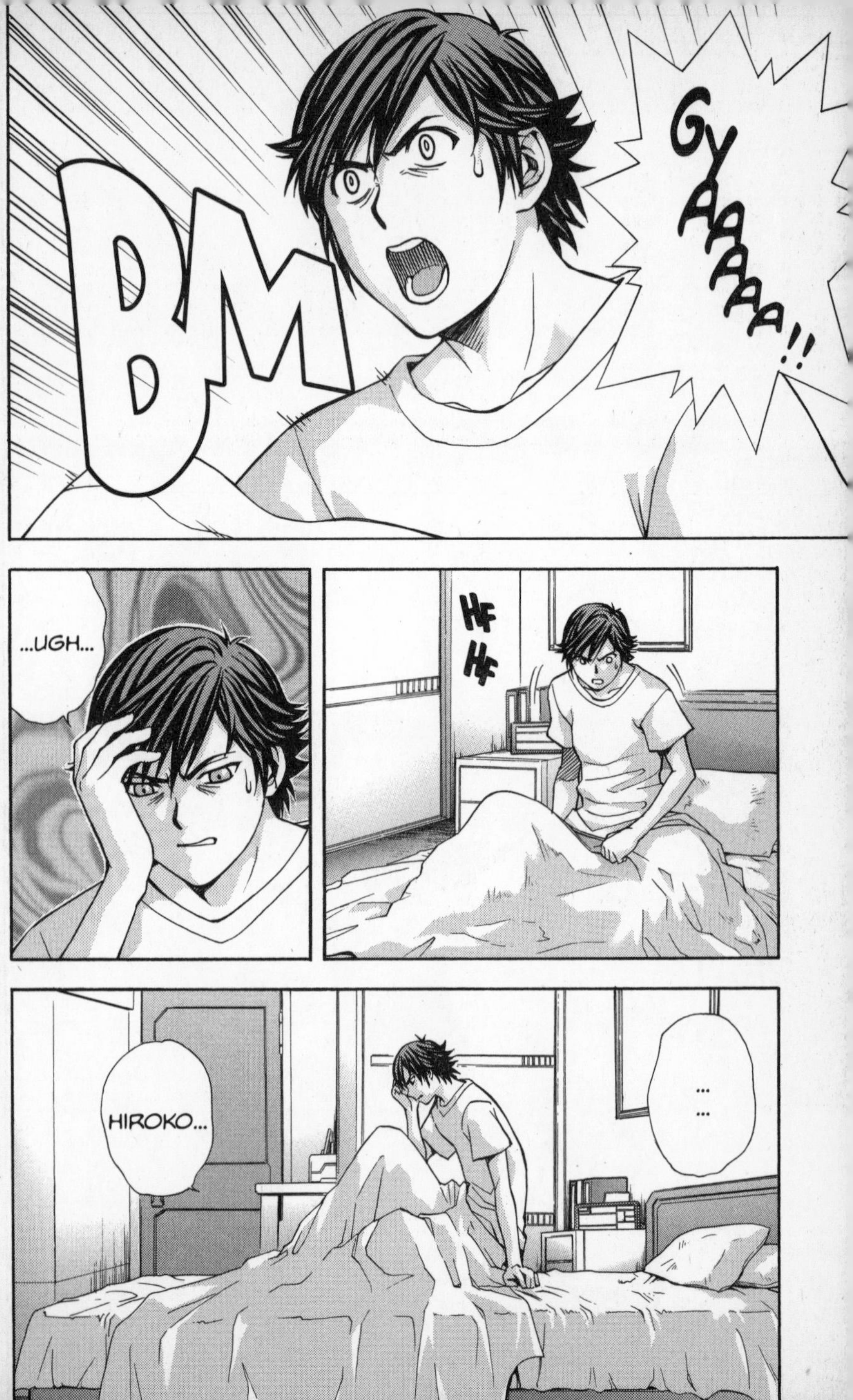
BM
GYAAAAA!!
HF
HF
...UGH...
...
...
HIROKO...

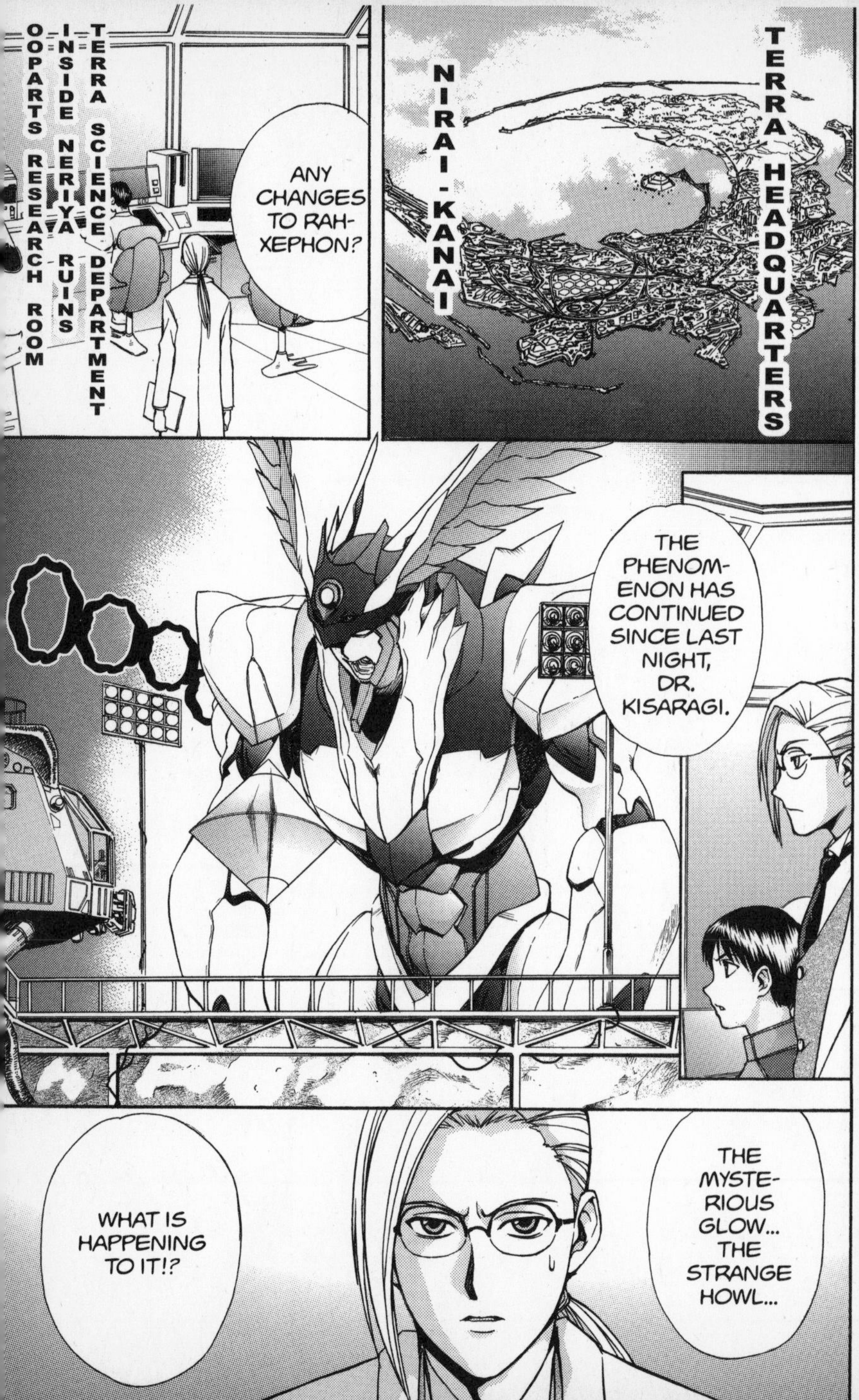
TERRA HEADQUARTERS
NIRAI-KANAI
TERRA SCIENCE DEPARTMENT
INSIDE NERIYA RUINS
OOPARTS RESEARCH ROOM
ANY CHANGES TO RAH-XEPHON?
THE PHENOM-ENON HAS CONTINUED SINCE LAST NIGHT, DR. KISARAGI.
OOO
THE MYSTE-RIOUS GLOW... THE STRANGE HOWL...
WHAT IS HAPPENING TO IT!?

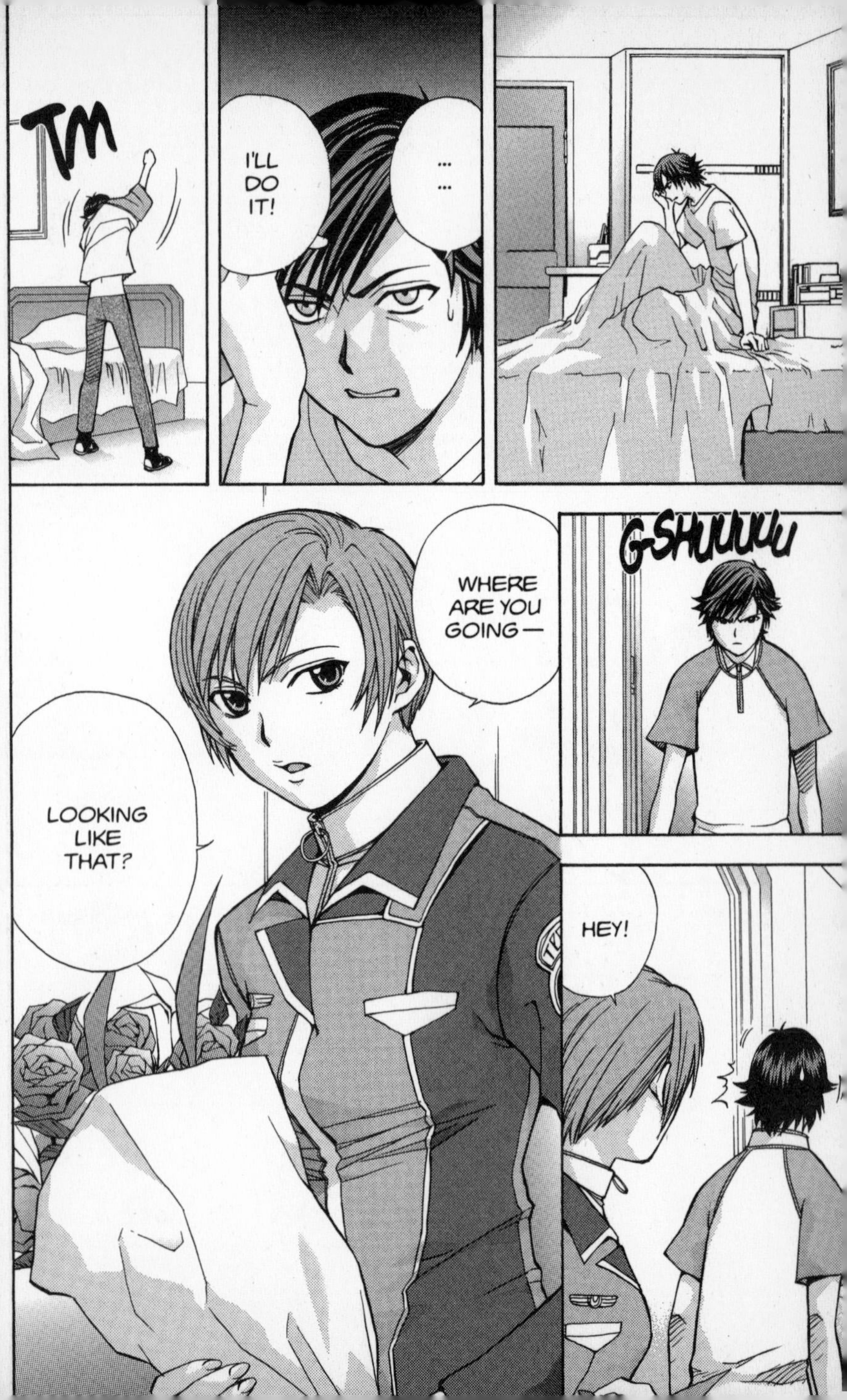

……
I'LL DO IT!
TM
G-SHUUUUU
HEY!
WHERE ARE YOU GOING—
LOOKING LIKE THAT?

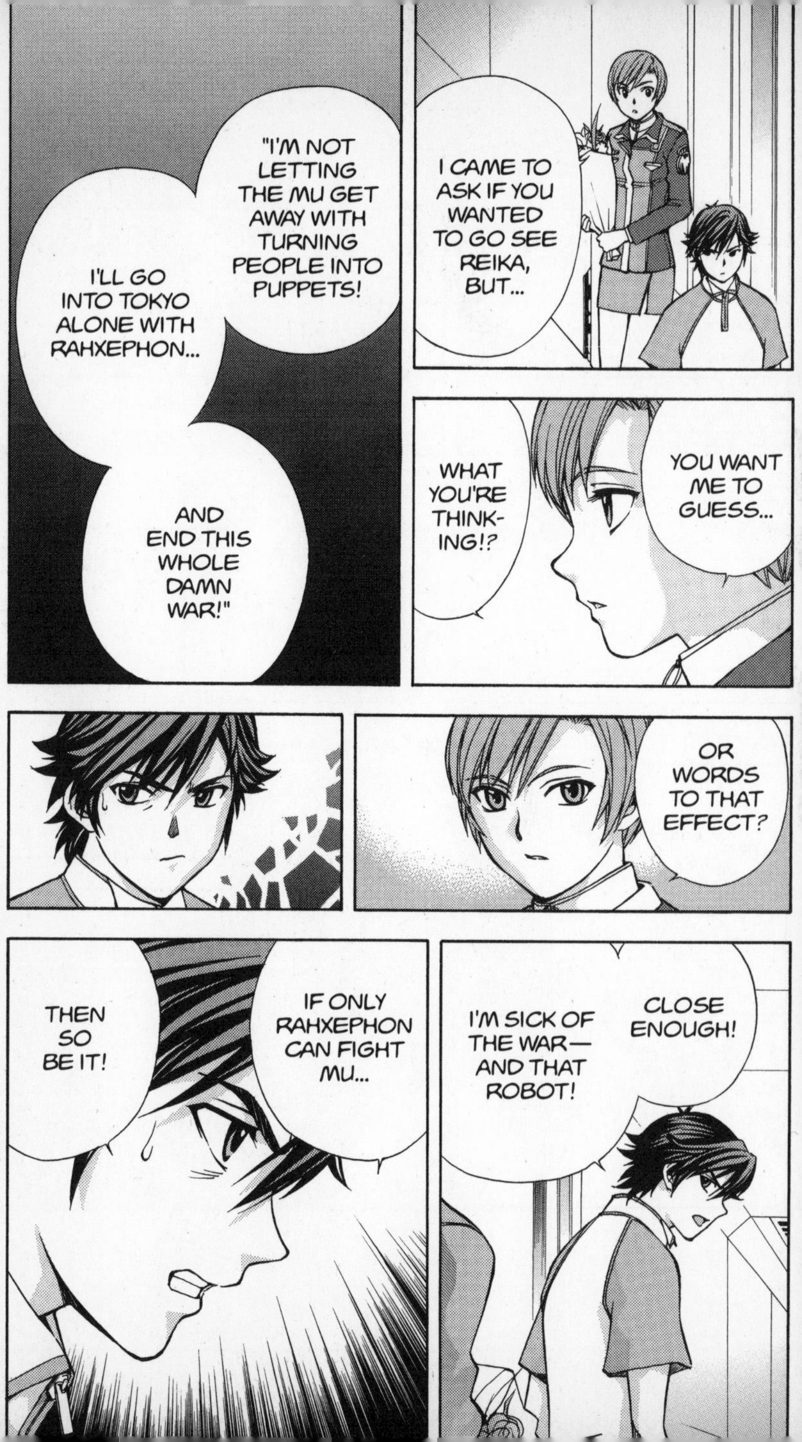
I CAME TO ASK IF YOU WANTED TO GO SEE REIKA, BUT...
YOU WANT ME TO GUESS...
WHAT YOU'RE THINK-ING!?
"I'M NOT LETTING THE MU GET AWAY WITH TURNING PEOPLE INTO PUPPETS!
I'LL GO INTO TOKYO ALONE WITH RAHXEPHON...
AND END THIS WHOLE DAMN WAR!"
OR WORDS TO THAT EFFECT?
CLOSE ENOUGH!
I'M SICK OF THE WAR— AND THAT ROBOT!
IF ONLY RAHXEPHON CAN FIGHT MU...
THEN SO BE IT!

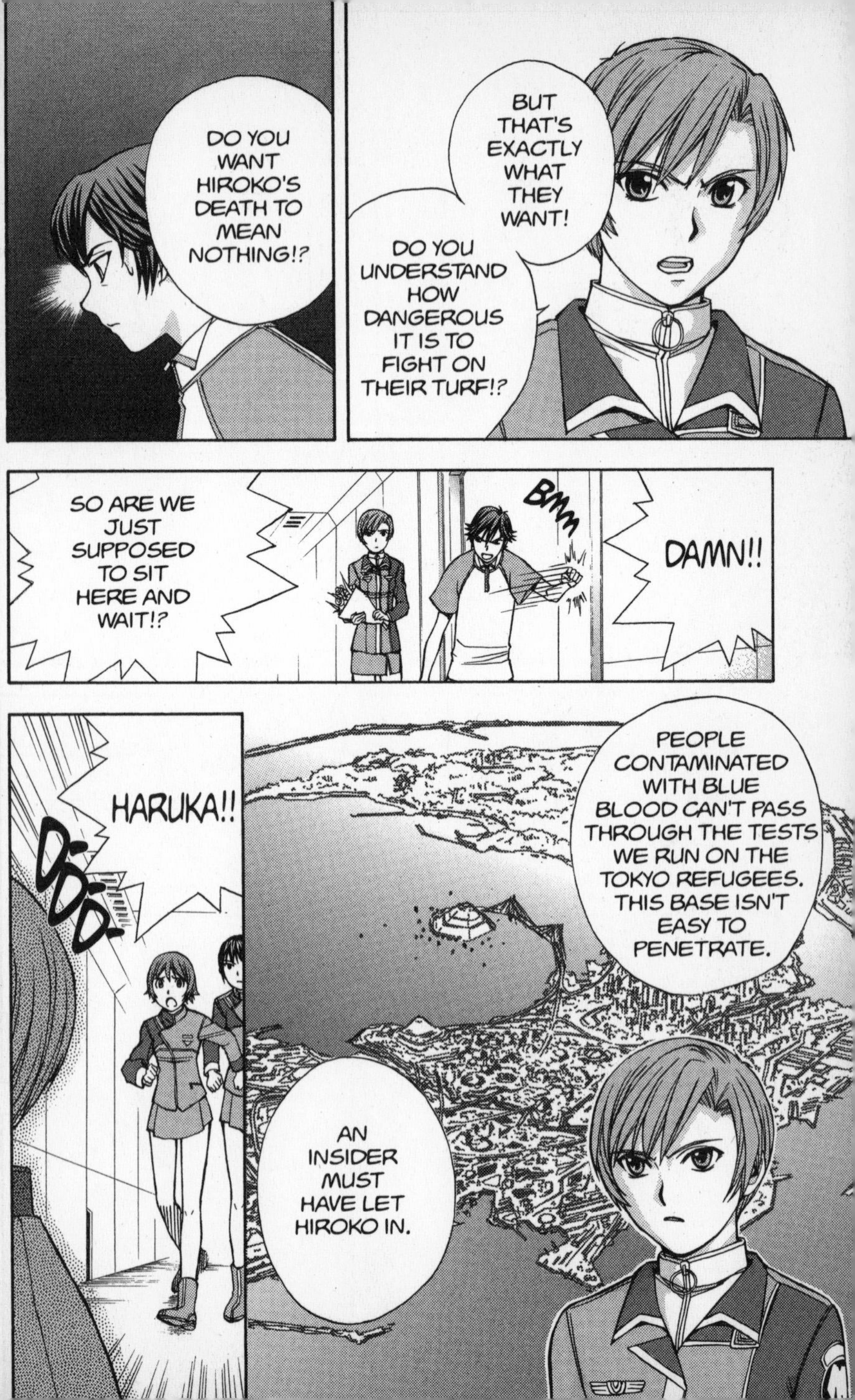
BUT THAT'S EXACTLY WHAT THEY WANT!
DO YOU UNDERSTAND HOW DANGEROUS IT IS TO FIGHT ON THEIR TURF!?
DO YOU WANT HIROKO'S DEATH TO MEAN NOTHING!?
DAMN!!
BMM
SO ARE WE JUST SUPPOSED TO SIT HERE AND WAIT!?
PEOPLE CONTAMINATED WITH BLUE BLOOD CAN'T PASS THROUGH THE TESTS WE RUN ON THE TOKYO REFUGEES. THIS BASE ISN'T EASY TO PENETRATE.
AN INSIDER MUST HAVE LET HIROKO IN.
HARUKA!!
D-D-D-

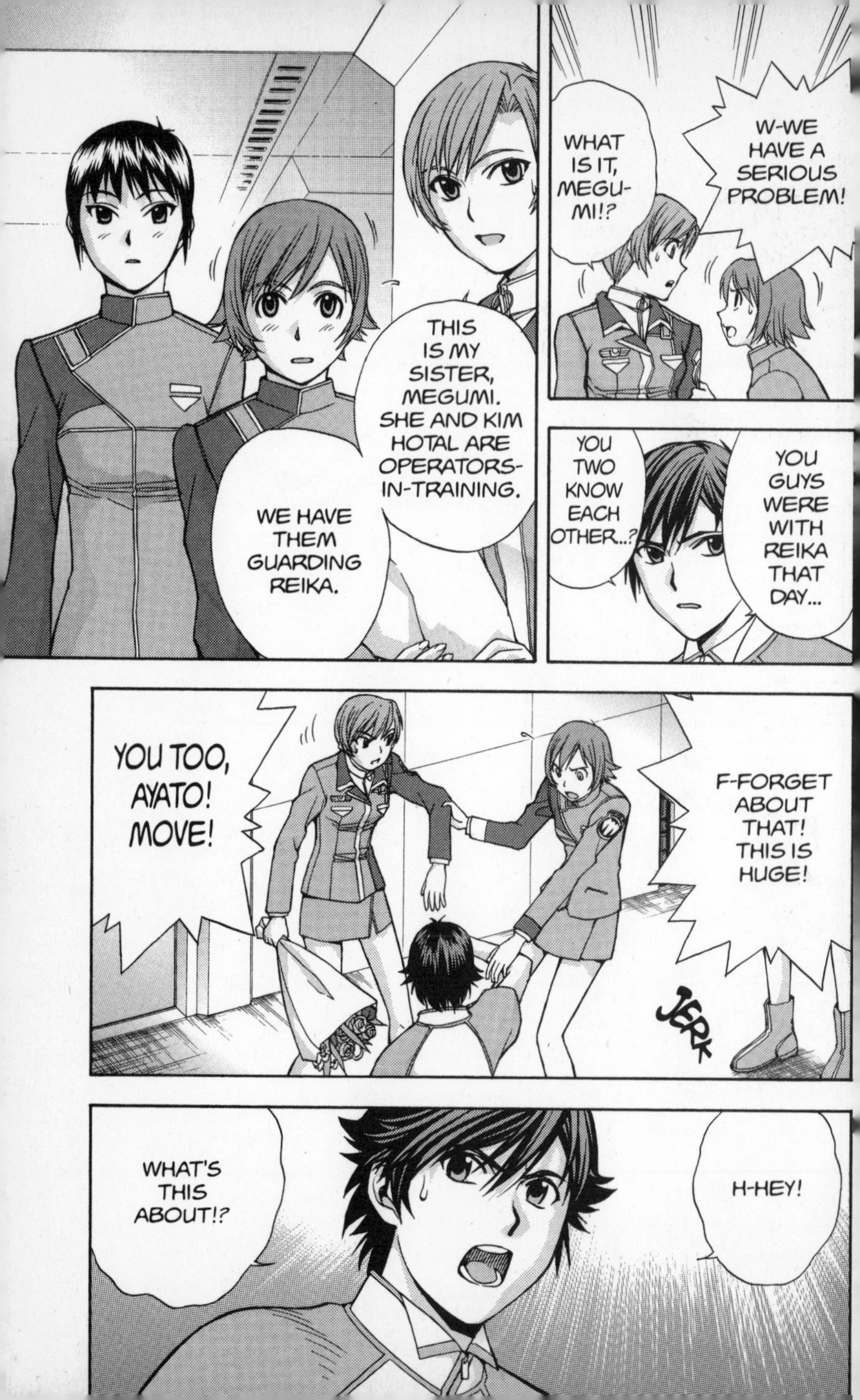
W-WE HAVE A SERIOUS PROBLEM!
WHAT IS IT, MEGU-MI!?
YOU GUYS WERE WITH REIKA THAT DAY...
YOU TWO KNOW EACH OTHER...?
THIS IS MY SISTER, MEGUMI. SHE AND KIM HOTAL ARE OPERATORS-IN-TRAINING.
WE HAVE THEM GUARDING REIKA.
F-FORGET ABOUT THAT! THIS IS HUGE!
JERK
YOU TOO, AYATO! MOVE!
H-HEY!
WHAT'S THIS ABOUT!?

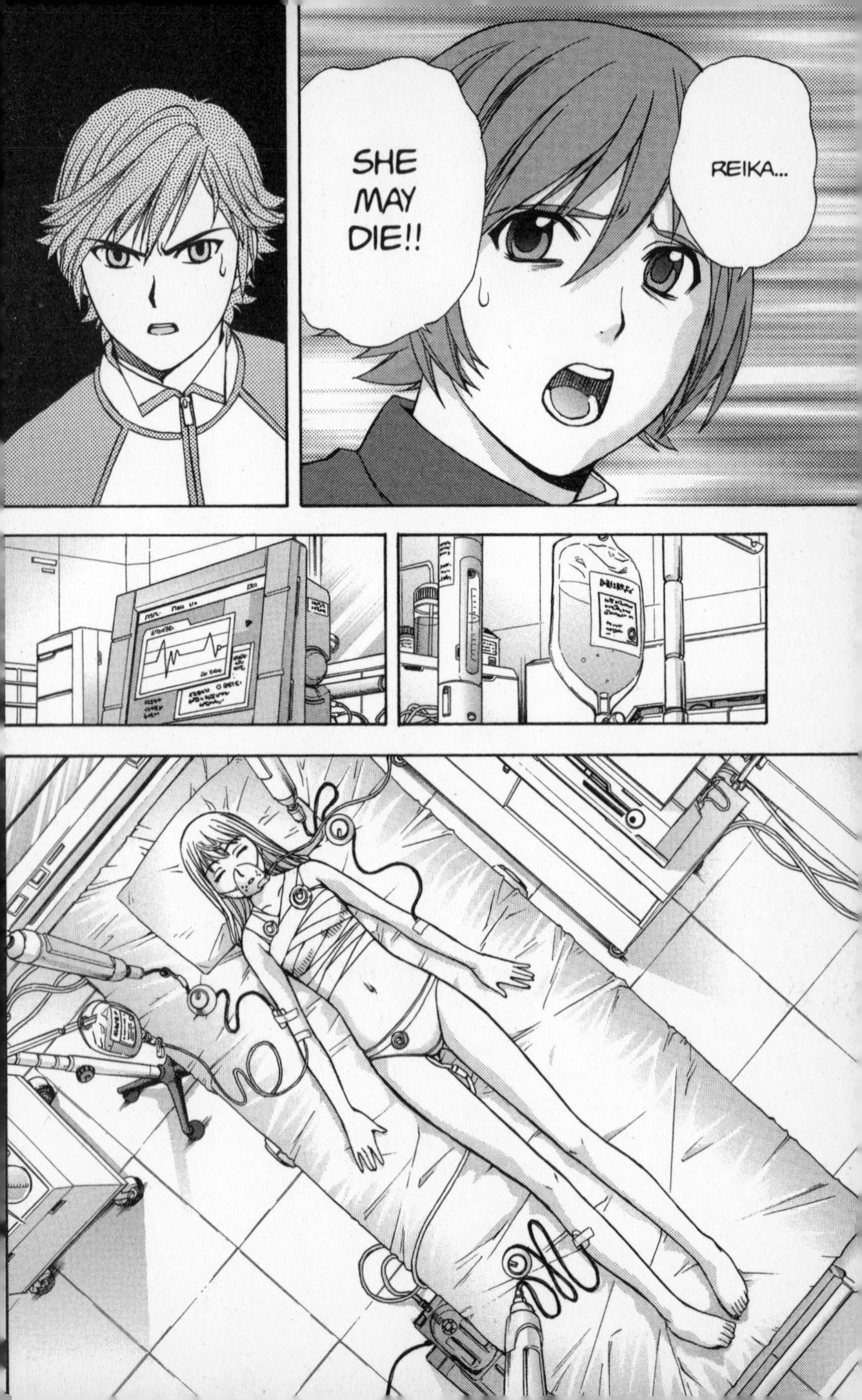
REIKA...
SHE MAY DIE!!

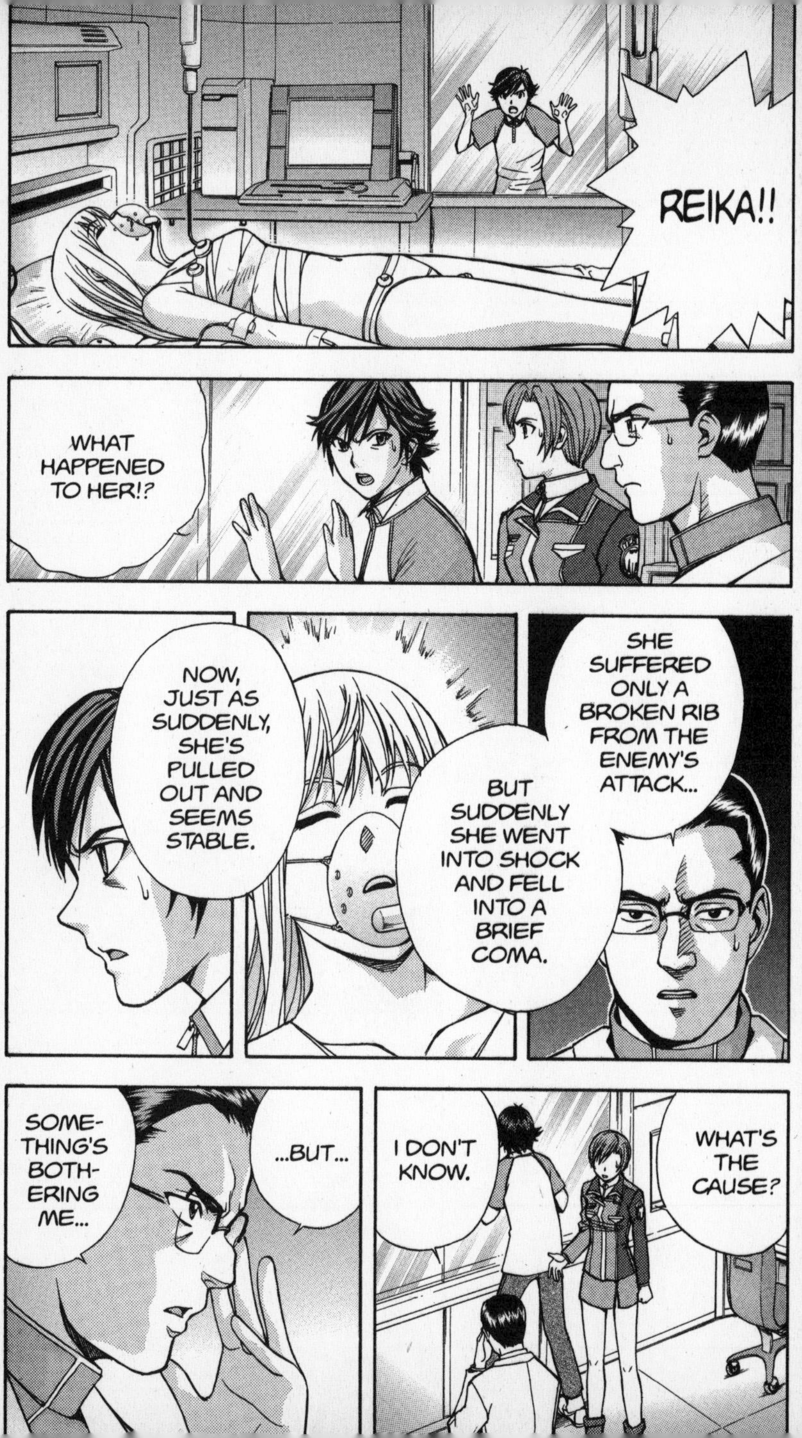
REIKA!!
WHAT HAPPENED TO HER!?
SHE SUFFERED ONLY A BROKEN RIB FROM THE ENEMY'S ATTACK...
BUT SUDDENLY SHE WENT INTO SHOCK AND FELL INTO A BRIEF COMA.
NOW, JUST AS SUDDENLY, SHE'S PULLED OUT AND SEEMS STABLE.
WHAT'S THE CAUSE?
I DON'T KNOW.
...BUT...
SOME-THING'S BOTH-ERING ME...

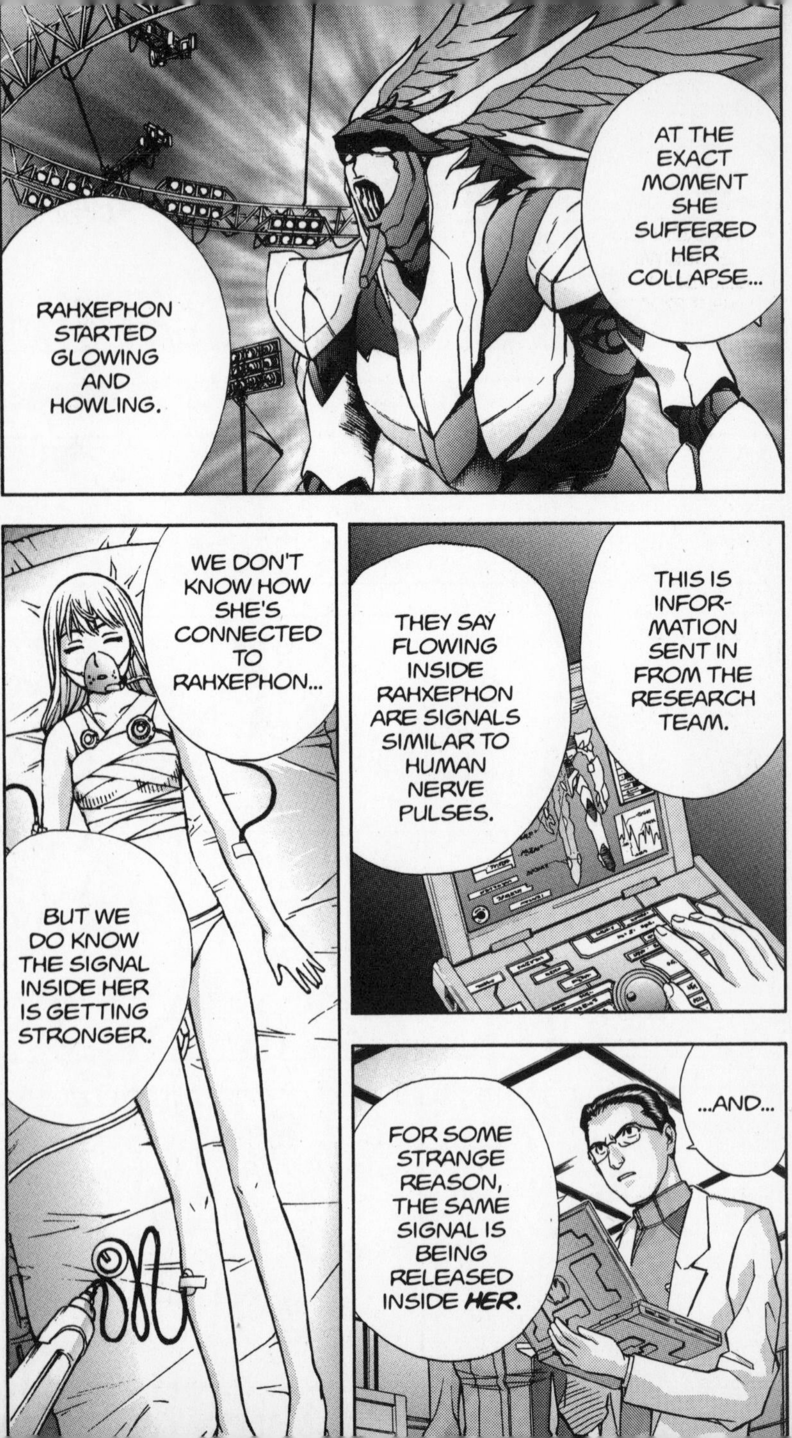
AT THE EXACT MOMENT SHE SUFFERED HER COLLAPSE...
RAHXEPHON STARTED GLOWING AND HOWLING.
THIS IS INFORMATION SENT IN FROM THE RESEARCH TEAM.
THEY SAY FLOWING INSIDE RAHXEPHON ARE SIGNALS SIMILAR TO HUMAN NERVE PULSES.
...AND...
FOR SOME STRANGE REASON, THE SAME SIGNAL IS BEING RELEASED INSIDE ***HER***.
WE DON'T KNOW HOW SHE'S CONNECTED TO RAHXEPHON...
BUT WE DO KNOW THE SIGNAL INSIDE HER IS GETTING STRONGER.

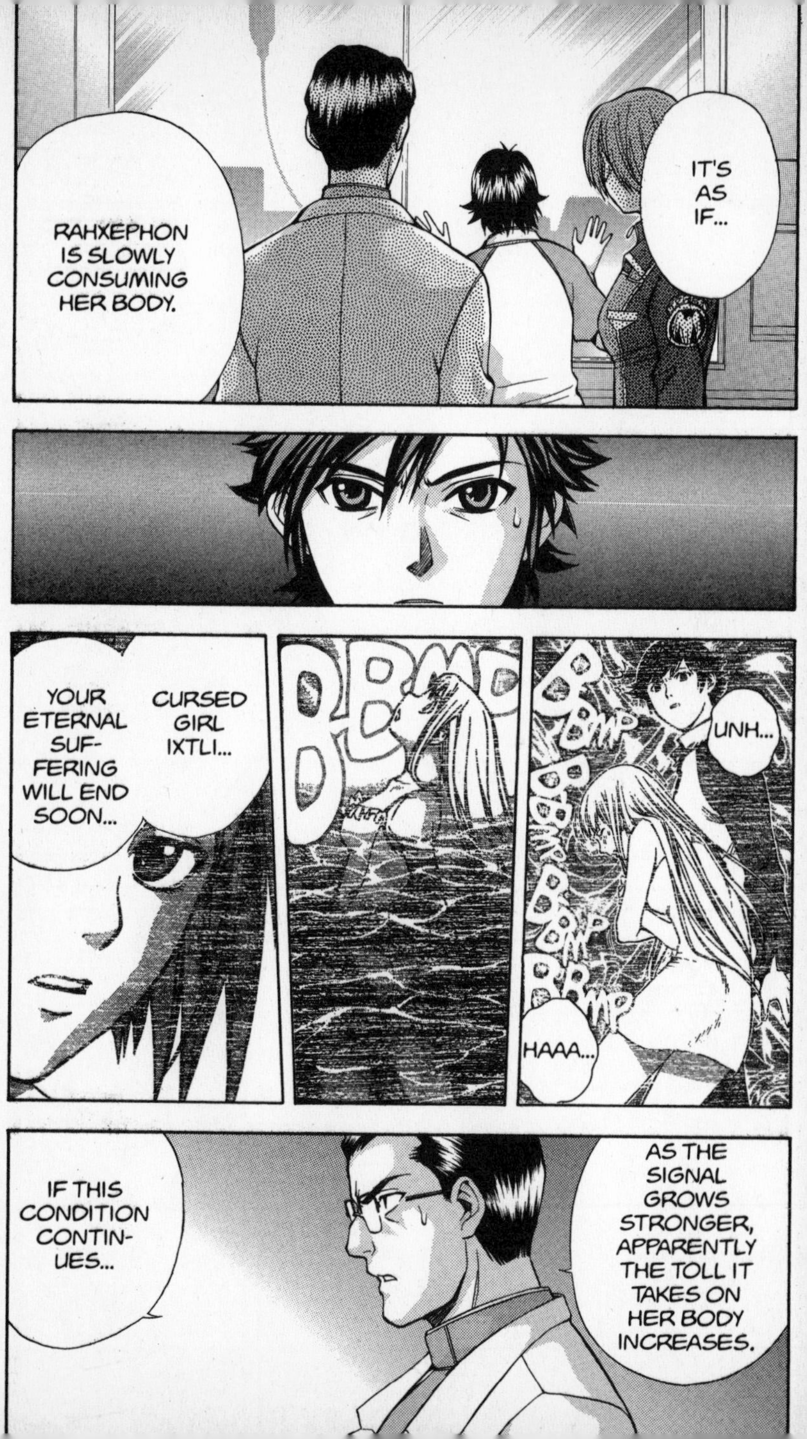
IT'S AS IF...
RAHXEPHON IS SLOWLY CONSUMING HER BODY.
BBMP BBMP BBMP BBMP BBMP
UNH...
HAAA...
CURSED GIRL IXTLI...
YOUR ETERNAL SUF-FERING WILL END SOON...
AS THE SIGNAL GROWS STRONGER, APPARENTLY THE TOLL IT TAKES ON HER BODY INCREASES.
IF THIS CONDITION CONTIN-UES...

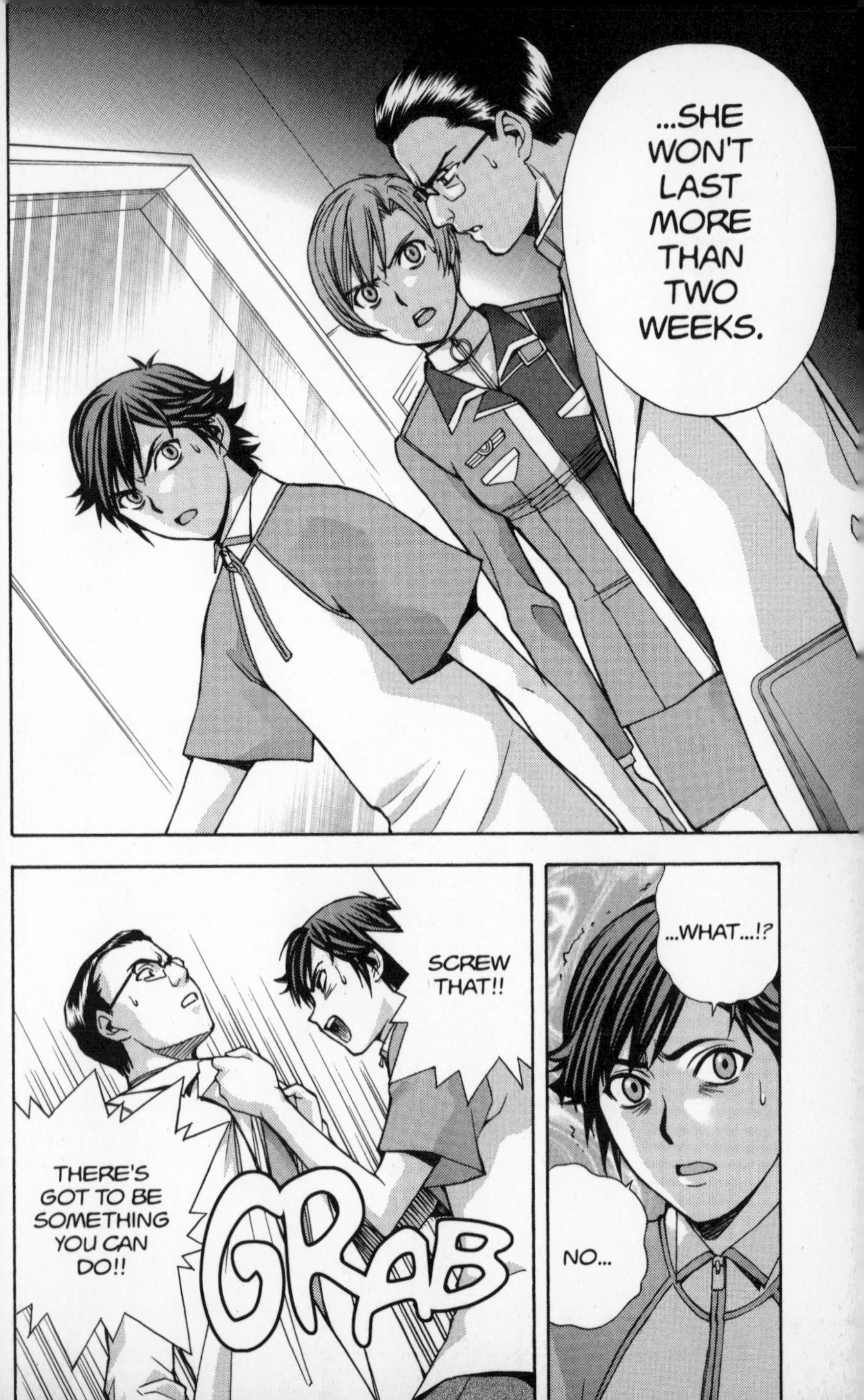
...SHE WON'T LAST MORE THAN TWO WEEKS.
...WHAT...!?
NO...
SCREW THAT!!
THERE'S GOT TO BE SOMETHING YOU CAN DO!!
GRAB

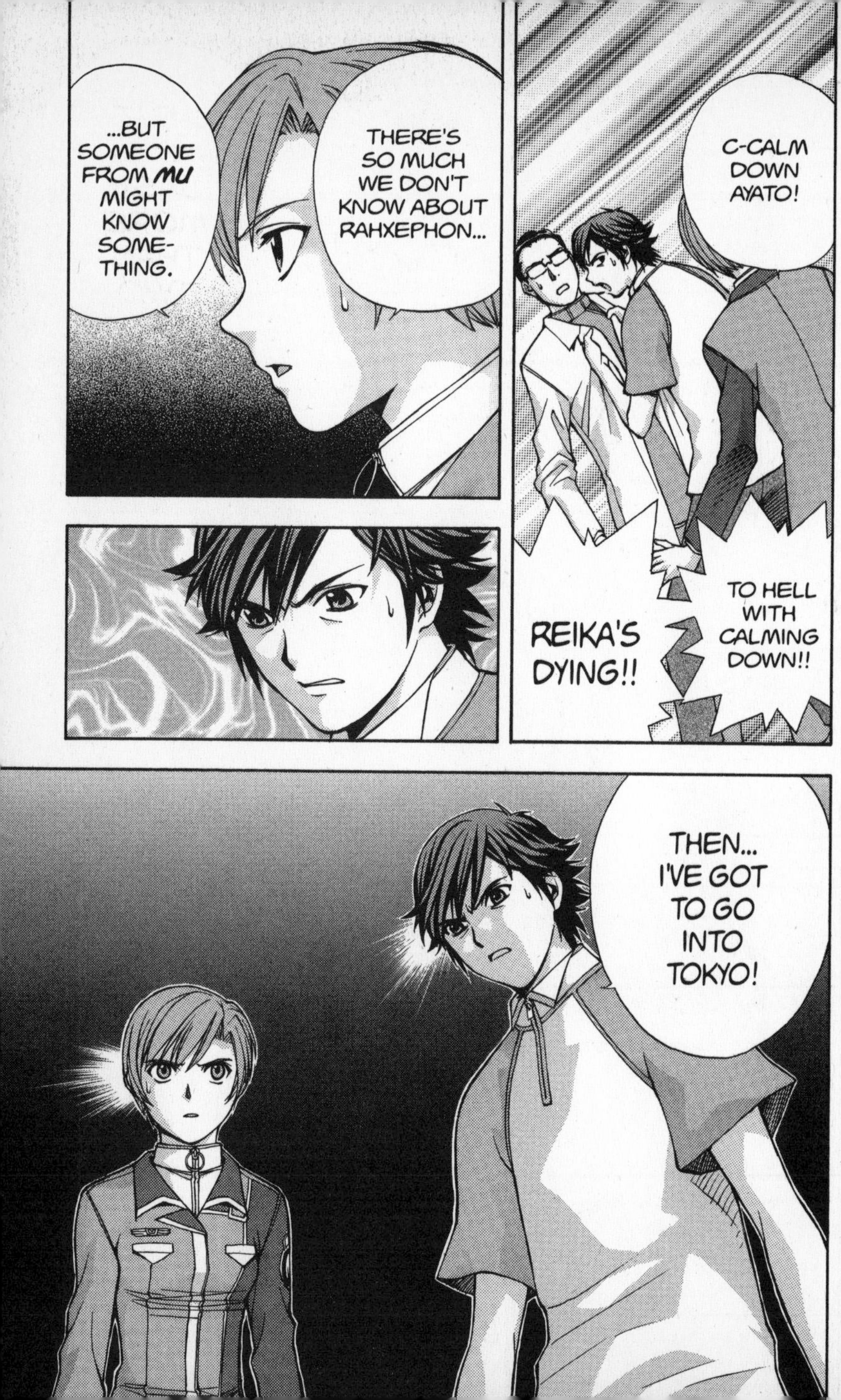
C-CALM DOWN AYATO!
TO HELL WITH CALMING DOWN!!
REIKA'S DYING!!
THERE'S SO MUCH WE DON'T KNOW ABOUT RAHXEPHON...
...BUT SOMEONE FROM MU MIGHT KNOW SOME-THING.
THEN... I'VE GOT TO GO INTO TOKYO!

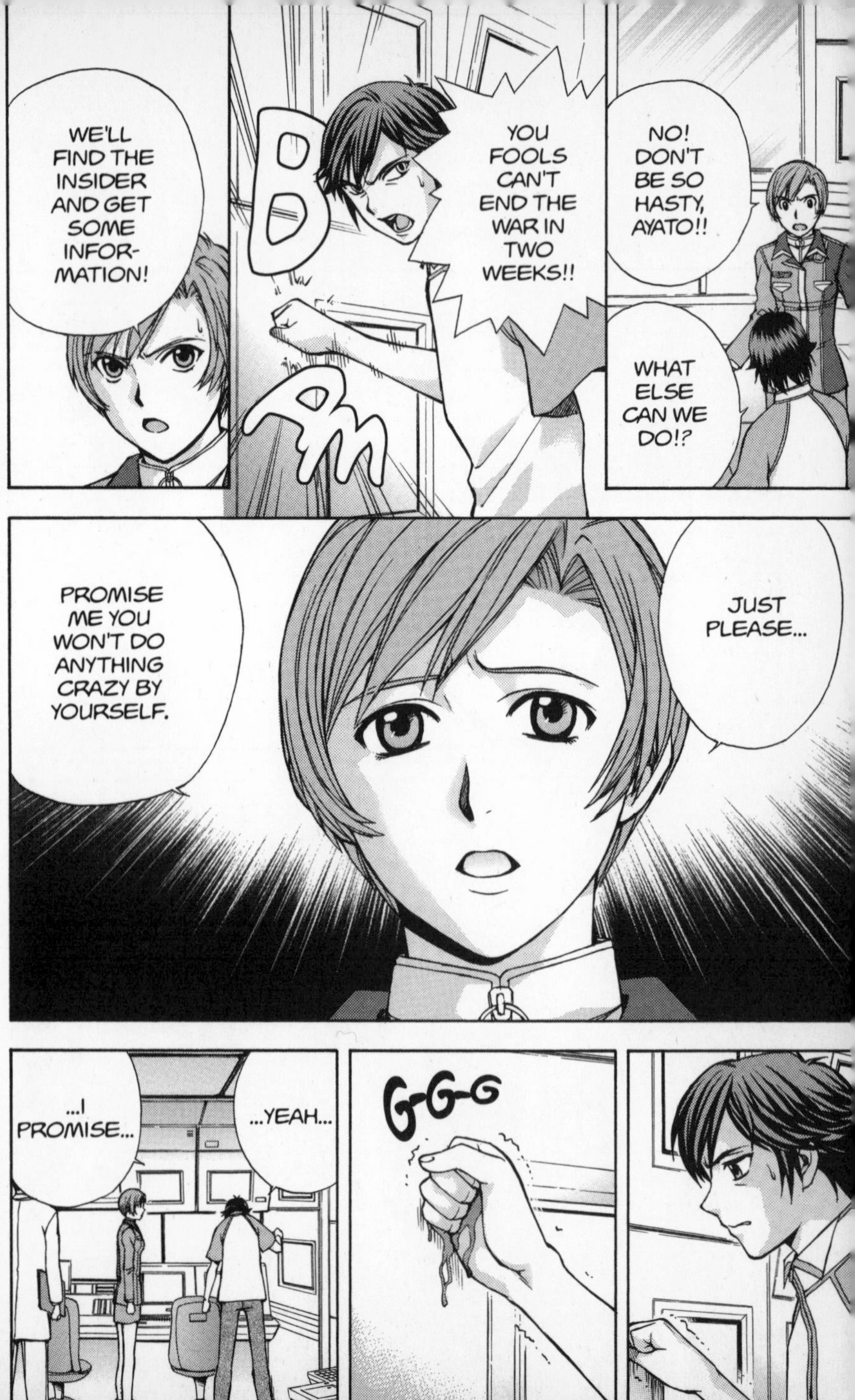
NO! DON'T BE SO HASTY, AYATO!!
WHAT ELSE CAN WE DO!?
BAM
YOU FOOLS CAN'T END THE WAR IN TWO WEEKS!!
WE'LL FIND THE INSIDER AND GET SOME INFOR-MATION!
JUST PLEASE...
PROMISE ME YOU WON'T DO ANYTHING CRAZY BY YOURSELF.
G-G-G
...YEAH...
...I PROMISE...

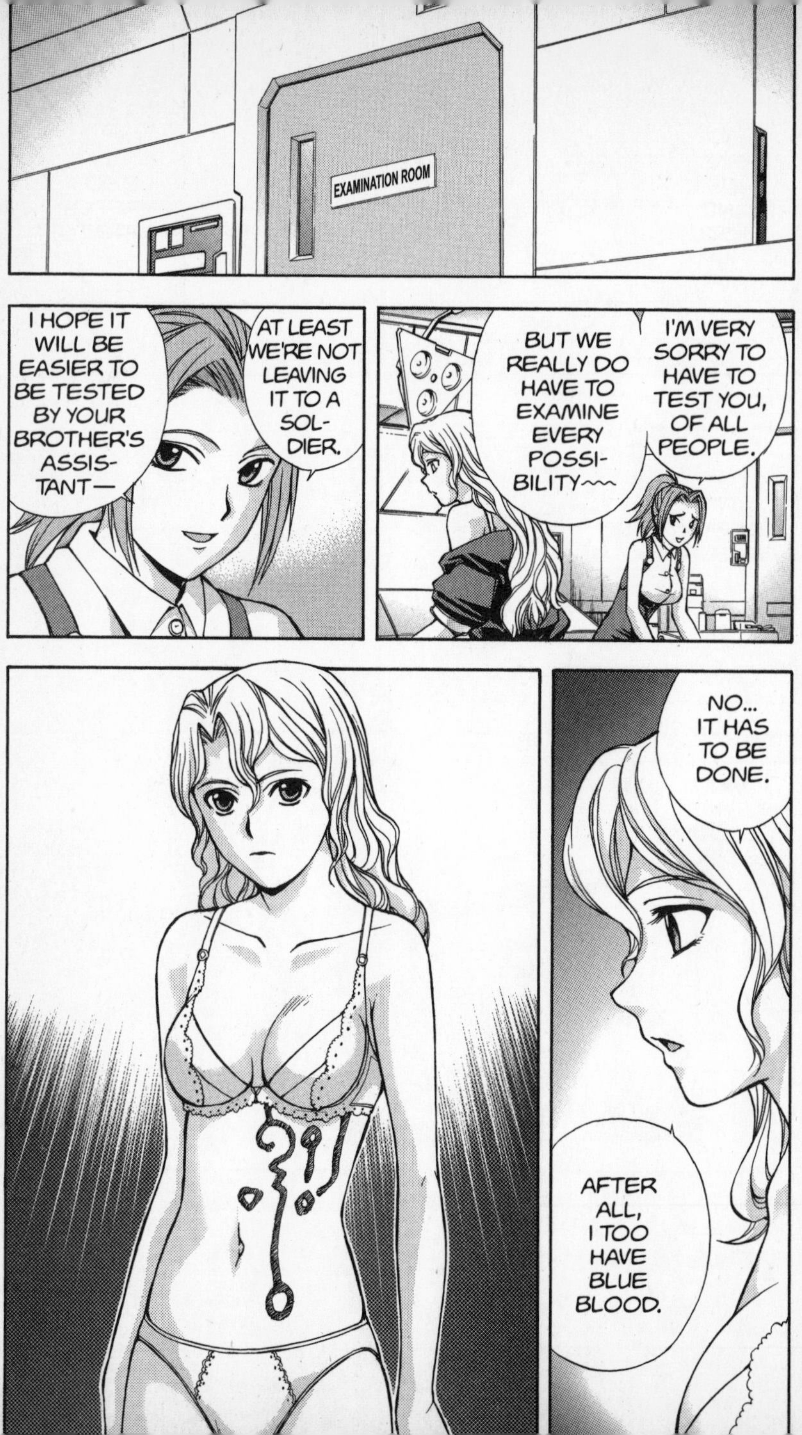
EXAMINATION ROOM
I'M VERY SORRY TO HAVE TO TEST YOU, OF ALL PEOPLE.
BUT WE REALLY DO HAVE TO EXAMINE EVERY POSSIBILITY~~~
AT LEAST WE'RE NOT LEAVING IT TO A SOLDIER.
I HOPE IT WILL BE EASIER TO BE TESTED BY YOUR BROTHER'S ASSISTANT—
NO... IT HAS TO BE DONE.
AFTER ALL, I TOO HAVE BLUE BLOOD.

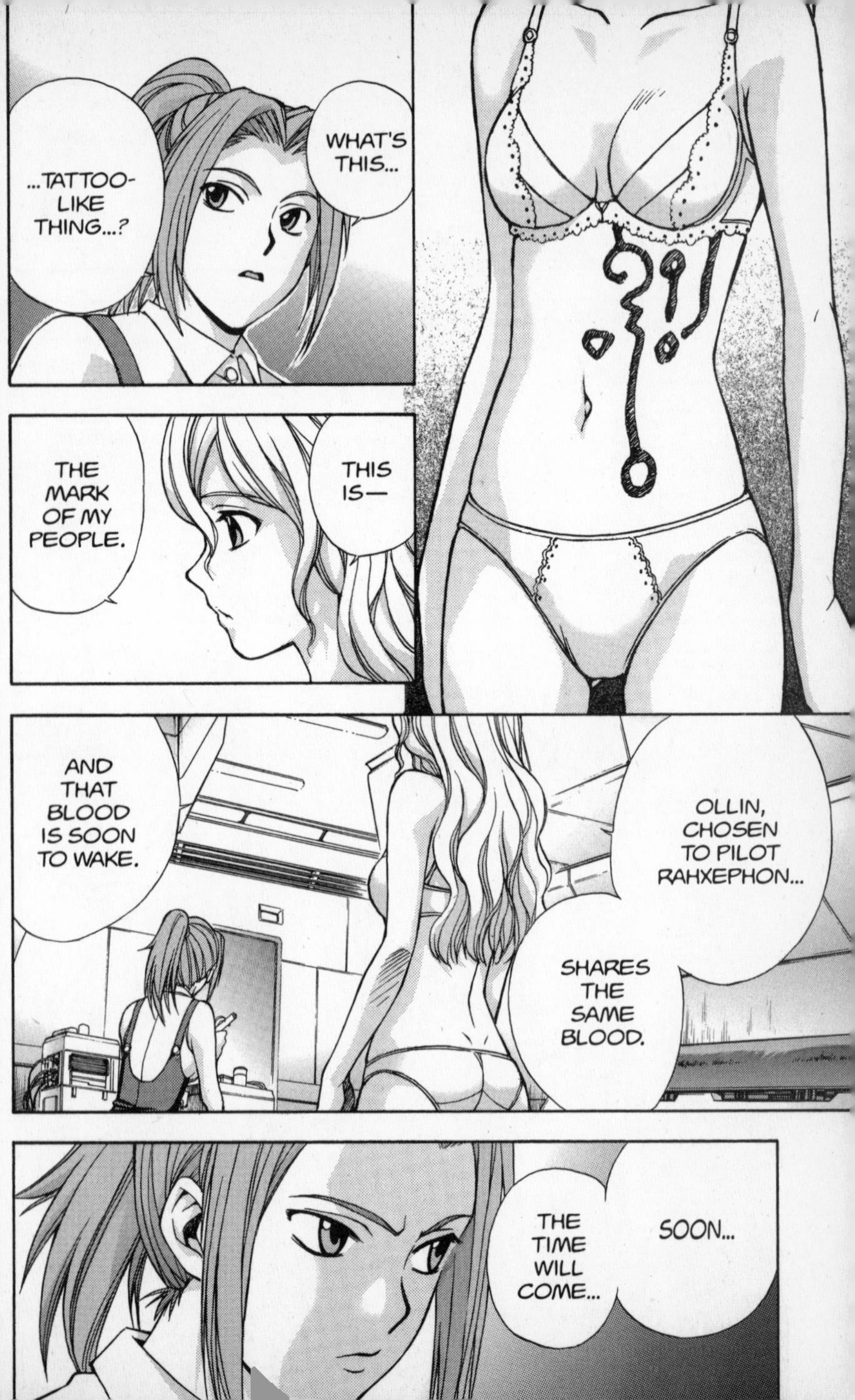
WHAT'S THIS...
...TATTOO-LIKE THING...?
THIS IS—
THE MARK OF MY PEOPLE.
OLLIN, CHOSEN TO PILOT RAHXEPHON...
SHARES THE SAME BLOOD.
AND THAT BLOOD IS SOON TO WAKE.
SOON...
THE TIME WILL COME...

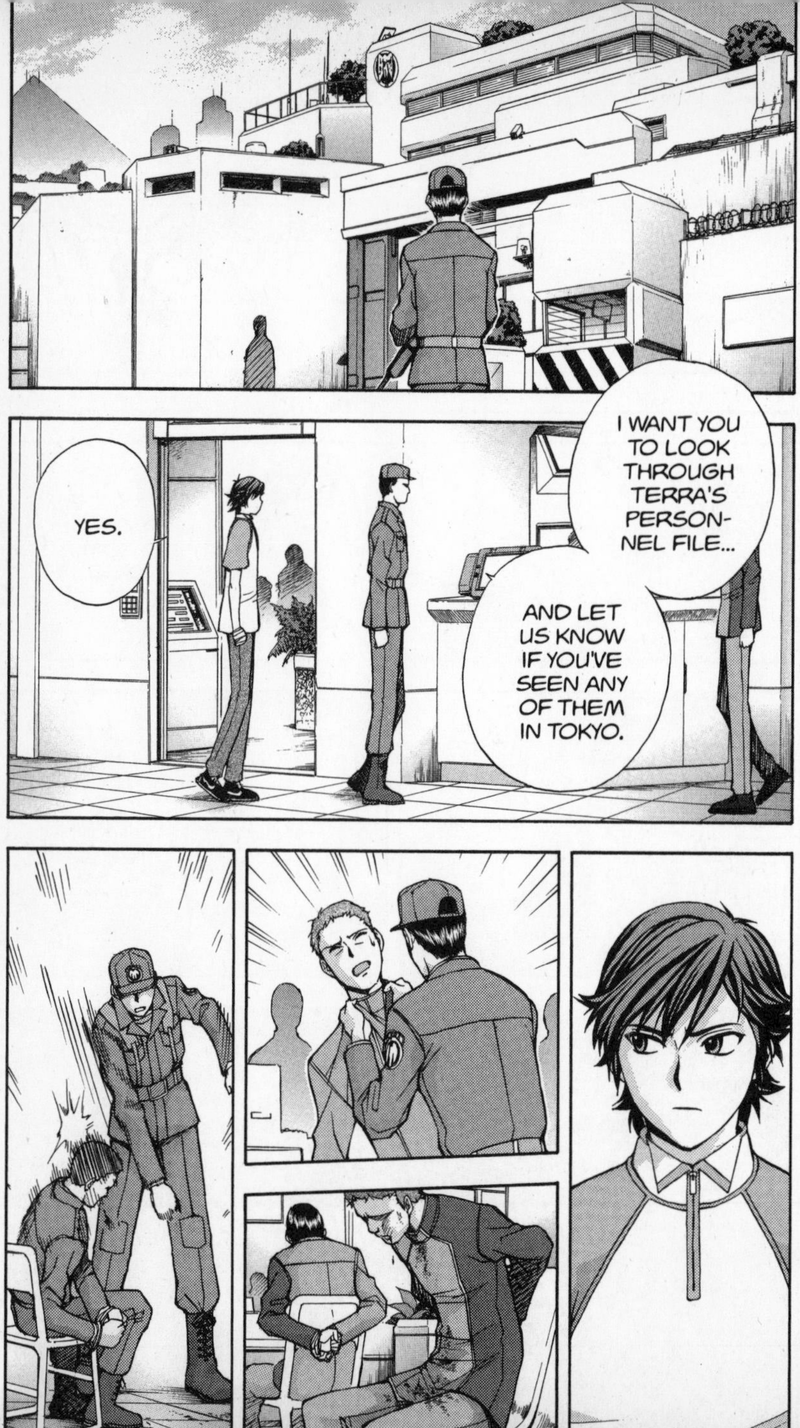
I WANT YOU TO LOOK THROUGH TERRA'S PERSON-NEL FILE...
AND LET US KNOW IF YOU'VE SEEN ANY OF THEM IN TOKYO.
YES.

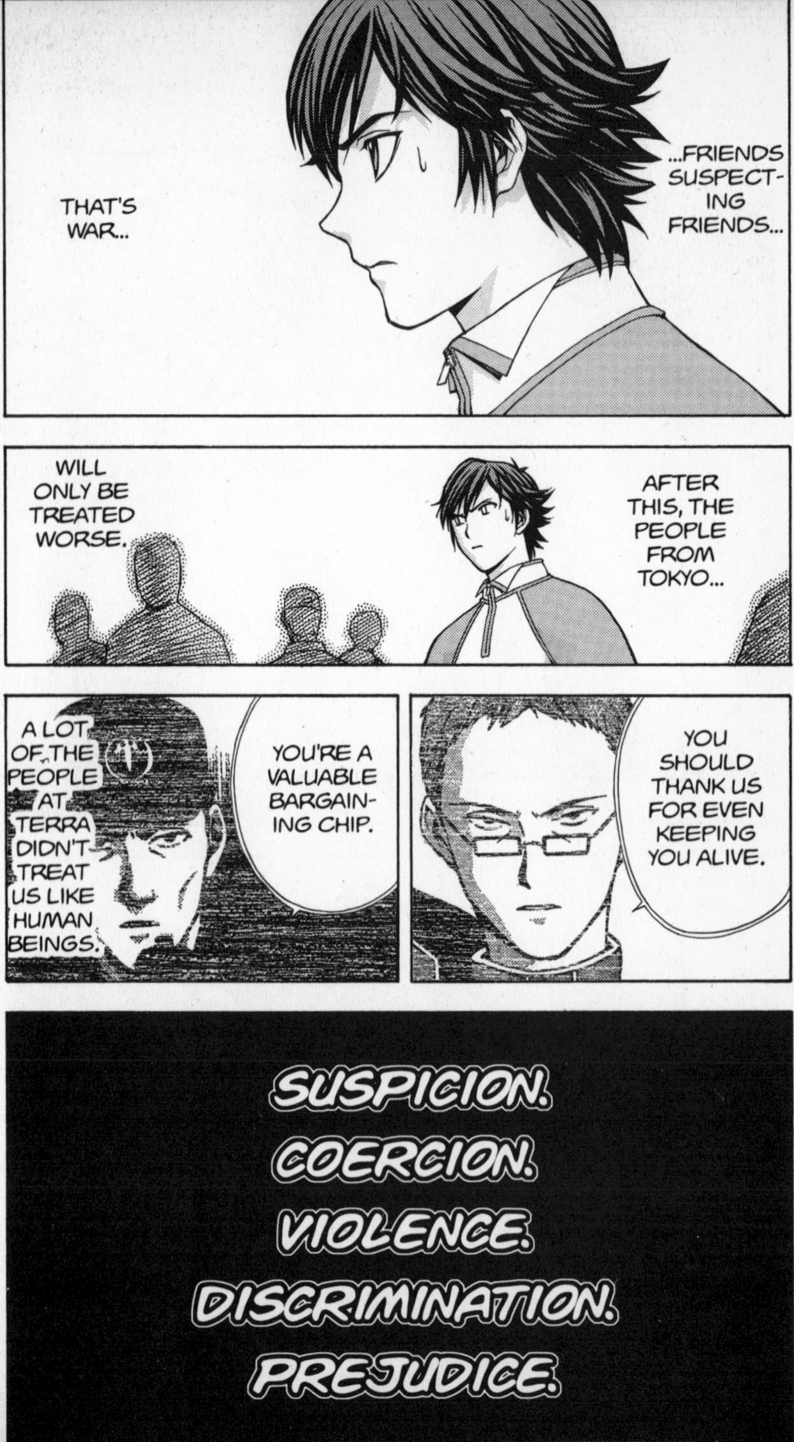
...FRIENDS SUSPECT-ING FRIENDS...
THAT'S WAR...
AFTER THIS, THE PEOPLE FROM TOKYO...
WILL ONLY BE TREATED WORSE.
YOU SHOULD THANK US FOR EVEN KEEPING YOU ALIVE.
YOU'RE A VALUABLE BARGAIN-ING CHIP.
A LOT OF THE PEOPLE AT TERRA DIDN'T TREAT US LIKE HUMAN BEINGS.
SUSPICION.
COERCION.
VIOLENCE.
DISCRIMINATION.
PREJUDICE.

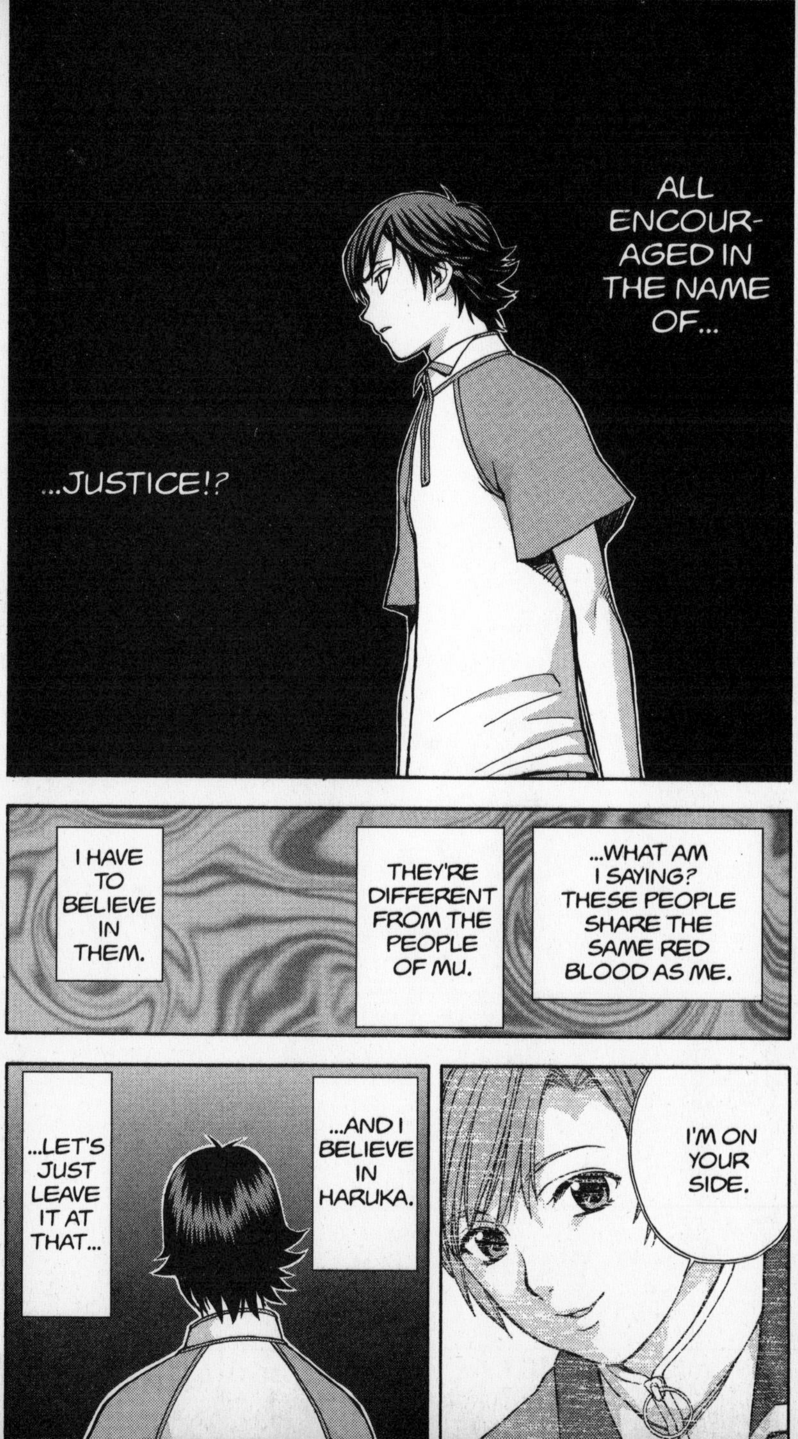
ALL ENCOURAGED IN THE NAME OF...
...JUSTICE!?
...WHAT AM I SAYING? THESE PEOPLE SHARE THE SAME RED BLOOD AS ME.
THEY'RE DIFFERENT FROM THE PEOPLE OF MU.
I HAVE TO BELIEVE IN THEM.
I'M ON YOUR SIDE.
...AND I BELIEVE IN HARUKA.
...LET'S JUST LEAVE IT AT THAT...

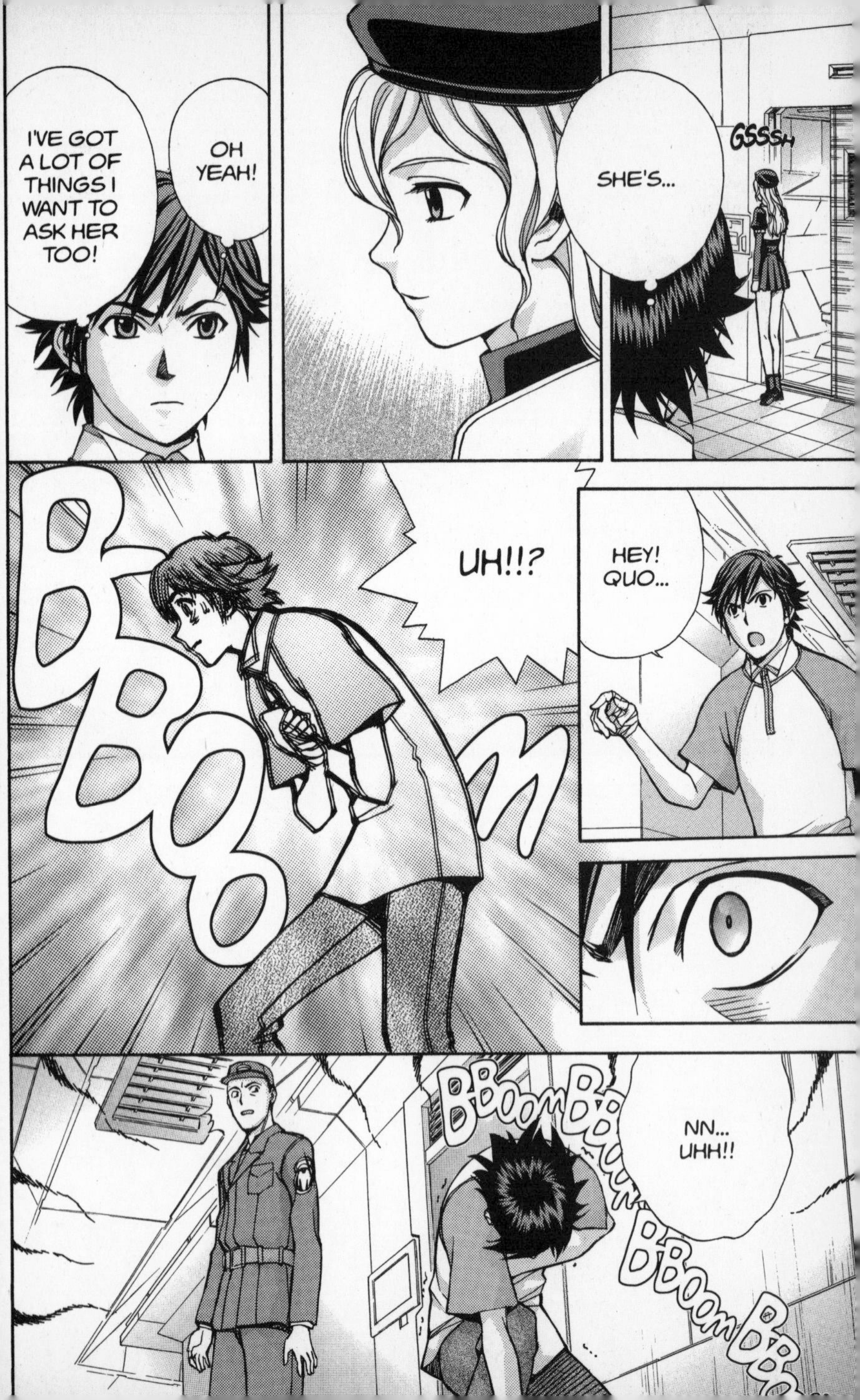
GSSSH
SHE'S...
OH YEAH!
I'VE GOT A LOT OF THINGS I WANT TO ASK HER TOO!
HEY! QUO...
UH!!?
BBOOM
NN... UHH!!
BBoomBBoom
BBoomBB

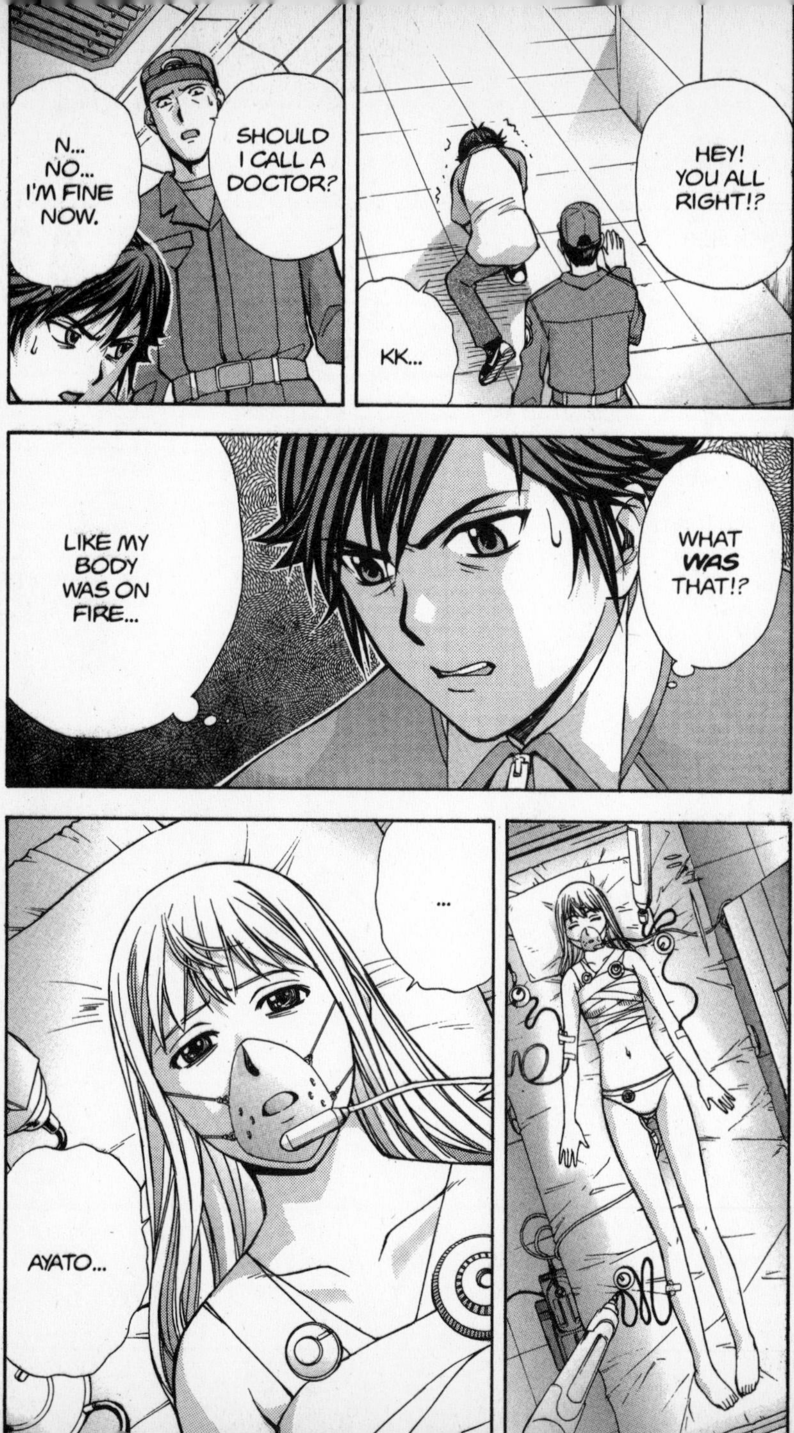
HEY! YOU ALL RIGHT!?
KK...
SHOULD I CALL A DOCTOR?
N... NO... I'M FINE NOW.
WHAT **WAS** THAT!?
LIKE MY BODY WAS ON FIRE...
...
AYATO...

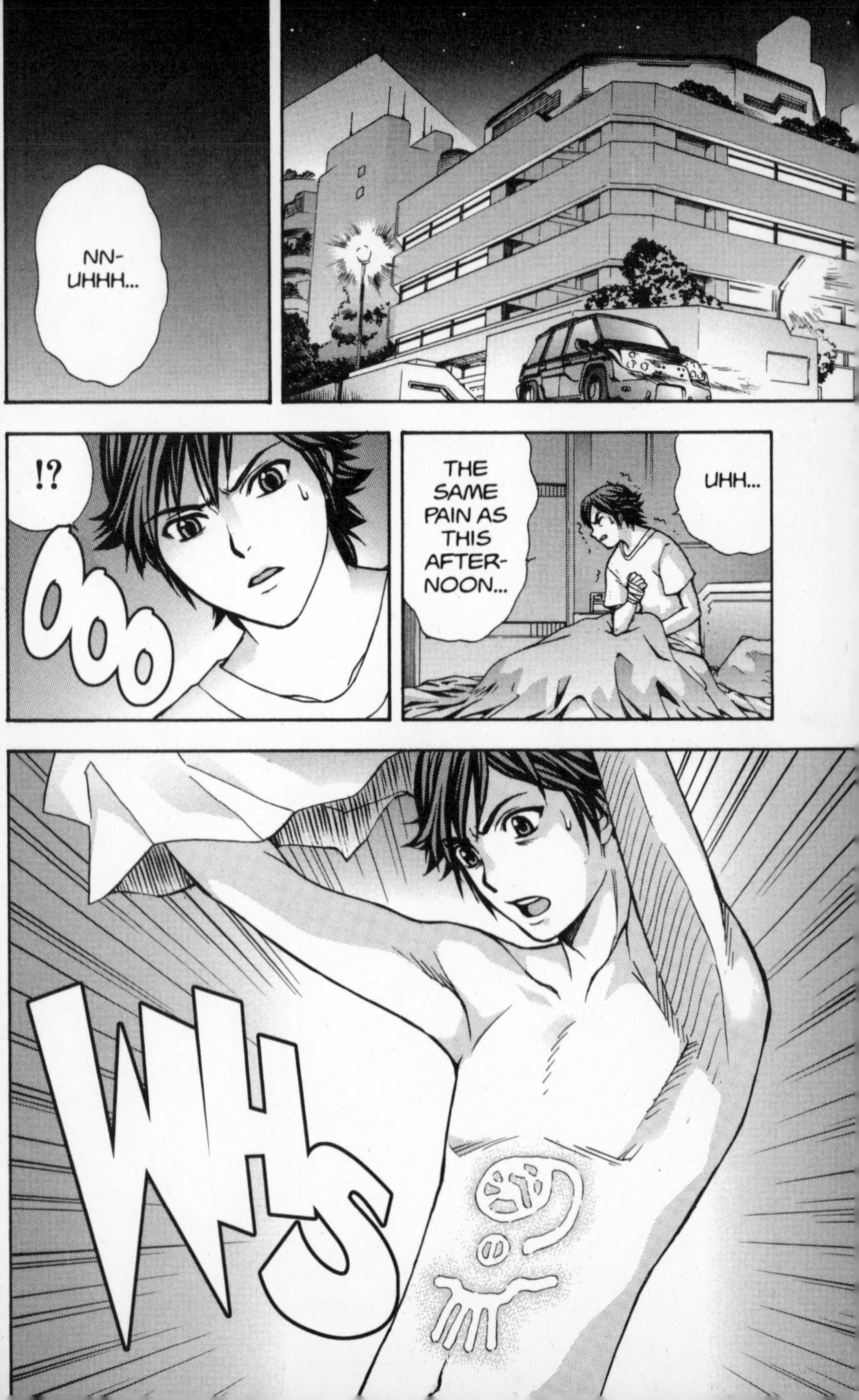
NN-UHHH...
UHH...
THE SAME PAIN AS THIS AFTERNOON...
!?
OOO
WHS

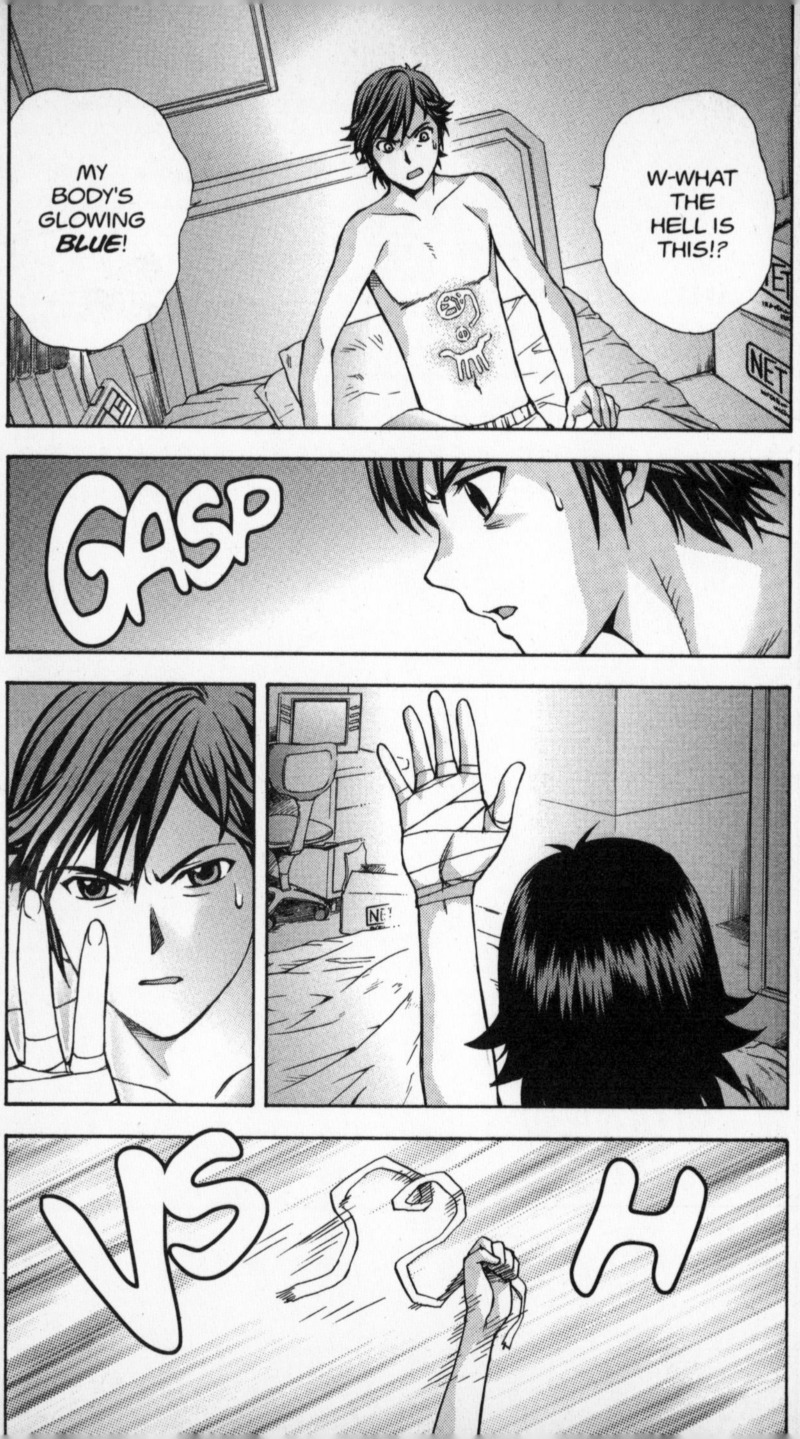
W-WHAT THE HELL IS THIS!?
MY BODY'S GLOWING **BLUE**!
GASP
VS H

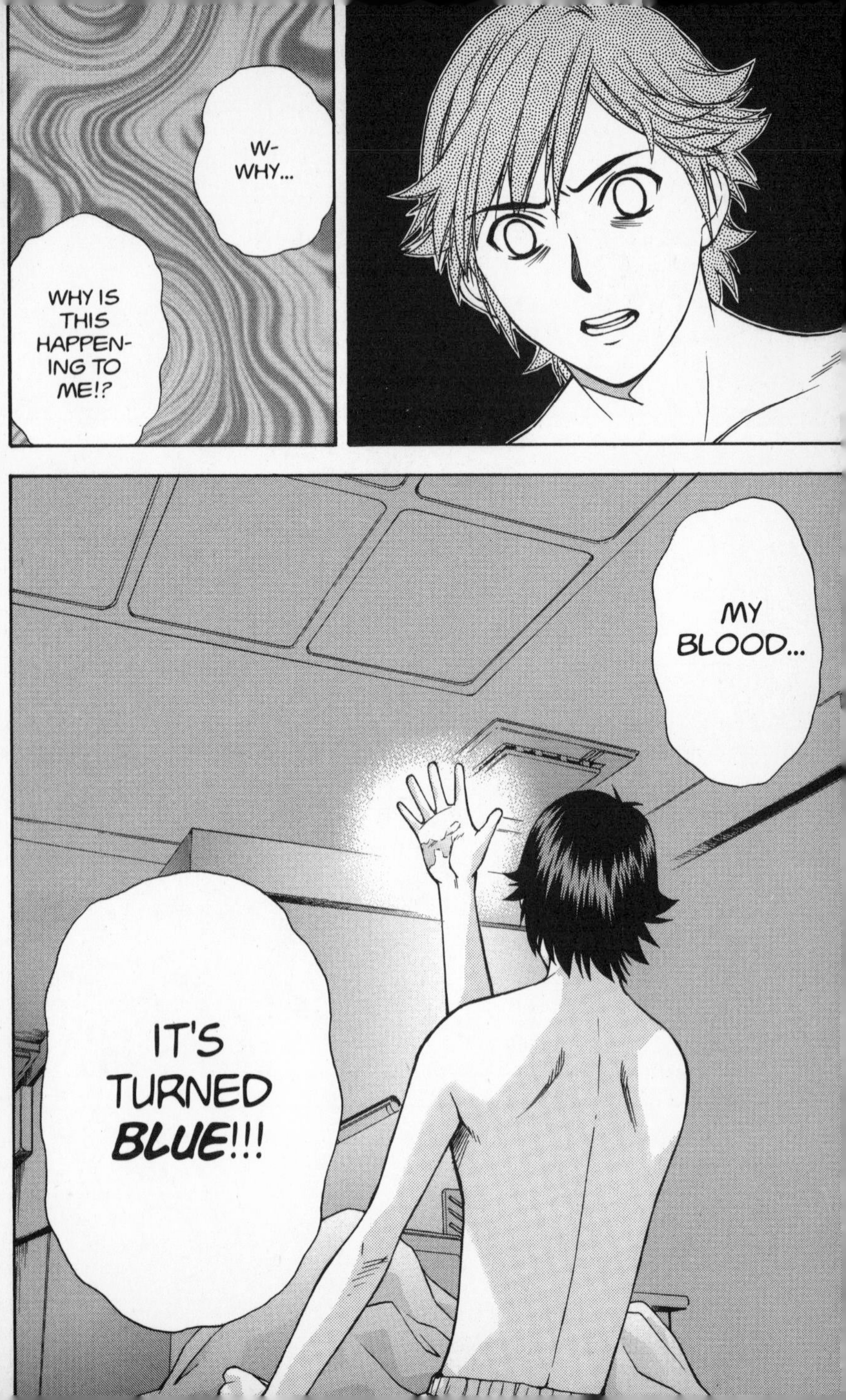
W-WHY...
WHY IS THIS HAPPENING TO ME!?
MY BLOOD...
IT'S TURNED **BLUE**!!!

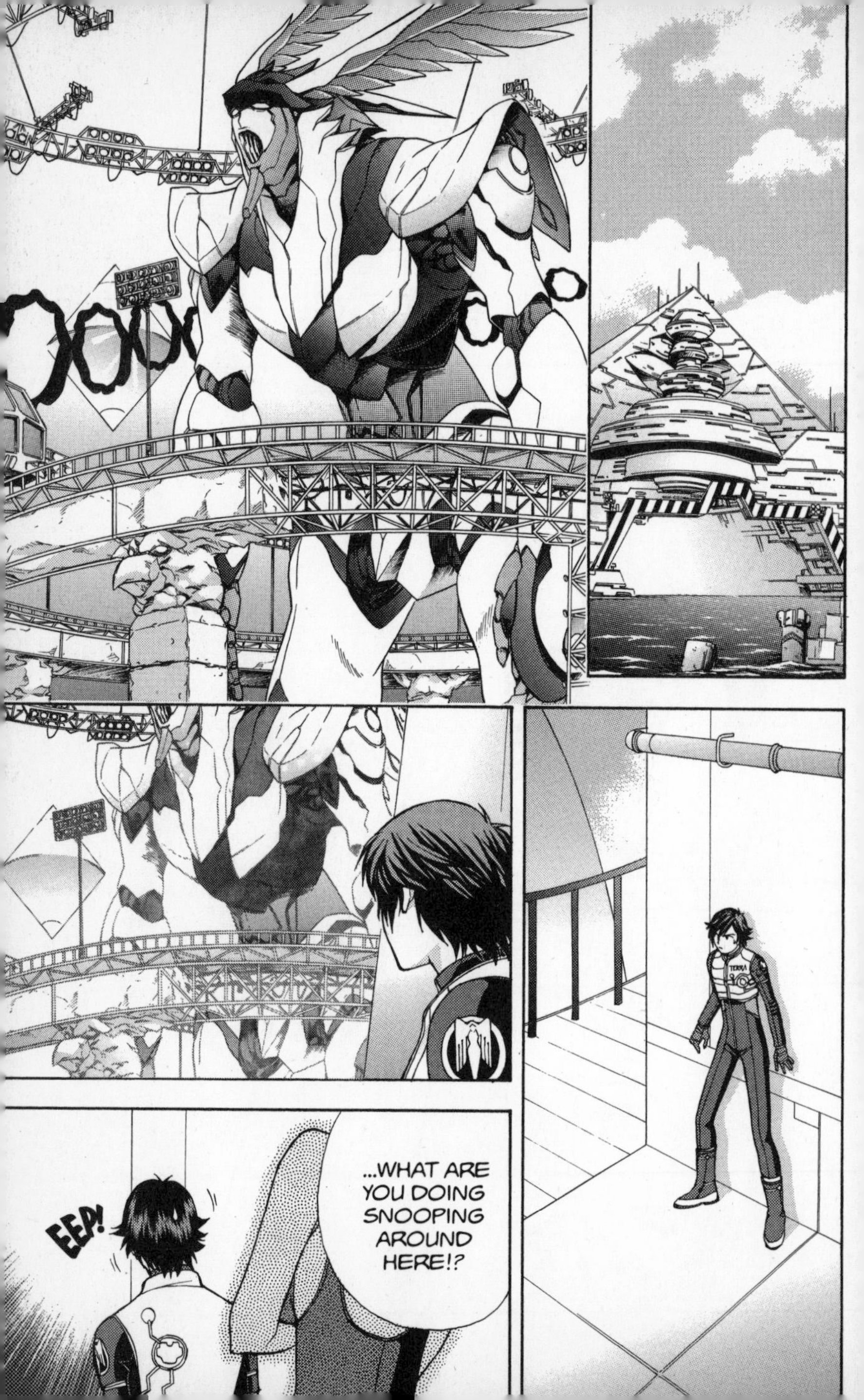
TERRA
...WHAT ARE YOU DOING SNOOPING AROUND HERE!?
EEP!

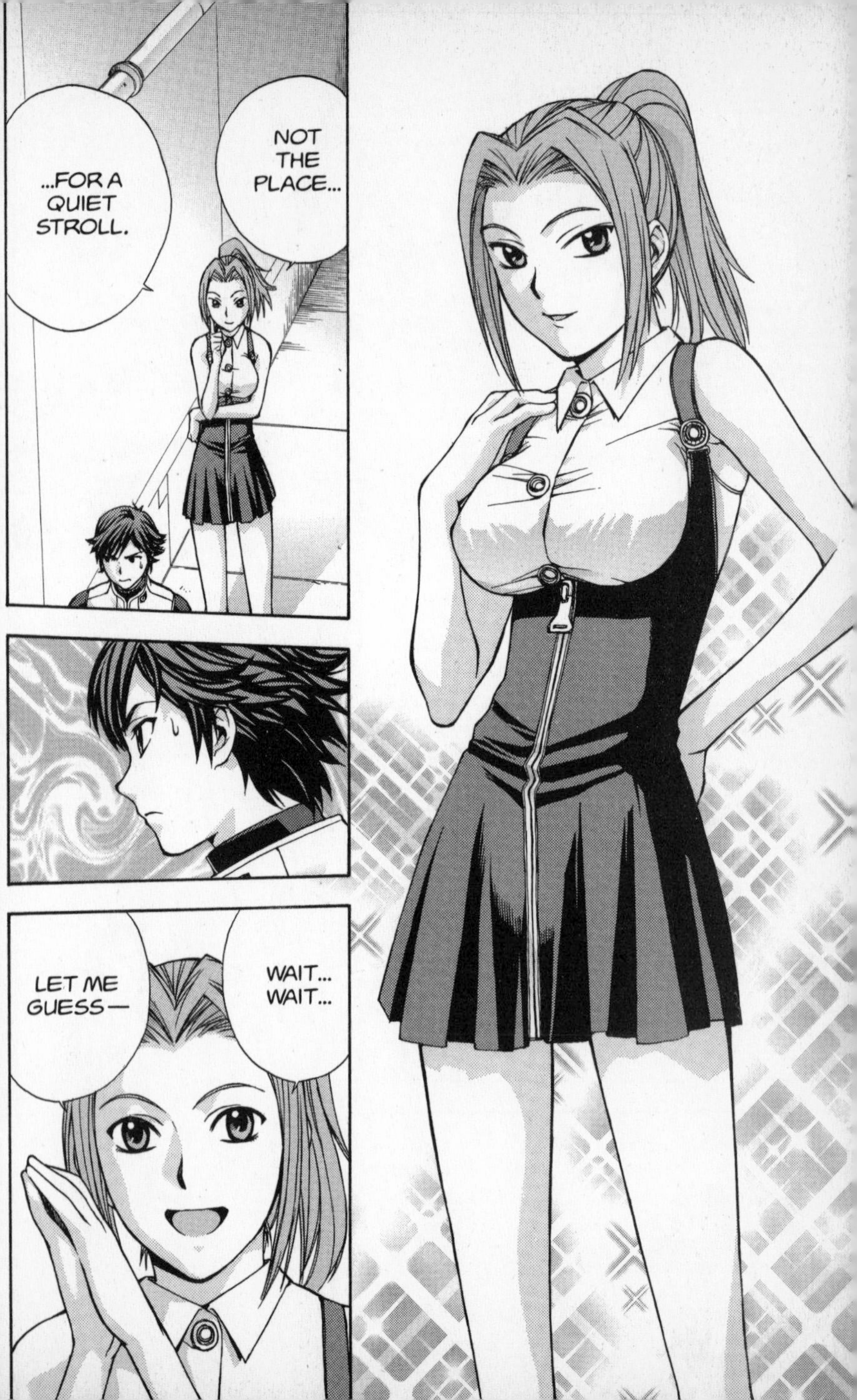
NOT THE PLACE...
...FOR A QUIET STROLL.
WAIT... WAIT...
LET ME GUESS—

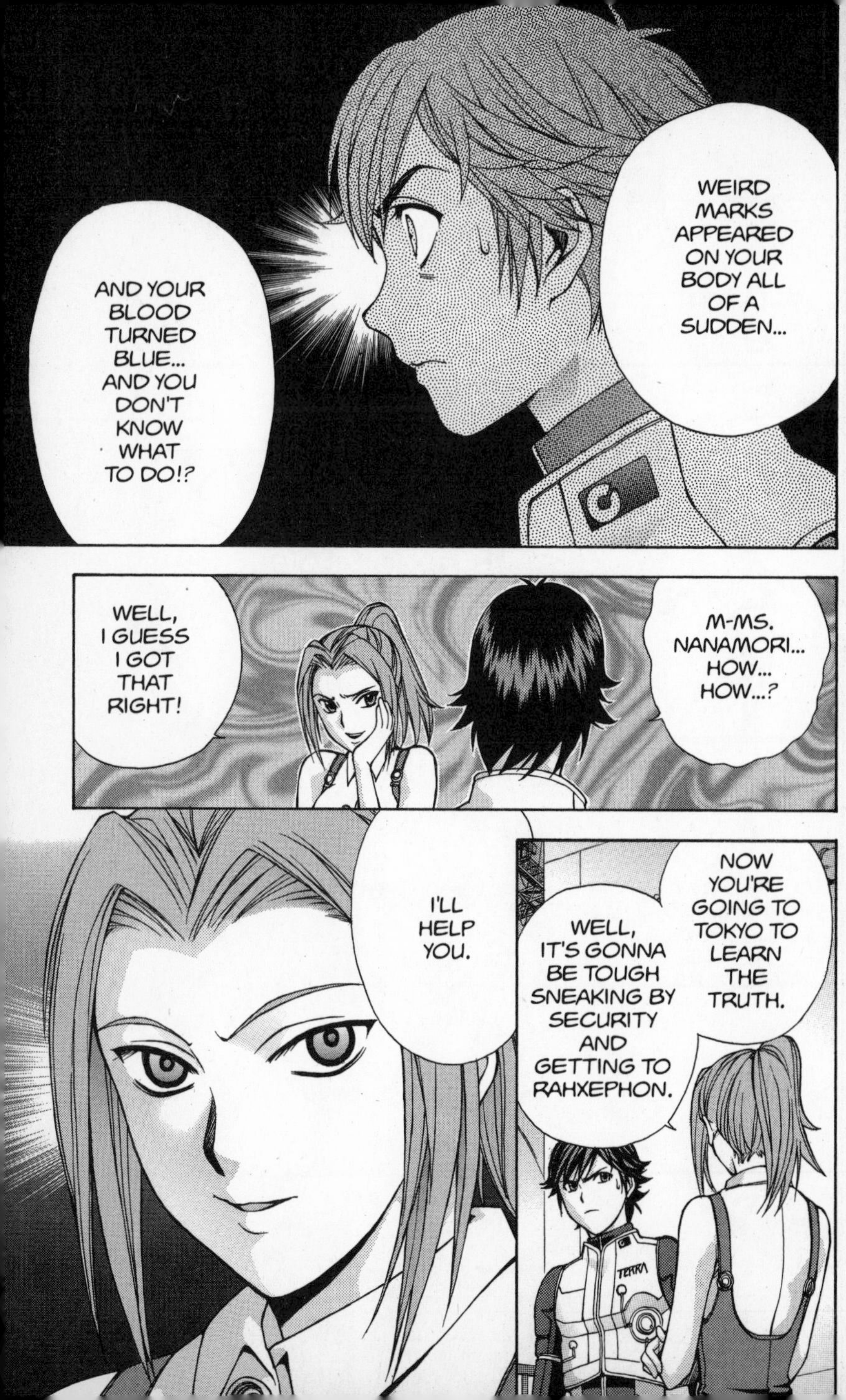
WEIRD MARKS APPEARED ON YOUR BODY ALL OF A SUDDEN...
AND YOUR BLOOD TURNED BLUE... AND YOU DON'T KNOW WHAT TO DO!?
M-MS. NANAMORI... HOW... HOW...?
WELL, I GUESS I GOT THAT RIGHT!
NOW YOU'RE GOING TO TOKYO TO LEARN THE TRUTH.
WELL, IT'S GONNA BE TOUGH SNEAKING BY SECURITY AND GETTING TO RAHXEPHON.
I'LL HELP YOU.

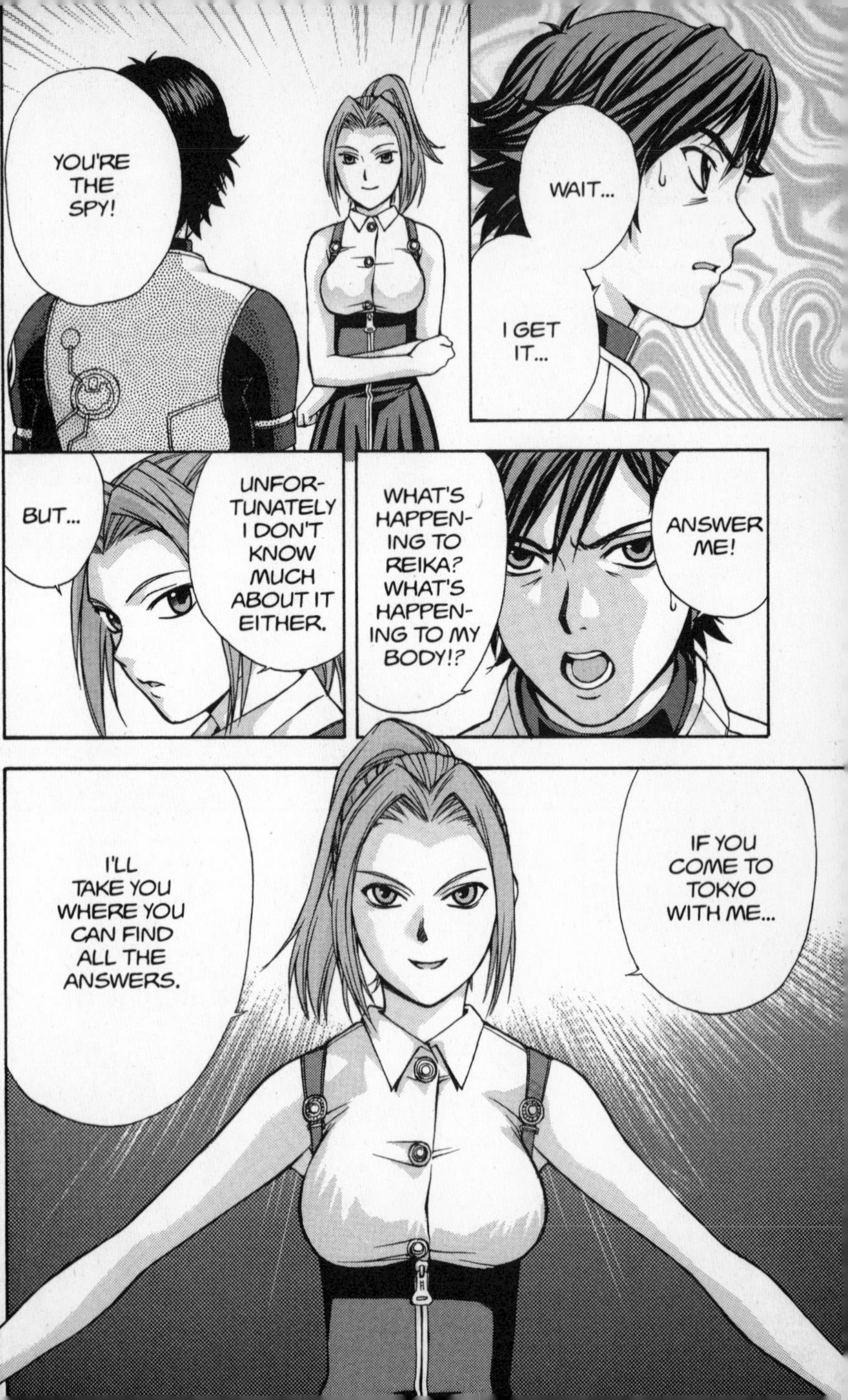
WAIT...
I GET IT...
YOU'RE THE SPY!
ANSWER ME!
WHAT'S HAPPENING TO REIKA? WHAT'S HAPPENING TO MY BODY!?
UNFORTUNATELY I DON'T KNOW MUCH ABOUT IT EITHER.
BUT...
IF YOU COME TO TOKYO WITH ME...
I'LL TAKE YOU WHERE YOU CAN FIND ALL THE ANSWERS.

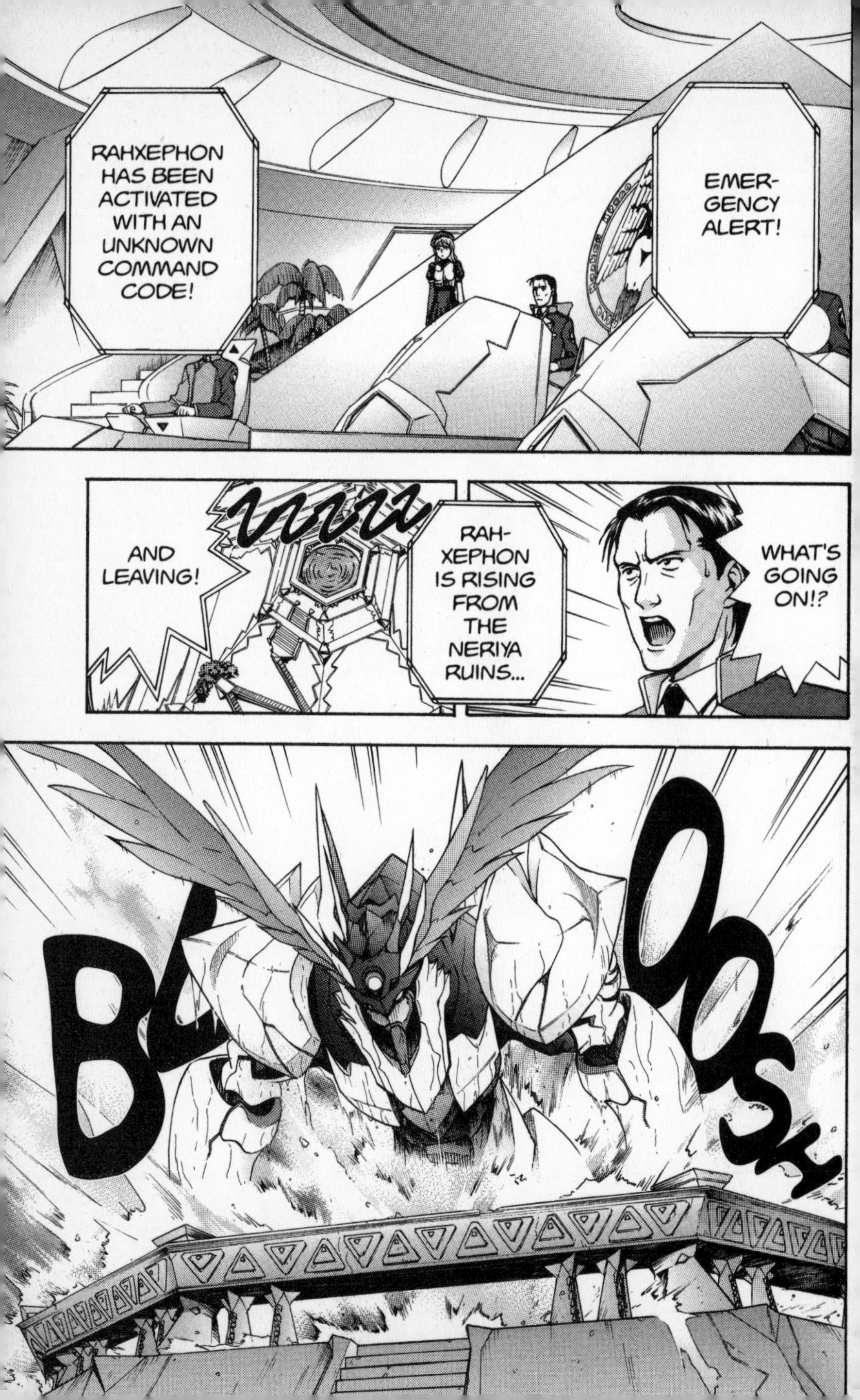
EMER-
GENCY
ALERT!
RAHXEPHON
HAS BEEN
ACTIVATED
WITH AN
UNKNOWN
COMMAND
CODE!
WHAT'S
GOING
ON!?
RAH-
XEPHON
IS RISING
FROM
THE
NERIYA
RUINS...
AND
LEAVING!

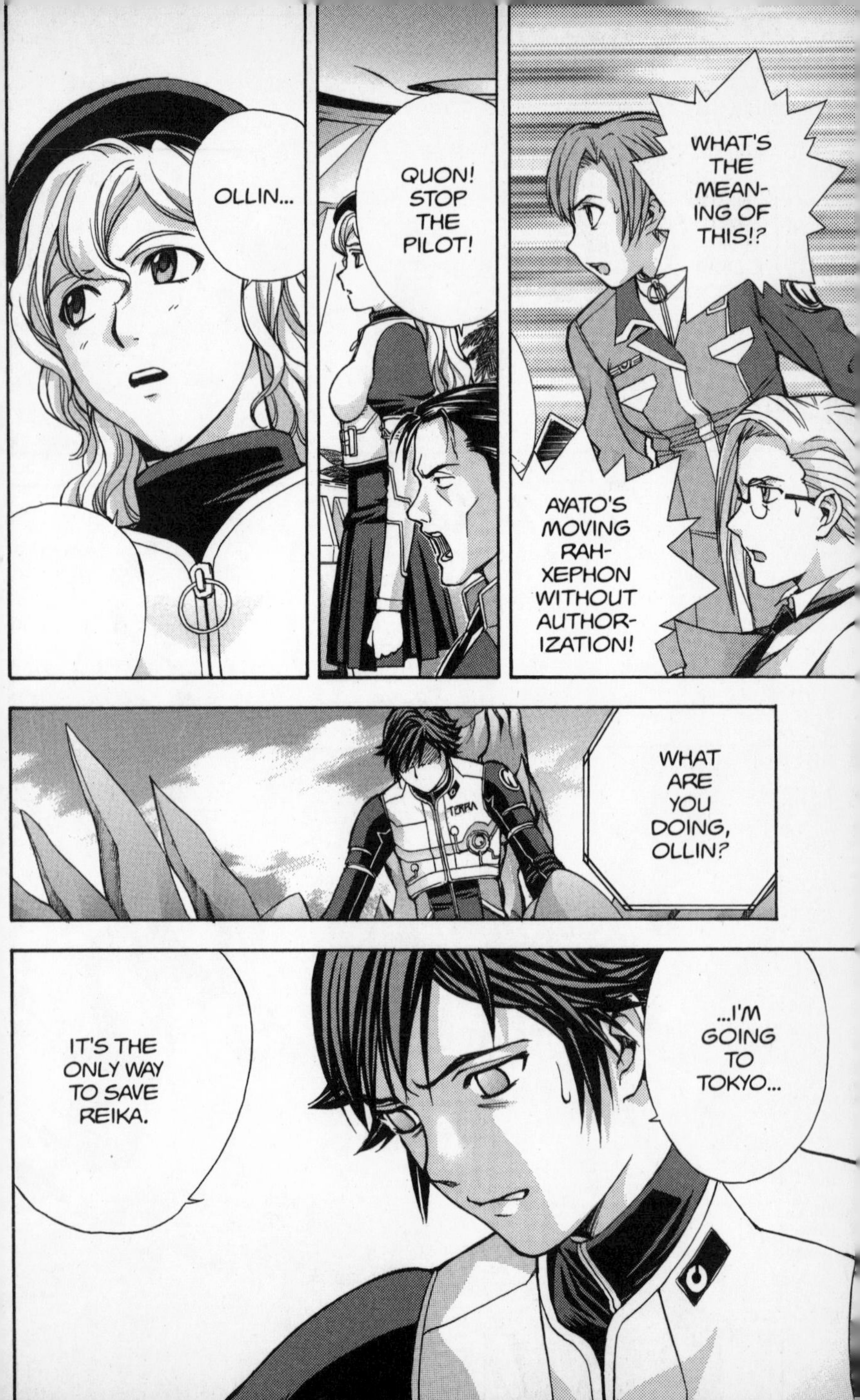
WHAT'S THE MEANING OF THIS!?
AYATO'S MOVING RAHXEPHON WITHOUT AUTHORIZATION!
QUON! STOP THE PILOT!
OLLIN...
WHAT ARE YOU DOING, OLLIN?
...I'M GOING TO TOKYO...
IT'S THE ONLY WAY TO SAVE REIKA.

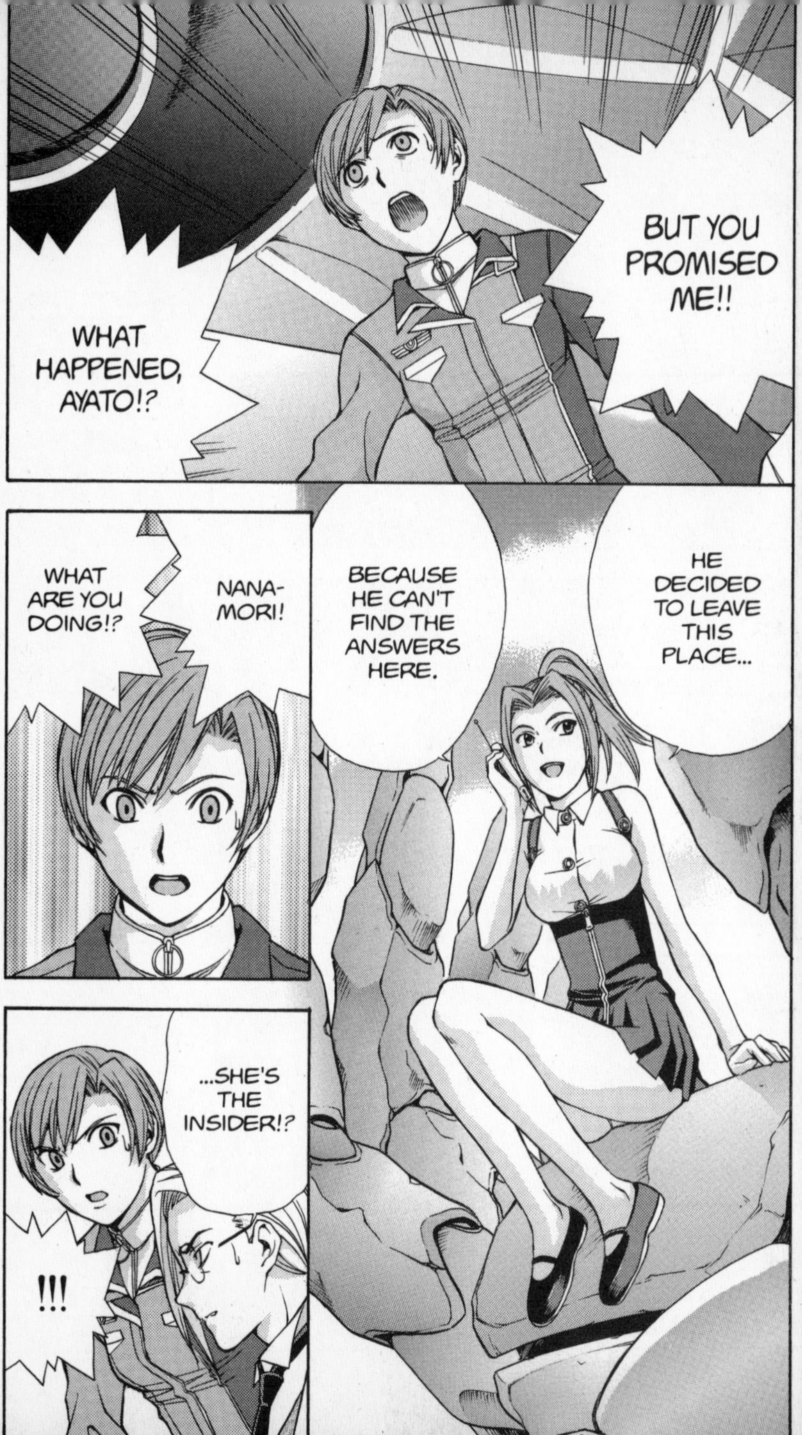
BUT YOU PROMISED ME!!
WHAT HAPPENED, AYATO!?
HE DECIDED TO LEAVE THIS PLACE...
BECAUSE HE CAN'T FIND THE ANSWERS HERE.
NANA-MORI!
WHAT ARE YOU DOING!?
...SHE'S THE INSIDER!?
!!!

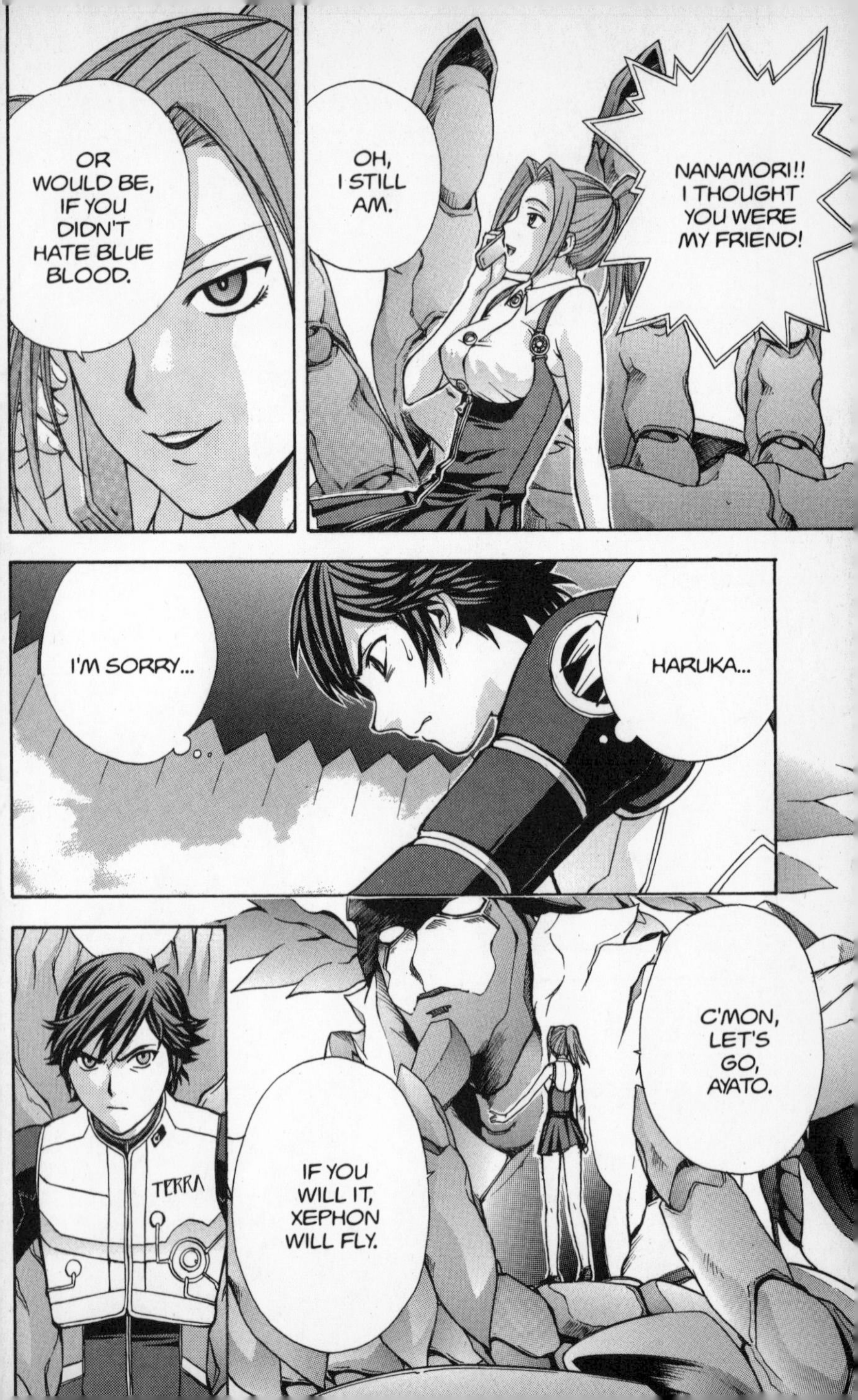
NANAMORI!! I THOUGHT YOU WERE MY FRIEND!
OH, I STILL AM.
OR WOULD BE, IF YOU DIDN'T HATE BLUE BLOOD.
HARUKA...
I'M SORRY...
C'MON, LET'S GO, AYATO.
IF YOU WILL IT, XEPHON WILL FLY.
TERRA

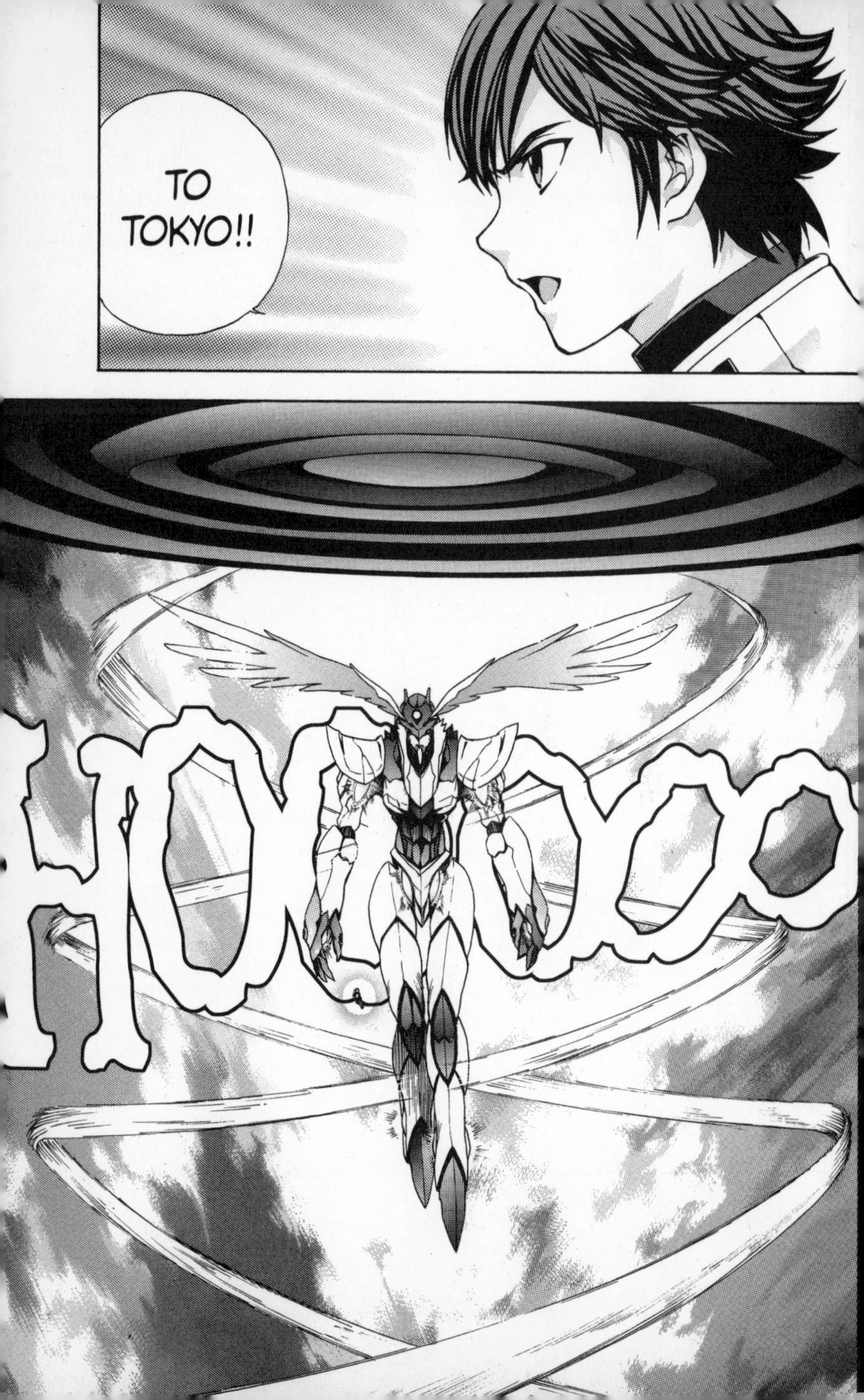
TO TOKYO!!

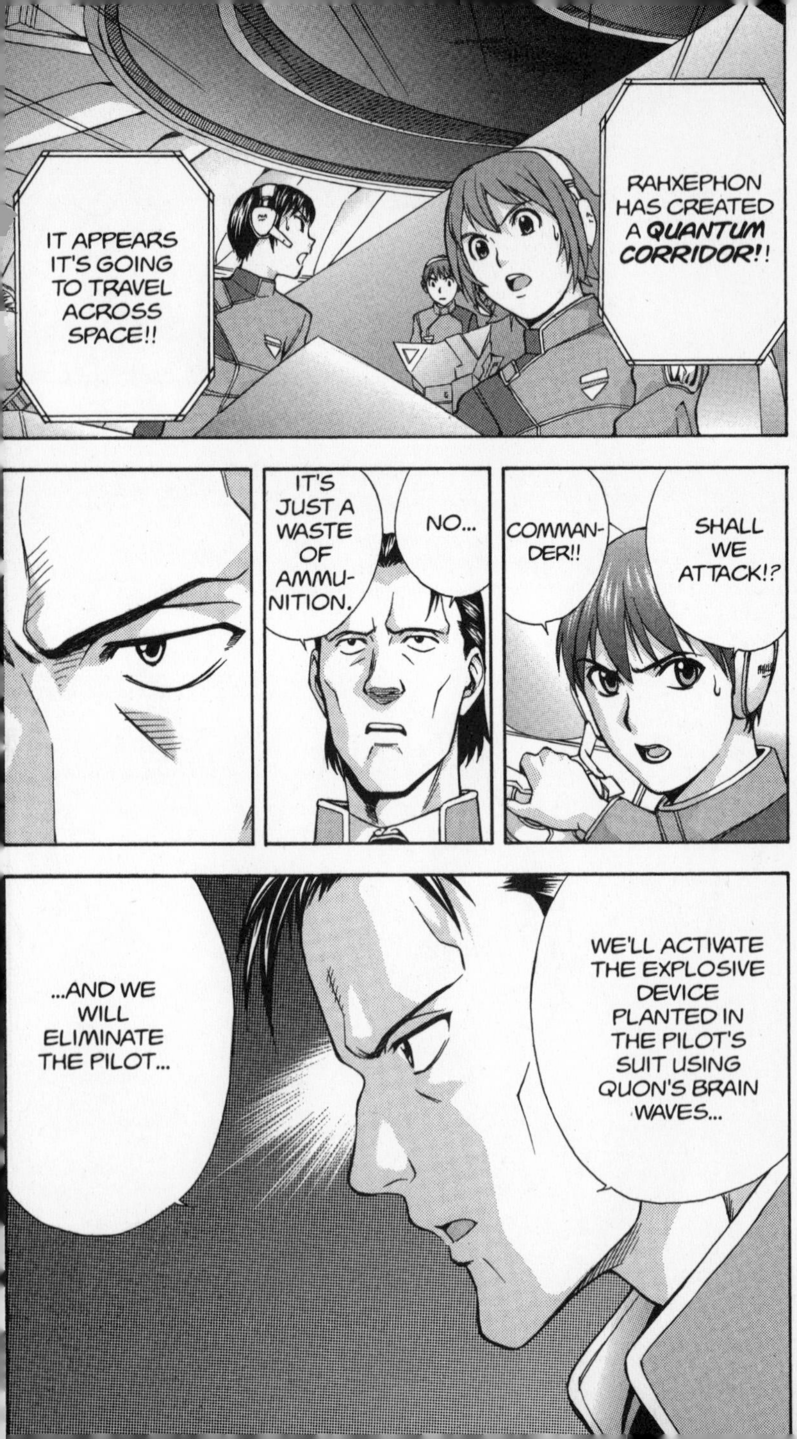
RAHXEPHON HAS CREATED A QUANTUM CORRIDOR!!
IT APPEARS IT'S GOING TO TRAVEL ACROSS SPACE!!
SHALL WE ATTACK!?
COMMAN-DER!!
NO...
IT'S JUST A WASTE OF AMMU-NITION.
WE'LL ACTIVATE THE EXPLOSIVE DEVICE PLANTED IN THE PILOT'S SUIT USING QUON'S BRAIN WAVES...
...AND WE WILL ELIMINATE THE PILOT...

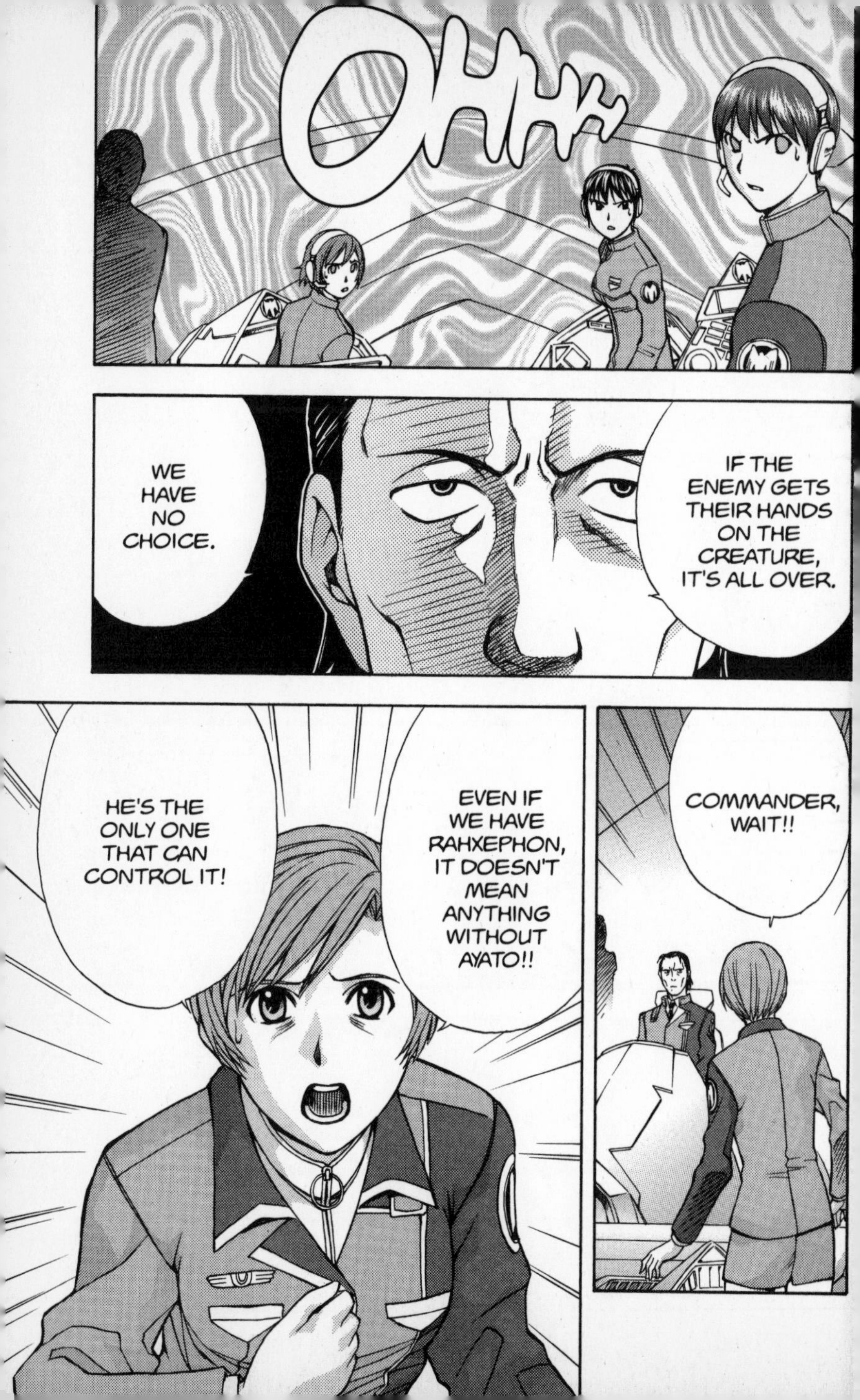
OHHH
IF THE ENEMY GETS THEIR HANDS ON THE CREATURE, IT'S ALL OVER.
WE HAVE NO CHOICE.
COMMANDER, WAIT!!
EVEN IF WE HAVE RAHXEPHON, IT DOESN'T MEAN ANYTHING WITHOUT AYATO!!
HE'S THE ONLY ONE THAT CAN CONTROL IT!

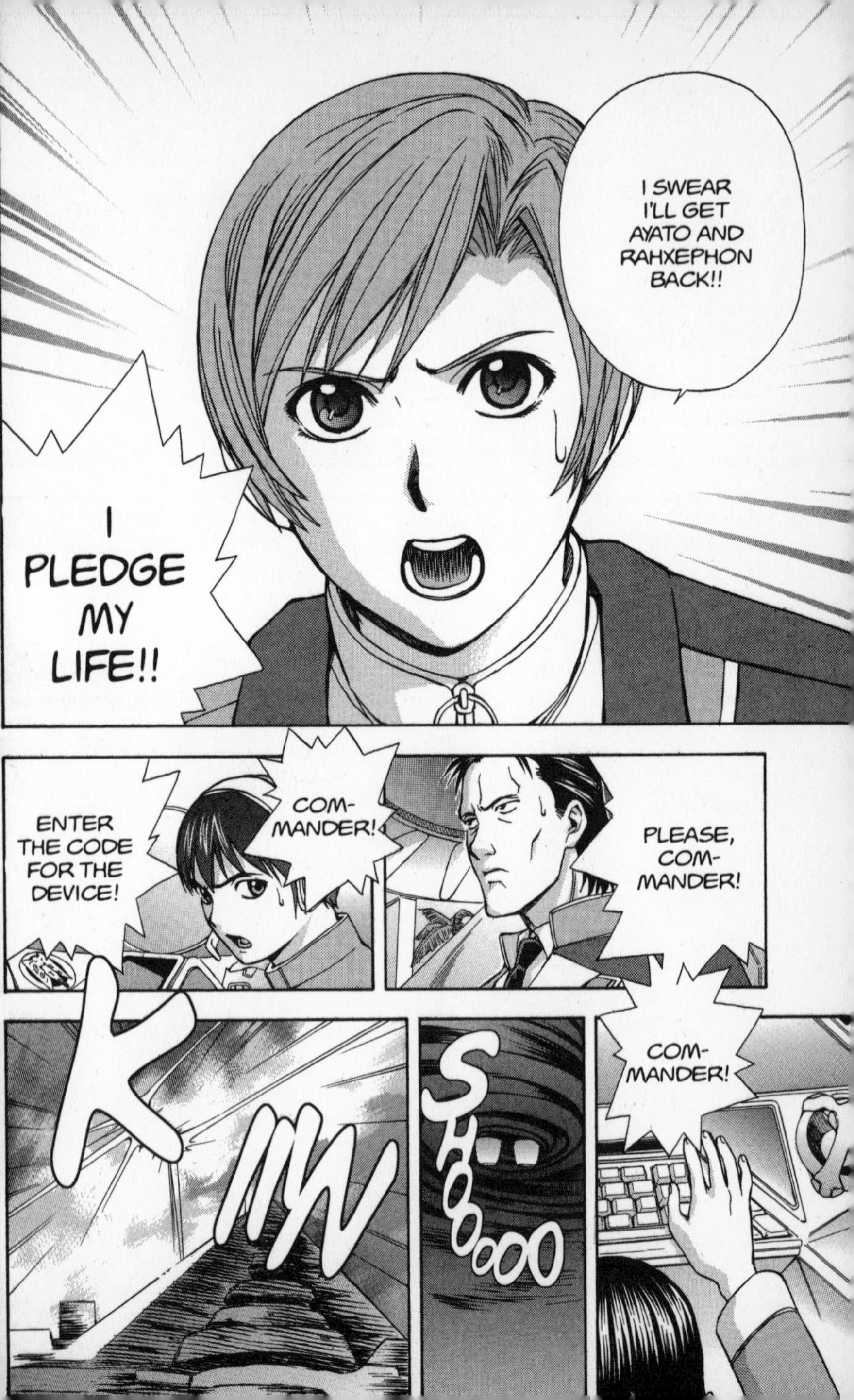
I SWEAR I'LL GET AYATO AND RAHXEPHON BACK!!
I PLEDGE MY LIFE!!
PLEASE, COM-MANDER!
COM-MANDER!
ENTER THE CODE FOR THE DEVICE!
COM-MANDER!
SHOOOOO
KIIIN

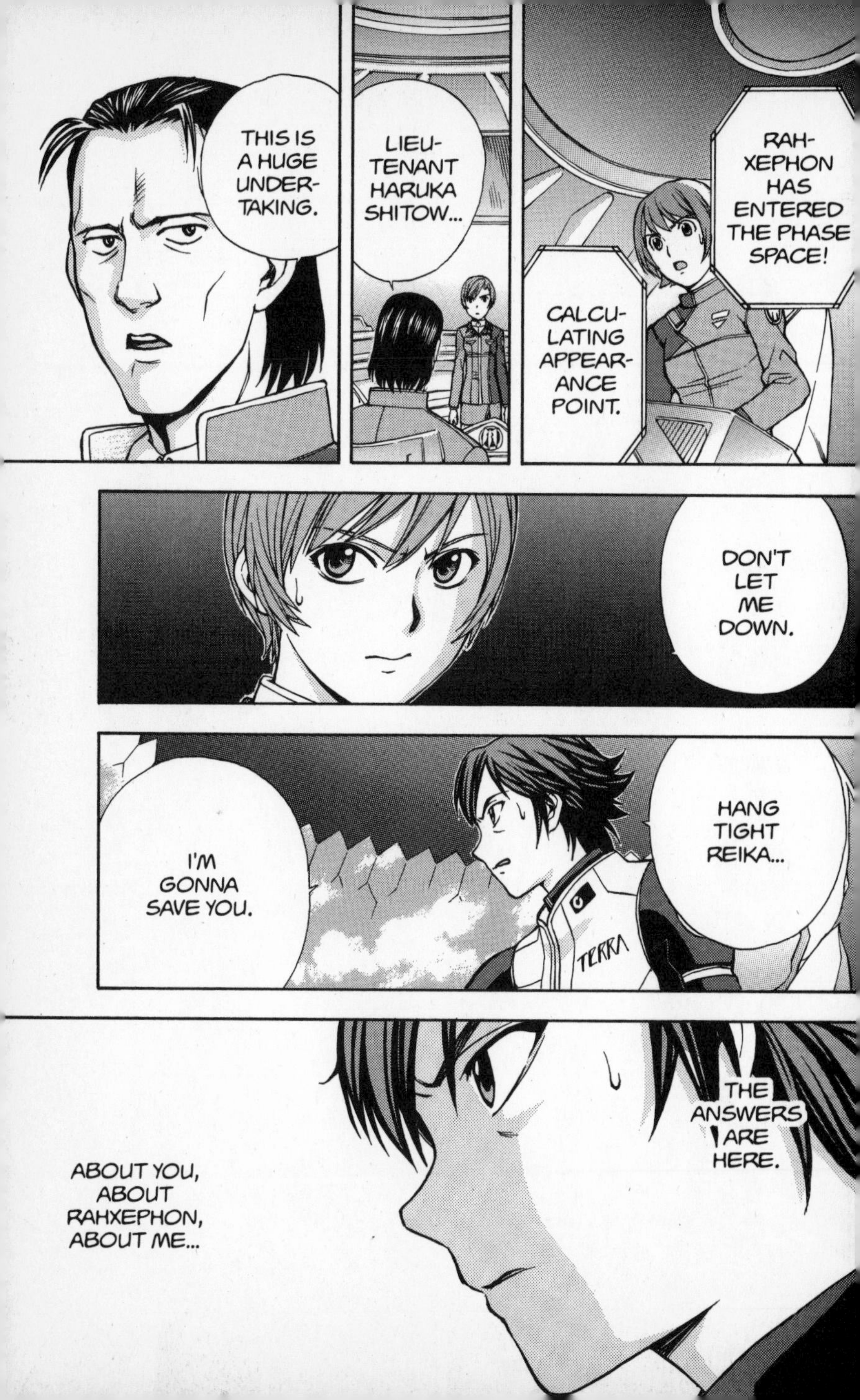
RAH-XEPHON HAS ENTERED THE PHASE SPACE!
CALCU-LATING APPEAR-ANCE POINT.
LIEU-TENANT HARUKA SHITOW...
THIS IS A HUGE UNDER-TAKING.
DON'T LET ME DOWN.
HANG TIGHT REIKA...
TERRA
I'M GONNA SAVE YOU.
THE ANSWERS ARE HERE.
ABOUT YOU, ABOUT RAHXEPHON, ABOUT ME...

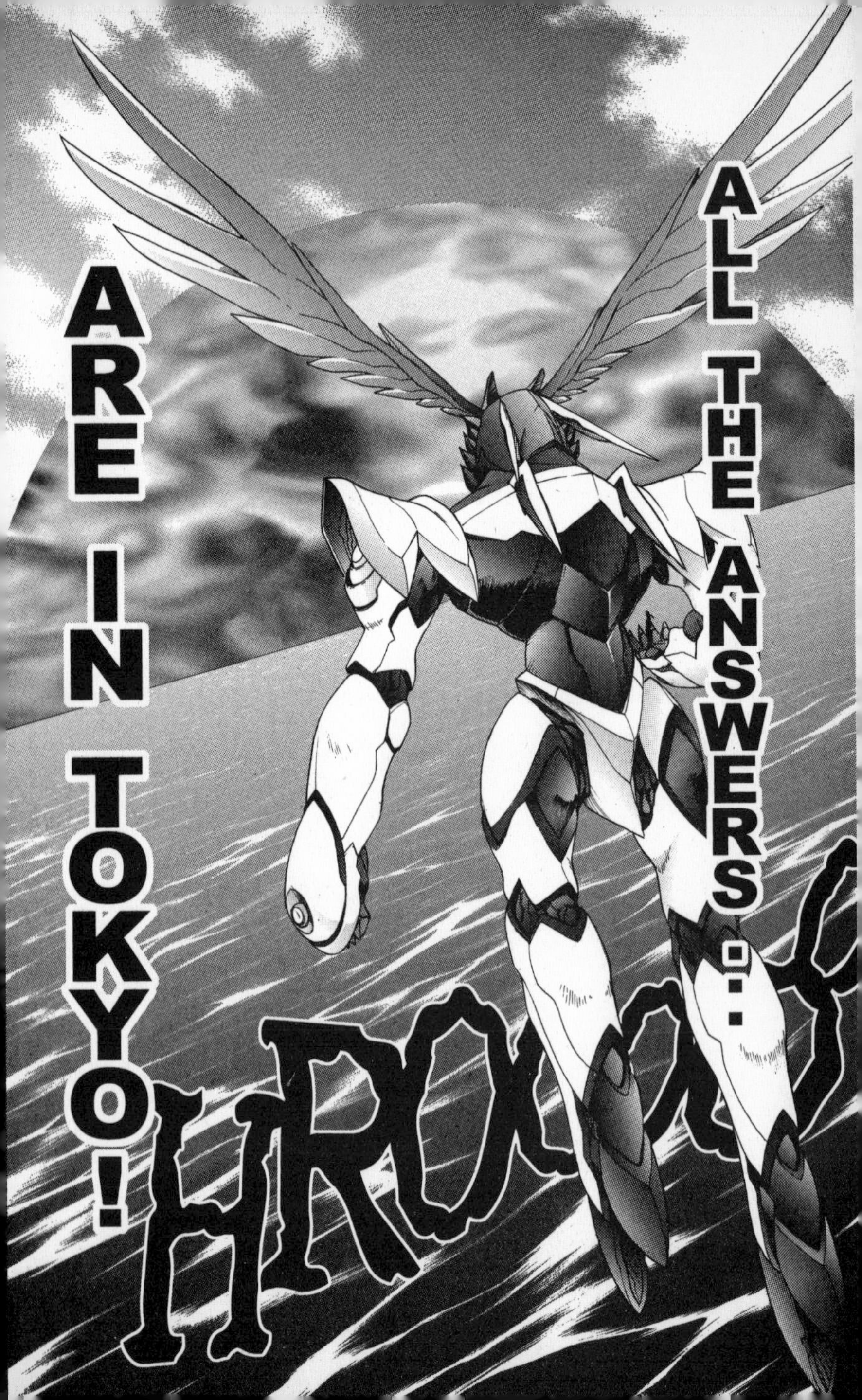
ALL THE ANSWERS...
ARE IN TOKYO!
HROOO

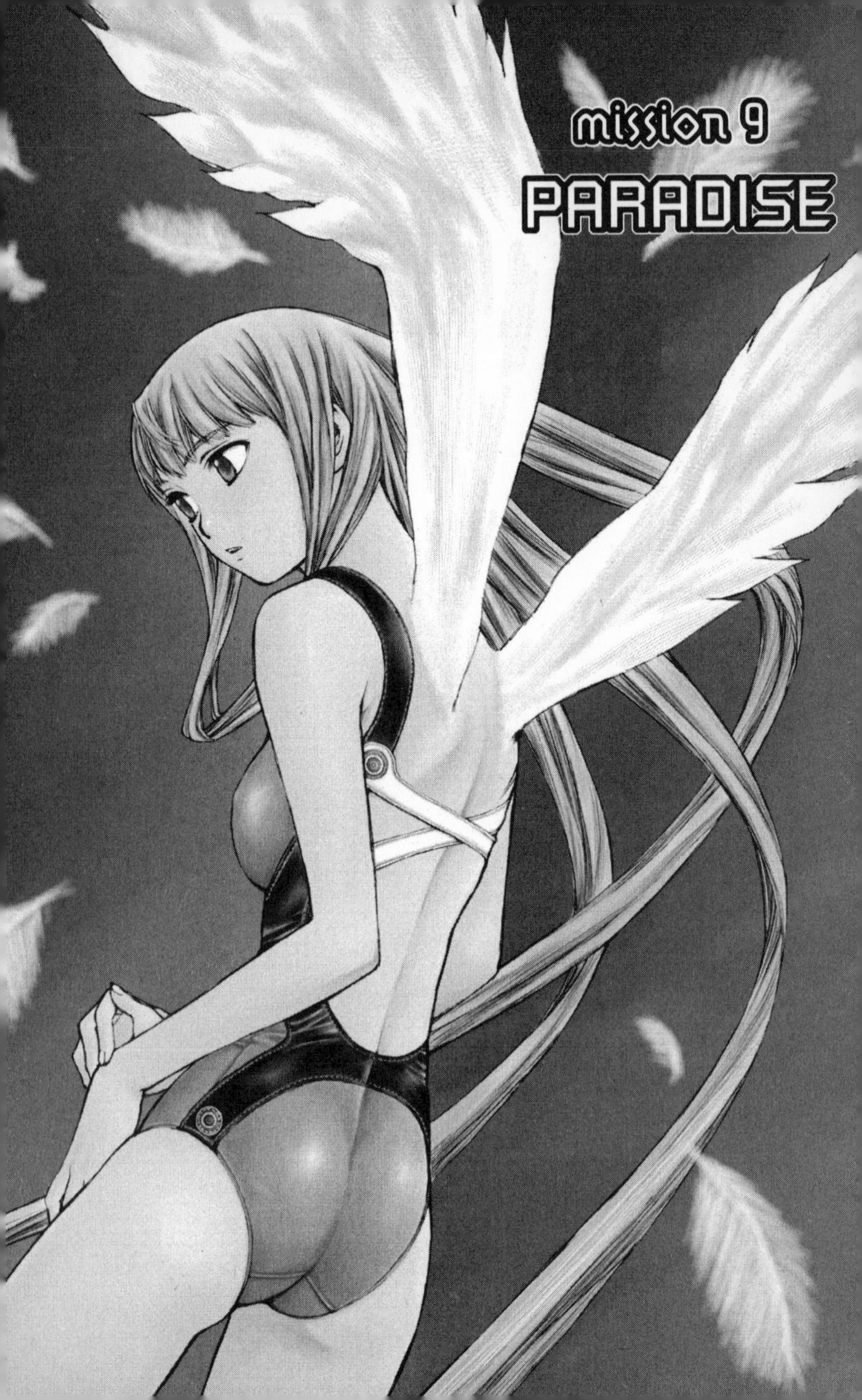
mission 9
PARADISE

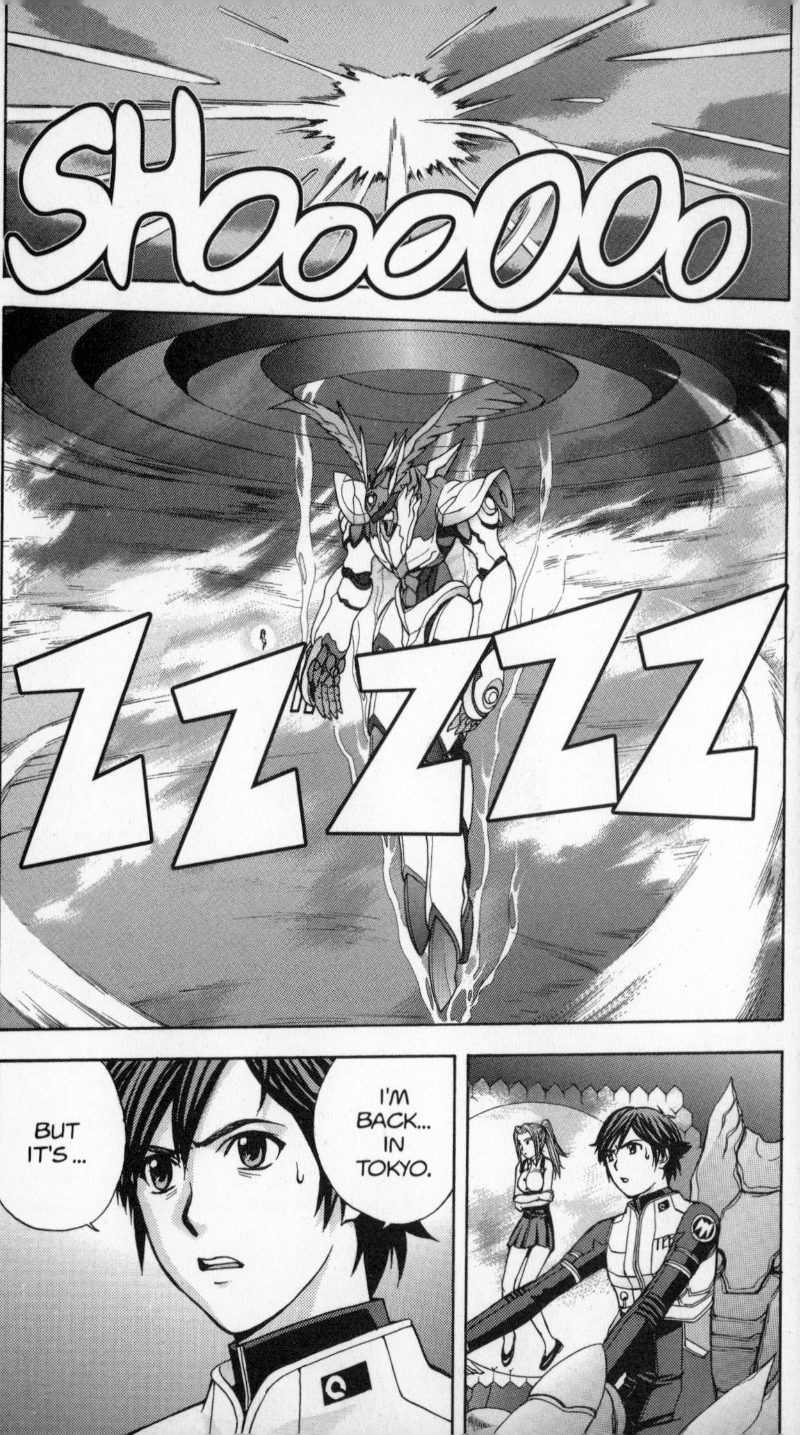
SHOOOOOO
ZZZZZ
I'M BACK... IN TOKYO.
BUT IT'S...

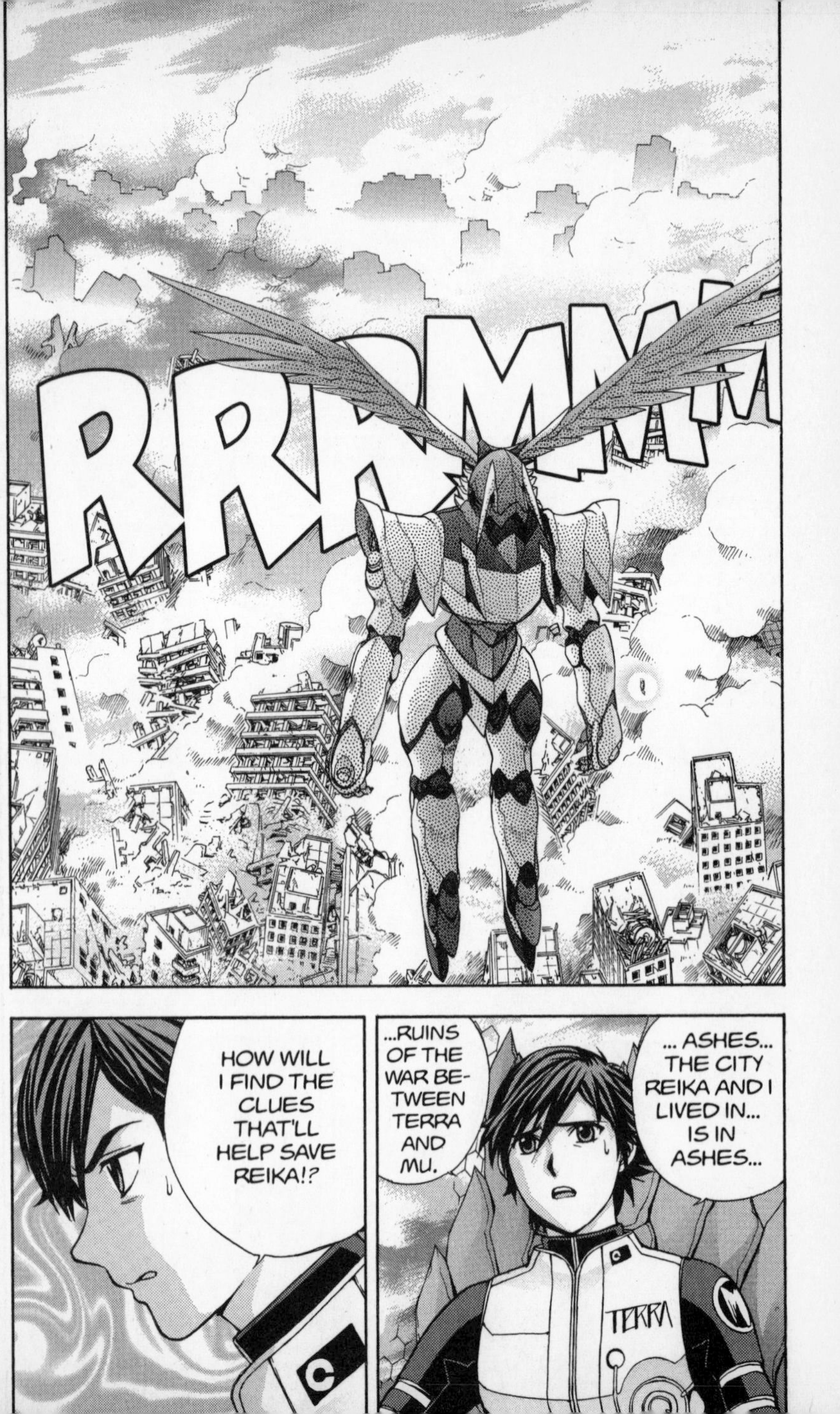

RRRMMMM
... ASHES... THE CITY REIKA AND I LIVED IN... IS IN ASHES...
...RUINS OF THE WAR BE- TWEEN TERRA AND MU.
TERRA
HOW WILL I FIND THE CLUES THAT'LL HELP SAVE REIKA!?

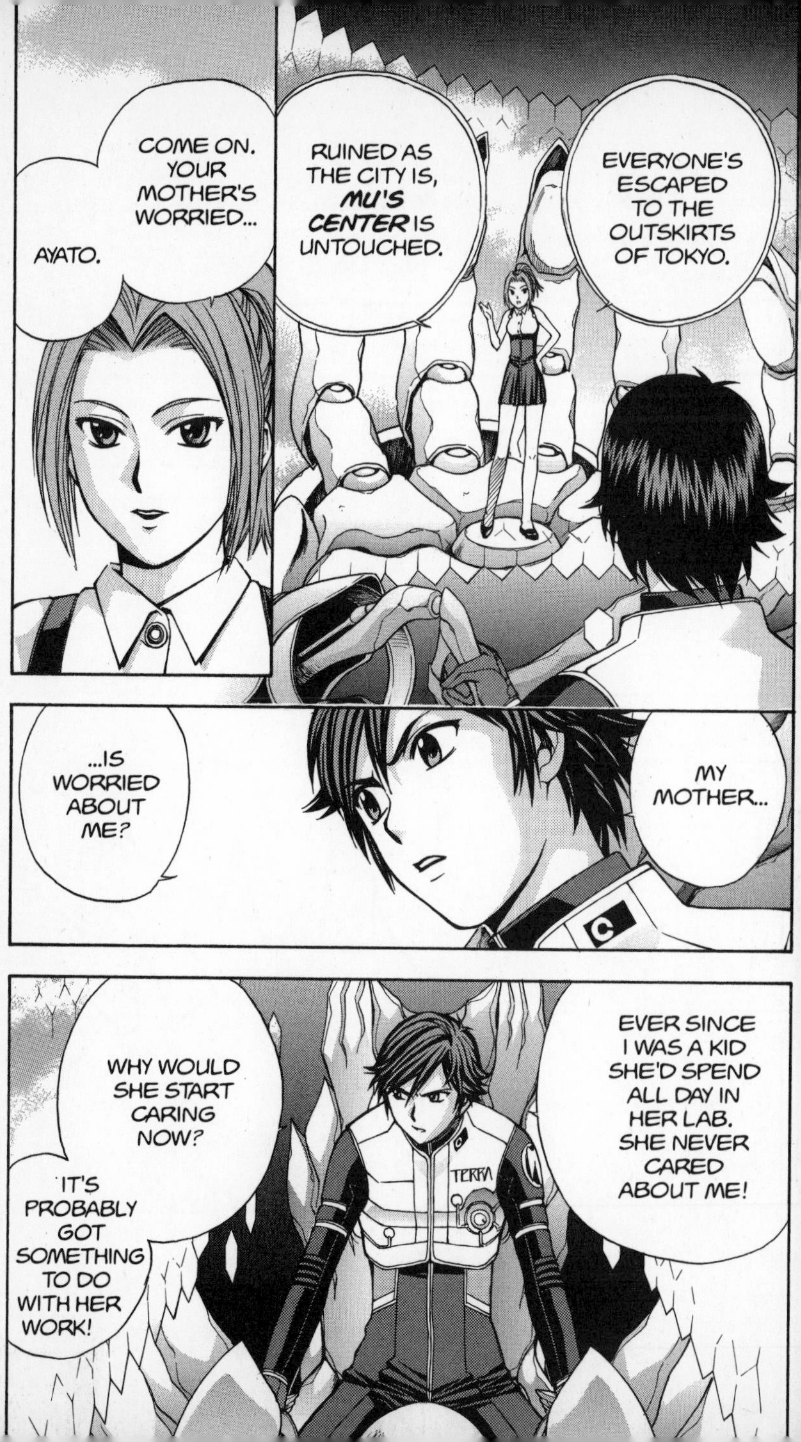
EVERYONE'S ESCAPED TO THE OUTSKIRTS OF TOKYO.
RUINED AS THE CITY IS, ***MU'S CENTER*** IS UNTOUCHED.
COME ON. YOUR MOTHER'S WORRIED... AYATO.
MY MOTHER...
...IS WORRIED ABOUT ME?
EVER SINCE I WAS A KID SHE'D SPEND ALL DAY IN HER LAB. SHE NEVER CARED ABOUT ME!
TERRA
WHY WOULD SHE START CARING NOW?
IT'S PROBABLY GOT SOMETHING TO DO WITH HER WORK!

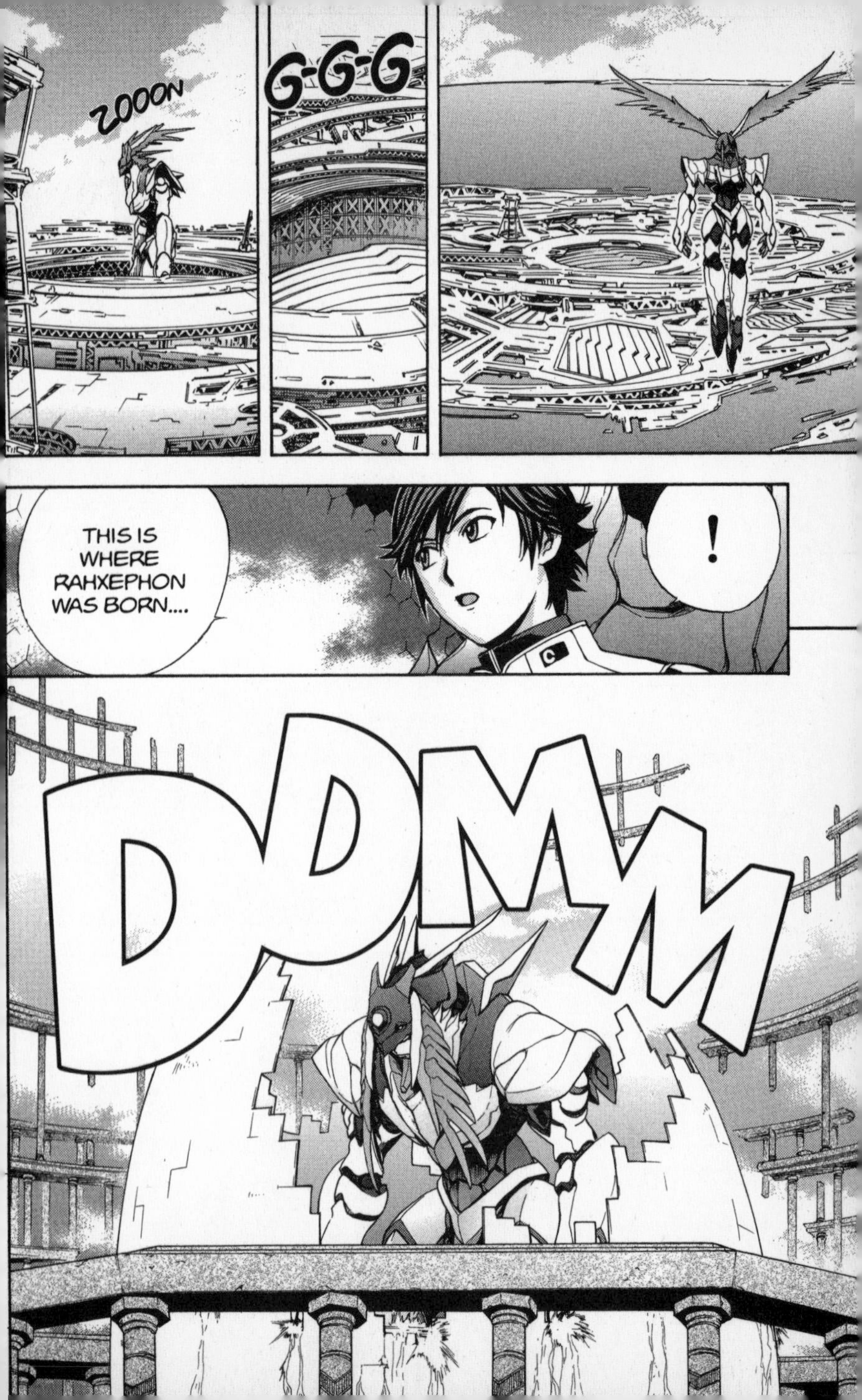
G-G-G
ZOOON
!
THIS IS WHERE RAHXEPHON WAS BORN....
DDMM

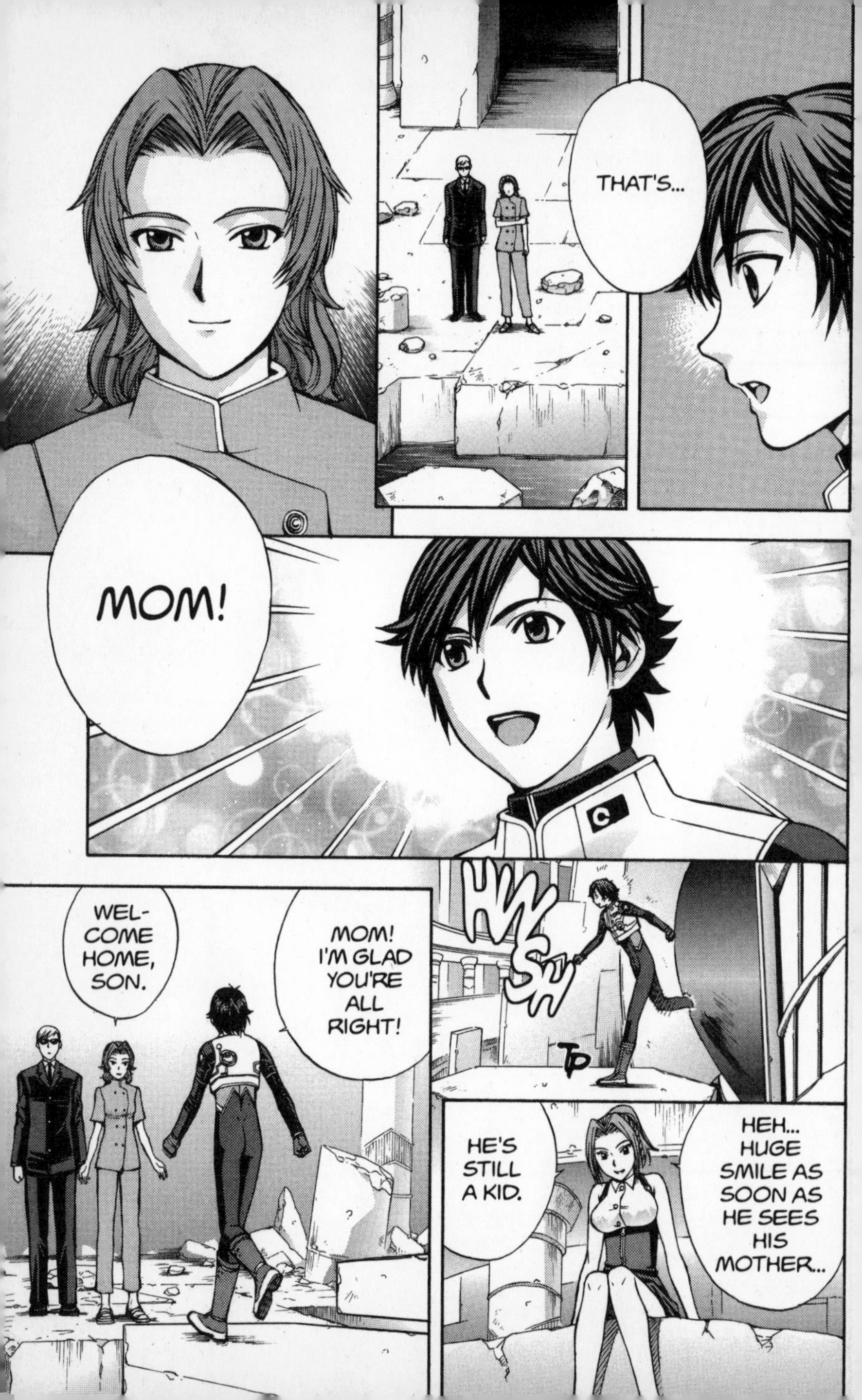
THAT'S...
MOM!
HWSH
TP
HEH... HUGE SMILE AS SOON AS HE SEES HIS MOTHER...
HE'S STILL A KID.
MOM! I'M GLAD YOU'RE ALL RIGHT!
WEL-COME HOME, SON.

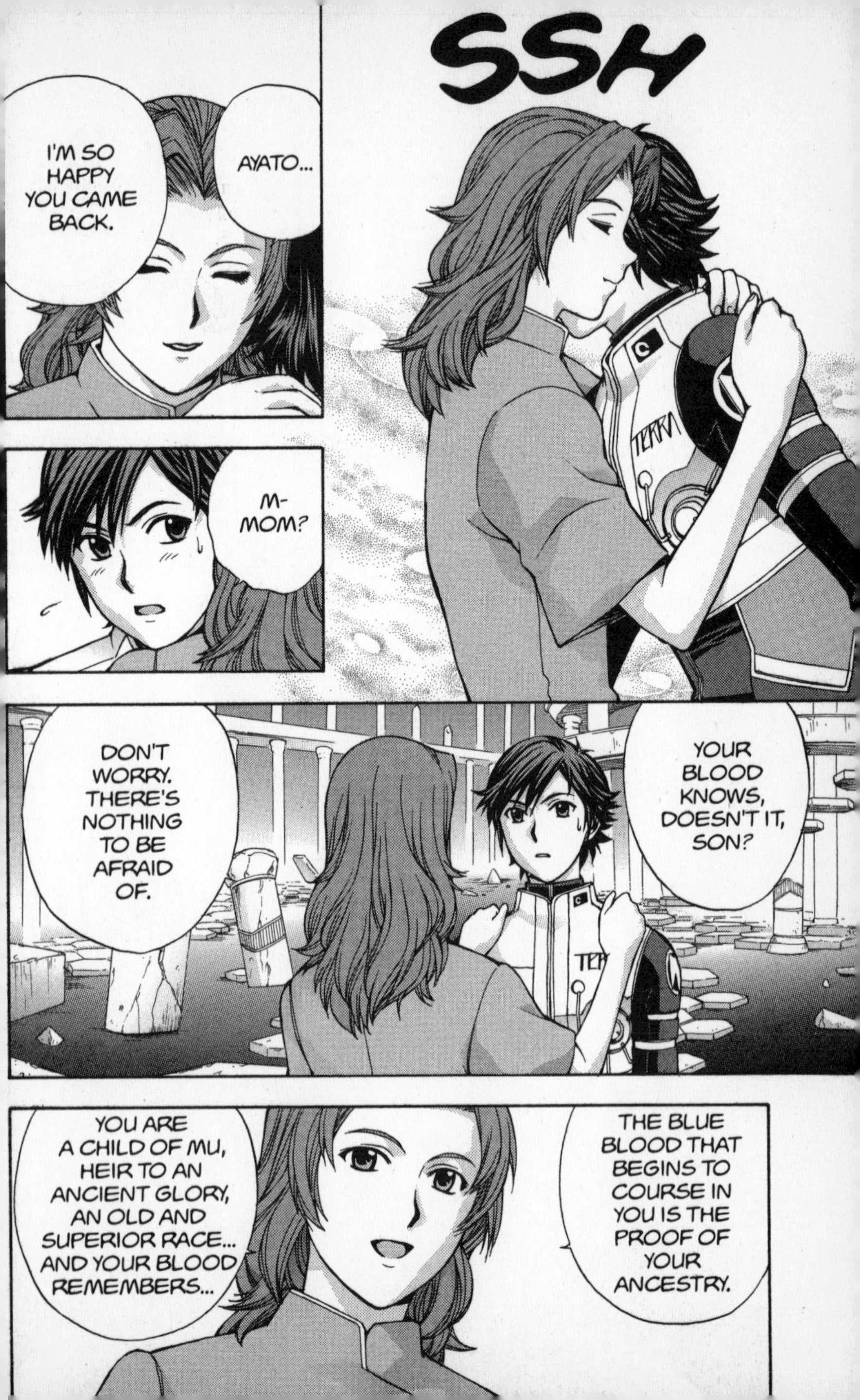
SSH
AYATO...
I'M SO HAPPY YOU CAME BACK.
M-MOM?
YOUR BLOOD KNOWS, DOESN'T IT, SON?
DON'T WORRY. THERE'S NOTHING TO BE AFRAID OF.
THE BLUE BLOOD THAT BEGINS TO COURSE IN YOU IS THE PROOF OF YOUR ANCESTRY.
YOU ARE A CHILD OF MU, HEIR TO AN ANCIENT GLORY, AN OLD AND SUPERIOR RACE... AND YOUR BLOOD REMEMBERS...

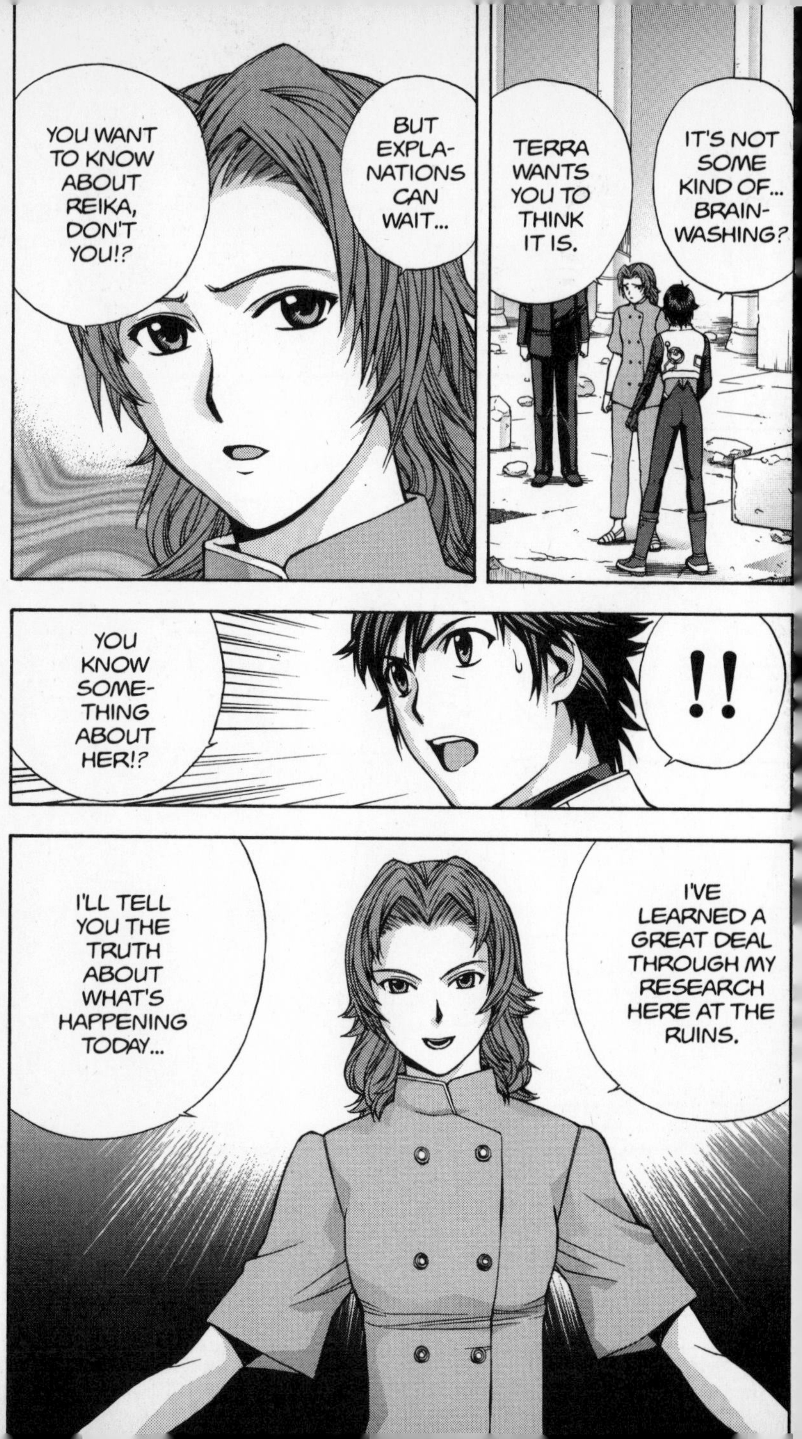
IT'S NOT SOME KIND OF... BRAIN-WASHING?
TERRA WANTS YOU TO THINK IT IS.
BUT EXPLANATIONS CAN WAIT...
YOU WANT TO KNOW ABOUT REIKA, DON'T YOU!?
!!
YOU KNOW SOMETHING ABOUT HER!?
I'VE LEARNED A GREAT DEAL THROUGH MY RESEARCH HERE AT THE RUINS.
I'LL TELL YOU THE TRUTH ABOUT WHAT'S HAPPENING TODAY...

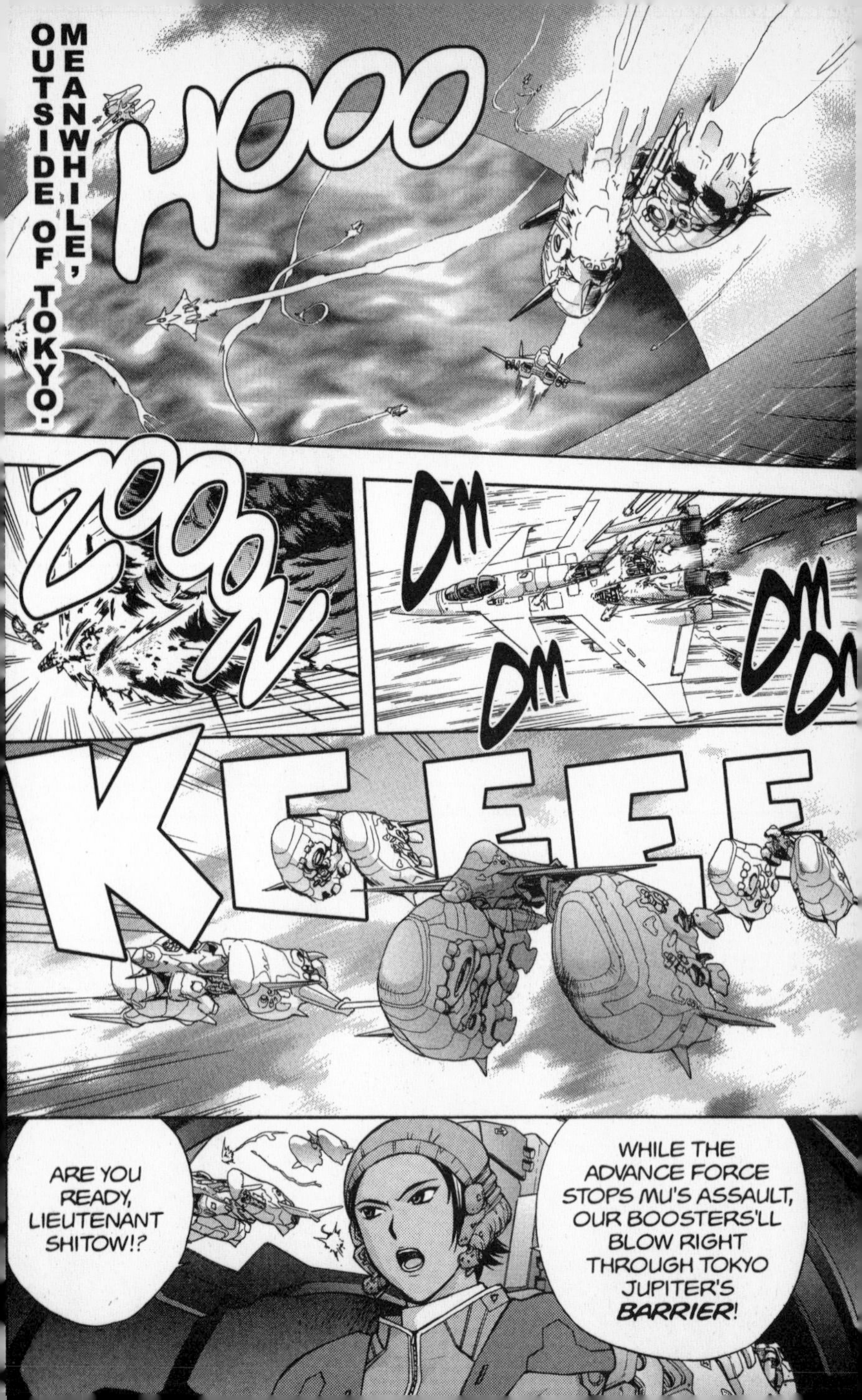
MEANWHILE, OUTSIDE OF TOKYO.
HOOOO
DM
DM
DM
DM
ZOOOON
KEEEE
WHILE THE ADVANCE FORCE STOPS MU'S ASSAULT, OUR BOOSTERS'LL BLOW RIGHT THROUGH TOKYO JUPITER'S ***BARRIER***!
ARE YOU READY, LIEUTENANT SHITOW!?

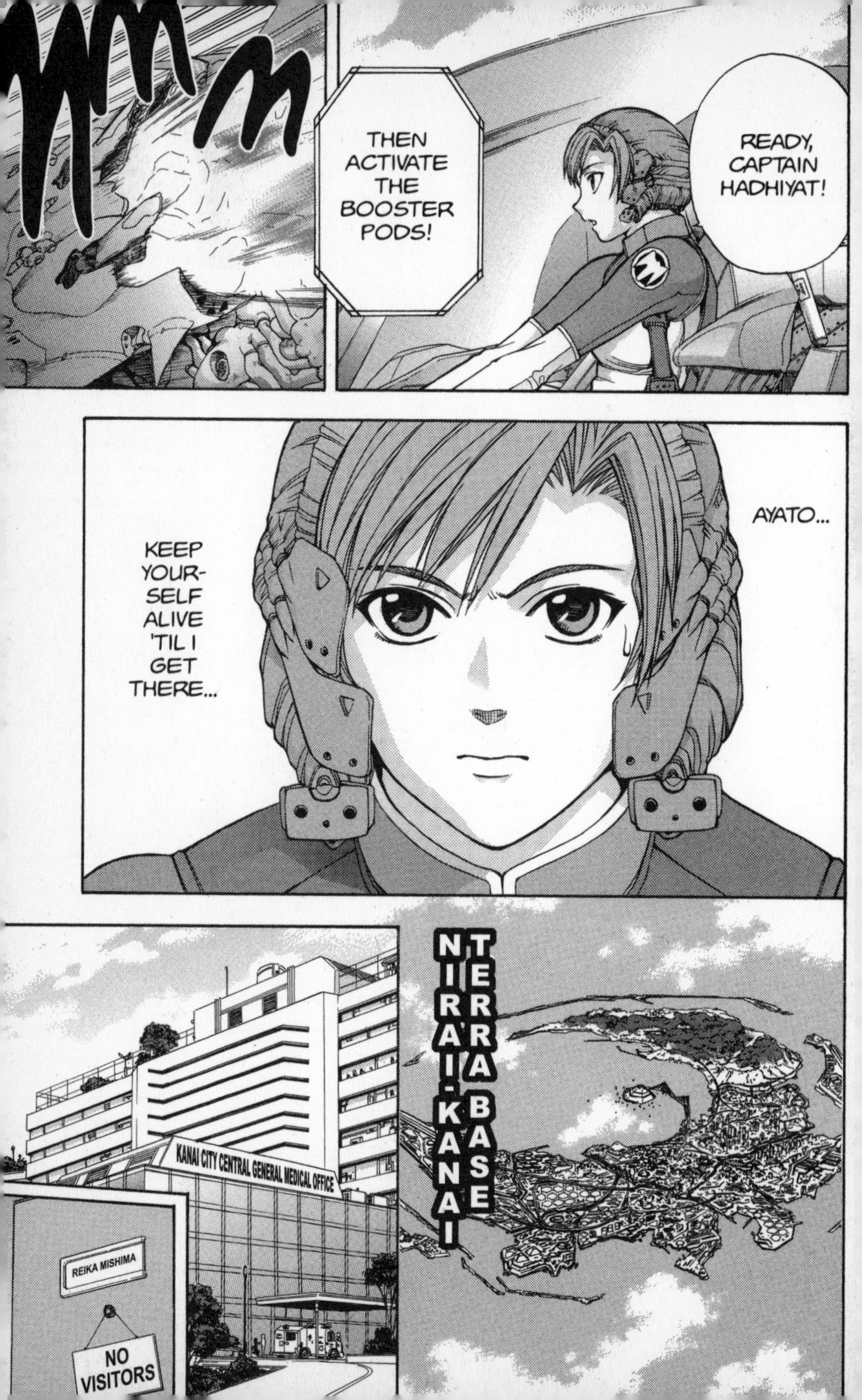
READY, CAPTAIN HADHIYAT!
THEN ACTIVATE THE BOOSTER PODS!
AYATO...
KEEP YOURSELF ALIVE 'TIL I GET THERE...
TERRA BASE
NIRAI-KANAI
KANAI CITY CENTRAL GENERAL MEDICAL OFFICE
REIKA MISHIMA
NO VISITORS

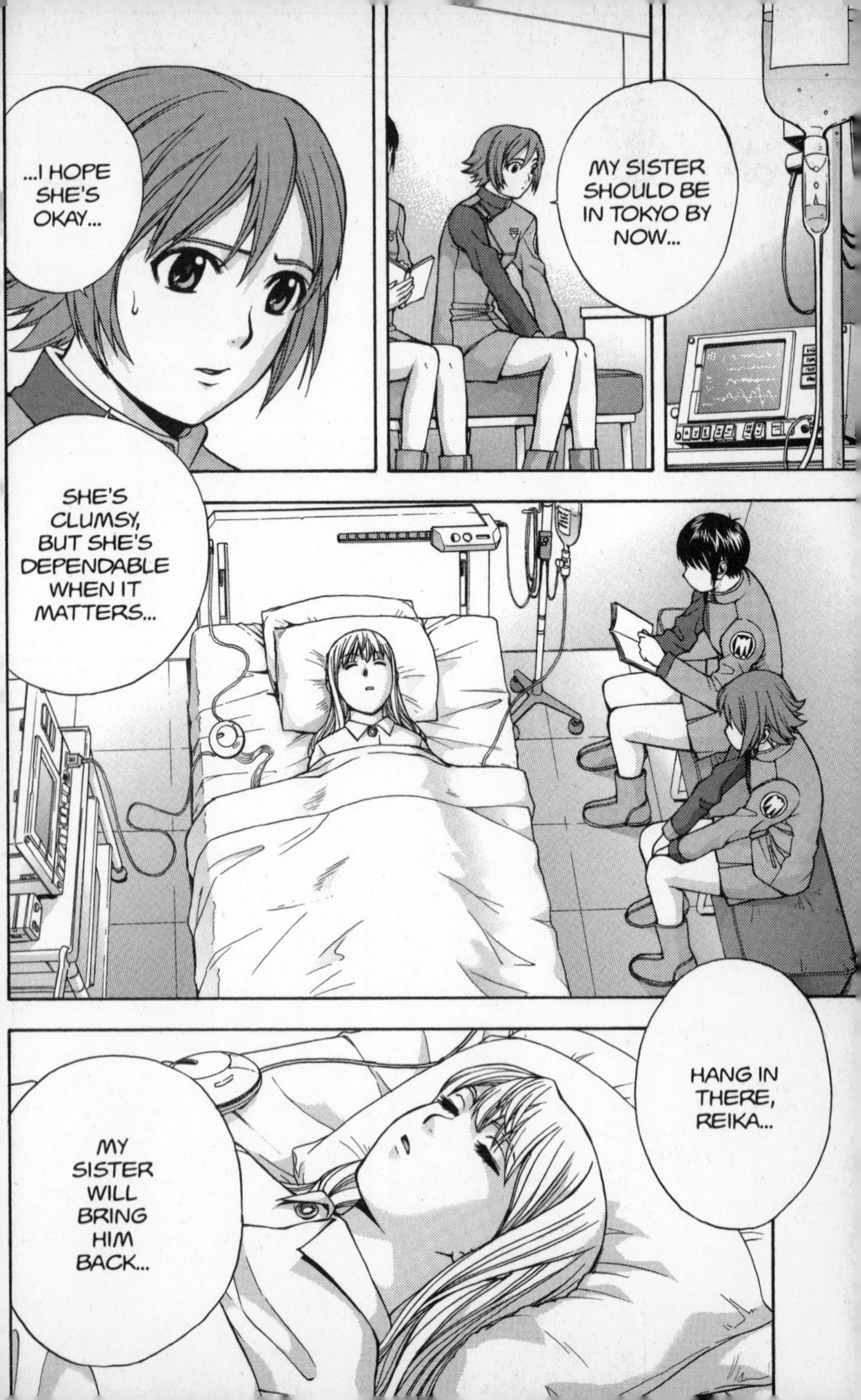
MY SISTER SHOULD BE IN TOKYO BY NOW...
...I HOPE SHE'S OKAY...
SHE'S CLUMSY, BUT SHE'S DEPENDABLE WHEN IT MATTERS...
HANG IN THERE, REIKA...
MY SISTER WILL BRING HIM BACK...

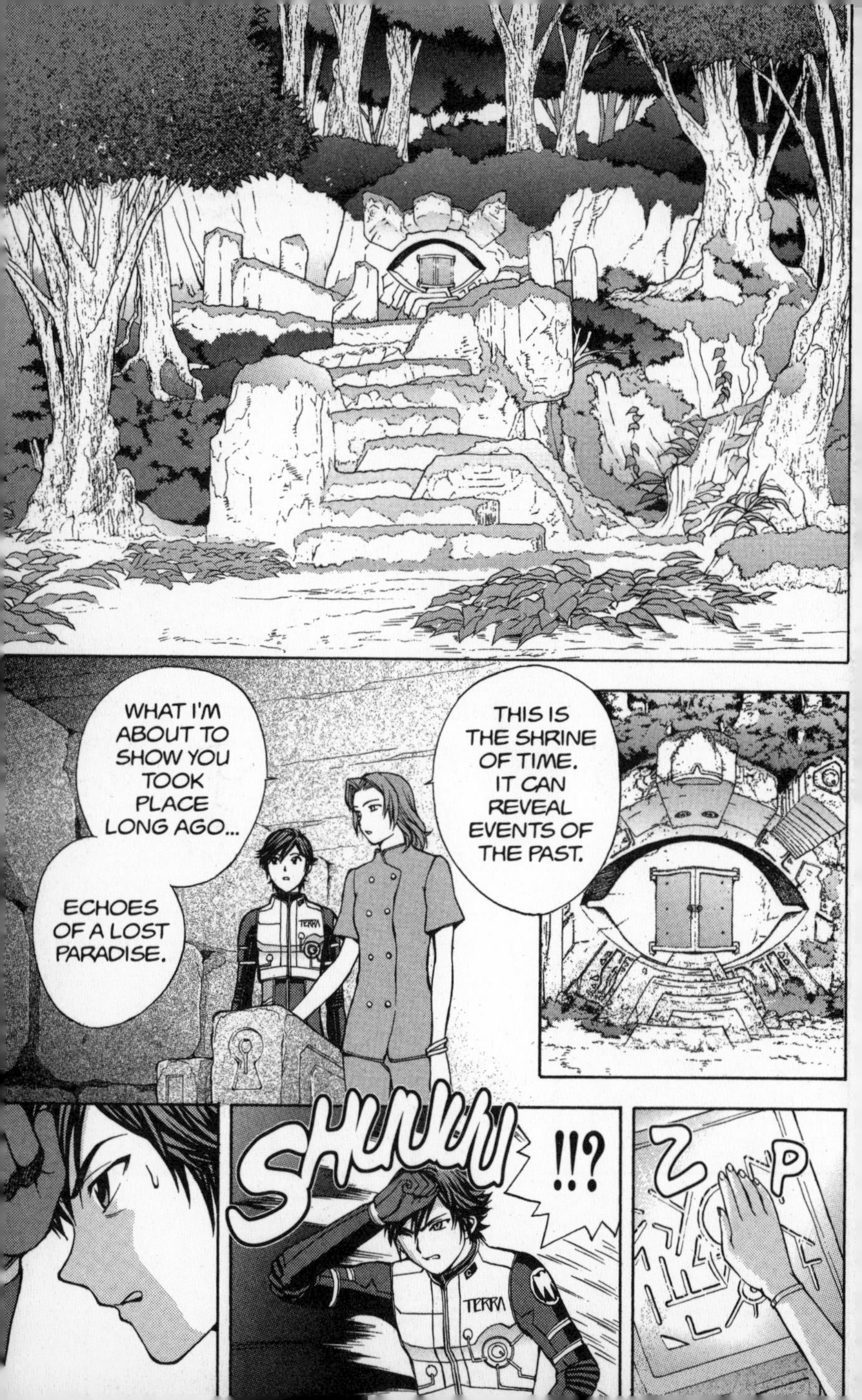
THIS IS THE SHRINE OF TIME. IT CAN REVEAL EVENTS OF THE PAST.
WHAT I'M ABOUT TO SHOW YOU TOOK PLACE LONG AGO...
ECHOES OF A LOST PARADISE.
TERRA
Z P
SHUUUU
!!?
TERRA

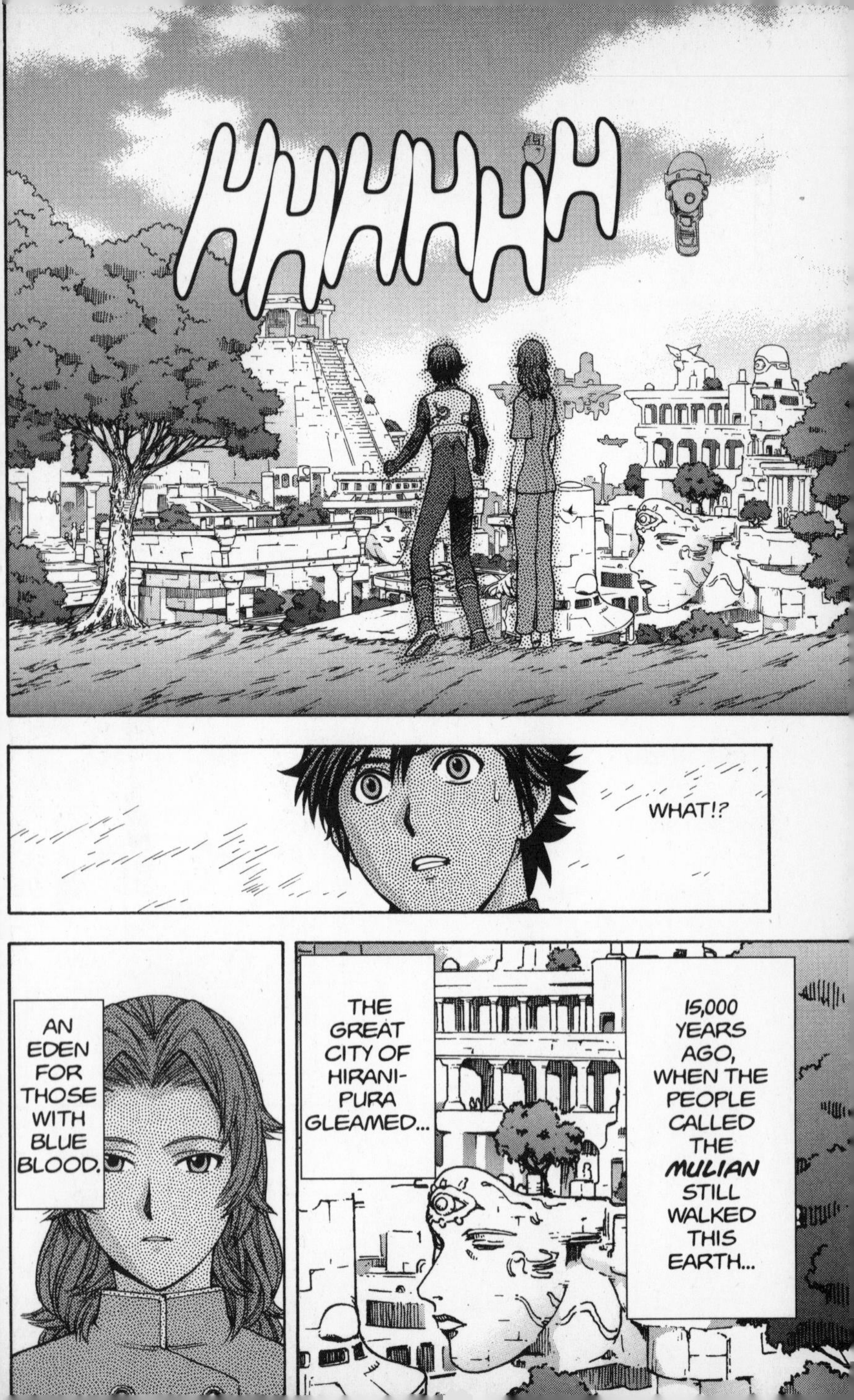

HHHHHH
WHAT!?
15,000 YEARS AGO, WHEN THE PEOPLE CALLED THE *MULIAN* STILL WALKED THIS EARTH...
THE GREAT CITY OF HIRANI-PURA GLEAMED...
AN EDEN FOR THOSE WITH BLUE BLOOD.

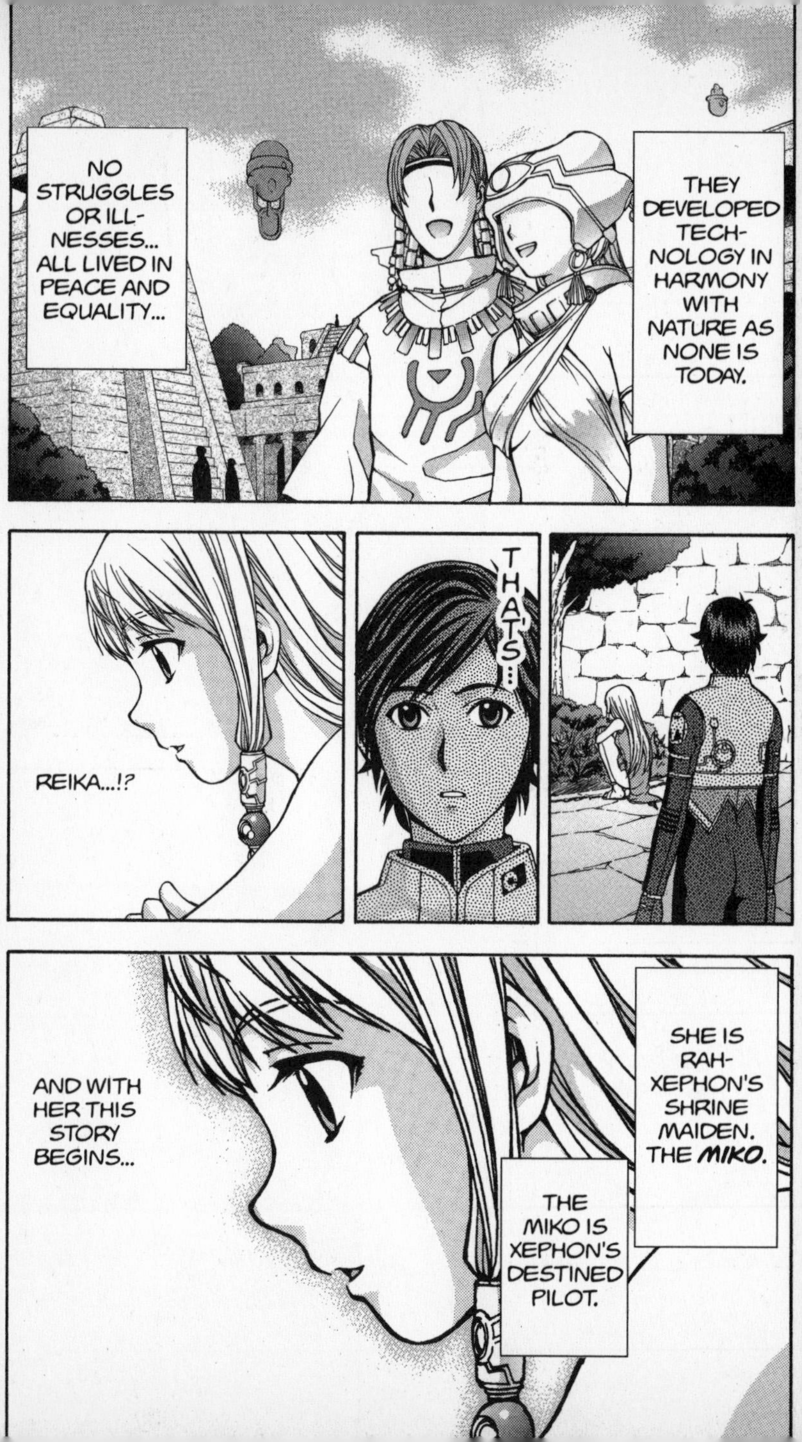
THEY DEVELOPED TECH-NOLOGY IN HARMONY WITH NATURE AS NONE IS TODAY.
NO STRUGGLES OR ILL-NESSES... ALL LIVED IN PEACE AND EQUALITY...
THAT'S...
REIKA...!?
SHE IS RAH-XEPHON'S SHRINE MAIDEN. THE *MIKO*.
THE MIKO IS XEPHON'S DESTINED PILOT.
AND WITH HER THIS STORY BEGINS...

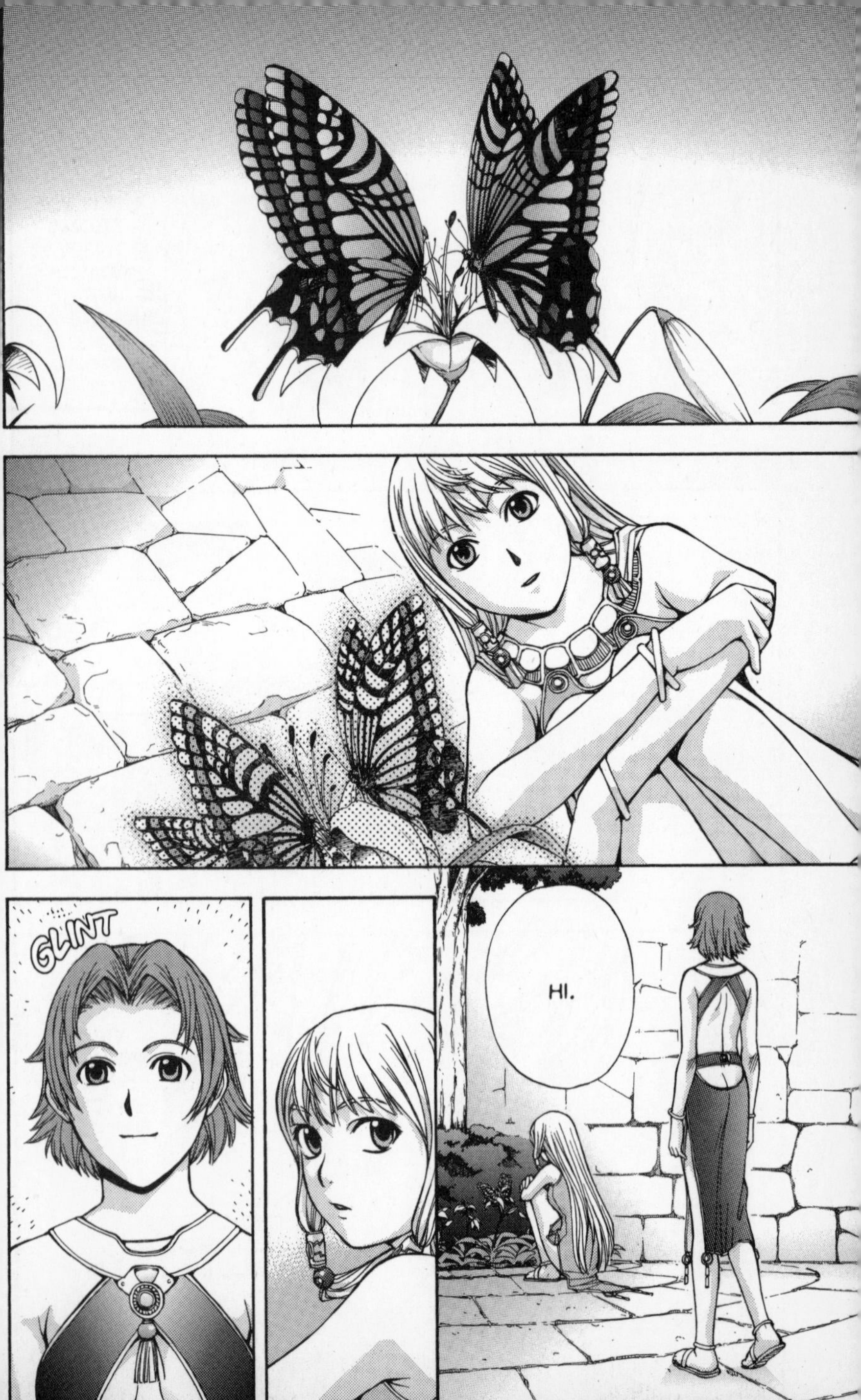
HI.
GLINT

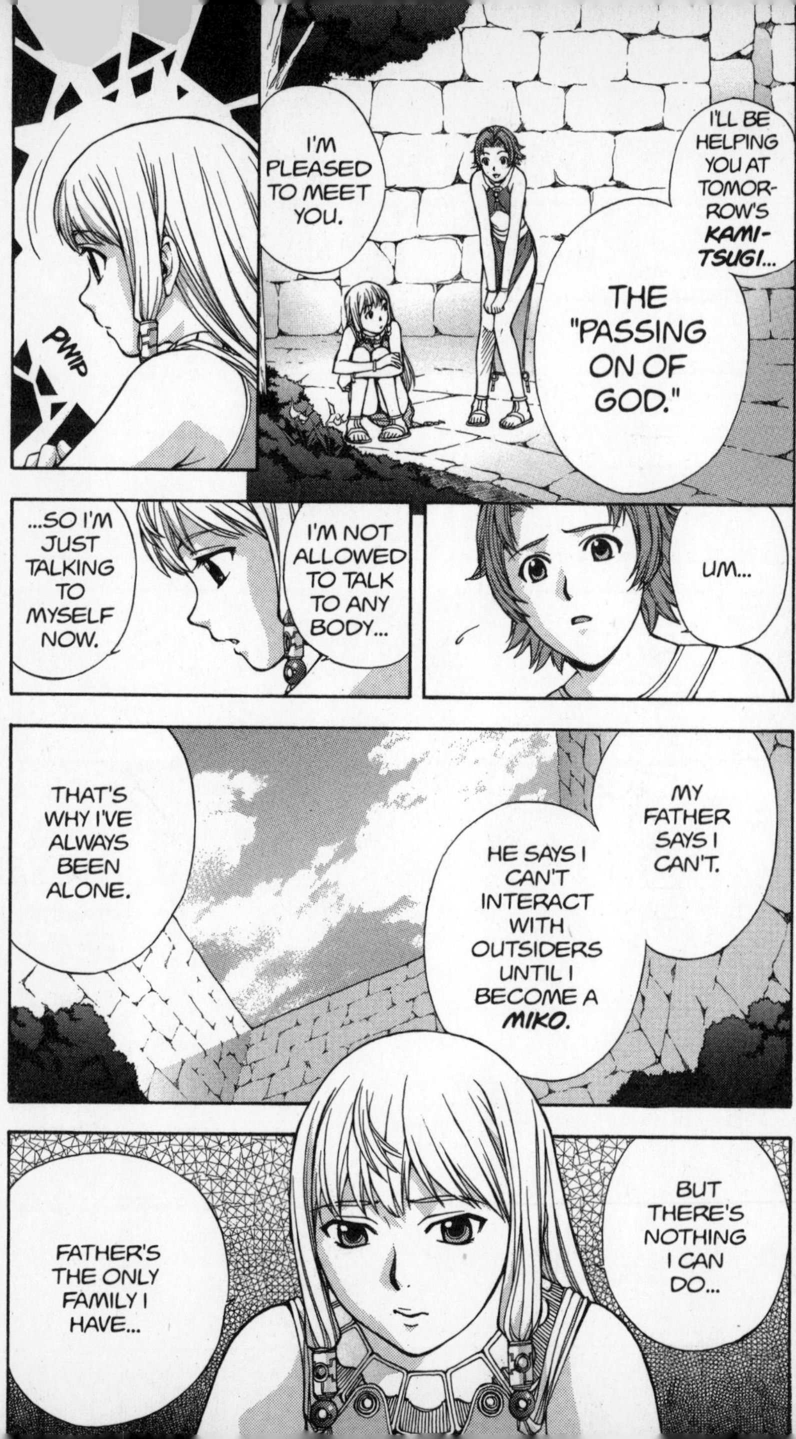
I'LL BE HELPING YOU AT TOMORROW'S KAMI-TSUGI...
THE "PASSING ON OF GOD."
I'M PLEASED TO MEET YOU.
PWIP
UM...
I'M NOT ALLOWED TO TALK TO ANY BODY...
...SO I'M JUST TALKING TO MYSELF NOW.
MY FATHER SAYS I CAN'T.
HE SAYS I CAN'T INTERACT WITH OUTSIDERS UNTIL I BECOME A MIKO.
THAT'S WHY I'VE ALWAYS BEEN ALONE.
BUT THERE'S NOTHING I CAN DO...
FATHER'S THE ONLY FAMILY I HAVE...

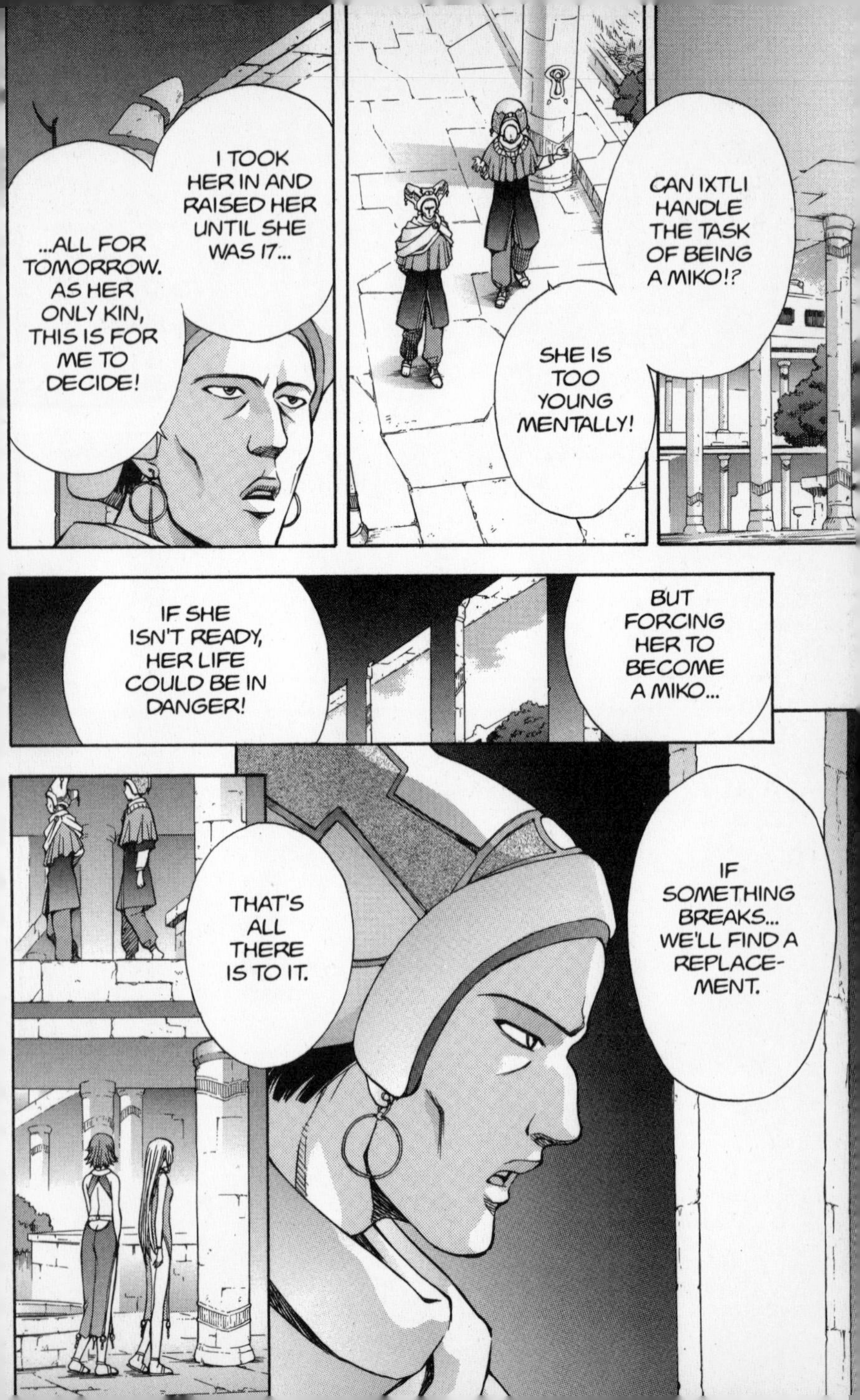
CAN IXTLI HANDLE THE TASK OF BEING A MIKO!?
SHE IS TOO YOUNG MENTALLY!
I TOOK HER IN AND RAISED HER UNTIL SHE WAS 17...
...ALL FOR TOMORROW. AS HER ONLY KIN, THIS IS FOR ME TO DECIDE!
BUT FORCING HER TO BECOME A MIKO...
IF SHE ISN'T READY, HER LIFE COULD BE IN DANGER!
IF SOMETHING BREAKS... WE'LL FIND A REPLACE- MENT.
THAT'S ALL THERE IS TO IT.

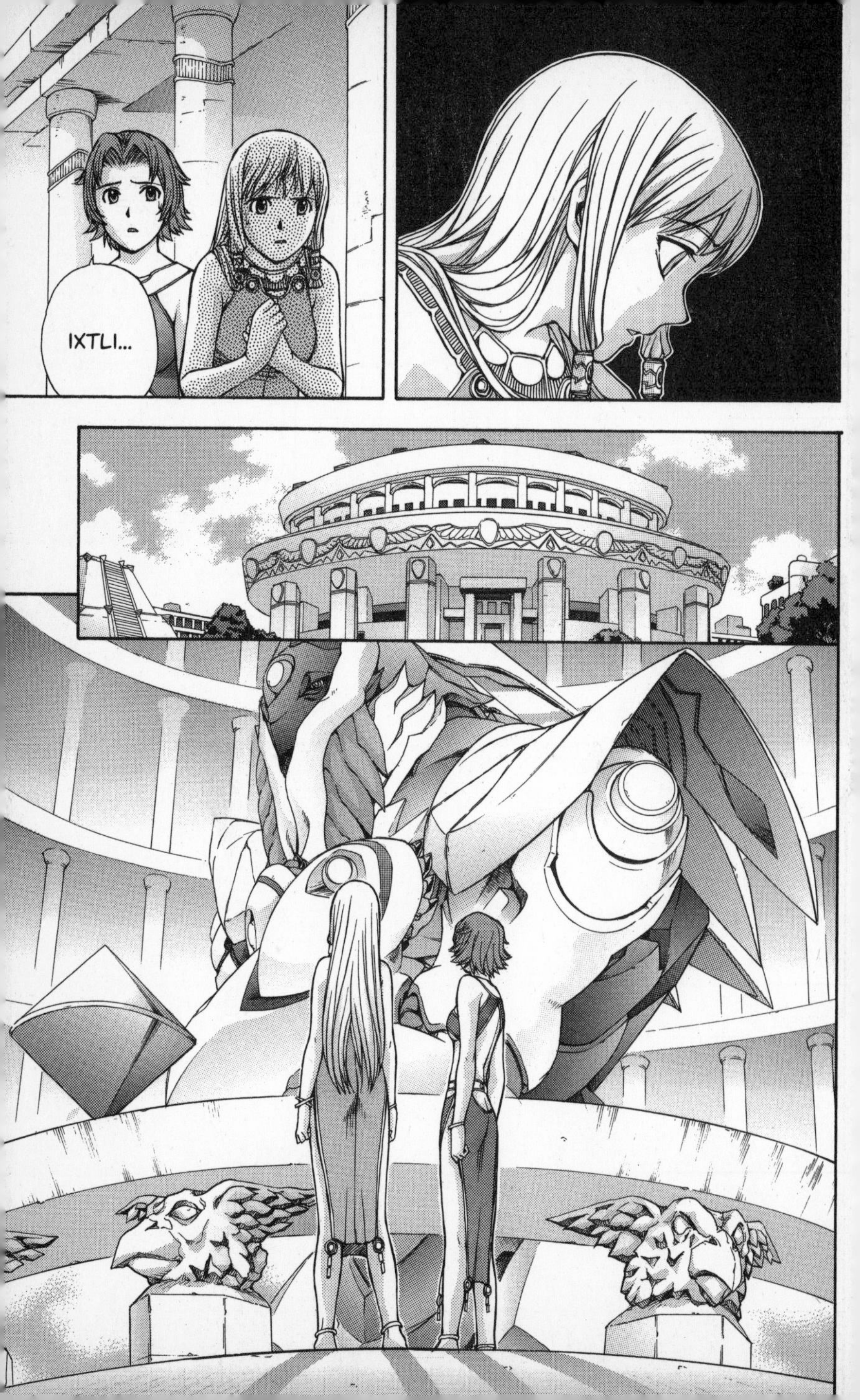
IXTLI...

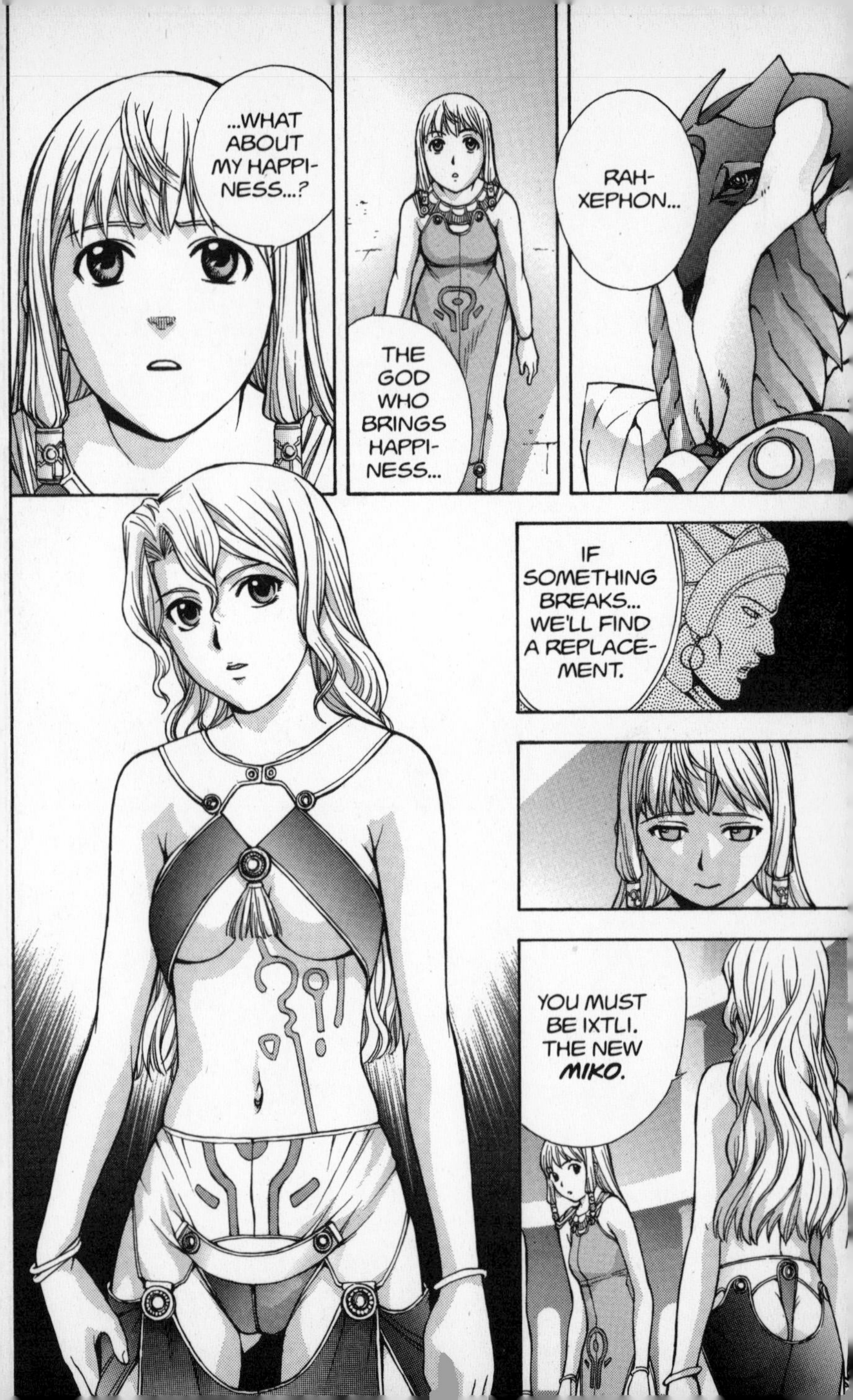
RAH-XEPHON...
THE GOD WHO BRINGS HAPPINESS...
...WHAT ABOUT MY HAPPINESS...?
IF SOMETHING BREAKS... WE'LL FIND A REPLACEMENT.
YOU MUST BE IXTLI. THE NEW *MIKO*.

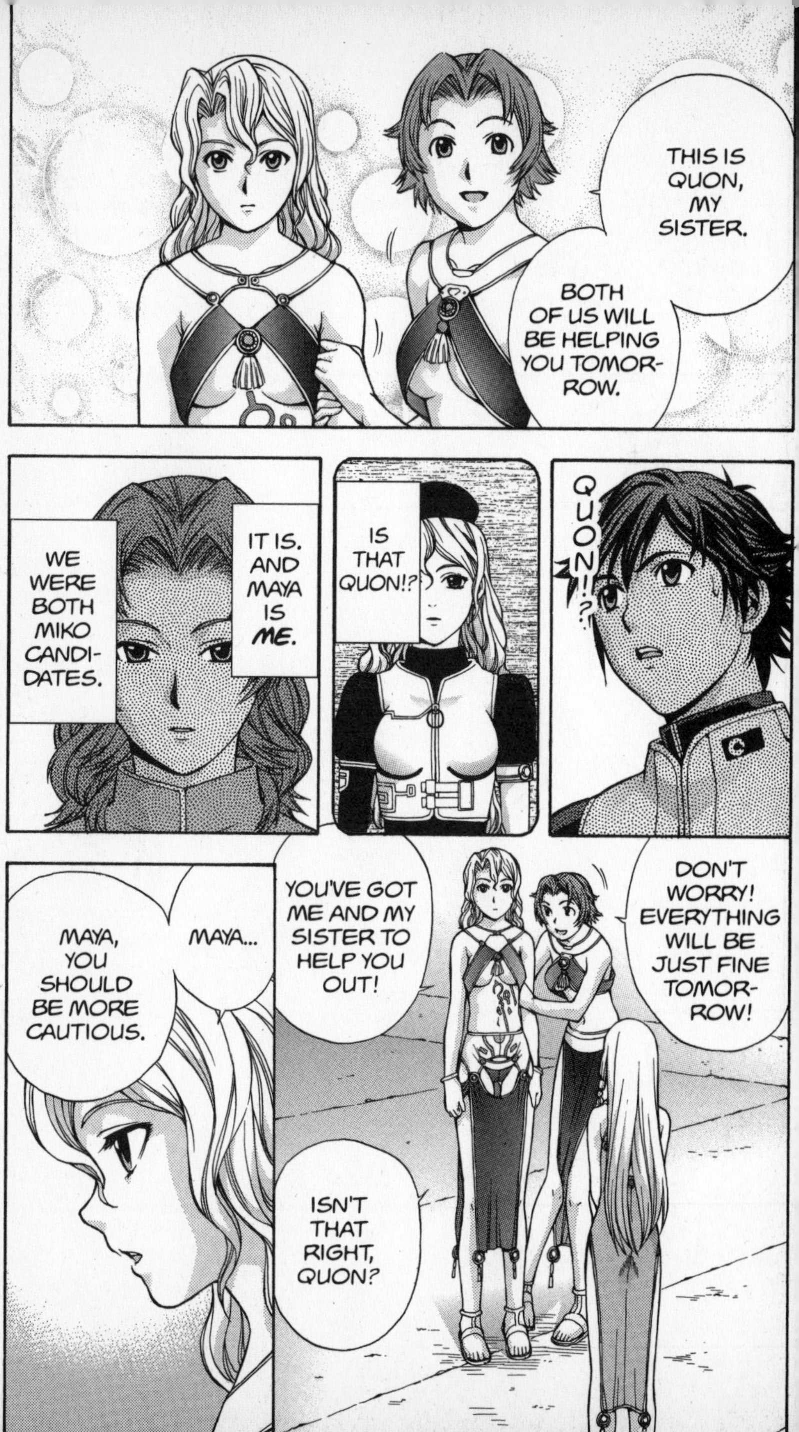

THIS IS QUON, MY SISTER.
BOTH OF US WILL BE HELPING YOU TOMOR-ROW.
QUON!?
IS THAT QUON!?
IT IS. AND MAYA IS *ME*.
WE WERE BOTH MIKO CANDI-DATES.
DON'T WORRY! EVERYTHING WILL BE JUST FINE TOMOR-ROW!
YOU'VE GOT ME AND MY SISTER TO HELP YOU OUT!
ISN'T THAT RIGHT, QUON?
MAYA...
MAYA, YOU SHOULD BE MORE CAUTIOUS.

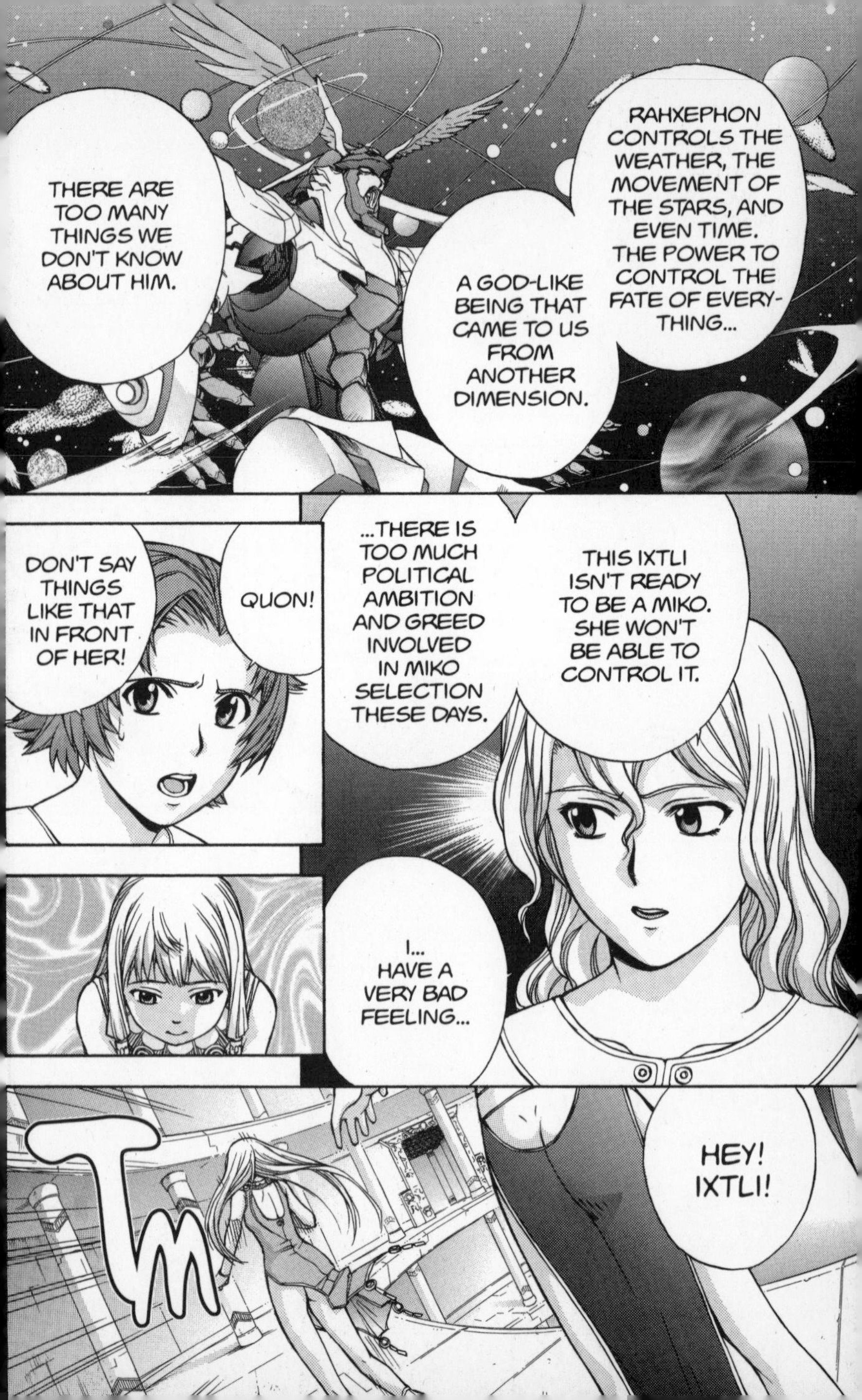
RAHXEPHON CONTROLS THE WEATHER, THE MOVEMENT OF THE STARS, AND EVEN TIME. THE POWER TO CONTROL THE FATE OF EVERY-THING...
A GOD-LIKE BEING THAT CAME TO US FROM ANOTHER DIMENSION.
THERE ARE TOO MANY THINGS WE DON'T KNOW ABOUT HIM.
THIS IXTLI ISN'T READY TO BE A MIKO. SHE WON'T BE ABLE TO CONTROL IT.
...THERE IS TOO MUCH POLITICAL AMBITION AND GREED INVOLVED IN MIKO SELECTION THESE DAYS.
I... HAVE A VERY BAD FEELING...
QUON!
DON'T SAY THINGS LIKE THAT IN FRONT OF HER!
HEY! IXTLI!
Tm

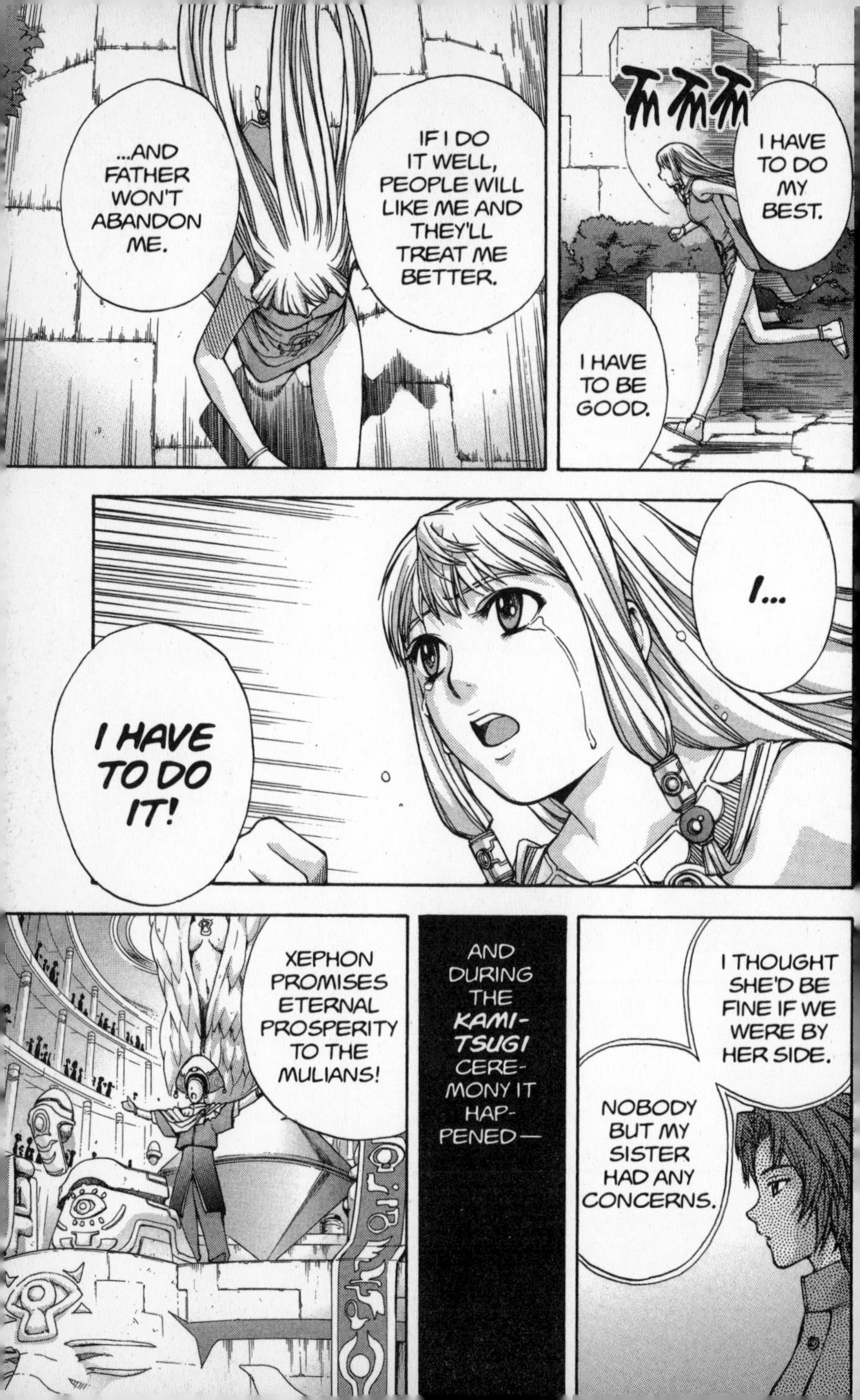
I HAVE TO DO MY BEST.
I HAVE TO BE GOOD.
IF I DO IT WELL, PEOPLE WILL LIKE ME AND THEY'LL TREAT ME BETTER.
...AND FATHER WON'T ABANDON ME.
I...
I HAVE TO DO IT!
I THOUGHT SHE'D BE FINE IF WE WERE BY HER SIDE.
NOBODY BUT MY SISTER HAD ANY CONCERNS.
AND DURING THE *KAMI-TSUGI* CEREMONY IT HAPPENED—
XEPHON PROMISES ETERNAL PROSPERITY TO THE MULIANS!

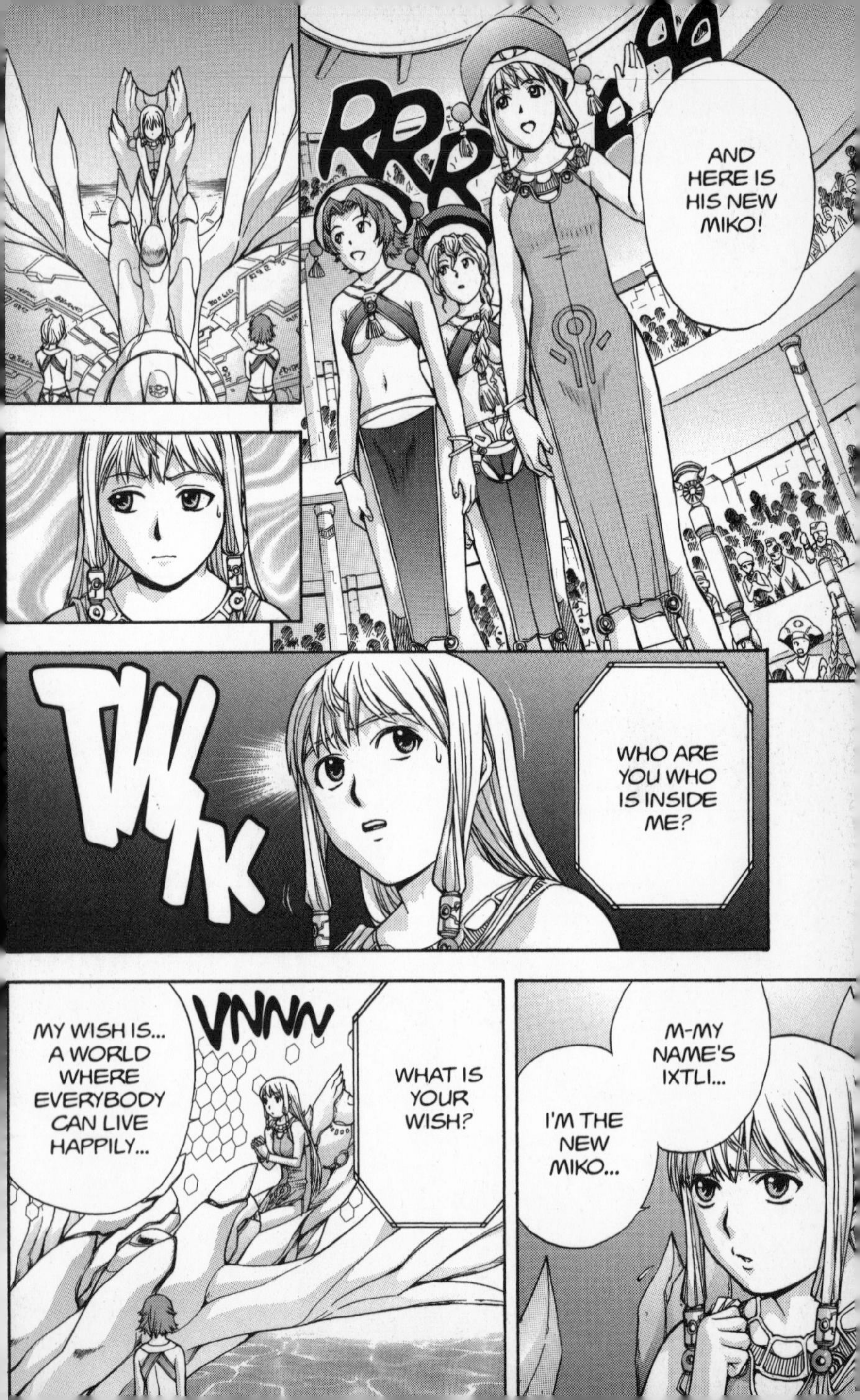
RRR
AND HERE IS HIS NEW MIKO!
WHO ARE YOU WHO IS INSIDE ME?
TWIK
M-MY NAME'S IXTLI...
I'M THE NEW MIKO...
WHAT IS YOUR WISH?
VNNN
MY WISH IS... A WORLD WHERE EVERYBODY CAN LIVE HAPPILY...

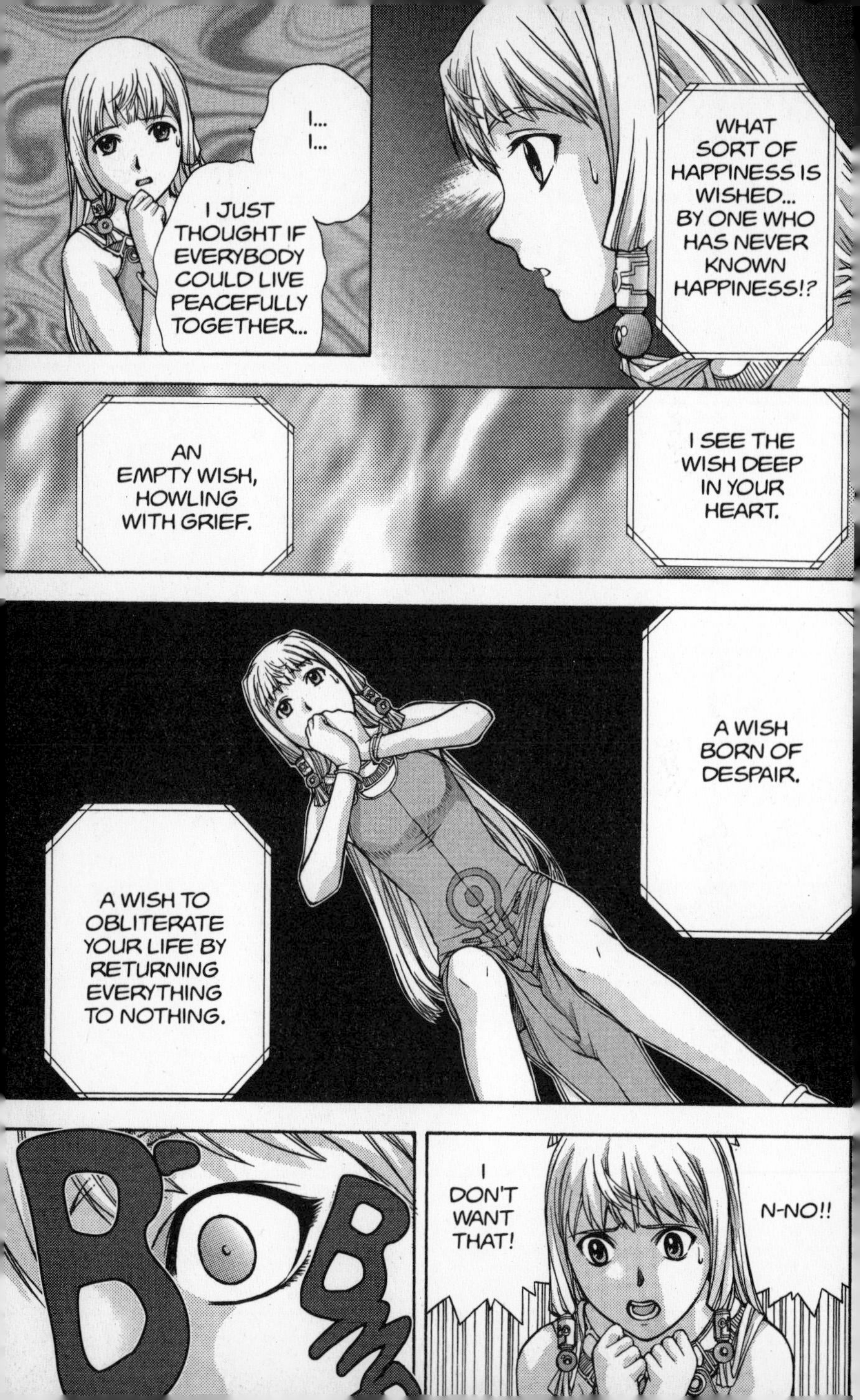
WHAT SORT OF HAPPINESS IS WISHED... BY ONE WHO HAS NEVER KNOWN HAPPINESS!?
I... I...
I JUST THOUGHT IF EVERYBODY COULD LIVE PEACEFULLY TOGETHER...
I SEE THE WISH DEEP IN YOUR HEART.
AN EMPTY WISH, HOWLING WITH GRIEF.
A WISH BORN OF DESPAIR.
A WISH TO OBLITERATE YOUR LIFE BY RETURNING EVERYTHING TO NOTHING.
N-NO!!
I DON'T WANT THAT!

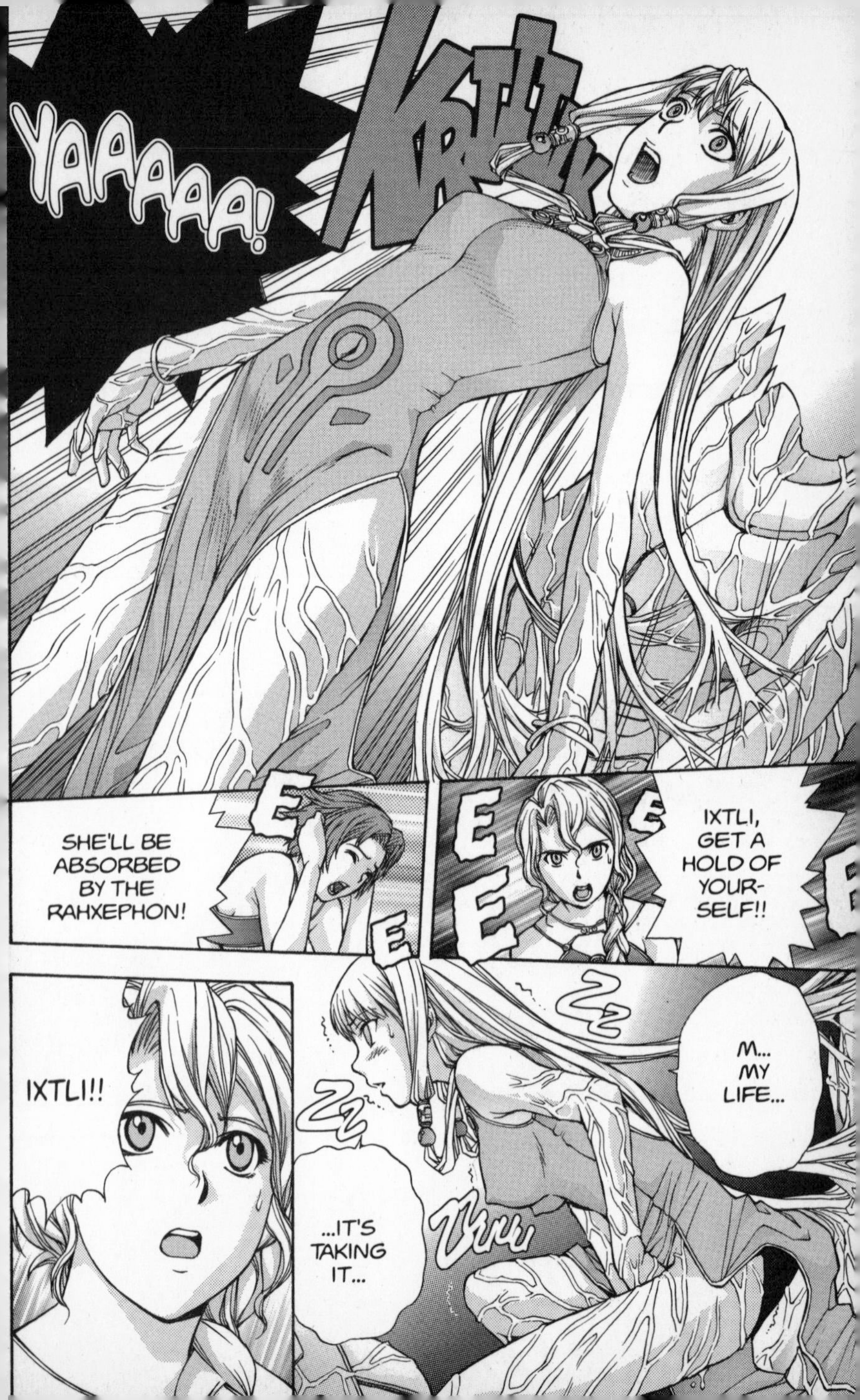
YAAAAAA!
IXTLI, GET A HOLD OF YOUR-SELF!!
SHE'LL BE ABSORBED BY THE RAHXEPHON!
M... MY LIFE...
...IT'S TAKING IT...
IXTLI!!

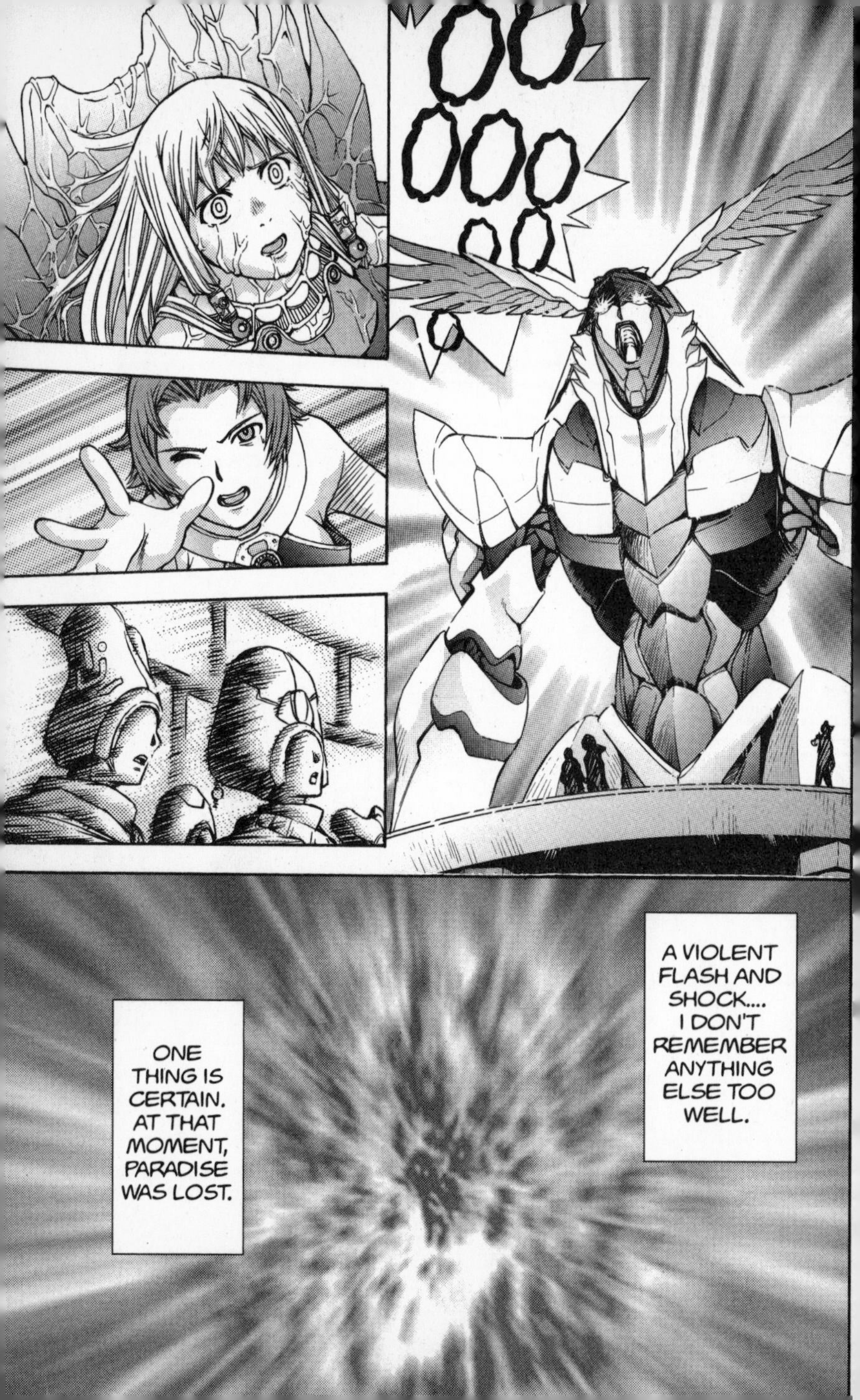
OOOOOOOO
A VIOLENT FLASH AND SHOCK.... I DON'T REMEMBER ANYTHING ELSE TOO WELL.
ONE THING IS CERTAIN. AT THAT MOMENT, PARADISE WAS LOST.

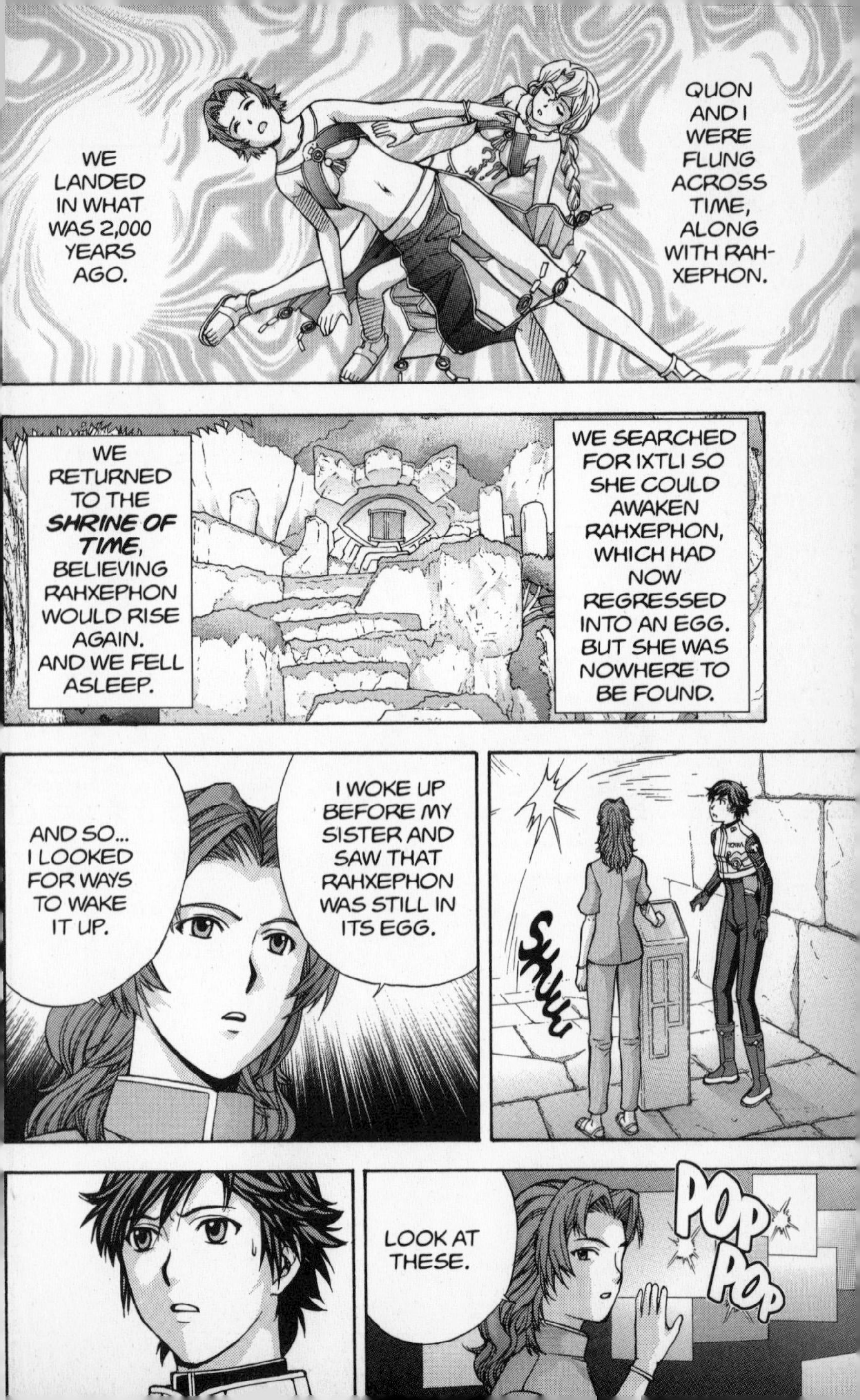
QUON AND I WERE FLUNG ACROSS TIME, ALONG WITH RAH-XEPHON.
WE LANDED IN WHAT WAS 2,000 YEARS AGO.
WE SEARCHED FOR IXTLI SO SHE COULD AWAKEN RAHXEPHON, WHICH HAD NOW REGRESSED INTO AN EGG. BUT SHE WAS NOWHERE TO BE FOUND.
WE RETURNED TO THE *SHRINE OF TIME*, BELIEVING RAHXEPHON WOULD RISE AGAIN. AND WE FELL ASLEEP.
SHUUU
I WOKE UP BEFORE MY SISTER AND SAW THAT RAHXEPHON WAS STILL IN ITS EGG.
AND SO... I LOOKED FOR WAYS TO WAKE IT UP.
POP POP
LOOK AT THESE.

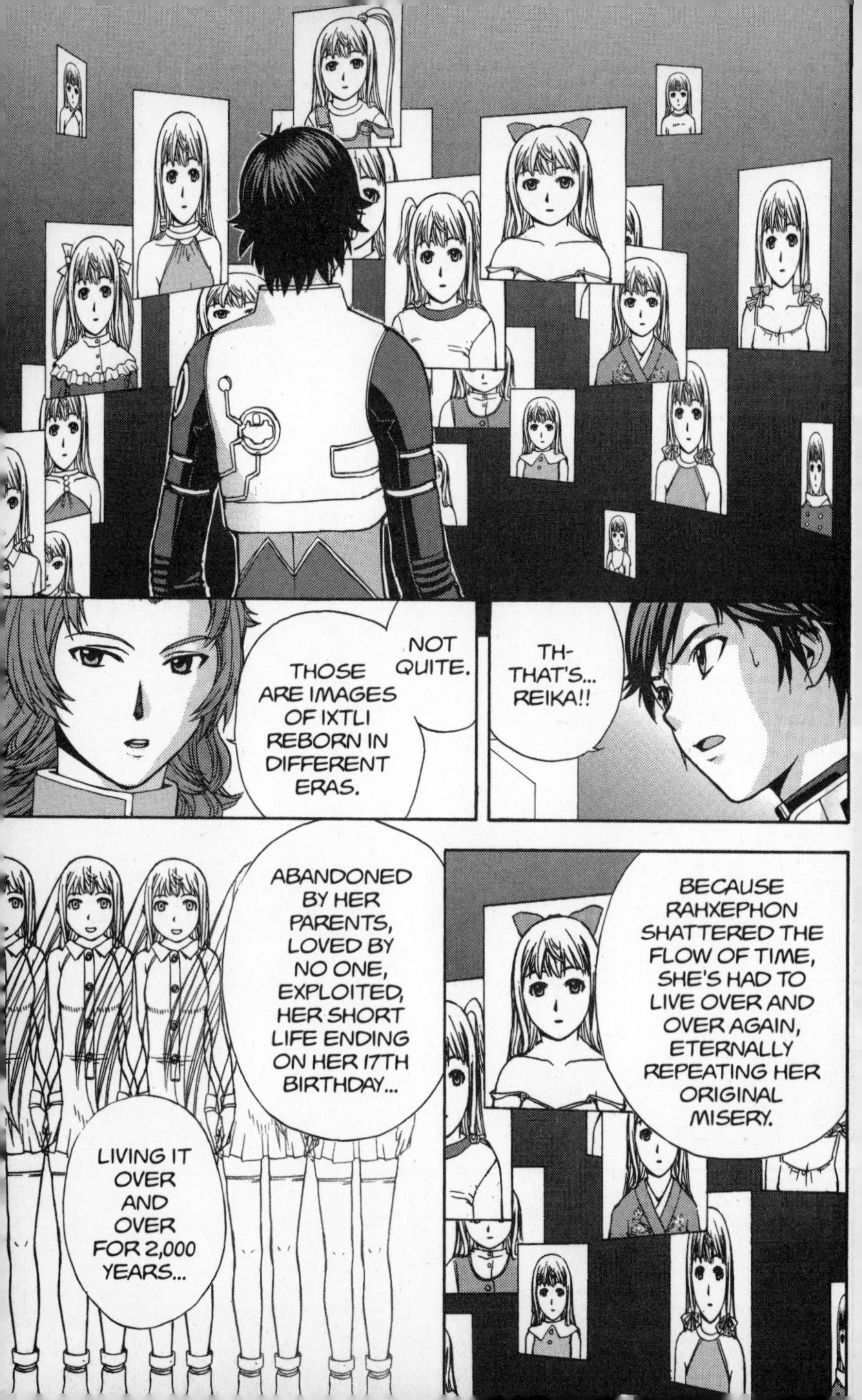
TH- THAT'S... REIKA!!
NOT QUITE.
THOSE ARE IMAGES OF IXTLI REBORN IN DIFFERENT ERAS.
BECAUSE RAHXEPHON SHATTERED THE FLOW OF TIME, SHE'S HAD TO LIVE OVER AND OVER AGAIN, ETERNALLY REPEATING HER ORIGINAL MISERY.
ABANDONED BY HER PARENTS, LOVED BY NO ONE, EXPLOITED, HER SHORT LIFE ENDING ON HER 17TH BIRTHDAY...
LIVING IT OVER AND OVER FOR 2,000 YEARS...

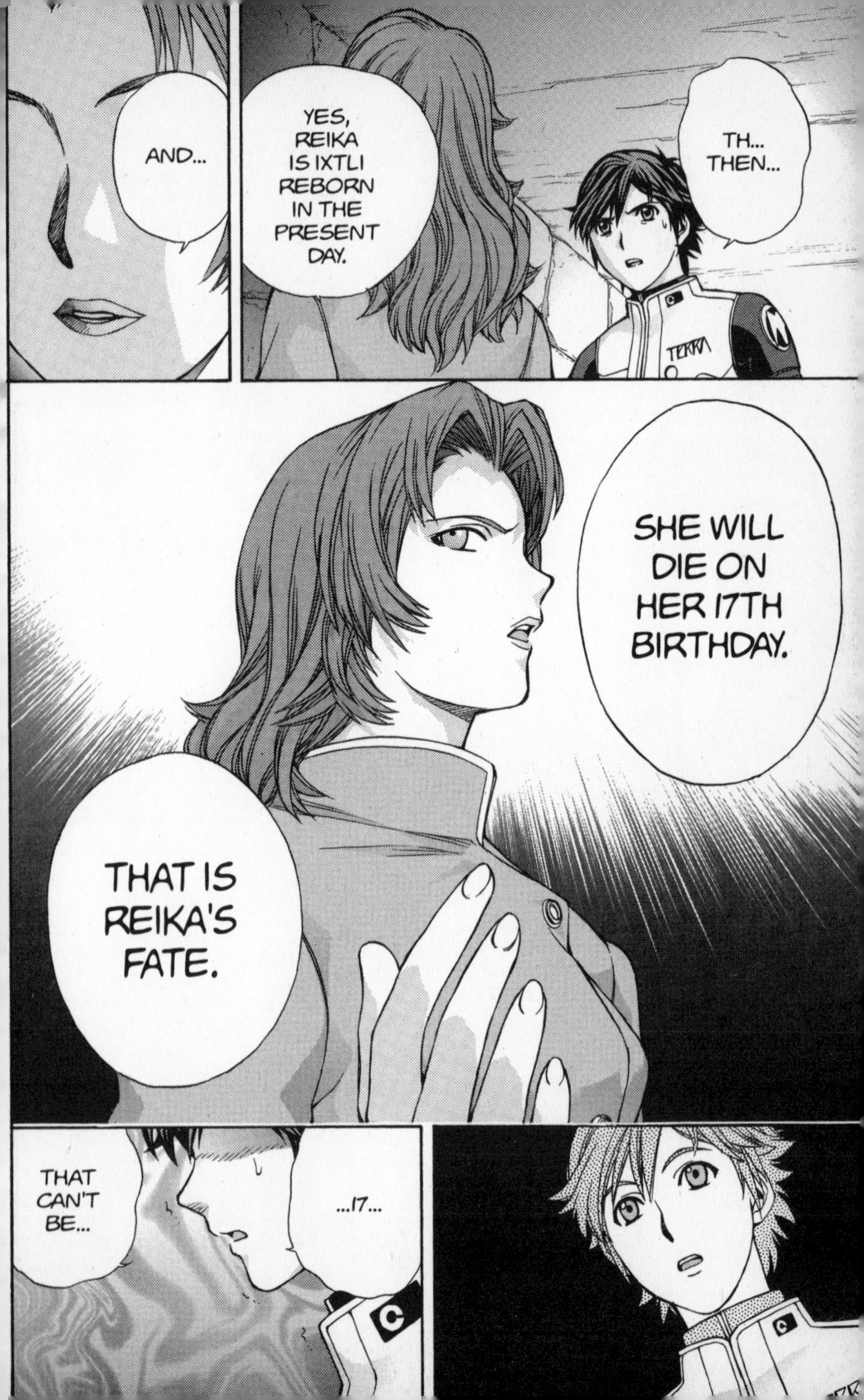
TH... THEN...
YES, REIKA IS IXTLI REBORN IN THE PRESENT DAY.
AND...
SHE WILL DIE ON HER 17TH BIRTHDAY.
THAT IS REIKA'S FATE.
...17...
THAT CAN'T BE...

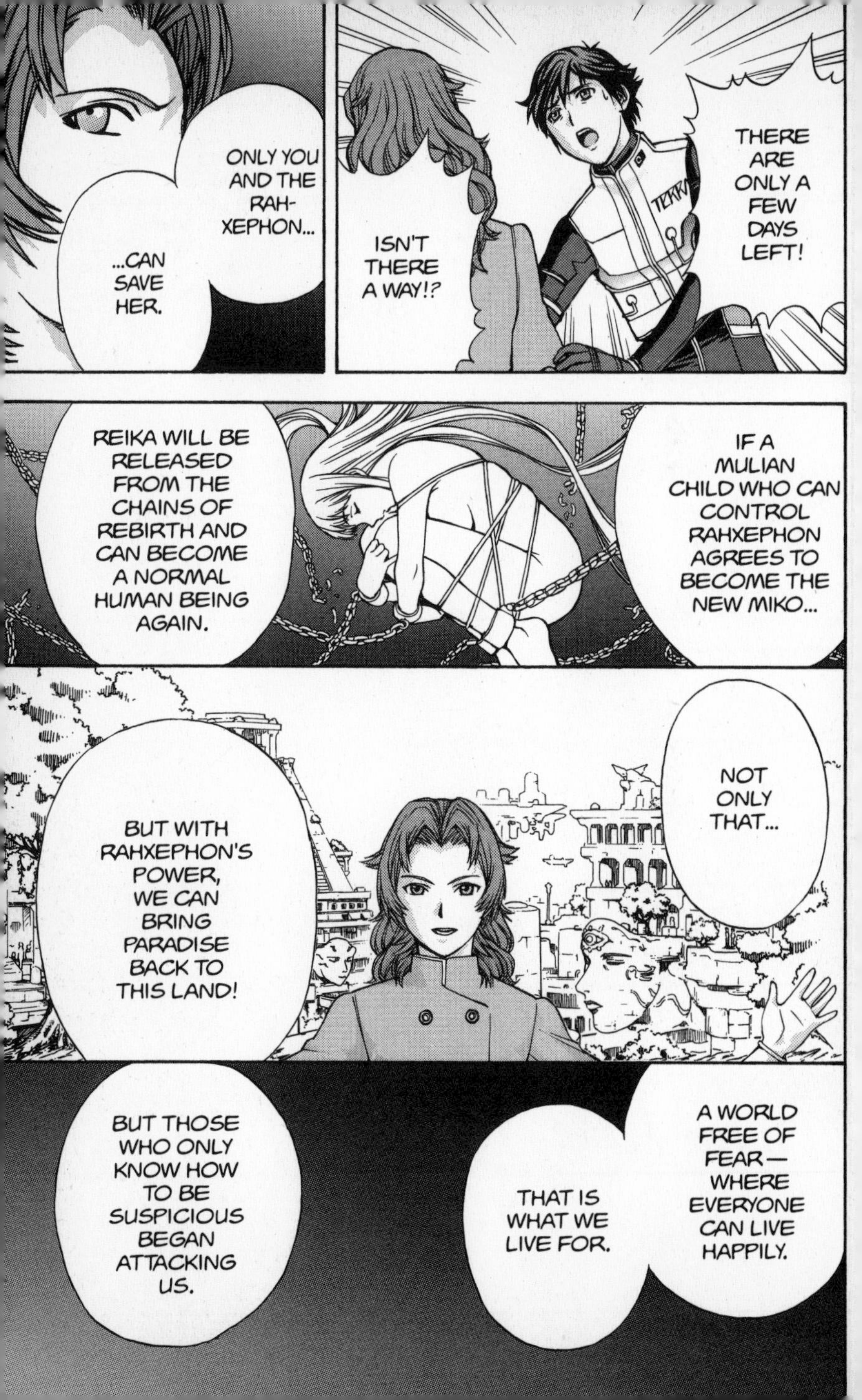
THERE ARE ONLY A FEW DAYS LEFT!
ISN'T THERE A WAY!?
ONLY YOU AND THE RAH-XEPHON...
...CAN SAVE HER.
IF A MULIAN CHILD WHO CAN CONTROL RAHXEPHON AGREES TO BECOME THE NEW MIKO...
REIKA WILL BE RELEASED FROM THE CHAINS OF REBIRTH AND CAN BECOME A NORMAL HUMAN BEING AGAIN.
NOT ONLY THAT...
BUT WITH RAHXEPHON'S POWER, WE CAN BRING PARADISE BACK TO THIS LAND!
A WORLD FREE OF FEAR—WHERE EVERYONE CAN LIVE HAPPILY.
THAT IS WHAT WE LIVE FOR.
BUT THOSE WHO ONLY KNOW HOW TO BE SUSPICIOUS BEGAN ATTACKING US.

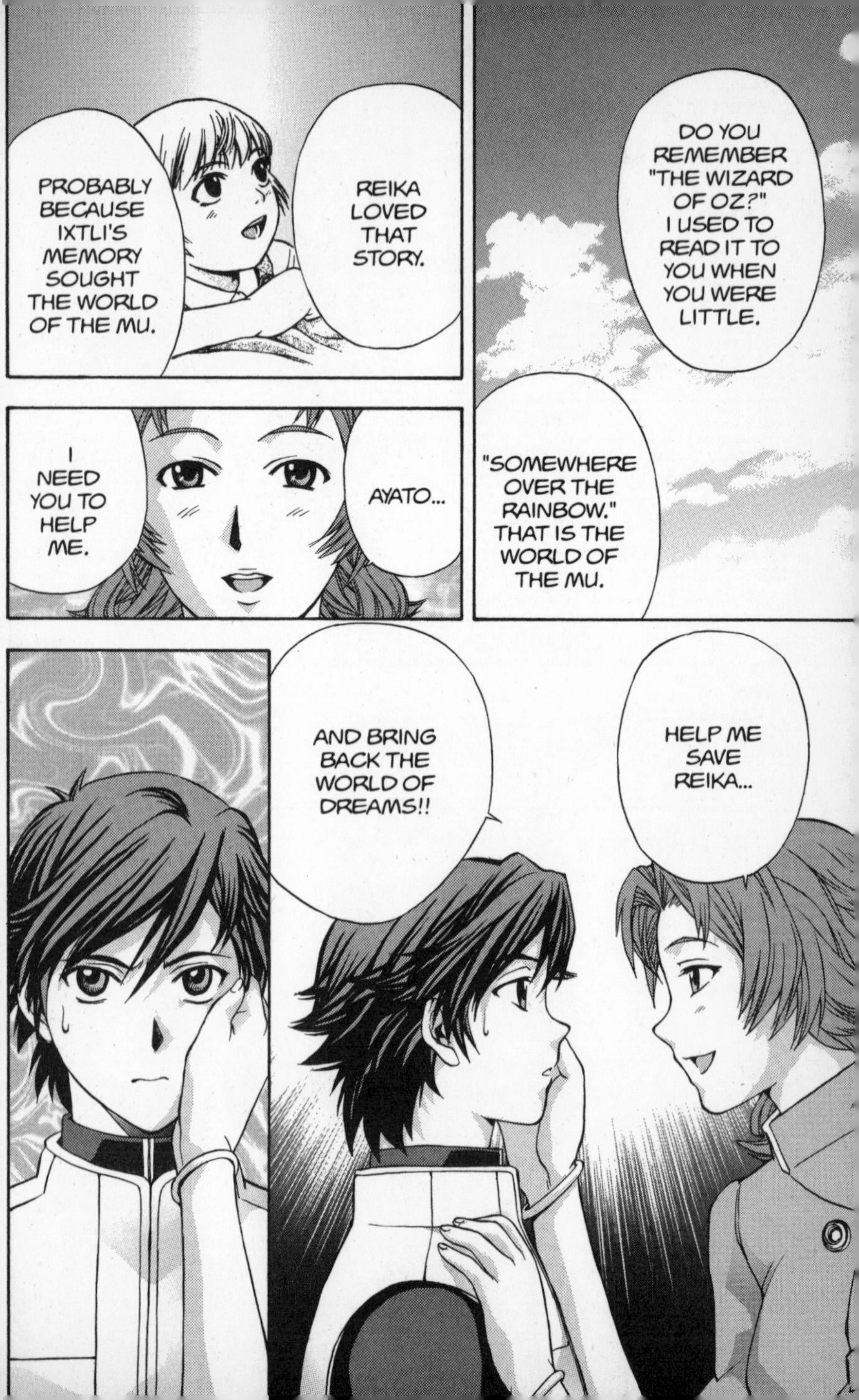
DO YOU REMEMBER "THE WIZARD OF OZ?" I USED TO READ IT TO YOU WHEN YOU WERE LITTLE.
"SOMEWHERE OVER THE RAINBOW." THAT IS THE WORLD OF THE MU.
REIKA LOVED THAT STORY.
PROBABLY BECAUSE IXTLI'S MEMORY SOUGHT THE WORLD OF THE MU.
AYATO...
I NEED YOU TO HELP ME.
HELP ME SAVE REIKA...
AND BRING BACK THE WORLD OF DREAMS!!

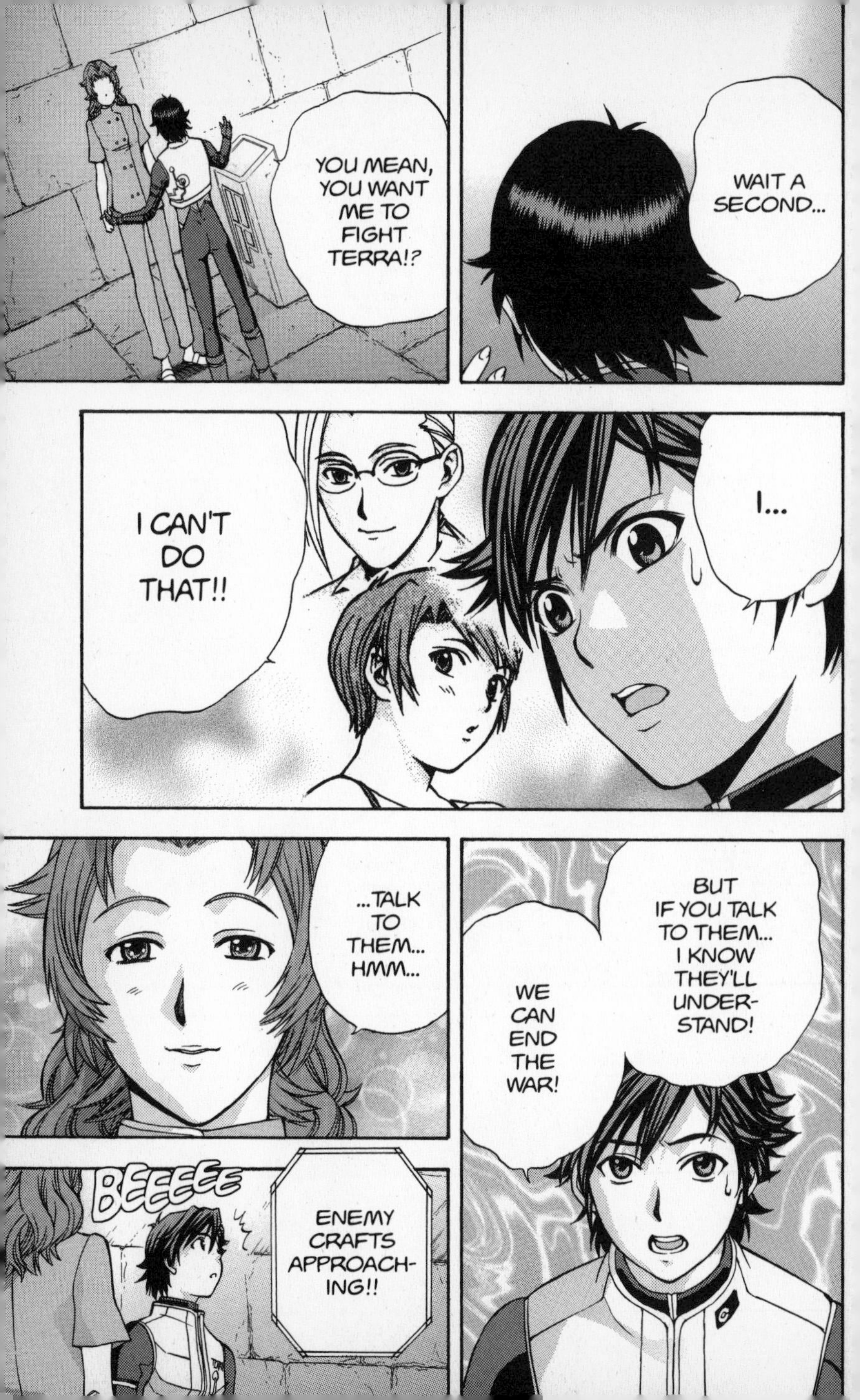
WAIT A SECOND...
YOU MEAN, YOU WANT ME TO FIGHT TERRA!?
I...
I CAN'T DO THAT!!
BUT IF YOU TALK TO THEM... I KNOW THEY'LL UNDER-STAND!
WE CAN END THE WAR!
...TALK TO THEM... HMM...
BEEEEEE
ENEMY CRAFTS APPROACH-ING!!

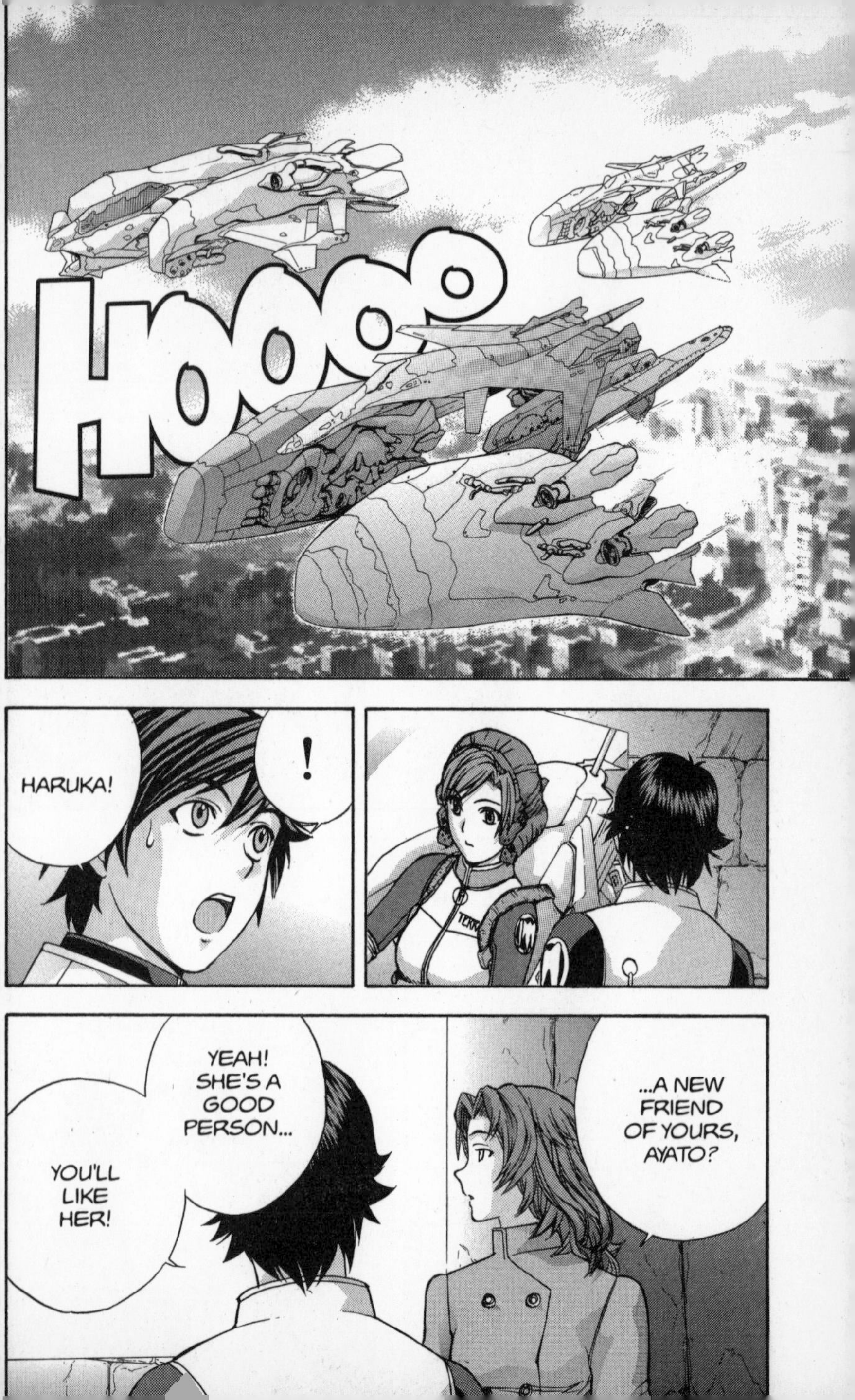
HOOOO
!
HARUKA!
...A NEW FRIEND OF YOURS, AYATO?
YEAH! SHE'S A GOOD PERSON...
YOU'LL LIKE HER!

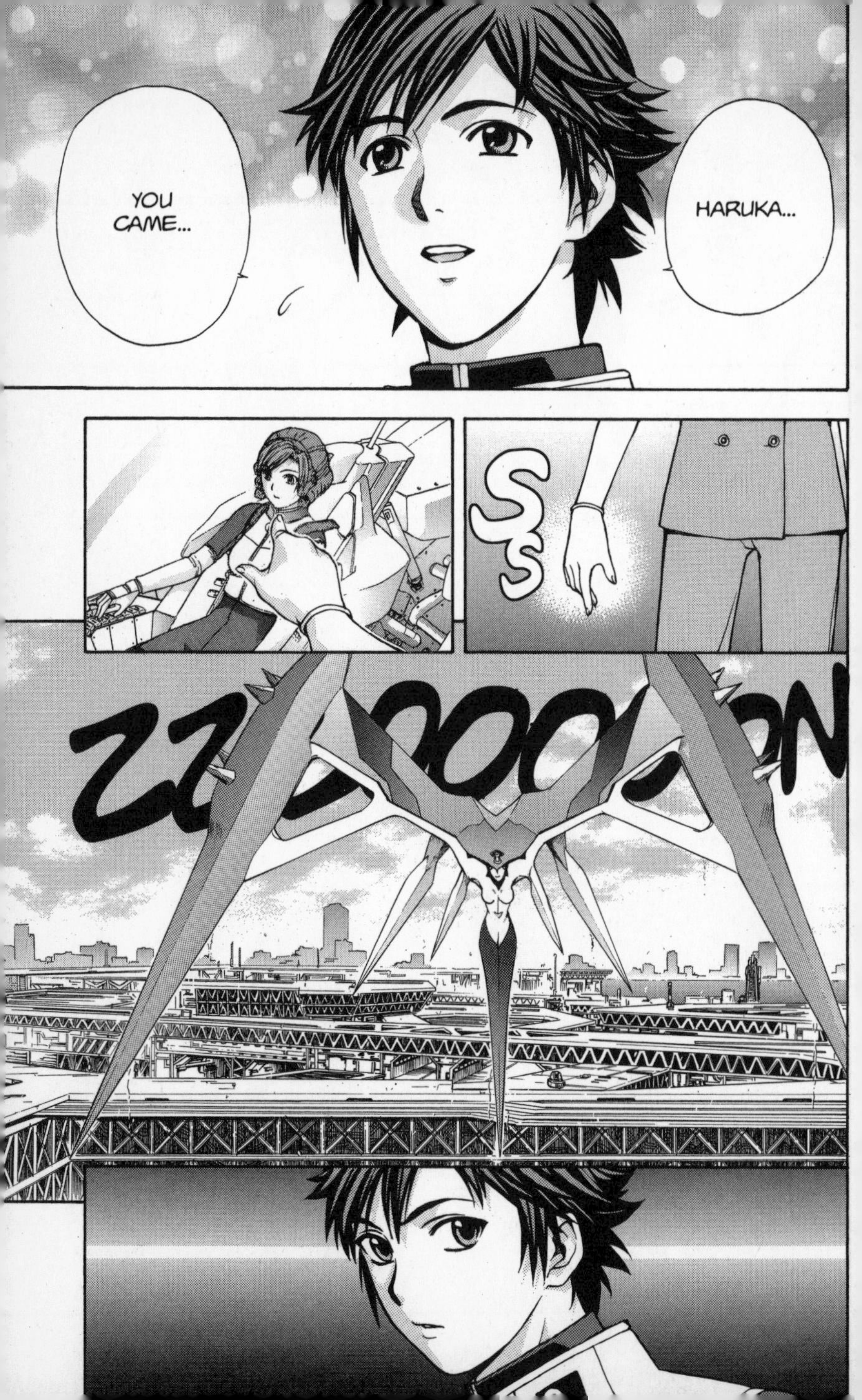
HARUKA...
YOU CAME...
SS
ZZZOOOOOON

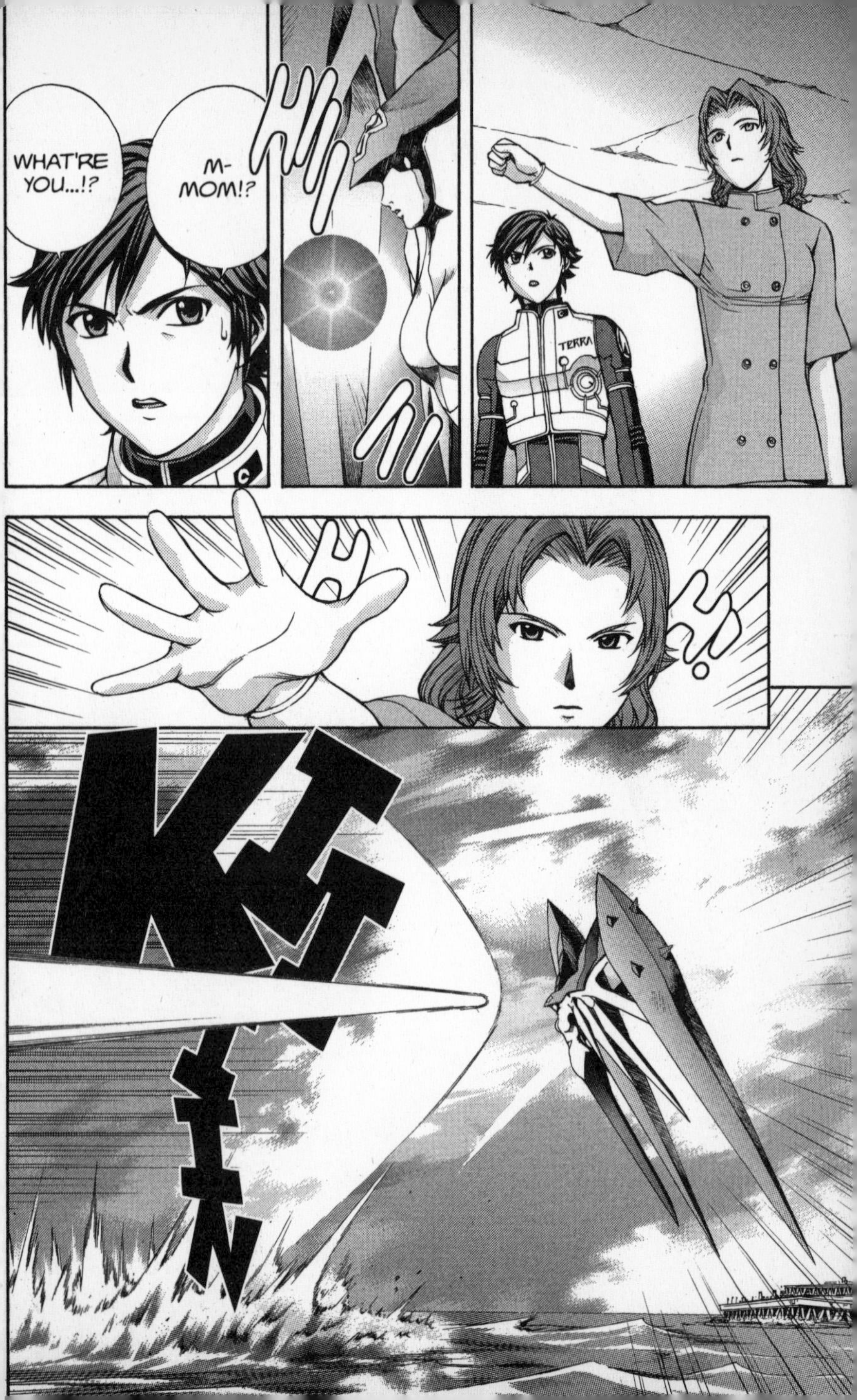
M-MOM!?
WHAT'RE YOU...!?

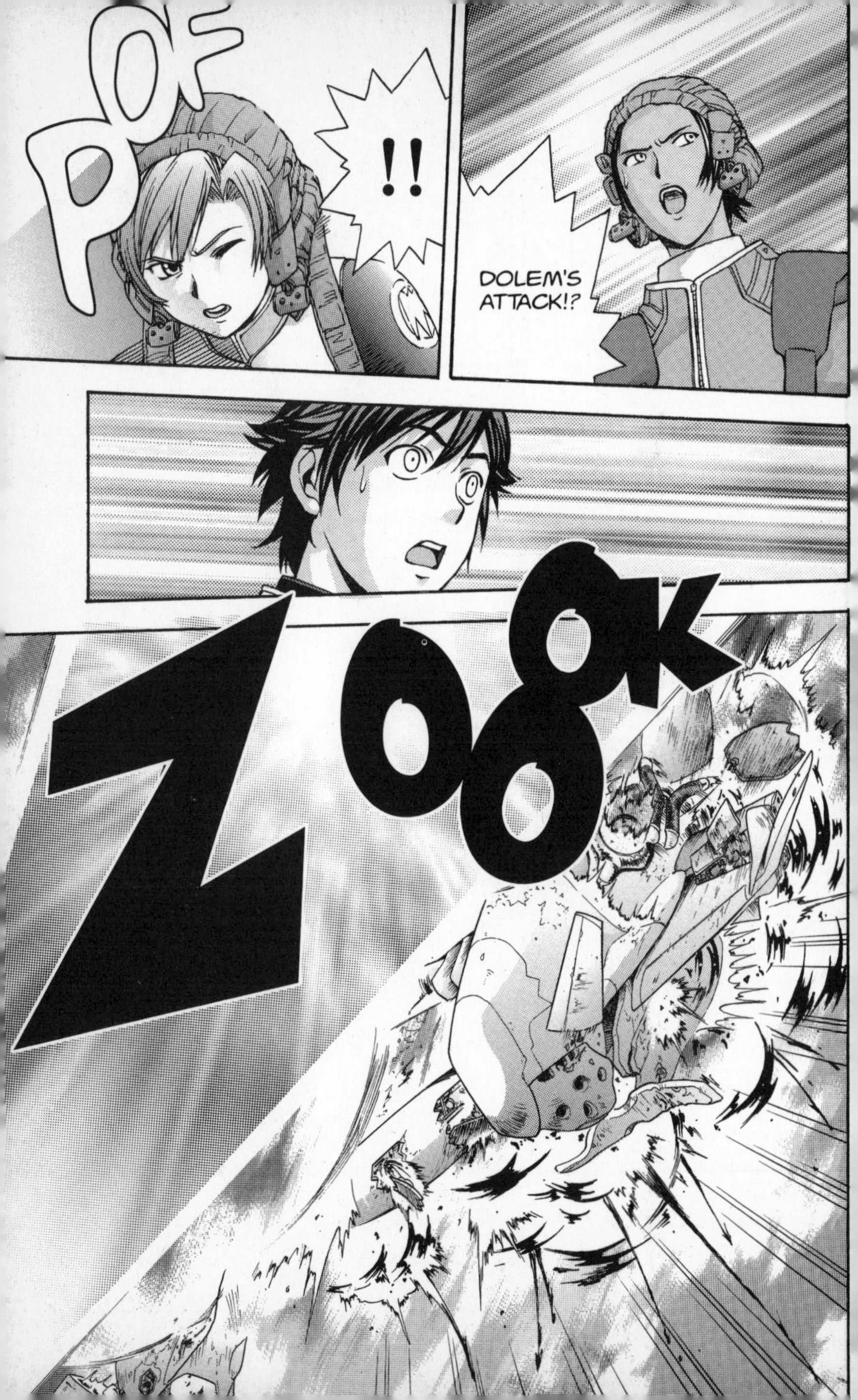
DOLEM'S ATTACK!?
POF
!!
ZOOOK

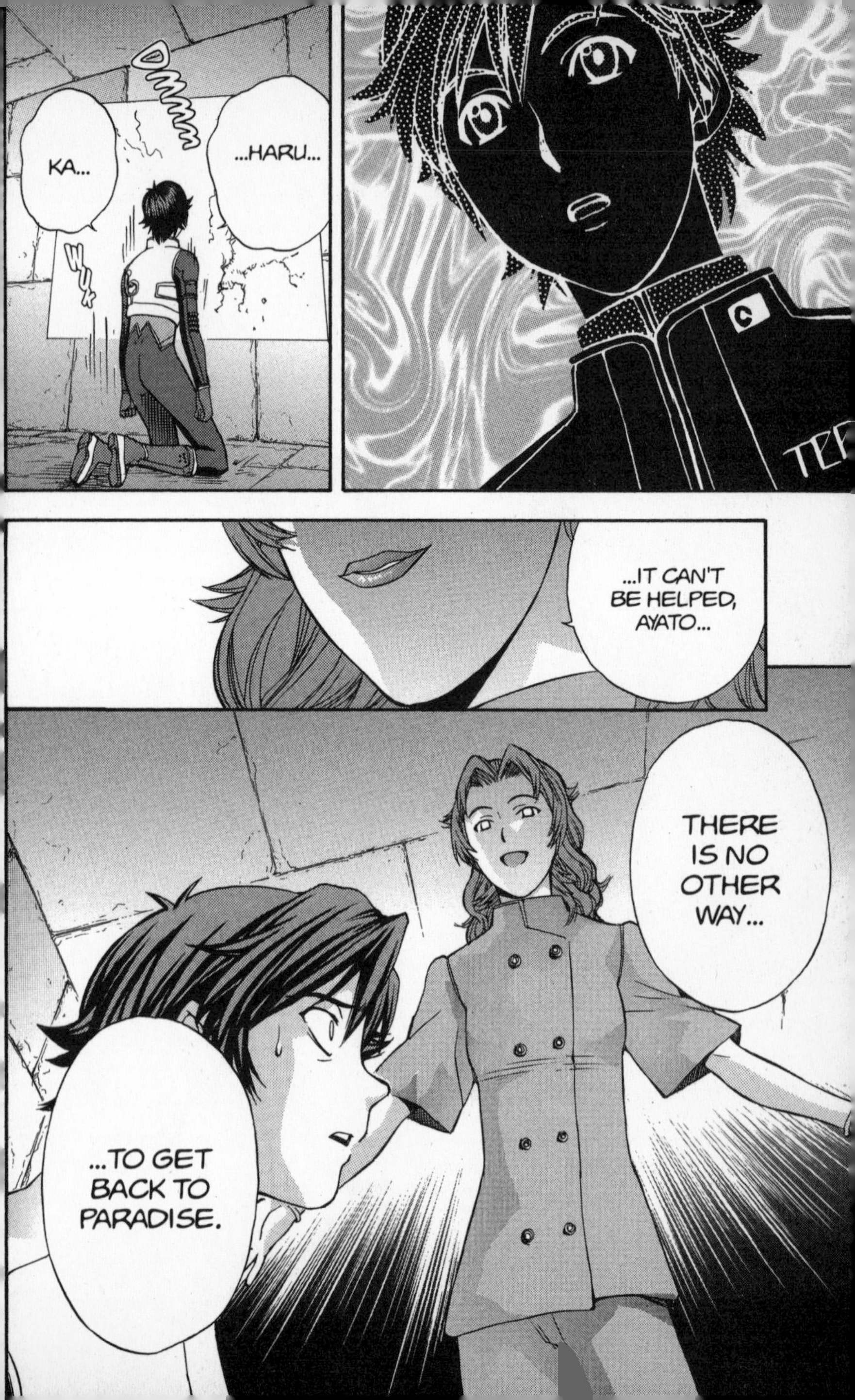
...HARU...
KA...
...IT CAN'T BE HELPED, AYATO...
THERE IS NO OTHER WAY...
...TO GET BACK TO PARADISE.

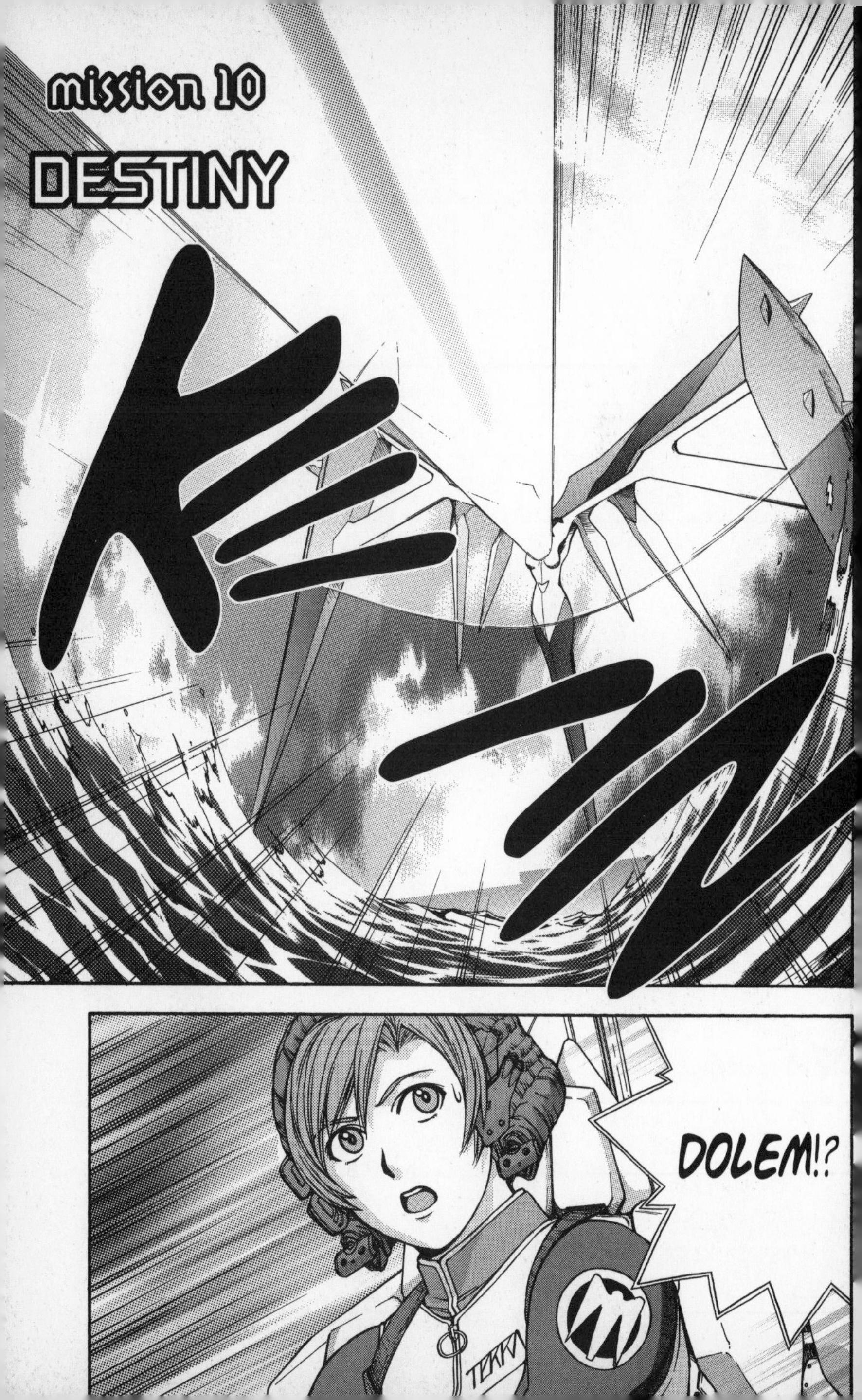
mission 10
DESTINY
DOLEM!?

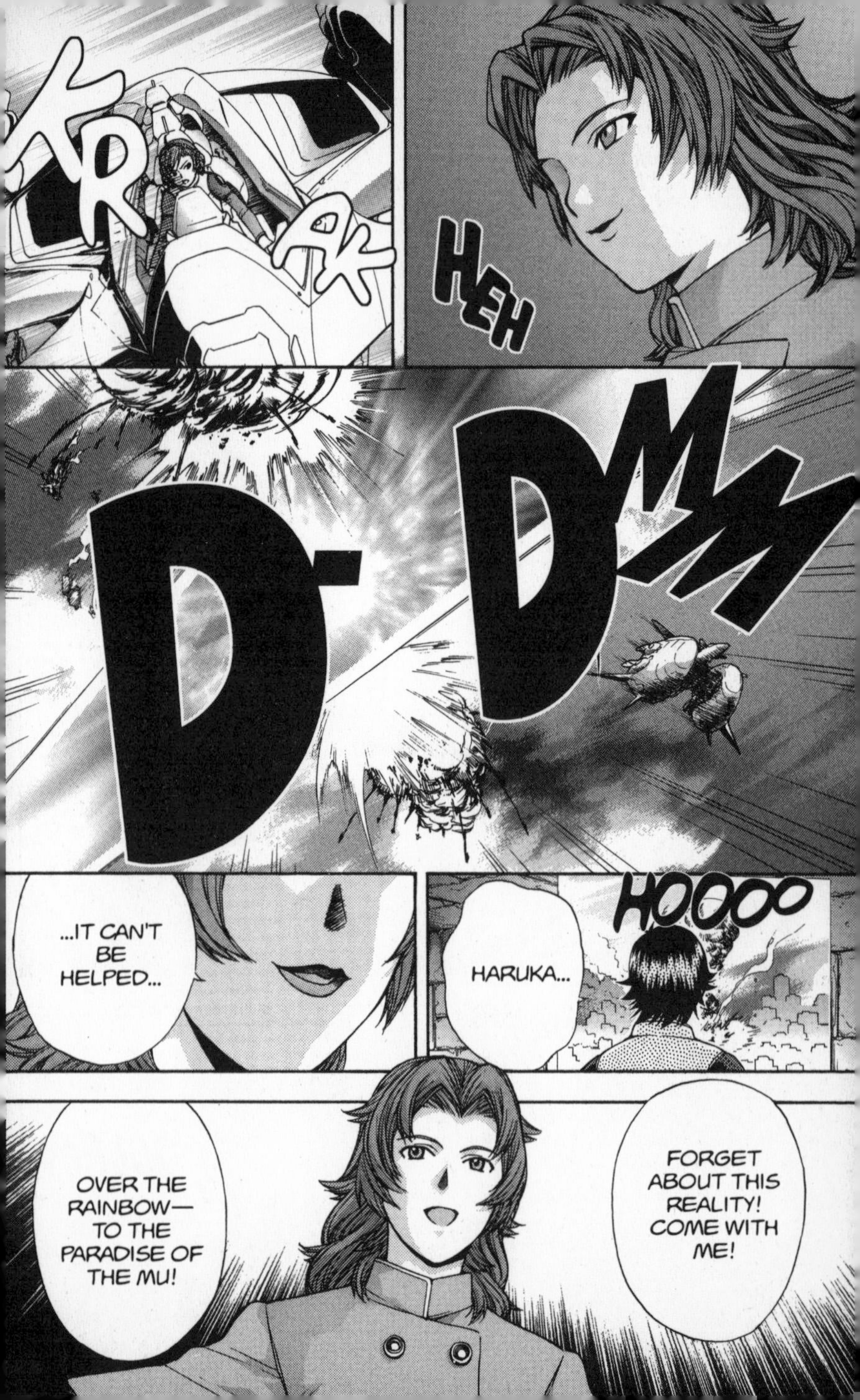
HEH
KRAK
D-DM
HOOOO
HARUKA...
...IT CAN'T BE HELPED...
FORGET ABOUT THIS REALITY! COME WITH ME!
OVER THE RAINBOW— TO THE PARADISE OF THE MU!

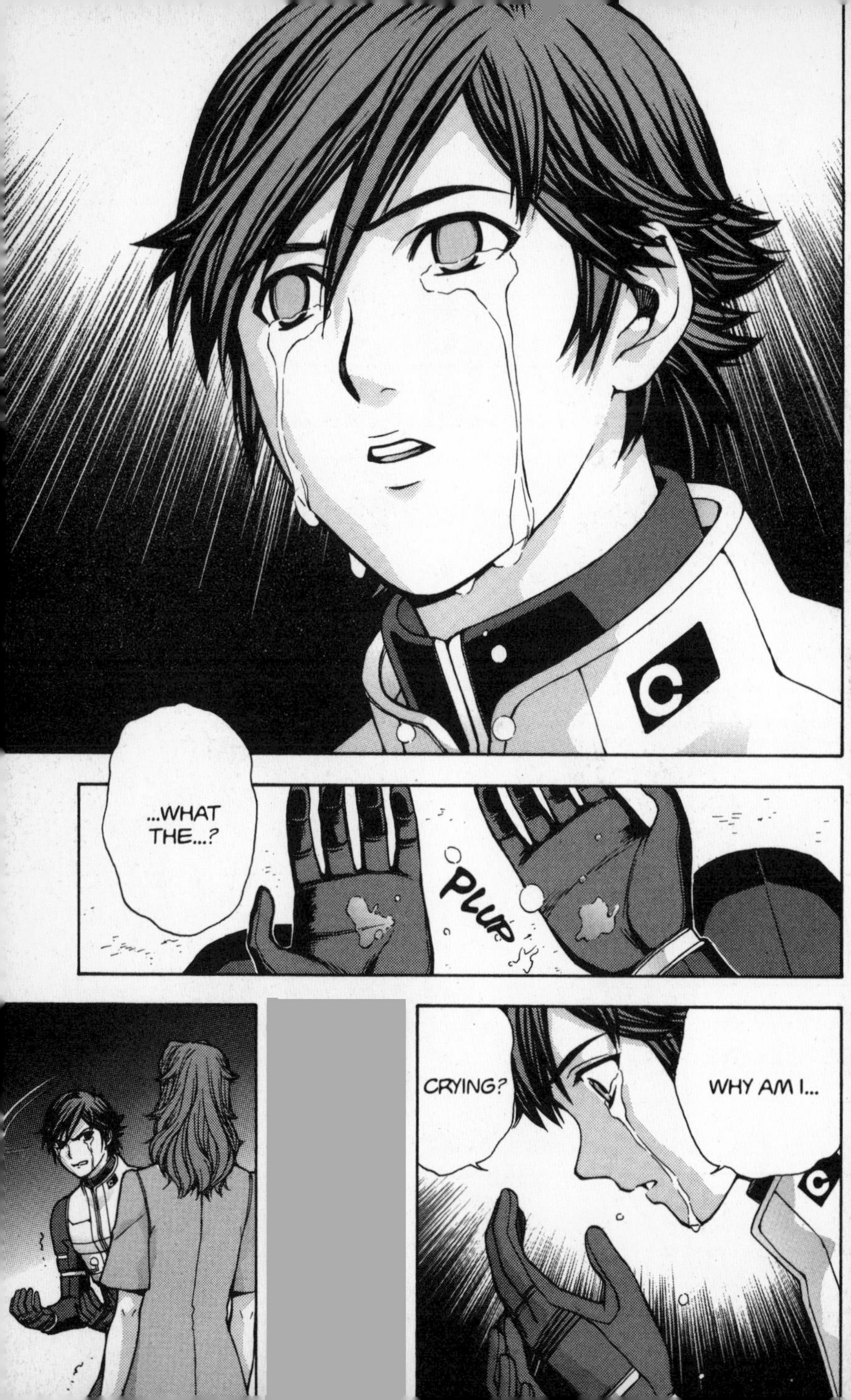
...WHAT THE...?
PLUP
WHY AM I...
CRYING?

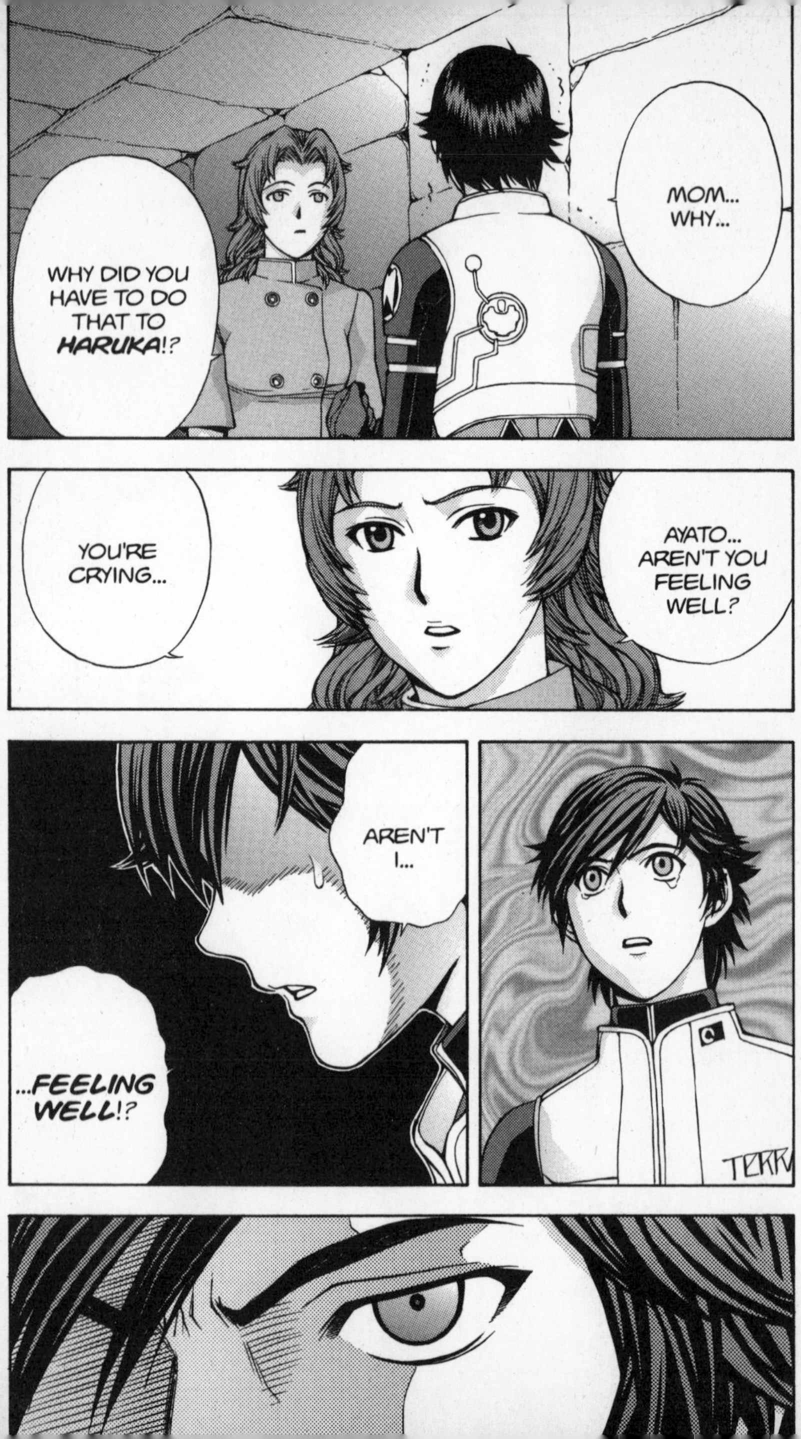
MOM... WHY...
WHY DID YOU HAVE TO DO THAT TO ***HARUKA***!?
AYATO... AREN'T YOU FEELING WELL?
YOU'RE CRYING...
TERR
AREN'T I...
...***FEELING WELL***!?

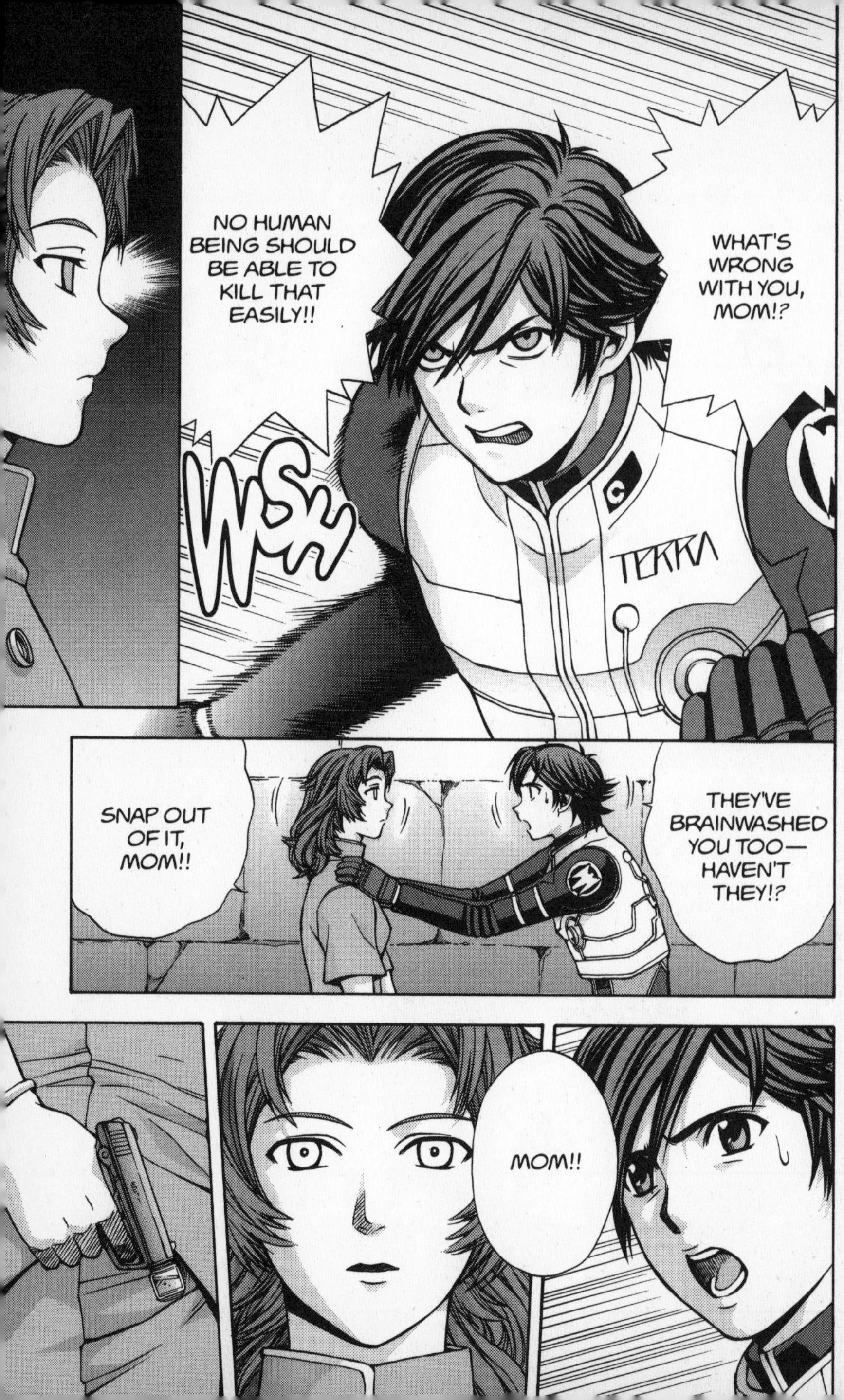
WHAT'S WRONG WITH YOU, MOM!?
NO HUMAN BEING SHOULD BE ABLE TO KILL THAT EASILY!!
WSHH
TERRA
THEY'VE BRAINWASHED YOU TOO—HAVEN'T THEY!?
SNAP OUT OF IT, MOM!!
MOM!!

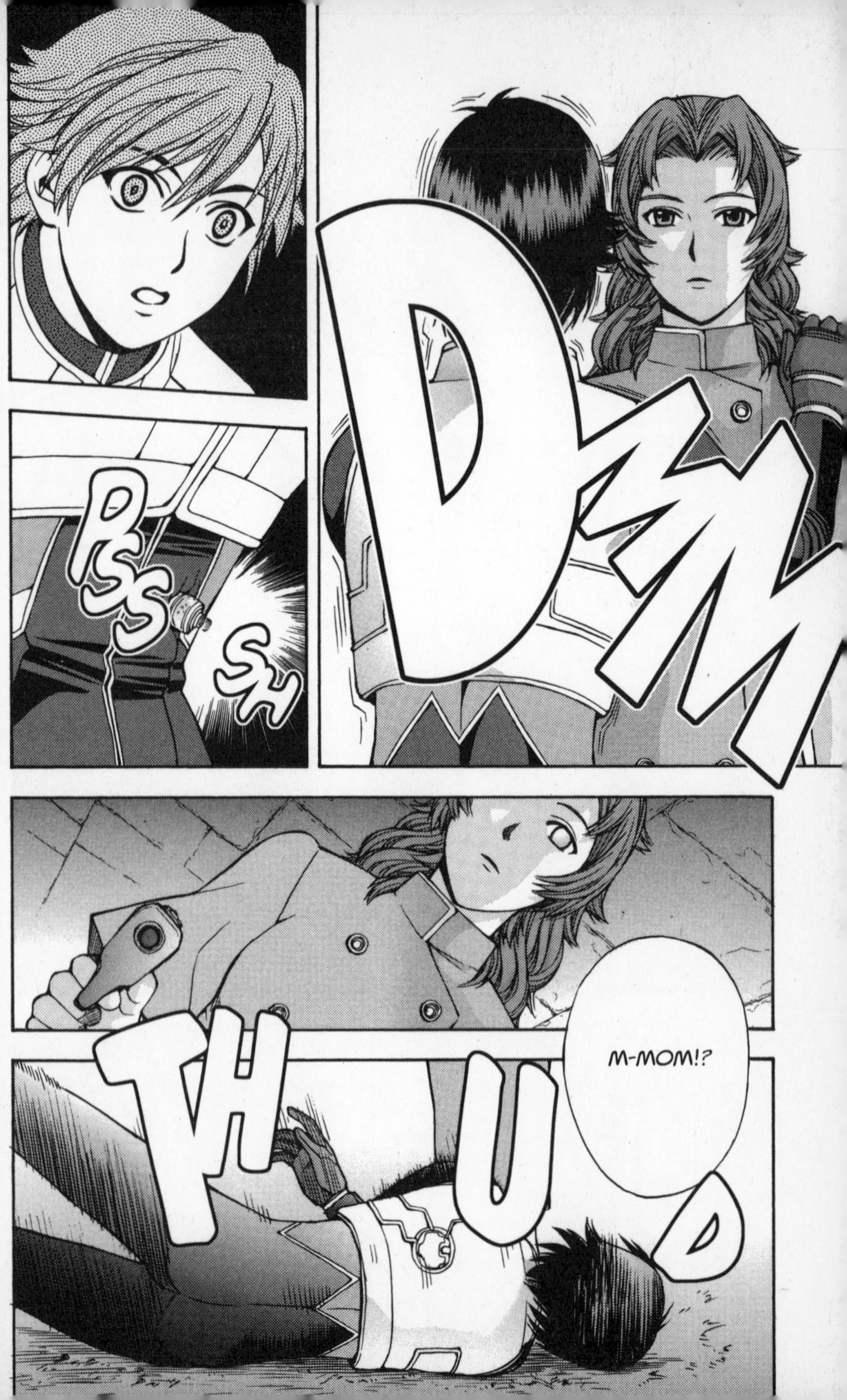
DMM
PSSS
SH
M-MOM!?
THUD

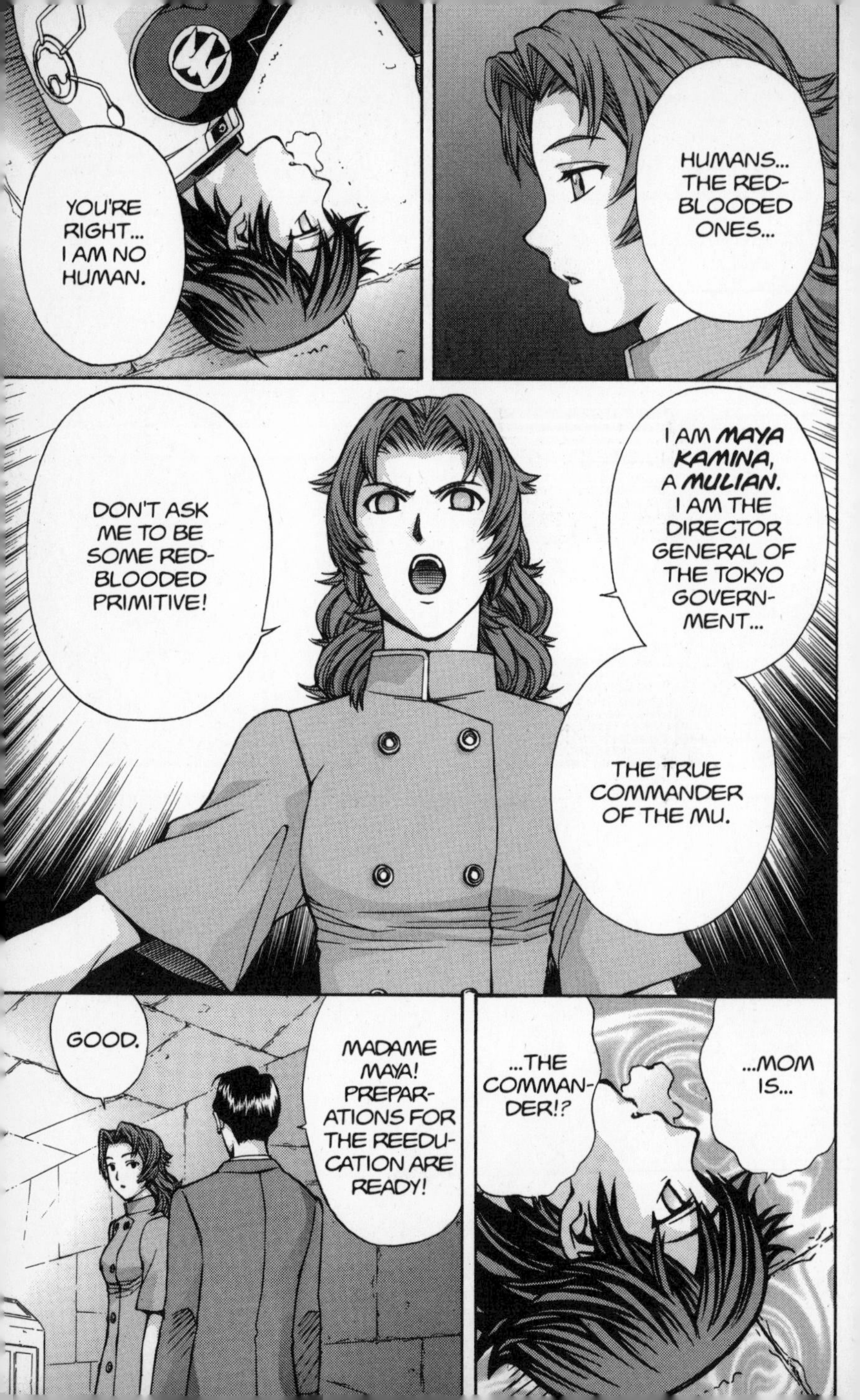
HUMANS... THE RED-BLOODED ONES...
YOU'RE RIGHT... I AM NO HUMAN.
I AM ***MAYA KAMINA***, A ***MULIAN***. I AM THE DIRECTOR GENERAL OF THE TOKYO GOVERNMENT...
THE TRUE COMMANDER OF THE MU.
DON'T ASK ME TO BE SOME RED-BLOODED PRIMITIVE!
...MOM IS...
...THE COMMANDER!?
MADAME MAYA! PREPARATIONS FOR THE REEDUCATION ARE READY!
GOOD.

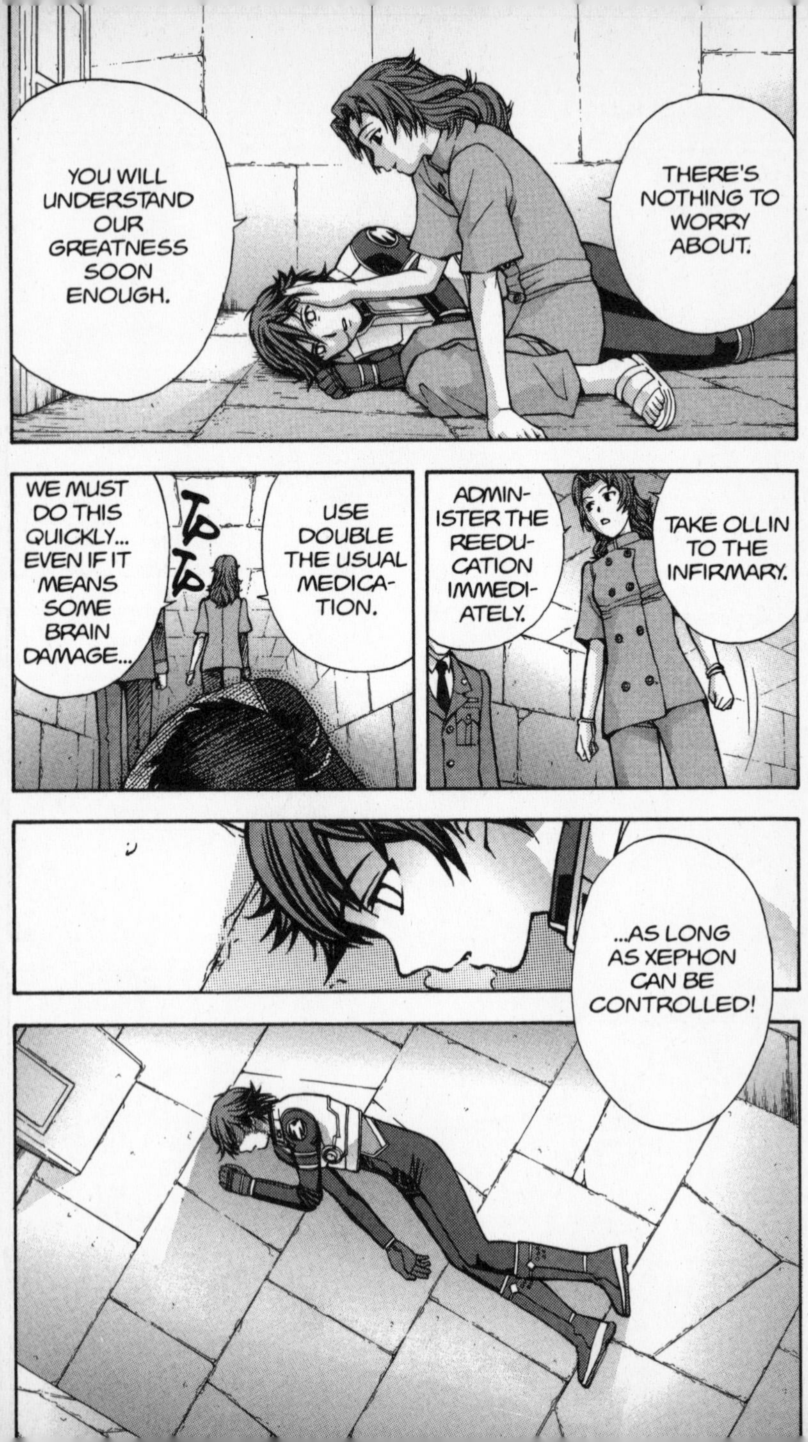
THERE'S NOTHING TO WORRY ABOUT.
YOU WILL UNDERSTAND OUR GREATNESS SOON ENOUGH.
TAKE OLLIN TO THE INFIRMARY.
ADMIN-ISTER THE REEDU-CATION IMMEDI-ATELY.
USE DOUBLE THE USUAL MEDICA-TION.
WE MUST DO THIS QUICKLY... EVEN IF IT MEANS SOME BRAIN DAMAGE...
...AS LONG AS XEPHON CAN BE CONTROLLED!

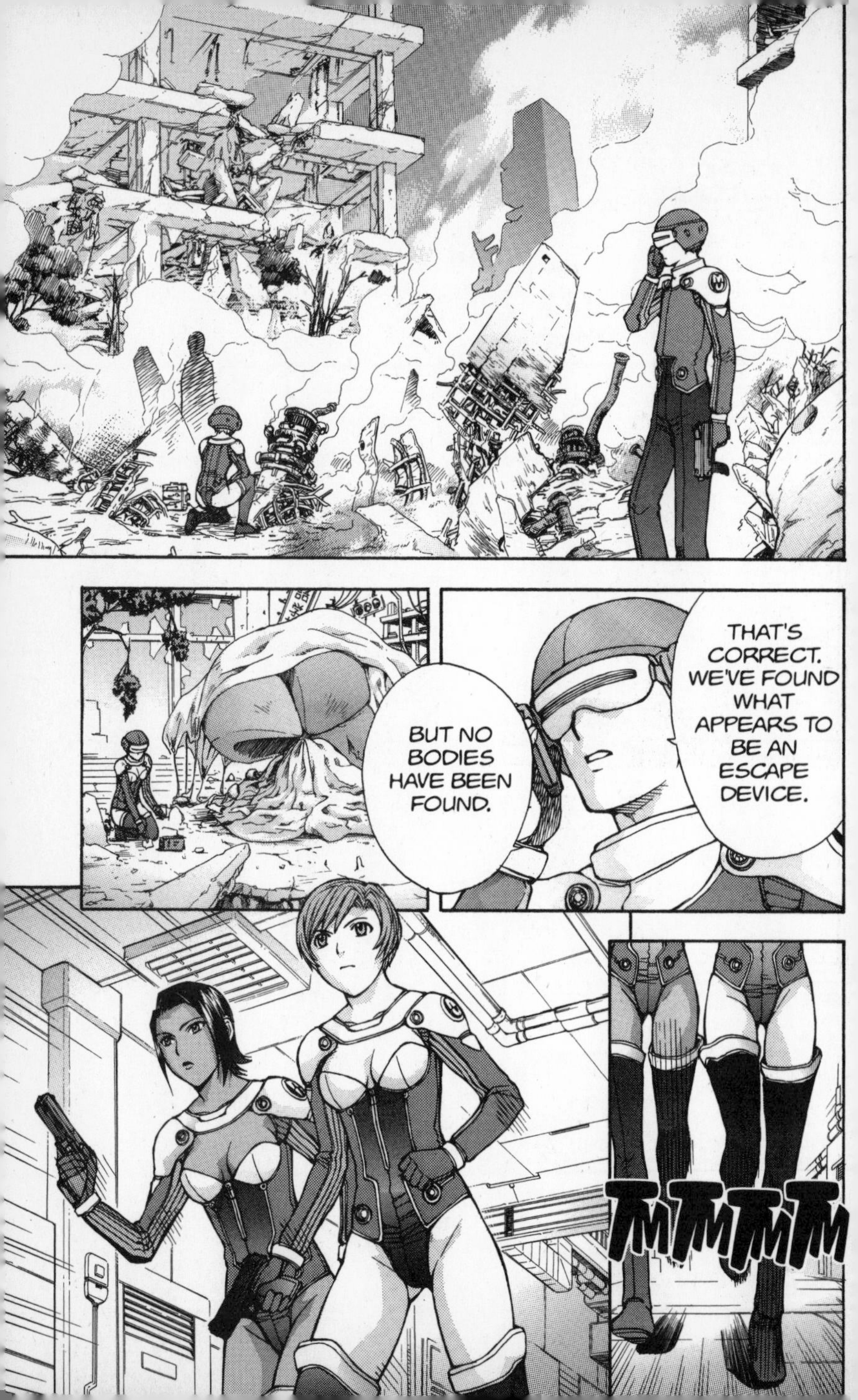
THAT'S CORRECT. WE'VE FOUND WHAT APPEARS TO BE AN ESCAPE DEVICE.
BUT NO BODIES HAVE BEEN FOUND.
TMTMTMTM

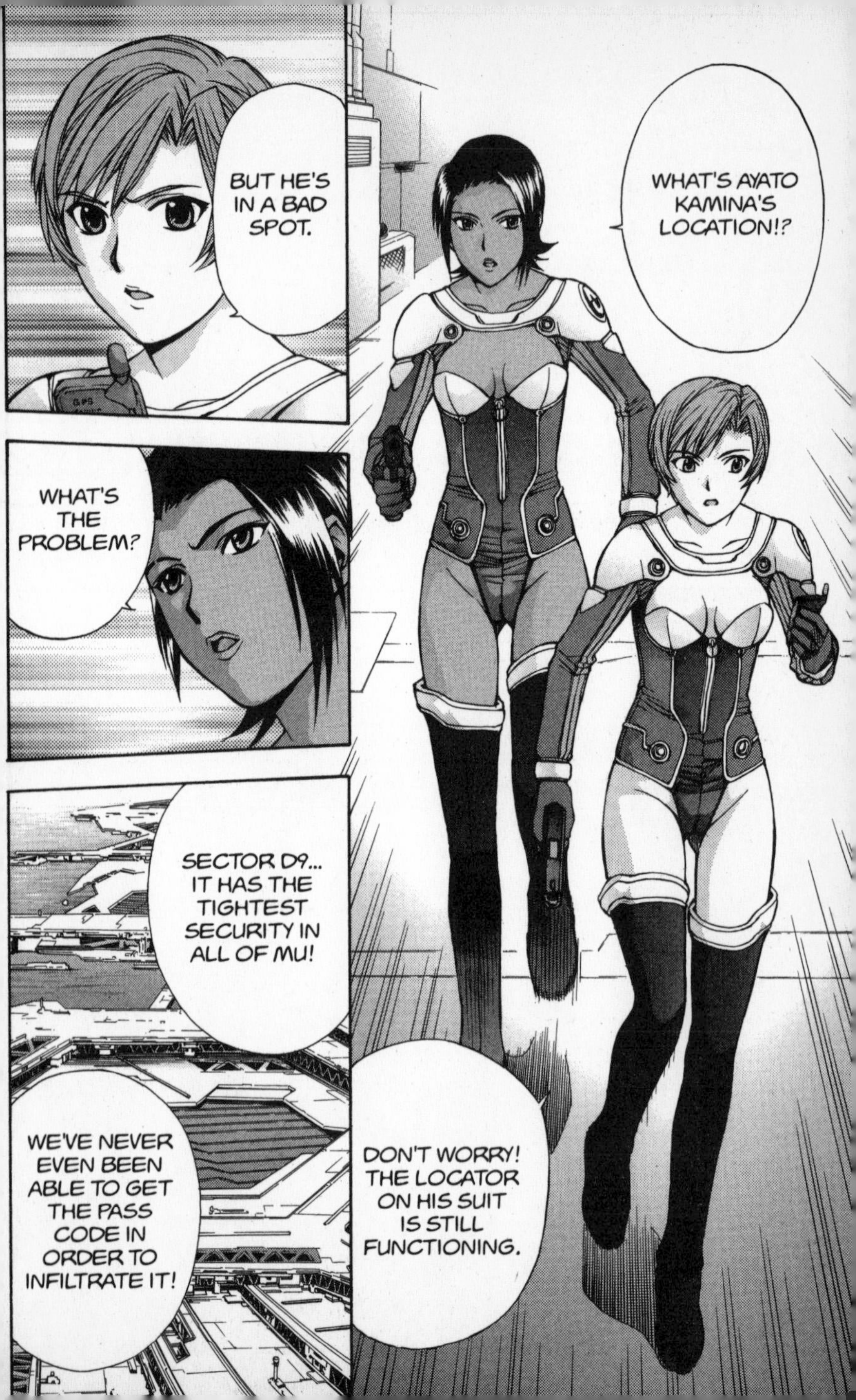
WHAT'S AYATO KAMINA'S LOCATION!?
DON'T WORRY! THE LOCATOR ON HIS SUIT IS STILL FUNCTIONING.
BUT HE'S IN A BAD SPOT.
WHAT'S THE PROBLEM?
SECTOR D9... IT HAS THE TIGHTEST SECURITY IN ALL OF MU!
WE'VE NEVER EVEN BEEN ABLE TO GET THE PASS CODE IN ORDER TO INFILTRATE IT!

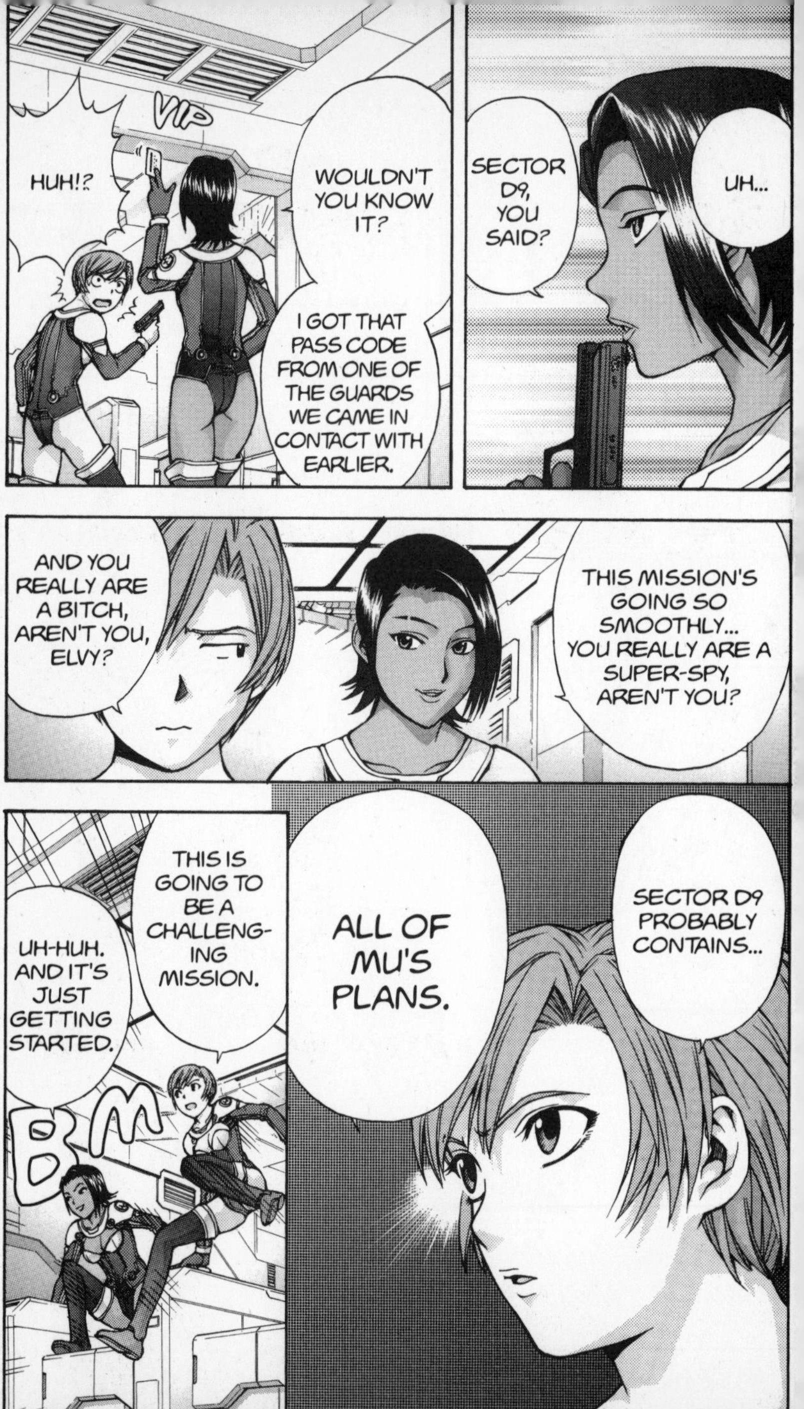
UH...
SECTOR D9, YOU SAID?
VIP
WOULDN'T YOU KNOW IT?
HUH!?
I GOT THAT PASS CODE FROM ONE OF THE GUARDS WE CAME IN CONTACT WITH EARLIER.
THIS MISSION'S GOING SO SMOOTHLY... YOU REALLY ARE A SUPER-SPY, AREN'T YOU?
AND YOU REALLY ARE A BITCH, AREN'T YOU, ELVY?
SECTOR D9 PROBABLY CONTAINS...
ALL OF MU'S PLANS.
THIS IS GOING TO BE A CHALLENG-ING MISSION.
UH-HUH. AND IT'S JUST GETTING STARTED.
BM

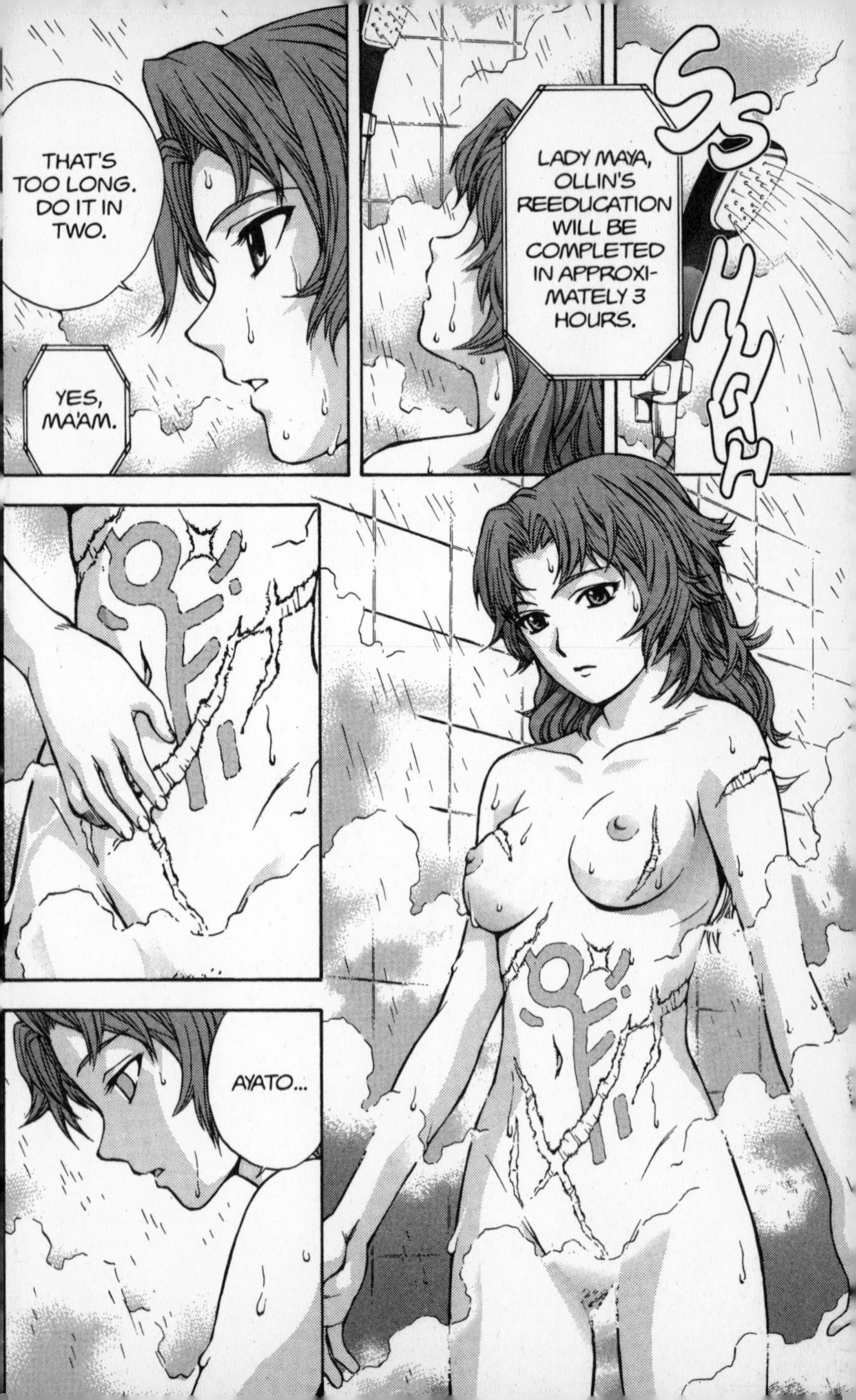
LADY MAYA, OLLIN'S REEDUCATION WILL BE COMPLETED IN APPROXI-MATELY 3 HOURS.
SSHHHH
THAT'S TOO LONG. DO IT IN TWO.
YES, MA'AM.
AYATO...

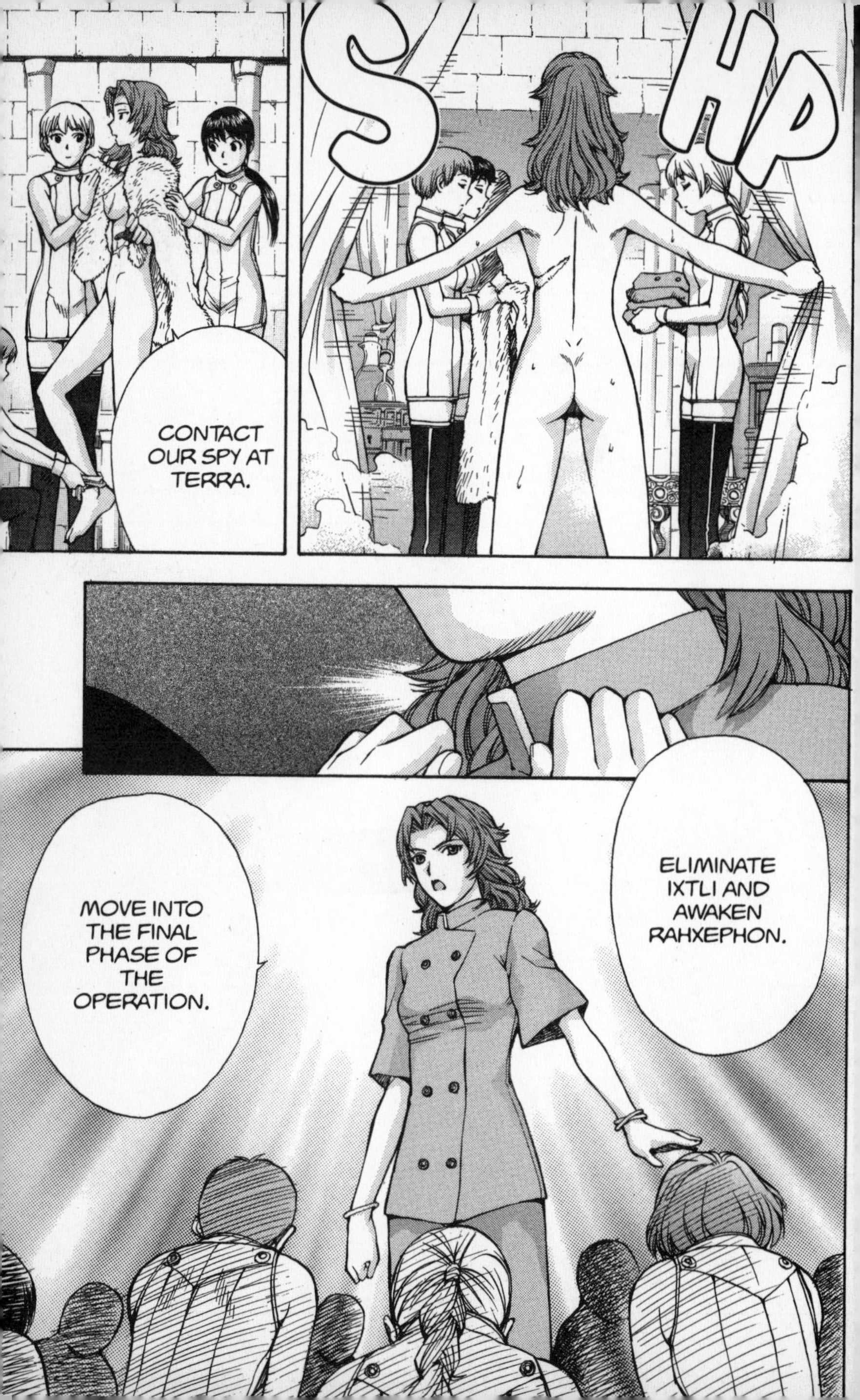
SHP
CONTACT OUR SPY AT TERRA.
ELIMINATE IXTLI AND AWAKEN RAHXEPHON.
MOVE INTO THE FINAL PHASE OF THE OPERATION.

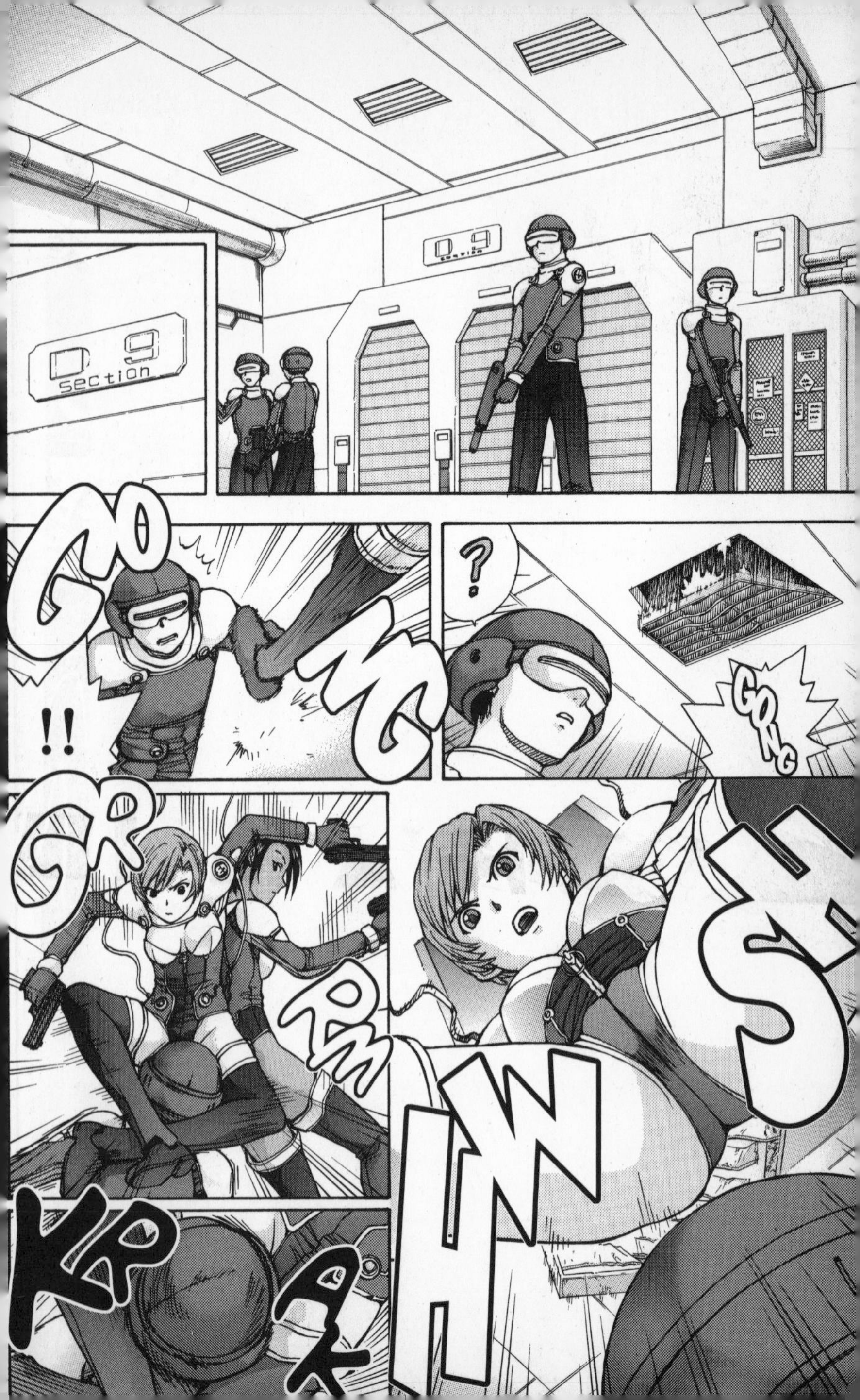
0 9 section
?
GONG
GO NG
!!
GR RM
KRAK

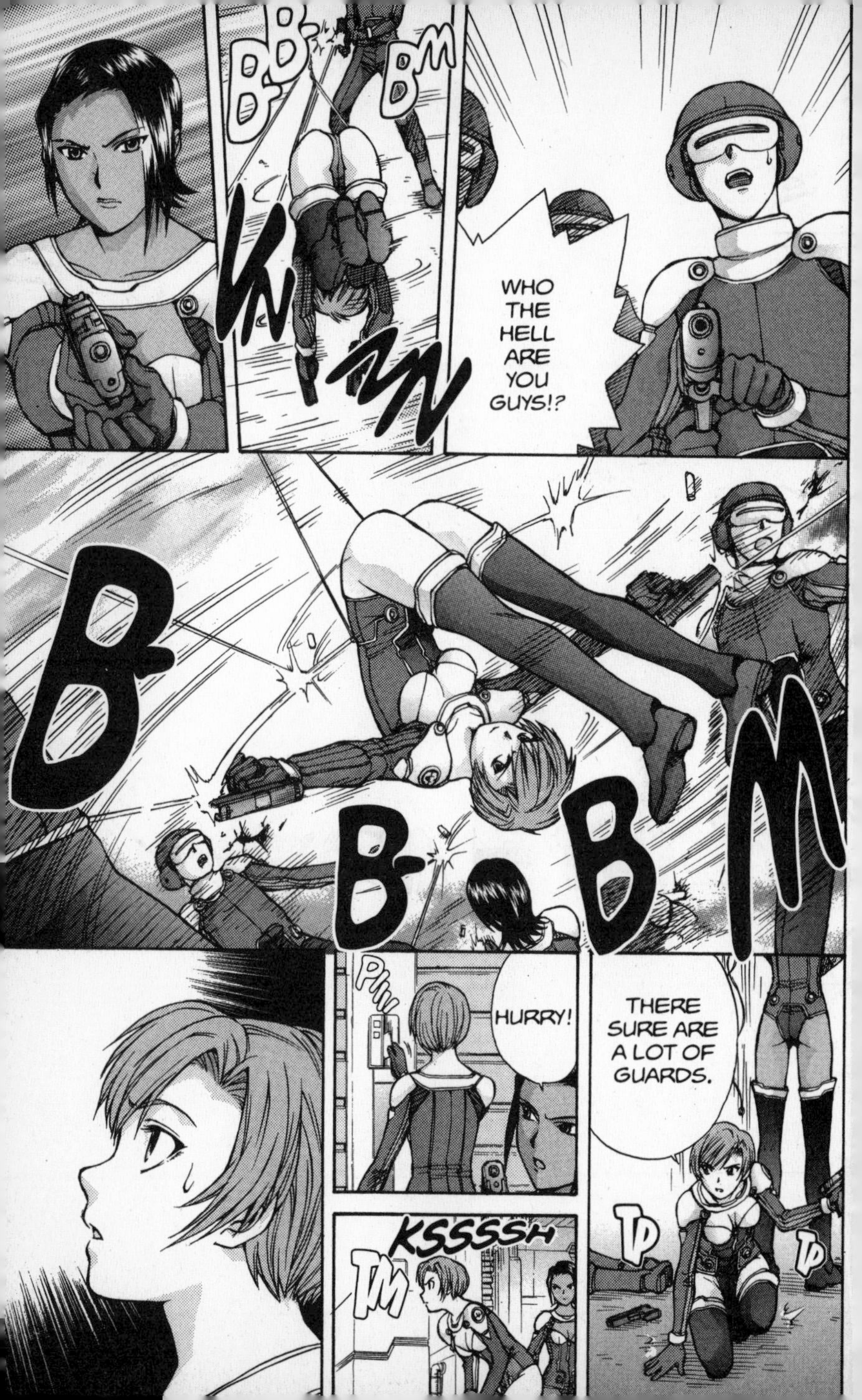
WHO THE HELL ARE YOU GUYS!?
BB-BM
BB-BBM
THERE SURE ARE A LOT OF GUARDS.
TP
TP
HURRY!
KSSSSH
TM

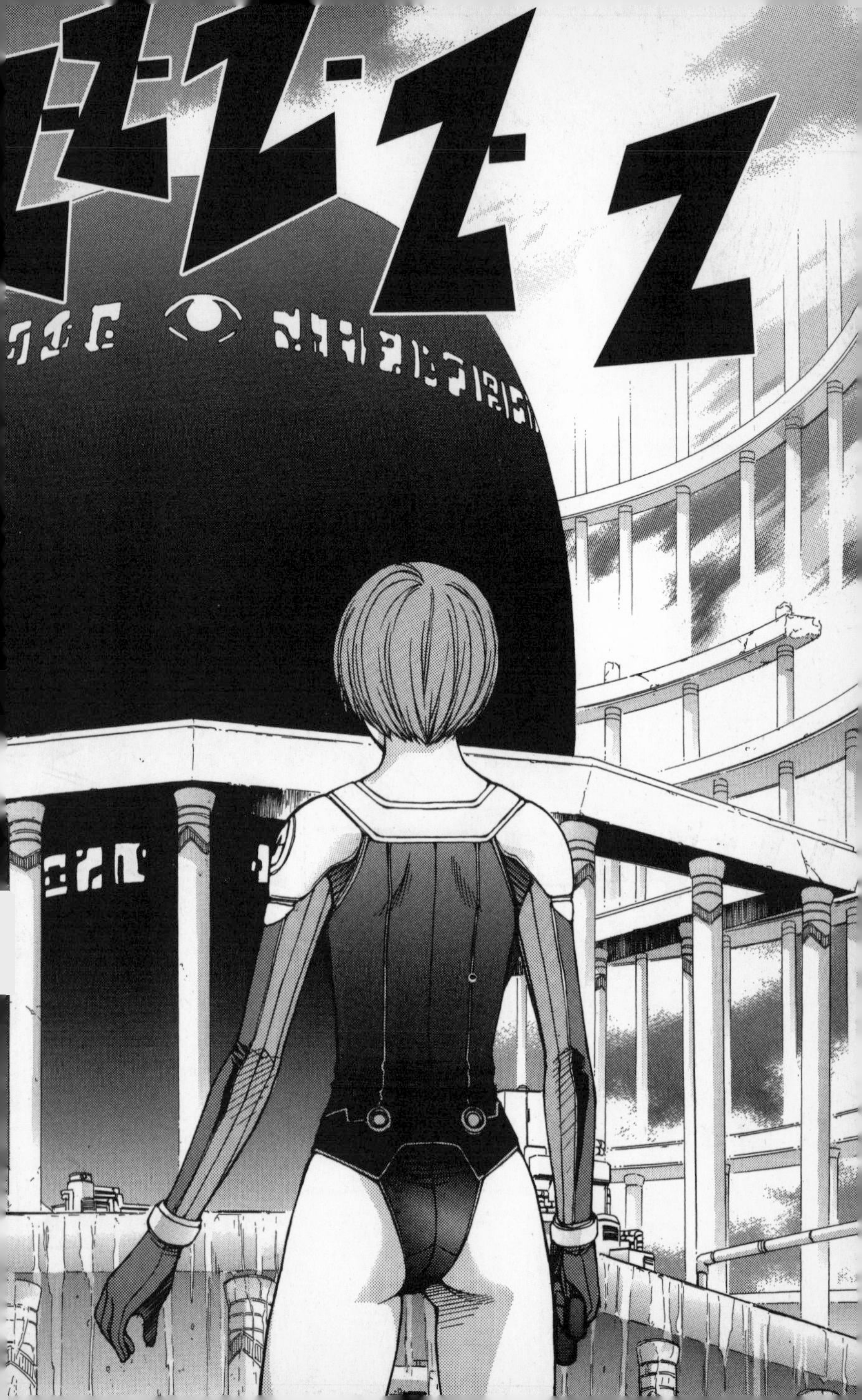

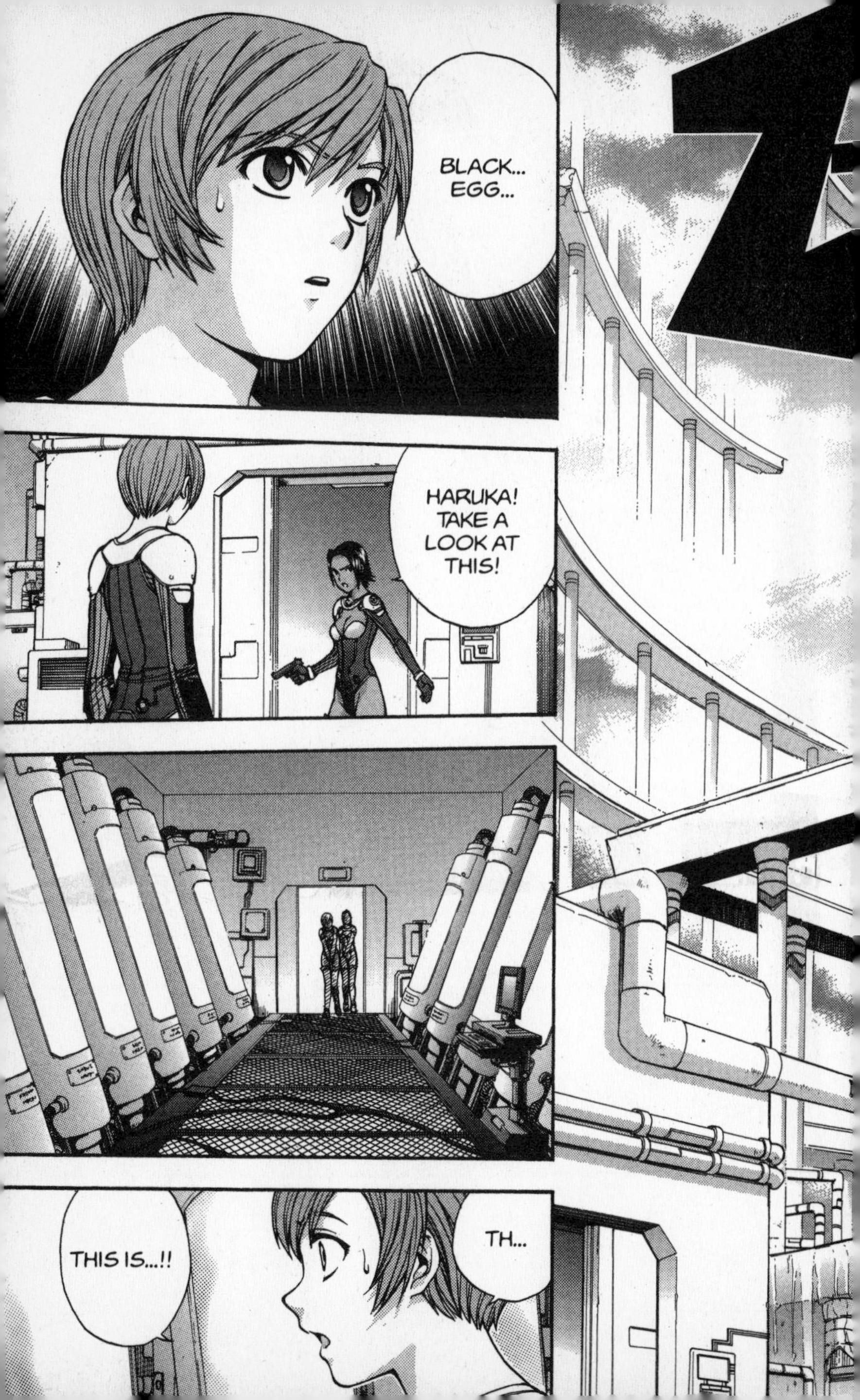
BLACK... EGG...
HARUKA! TAKE A LOOK AT THIS!
TH...
THIS IS...!!

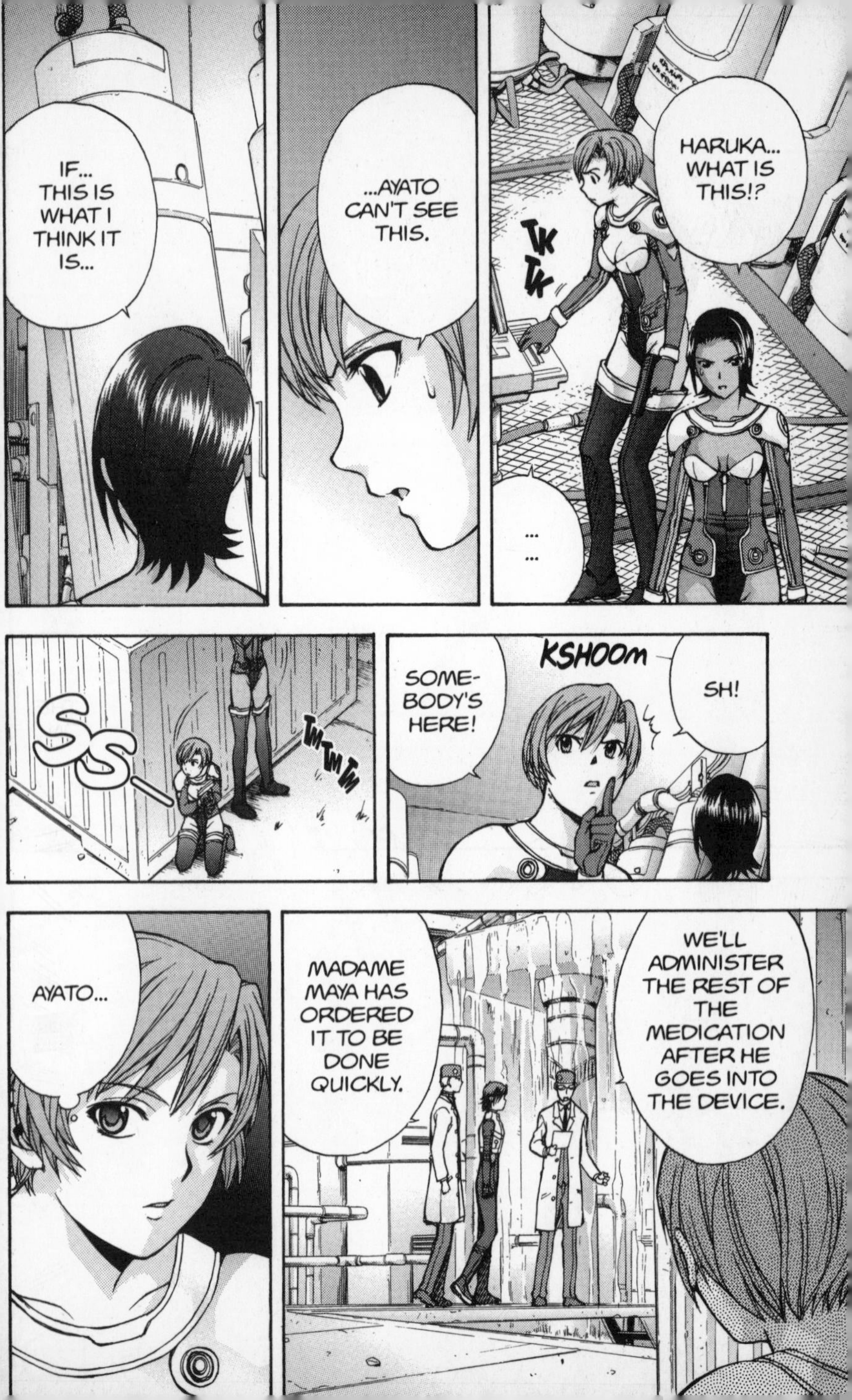
HARUKA... WHAT IS THIS!?
TK TK
...
...
...AYATO CAN'T SEE THIS.
IF... THIS IS WHAT I THINK IT IS...
SH!
KSHOOM
SOME-BODY'S HERE!
TM TM TM
SS-
WE'LL ADMINISTER THE REST OF THE MEDICATION AFTER HE GOES INTO THE DEVICE.
MADAME MAYA HAS ORDERED IT TO BE DONE QUICKLY.
AYATO...

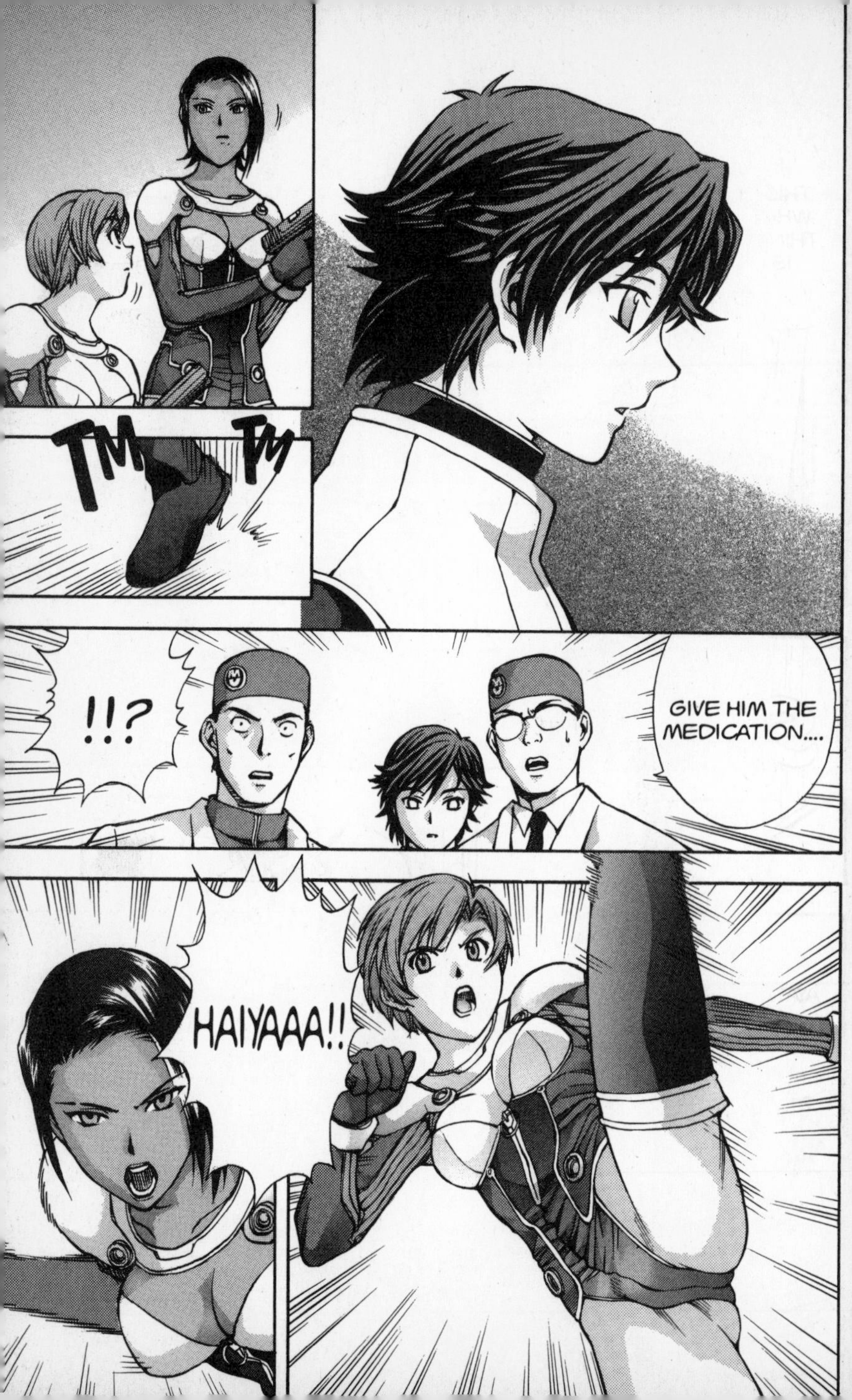
TM
TM
GIVE HIM THE MEDICATION....
!!?
HAIYAAA!!

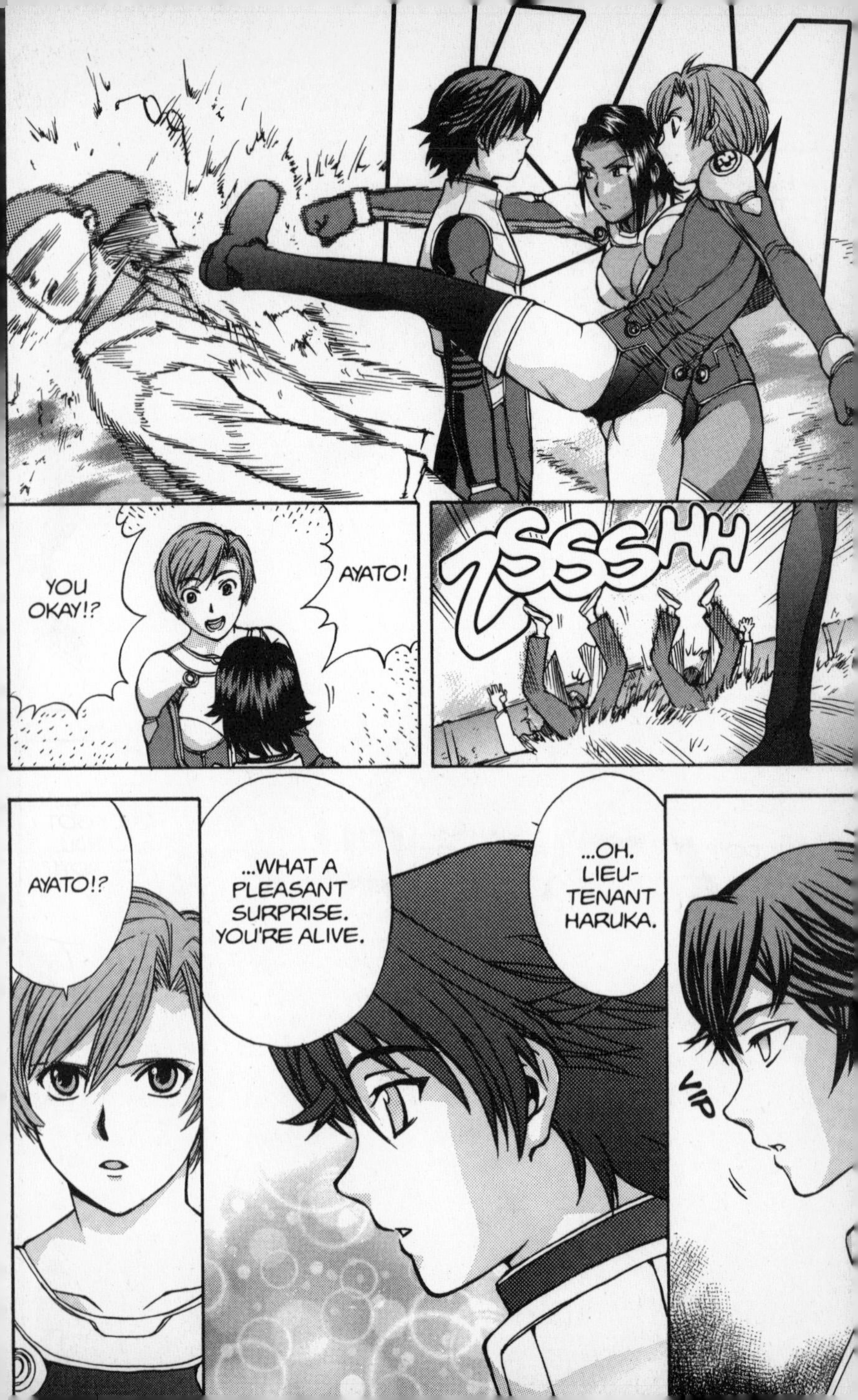
ZSSSHH
AYATO!
YOU OKAY!?
...OH. LIEU-TENANT HARUKA.
VIP
...WHAT A PLEASANT SURPRISE. YOU'RE ALIVE.
AYATO!?

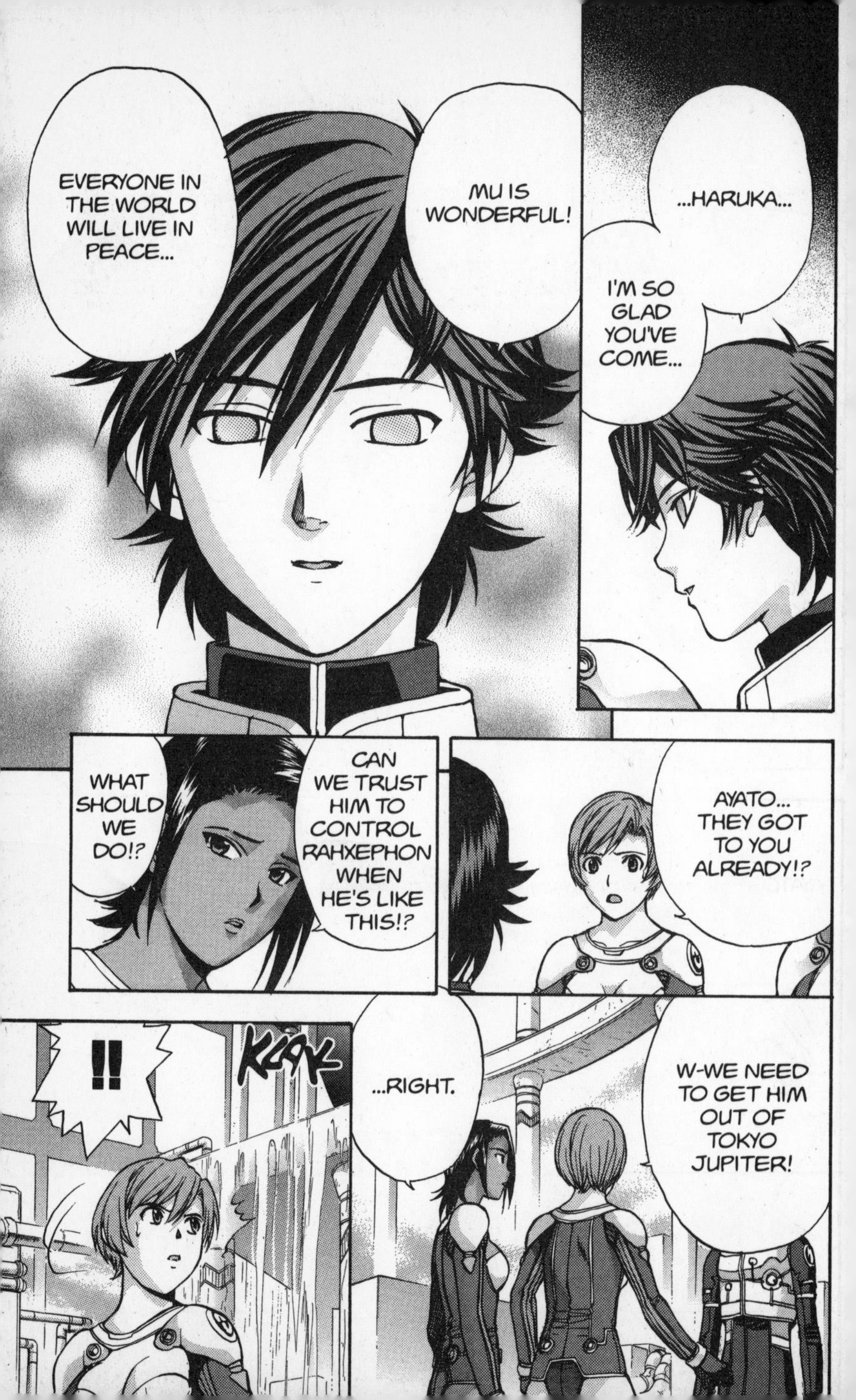
...HARUKA...
I'M SO GLAD YOU'VE COME...
MU IS WONDERFUL!
EVERYONE IN THE WORLD WILL LIVE IN PEACE...
AYATO... THEY GOT TO YOU ALREADY!?
CAN WE TRUST HIM TO CONTROL RAHXEPHON WHEN HE'S LIKE THIS!?
WHAT SHOULD WE DO!?
W-WE NEED TO GET HIM OUT OF TOKYO JUPITER!
...RIGHT.
KLAK
!!

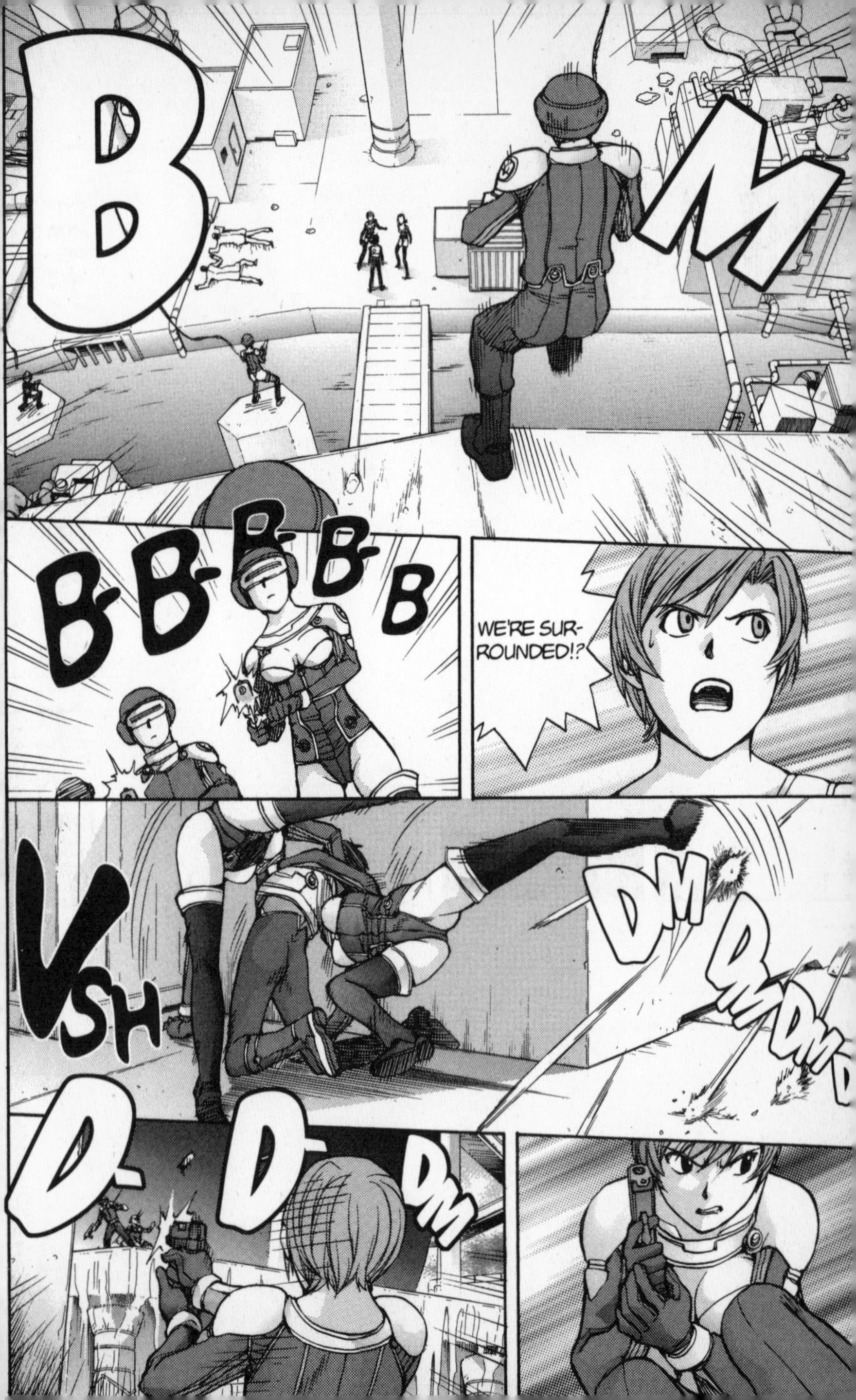
B M
WE'RE SUR-ROUNDED!?
B-B-B-B-B
DM DMDMDMD
VSH
D-D-DM

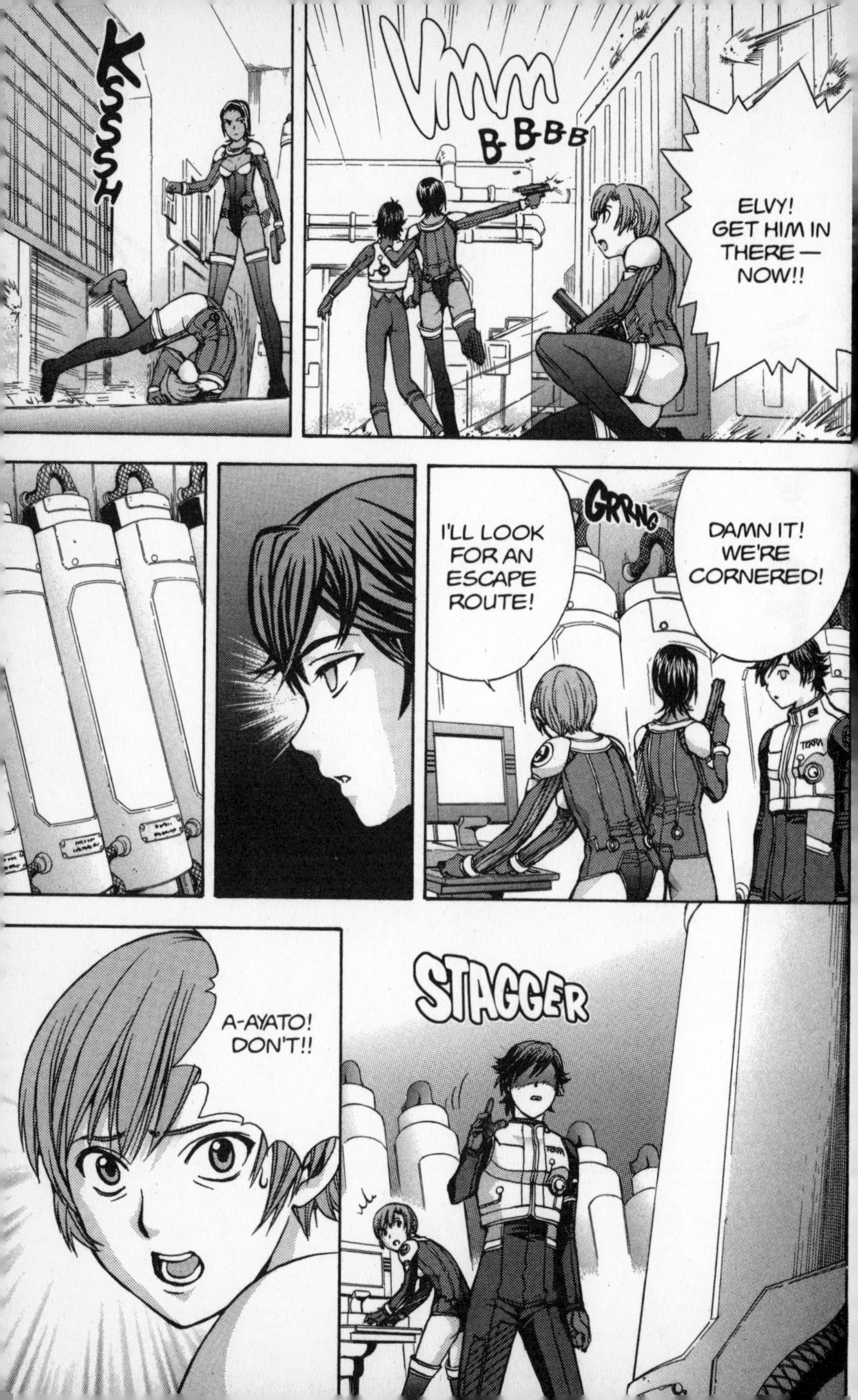
VMMM
B-B-B-B
ELVY! GET HIM IN THERE — NOW!!
KSSSSH
DAMN IT! WE'RE CORNERED!
GRRNG
I'LL LOOK FOR AN ESCAPE ROUTE!
STAGGER
A-AYATO! DON'T!!

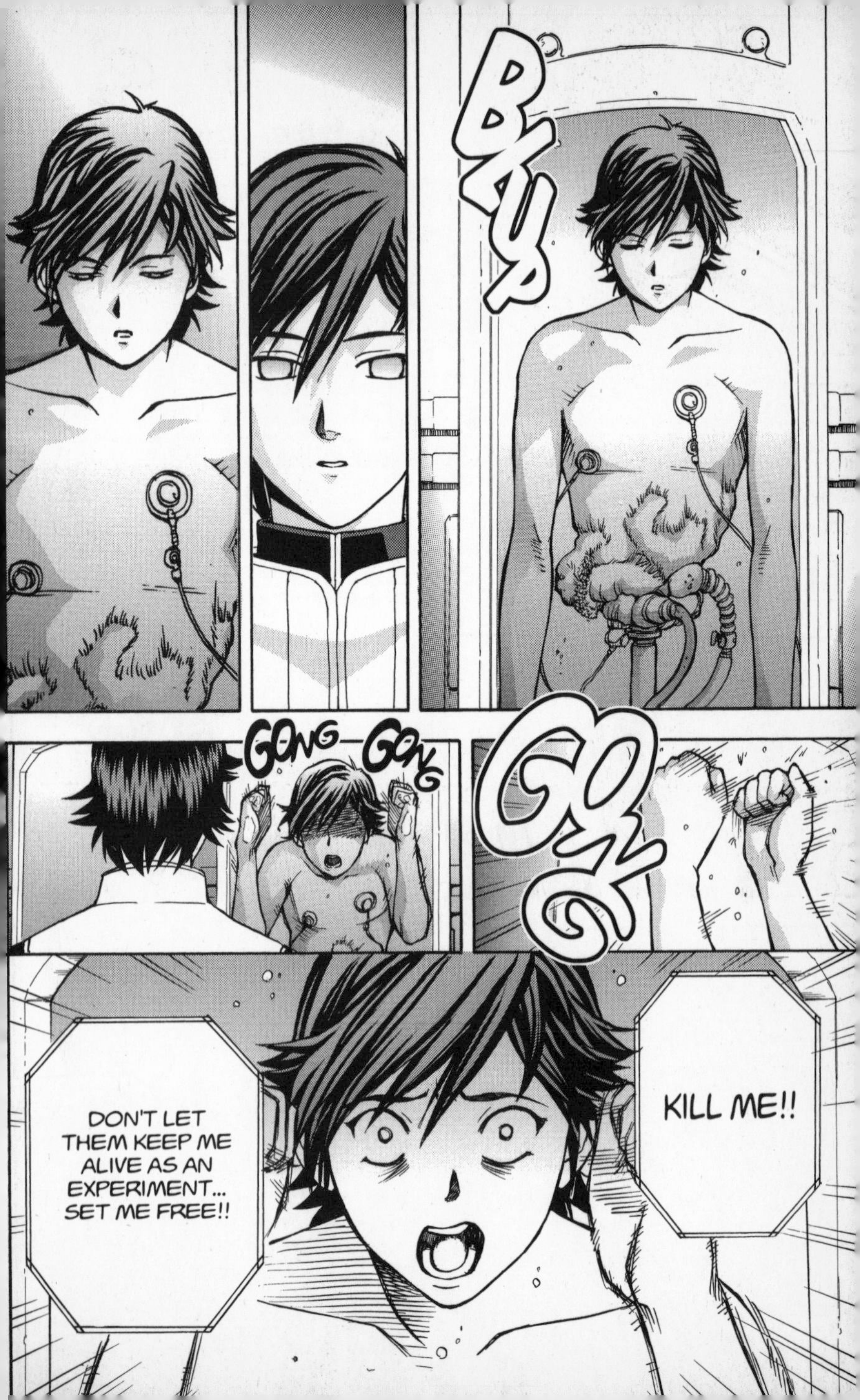
BLUP
GONG
GONG GONG
KILL ME!!
DON'T LET THEM KEEP ME ALIVE AS AN EXPERIMENT... SET ME FREE!!

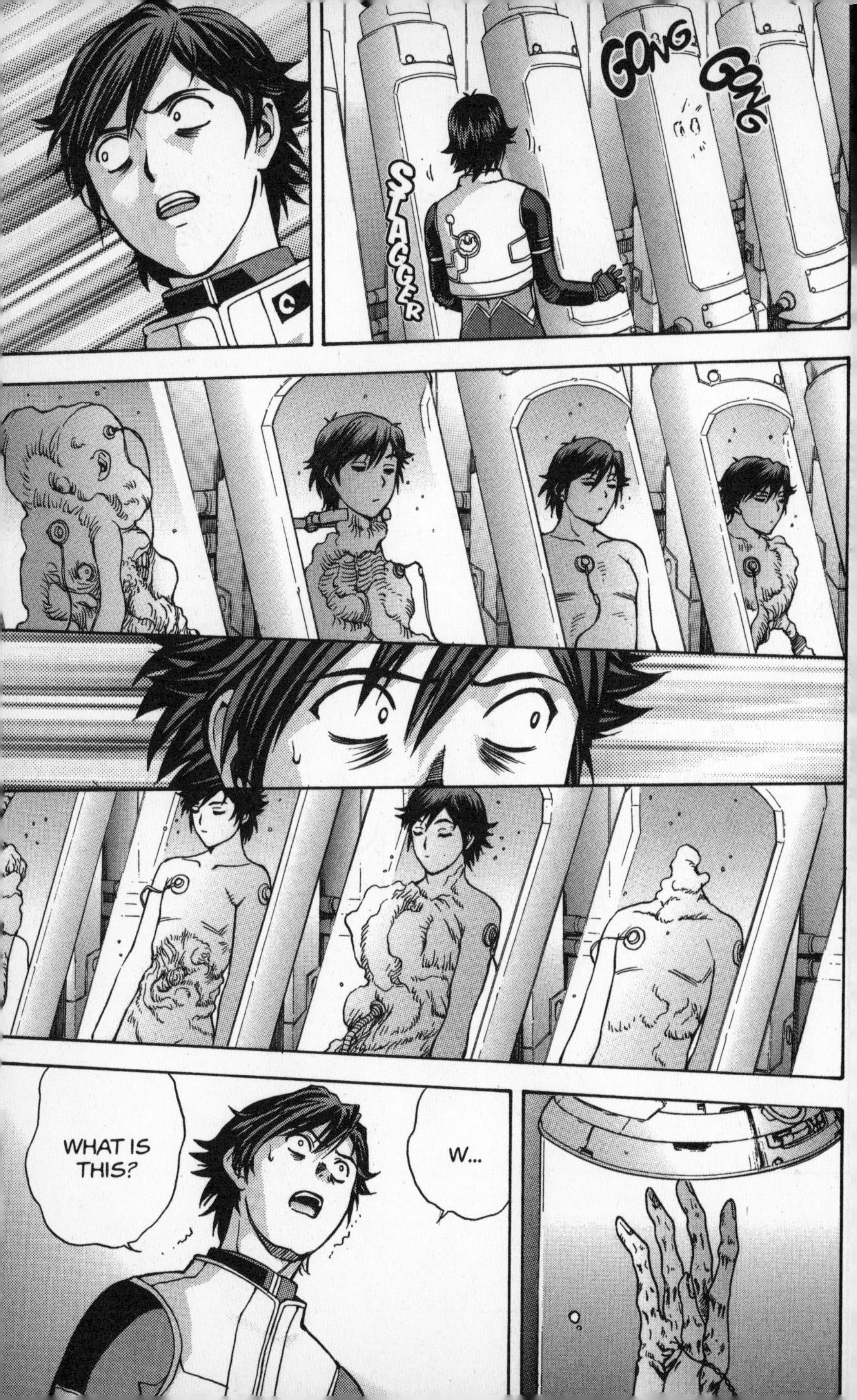
GONG GONG
STAGGER
W...
WHAT IS THIS?

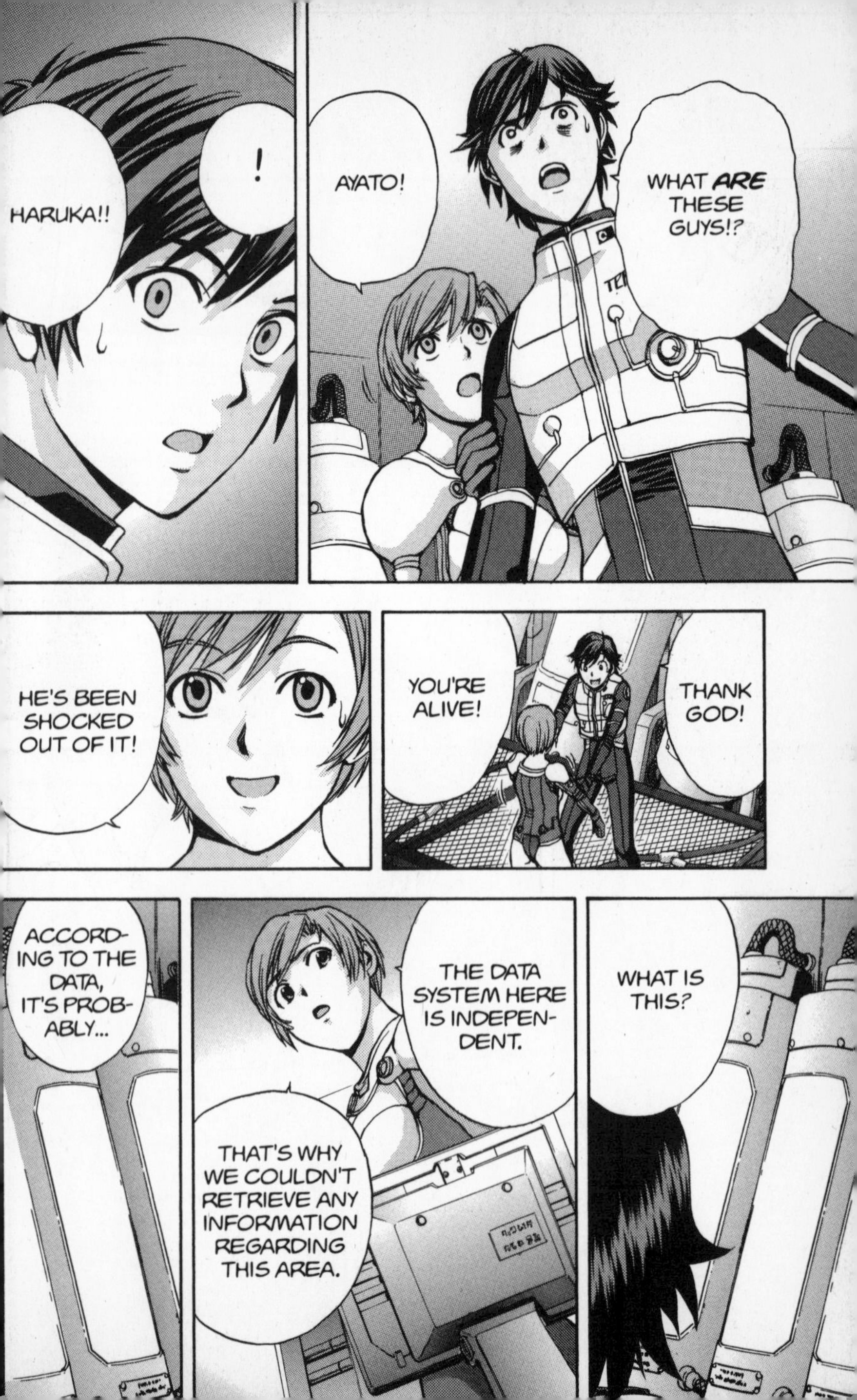
WHAT ARE THESE GUYS!?
AYATO!
!
HARUKA!!
THANK GOD!
YOU'RE ALIVE!
HE'S BEEN SHOCKED OUT OF IT!
WHAT IS THIS?
THE DATA SYSTEM HERE IS INDEPENDENT.
THAT'S WHY WE COULDN'T RETRIEVE ANY INFORMATION REGARDING THIS AREA.
ACCORDING TO THE DATA, IT'S PROBABLY...

...WHERE YOU WERE BORN, AYATO.

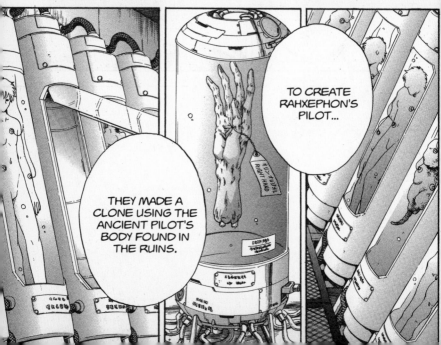

TO CREATE RAHXEPHON'S PILOT...

THEY MADE A CLONE USING THE ANCIENT PILOT'S BODY FOUND IN THE RUINS.

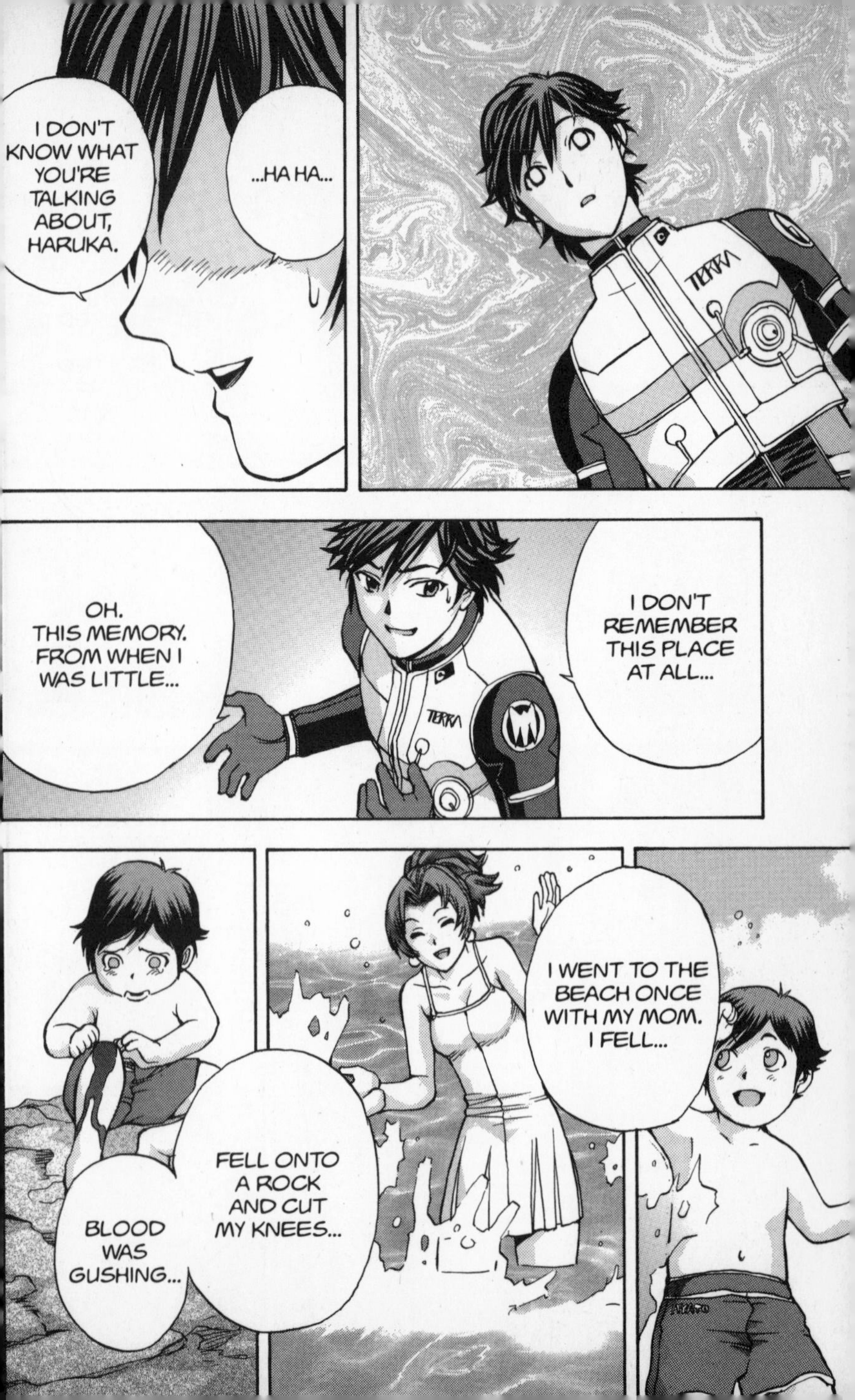
...HA HA...
I DON'T KNOW WHAT YOU'RE TALKING ABOUT, HARUKA.
I DON'T REMEMBER THIS PLACE AT ALL...
OH. THIS MEMORY. FROM WHEN I WAS LITTLE...
I WENT TO THE BEACH ONCE WITH MY MOM. I FELL...
FELL ONTO A ROCK AND CUT MY KNEES...
BLOOD WAS GUSHING...

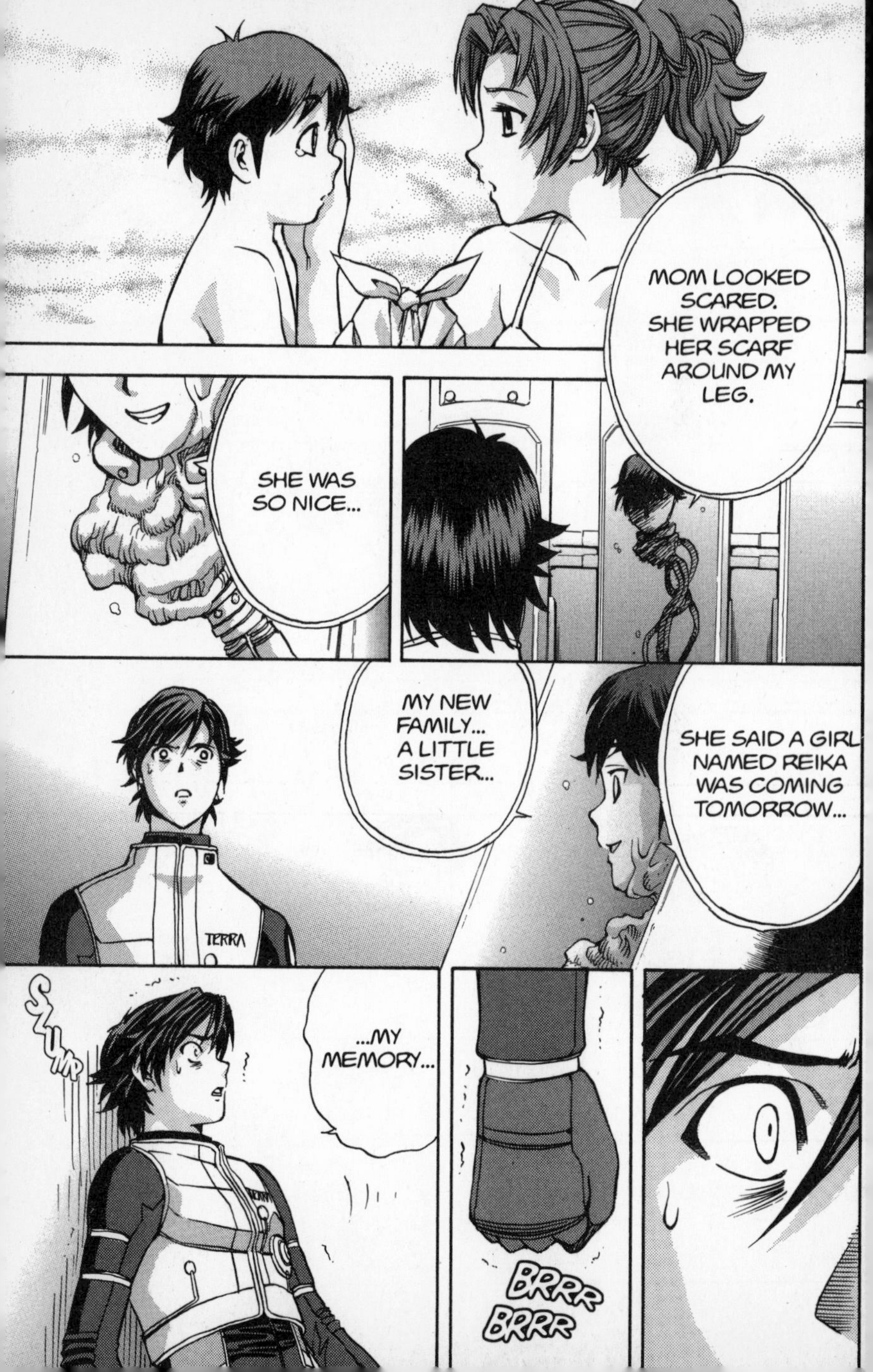
MOM LOOKED SCARED. SHE WRAPPED HER SCARF AROUND MY LEG.
SHE WAS SO NICE...
SHE SAID A GIRL NAMED REIKA WAS COMING TOMORROW...
MY NEW FAMILY... A LITTLE SISTER...
TERRA
BRRR BRRR
...MY MEMORY...
SLUMP

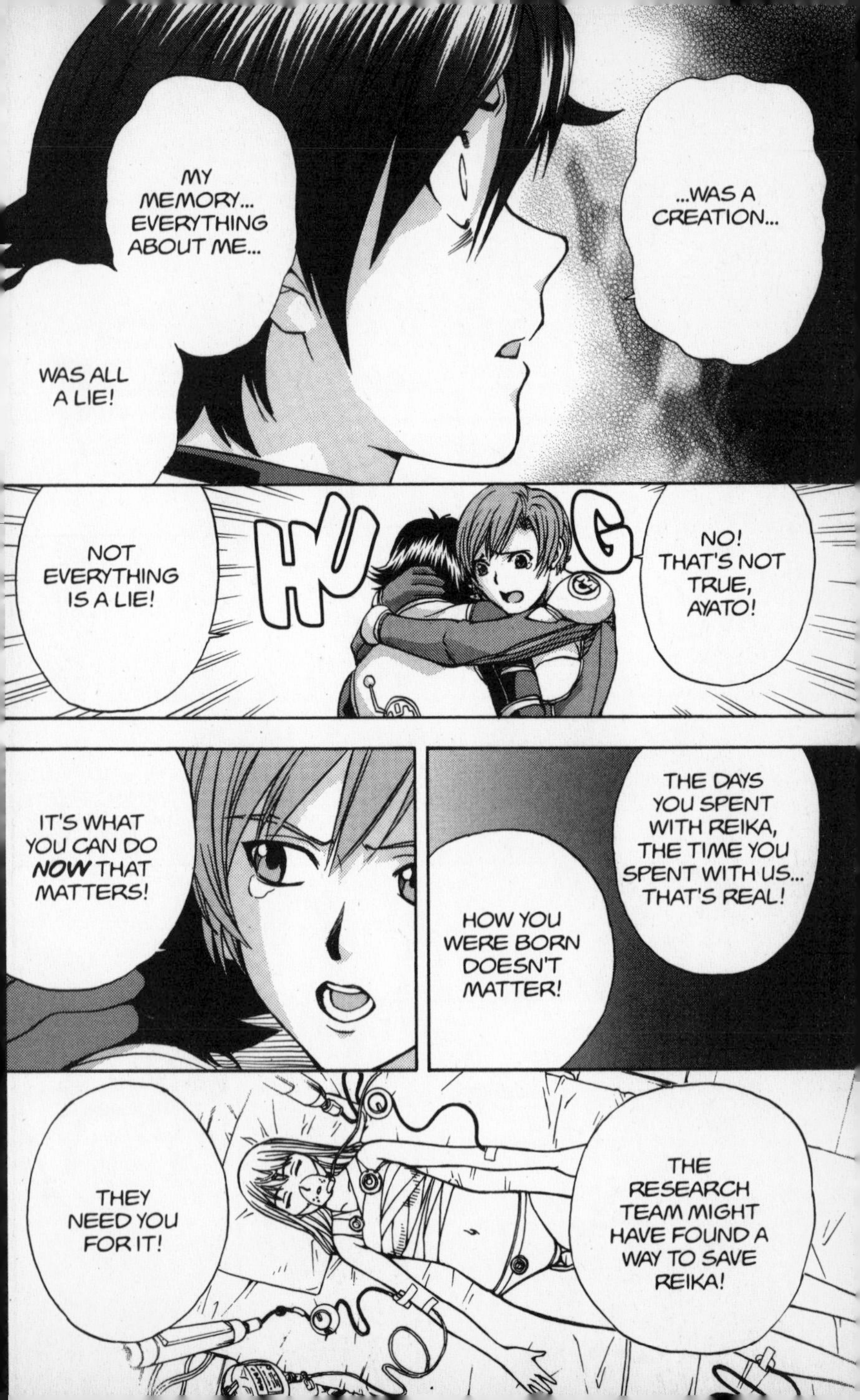
...WAS A CREATION...
MY MEMORY... EVERYTHING ABOUT ME...
WAS ALL A LIE!
NO! THAT'S NOT TRUE, AYATO!
HUG
NOT EVERYTHING IS A LIE!
THE DAYS YOU SPENT WITH REIKA, THE TIME YOU SPENT WITH US... THAT'S REAL!
HOW YOU WERE BORN DOESN'T MATTER!
IT'S WHAT YOU CAN DO *NOW* THAT MATTERS!
THE RESEARCH TEAM MIGHT HAVE FOUND A WAY TO SAVE REIKA!
THEY NEED YOU FOR IT!

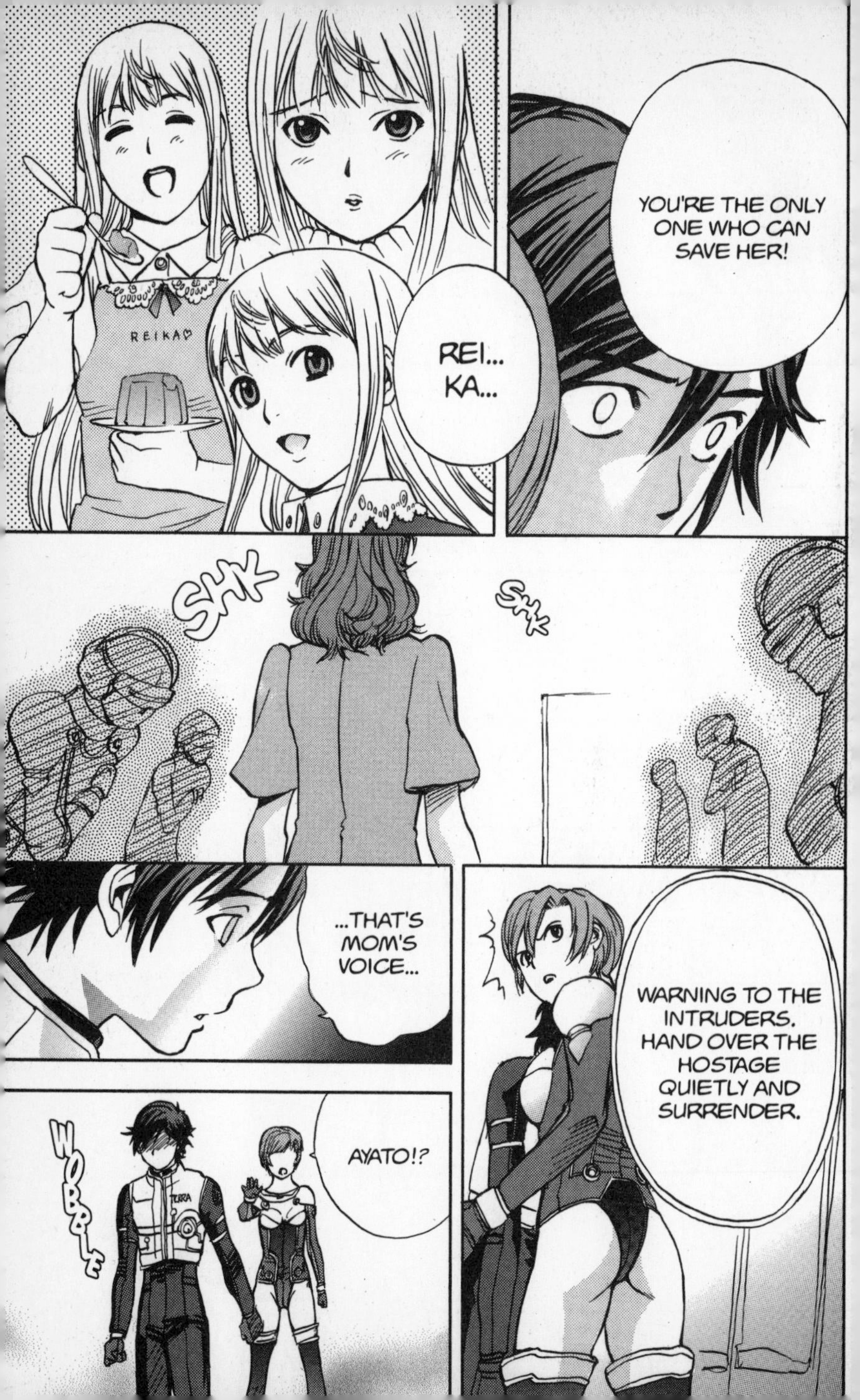
YOU'RE THE ONLY ONE WHO CAN SAVE HER!
REI... KA...
REIKA
SHK
SHK
WARNING TO THE INTRUDERS. HAND OVER THE HOSTAGE QUIETLY AND SURRENDER.
...THAT'S MOM'S VOICE...
AYATO!?
WOBBLE

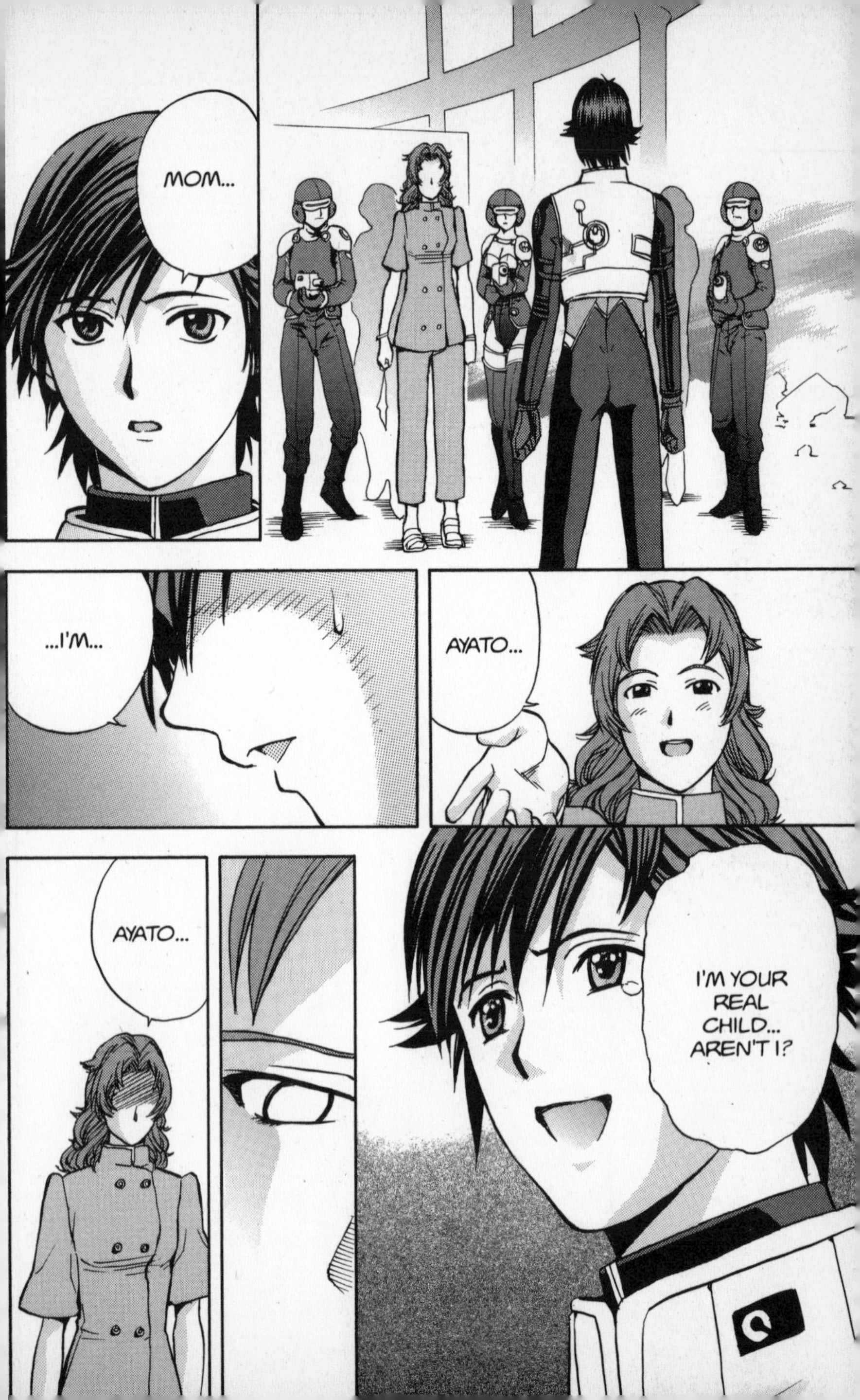
MOM...
AYATO...
...I'M...
I'M YOUR REAL CHILD... AREN'T I?
AYATO...

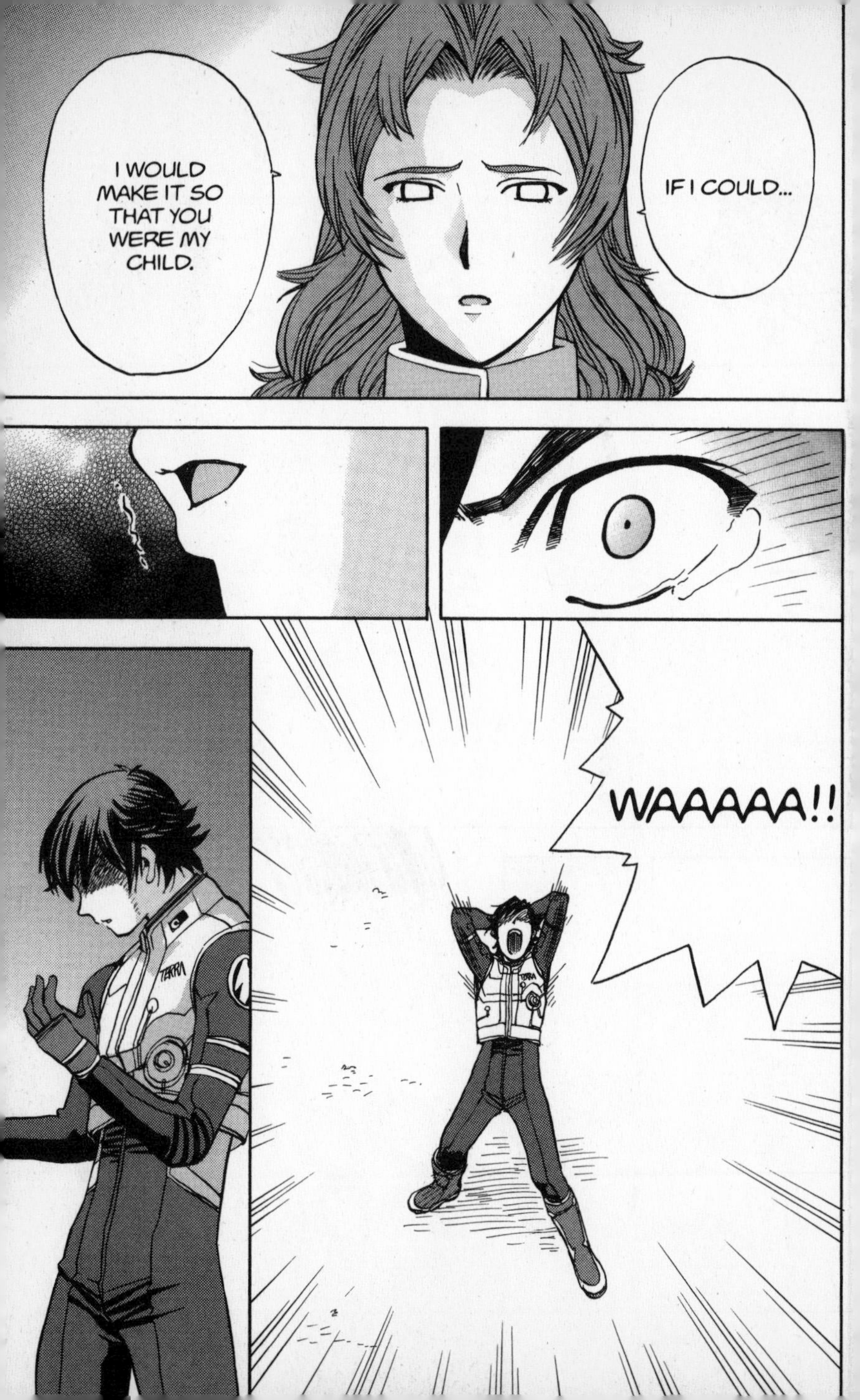
IF I COULD...
I WOULD MAKE IT SO THAT YOU WERE MY CHILD.
WAAAAAA!!

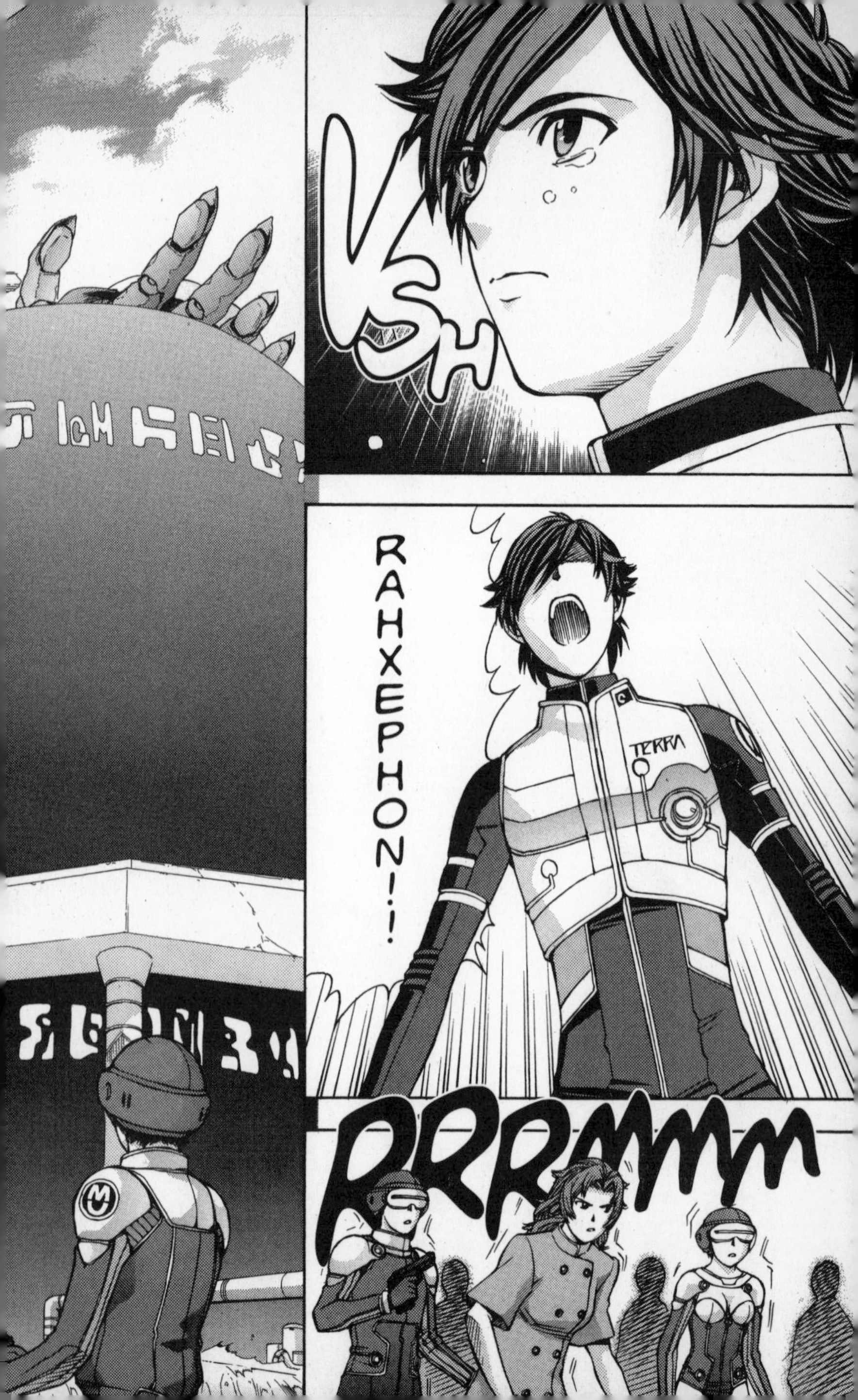
VSH
RAHXEPHON!!
TERRA
PRRMMM

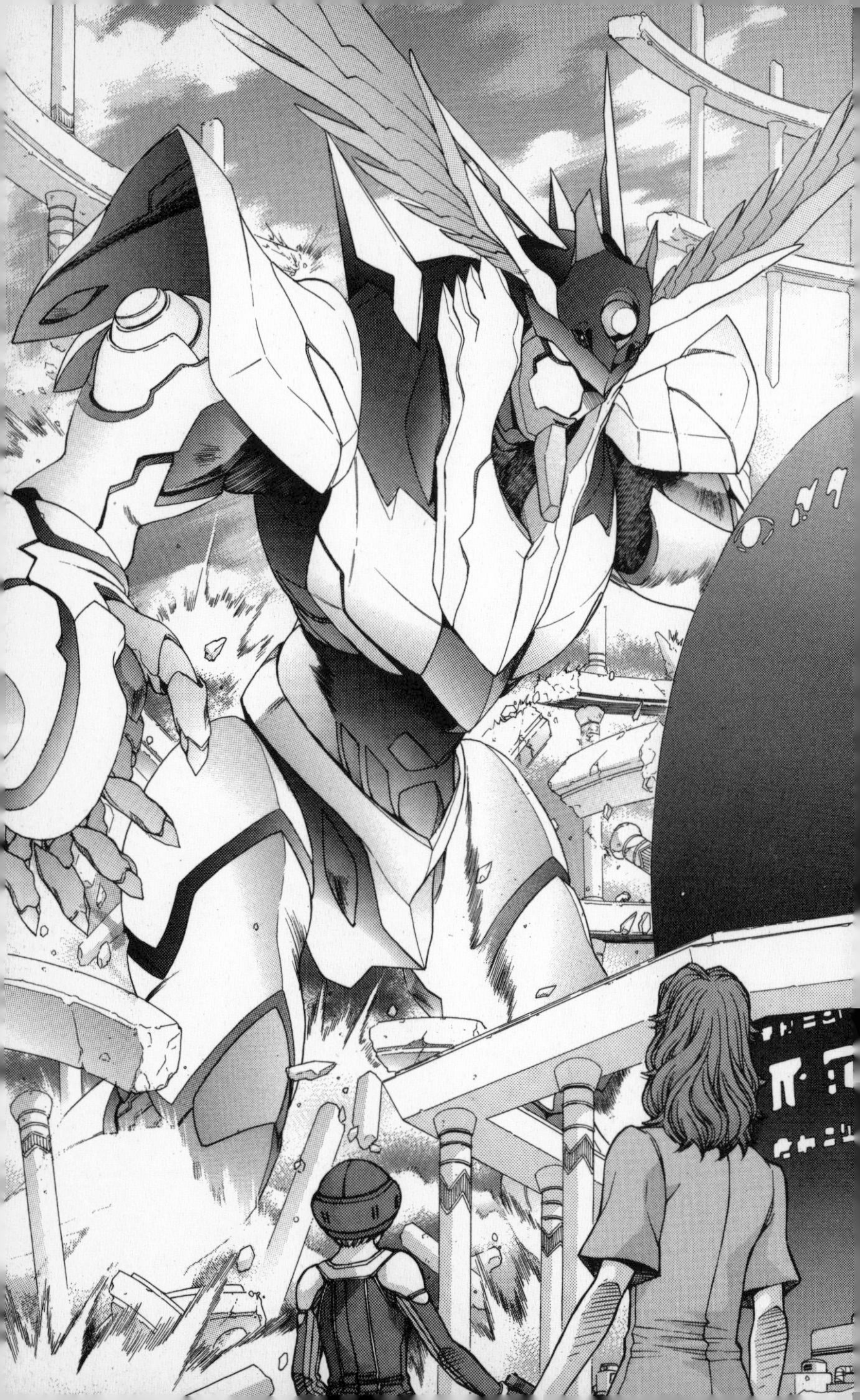

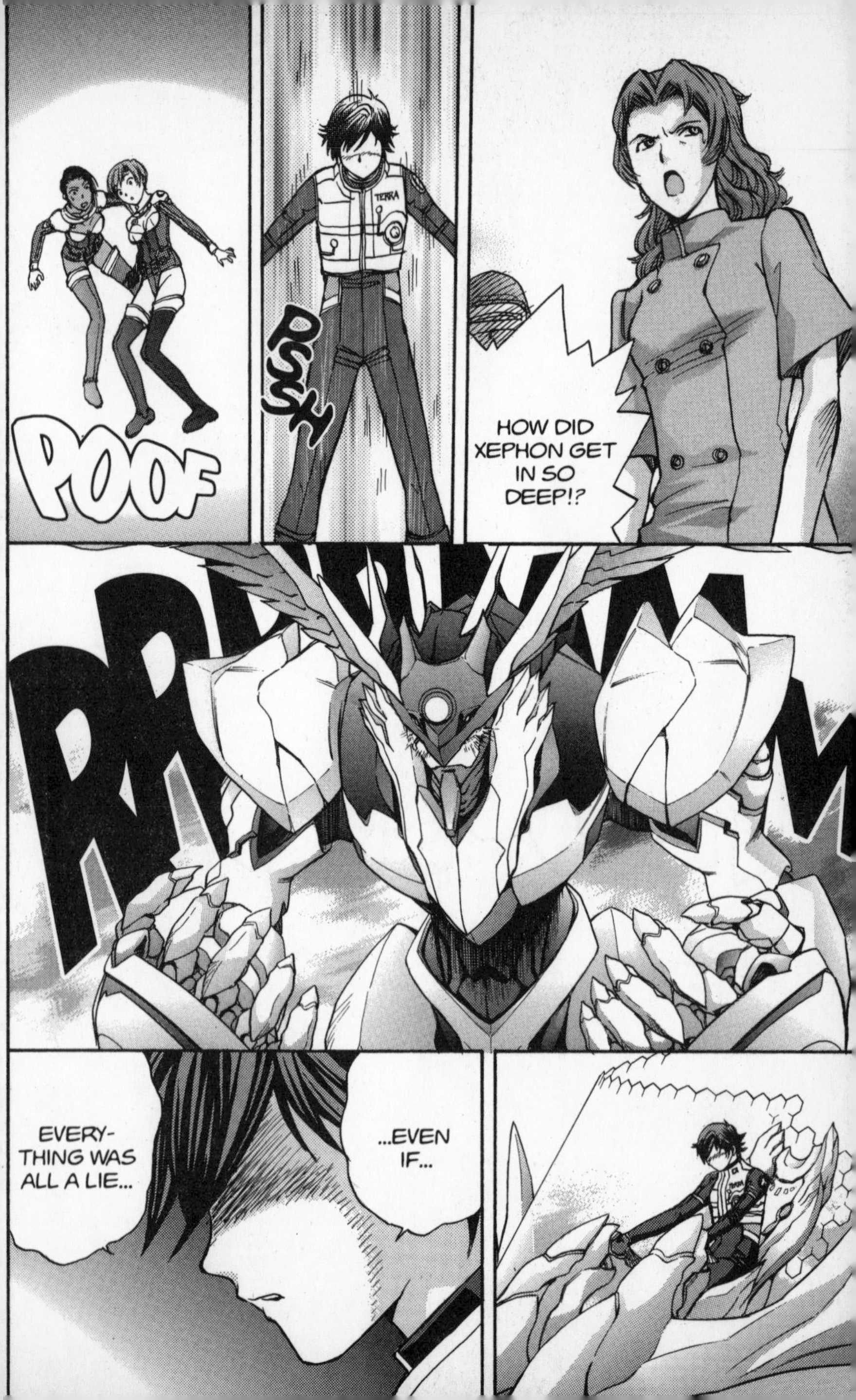
HOW DID XEPHON GET IN SO DEEP!?
PSSH
POOF
...EVEN IF...
EVERY-THING WAS ALL A LIE...

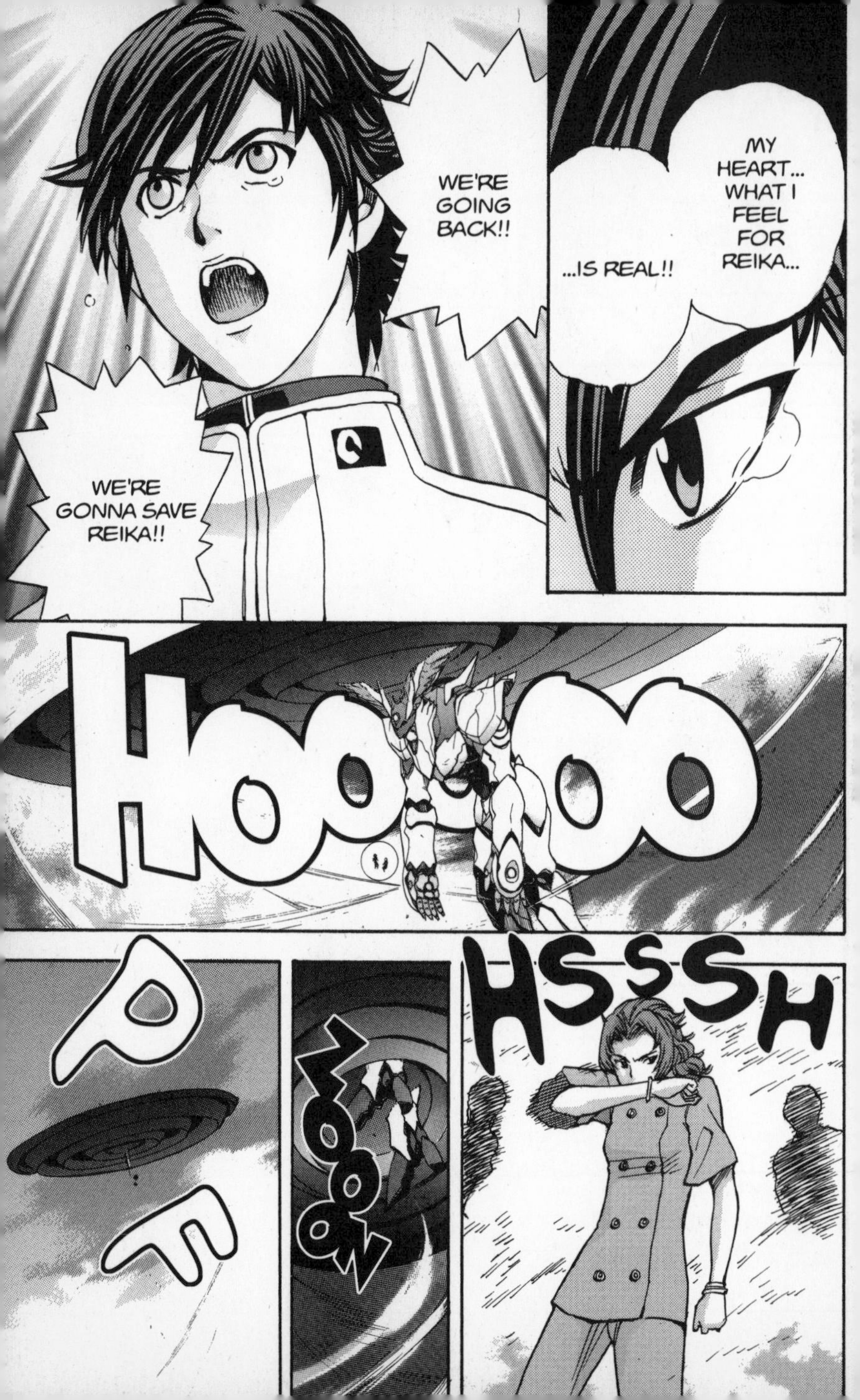
MY HEART... WHAT I FEEL FOR REIKA...
...IS REAL!!
WE'RE GOING BACK!!
WE'RE GONNA SAVE REIKA!!
HOOOOO
HSSSH
ZOOON
PF

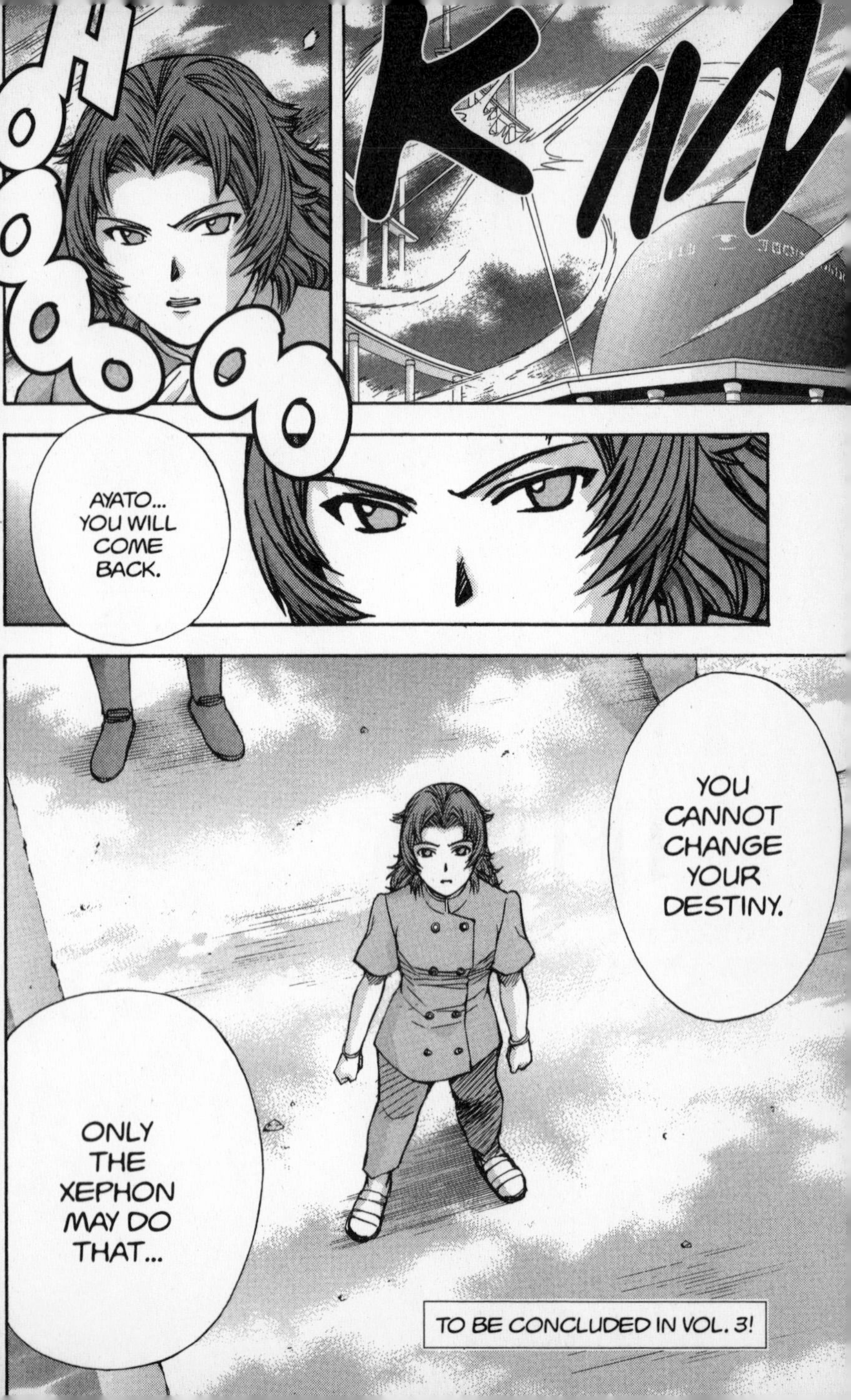
AYATO... YOU WILL COME BACK.
YOU CANNOT CHANGE YOUR DESTINY.
ONLY THE XEPHON MAY DO THAT...
TO BE CONCLUDED IN VOL. 3!

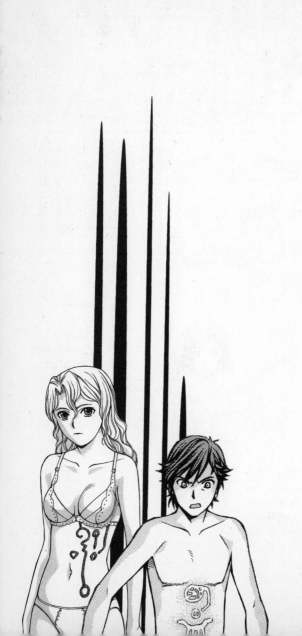

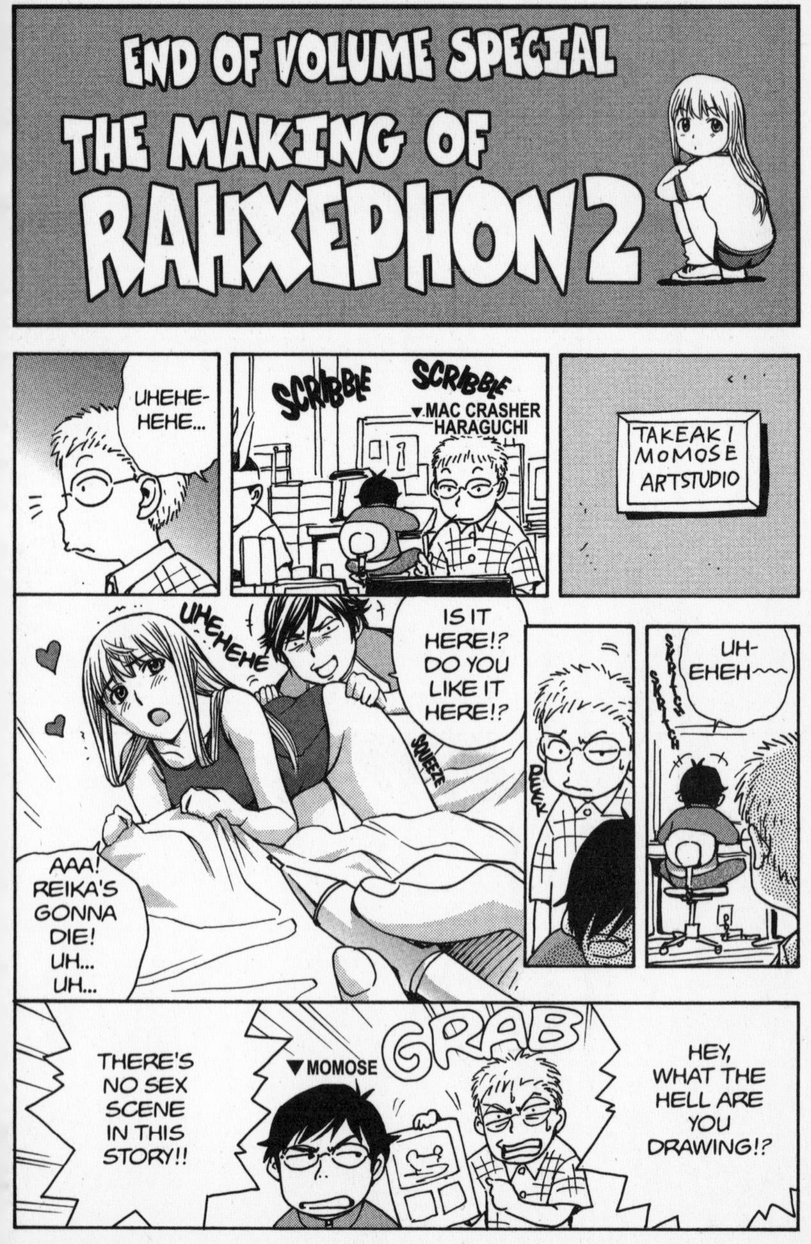
END OF VOLUME SPECIAL
THE MAKING OF RAHXEPHON 2
TAKEAKI MOMOSE ARTSTUDIO
SCRIBBLE
SCRIBBLE
▼MAC CRASHER HARAGUCHI
UHEHE-HEHE...
UH-EHEH~~~
SKRITCH
SKRITCH
UHEHEHE
IS IT HERE!? DO YOU LIKE IT HERE!?
SQUEEZE
AAA! REIKA'S GONNA DIE! UH... UH...
HEY, WHAT THE HELL ARE YOU DRAWING!?
GRAB
▼MOMOSE
THERE'S NO SEX SCENE IN THIS STORY!!

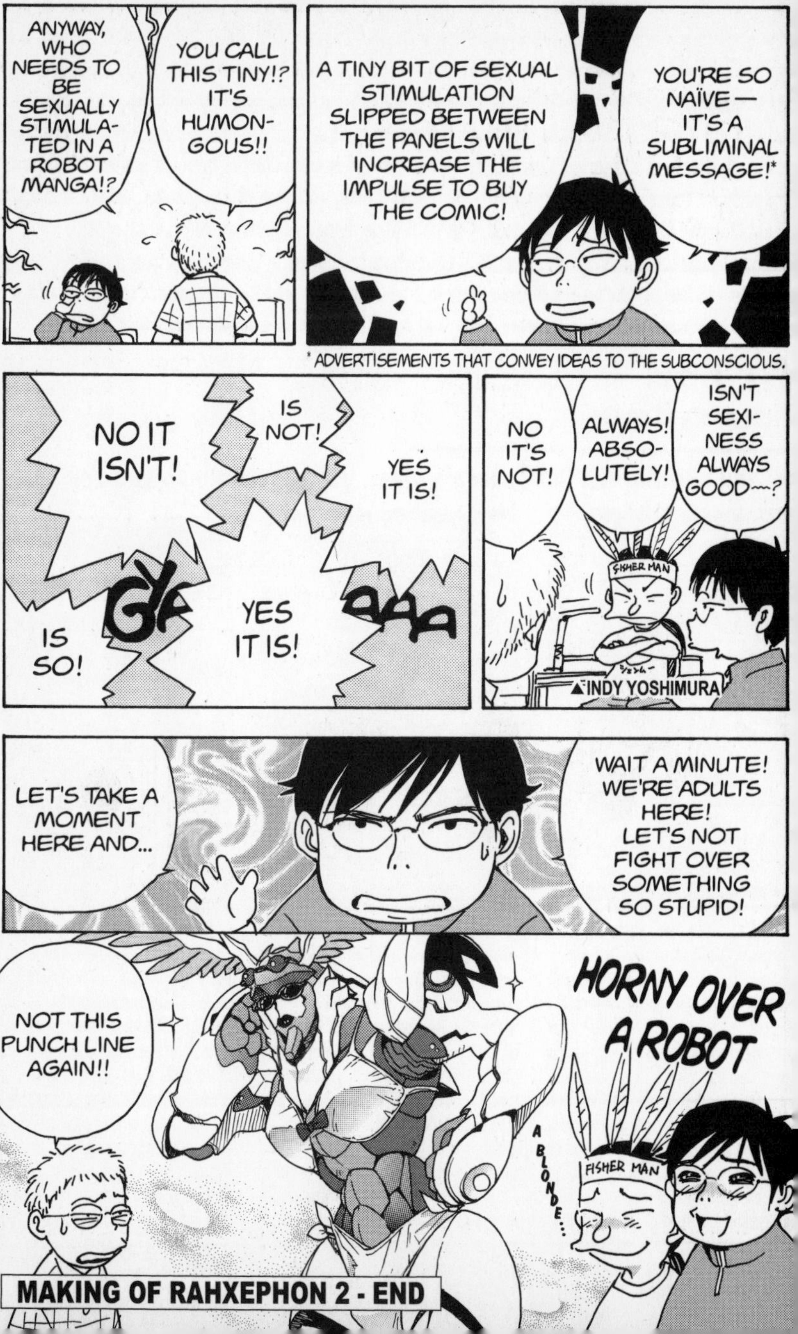
YOU'RE SO NAÏVE— IT'S A SUBLIMINAL MESSAGE!*
A TINY BIT OF SEXUAL STIMULATION SLIPPED BETWEEN THE PANELS WILL INCREASE THE IMPULSE TO BUY THE COMIC!
YOU CALL THIS TINY!? IT'S HUMONGOUS!!
ANYWAY, WHO NEEDS TO BE SEXUALLY STIMULATED IN A ROBOT MANGA!?
* ADVERTISEMENTS THAT CONVEY IDEAS TO THE SUBCONSCIOUS.
ISN'T SEXINESS ALWAYS GOOD~?
ALWAYS! ABSOLUTELY!
NO IT'S NOT!
FISHER MAN
▲INDY YOSHIMURA
YES IT IS!
IS NOT!
NO IT ISN'T!
AAA
YES IT IS!
GYA
IS SO!
WAIT A MINUTE! WE'RE ADULTS HERE! LET'S NOT FIGHT OVER SOMETHING SO STUPID!
LET'S TAKE A MOMENT HERE AND...
HORNY OVER A ROBOT
FISHER MAN
A BLONDE...
NOT THIS PUNCH LINE AGAIN!!
MAKING OF RAHXEPHON 2 - END

Two volumes down, one to go. Life just gets more and more hectic for poor Ayato, and it seems like it's all accelerating. Last year when I saw the first volume of the *RahXephon* anime, the show struck me ; being nothing more than another *Evangelion*-manque. You know the kind, some reluctant 14-year-old boy girl finds themselves at the helm of a giant robot (usually at their parents behest), and must fight to either: save mankind from space invaders; b) save just Tokyo from space invaders; or c) use the experience of loting a giant robot as a catalyst for personal growth, because that's really all that's important in the end. ; I watched more of the series, I really started to enjoy the nuances Yutaka Izubuchi infused his giant robot ıow with. As was the case with Yoshiyuki Sadamoto's manga version of *Evangelion*, Yutaka Izubuchi and ıkeaki Momose are now able, vis-à-vis this three volume manga adaptation, to experiment with other story ıeas and character conflicts they either didn't have time to address in the anime, or just never got around to ıtting in. It's fun to take an established story in a new direction, and it's a testament to the old adage that ıery end is just another new beginning. Well, that does it for now. See all you mecha fans in volume 3!

Kit Fox

ditor of *RahXephon*

id you like *RahXephon*? Here's what VIZ recommends you try next:

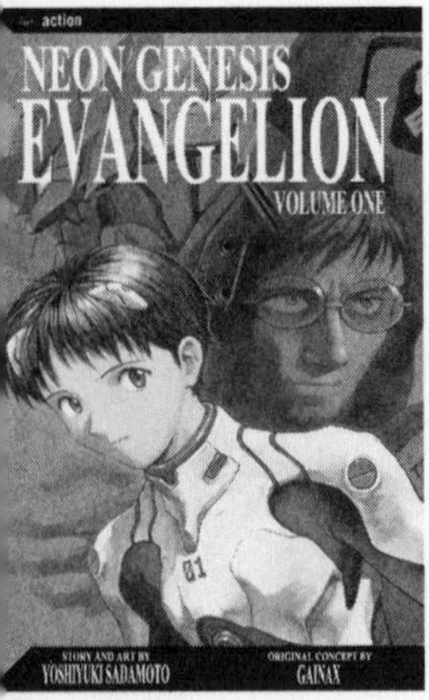

action
NEON GENESIS EVANGELION
VOLUME ONE
STORY AND ART BY YOSHIYUKI SADAMOTO
ORIGINAL CONCEPT BY GAINAX

Evangelion vol. 1

ıaracter designer extraordinaire Yoshiyuki ıdamoto—whose work has appeared in such ıimated fan favorites as *Nadia-Secret of ıue Water* and most recently *FLCL*—adapts *ıeon Genesis Evangelion*, the most ıntroversial and heavily influential anime of ıe 1990s, into an equally awe-inspiring ıanga. Shinji Ikari must help Nerv fend off ıe Angels, adapt to a new life with his ıtranged father, and come to grips with ıthing more than mankind's ultimate fate. All ıis and more rests on the shoulders of a ıung man who isn't even old enough to drive.

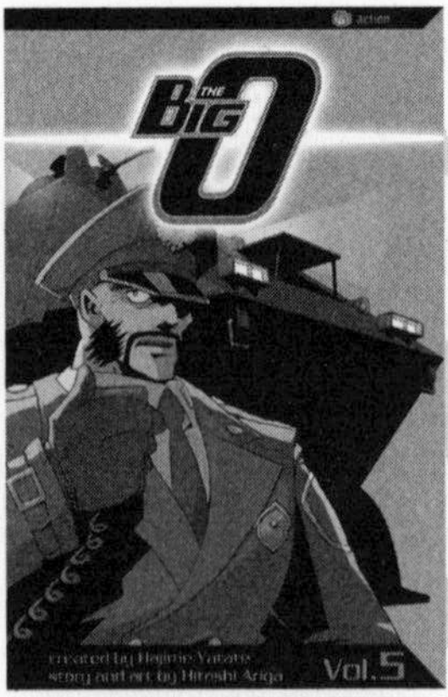

action
THE BIG O
Vol.5

The Big O vol. 5

Forty years ago the citizenry of Paradigm City all had their memories erased and were forced to begin their lives anew. Enter Roger Smith, a "negotiator" for anyone and everyone—criminals and citizens alike—who, along with a giant robot dubbed "the Big O," dishes out action-infused justice. From the folks who brought us *Gundam Wing* comes *The Big O*, a manga with giant robot action on a gargantuan scale.

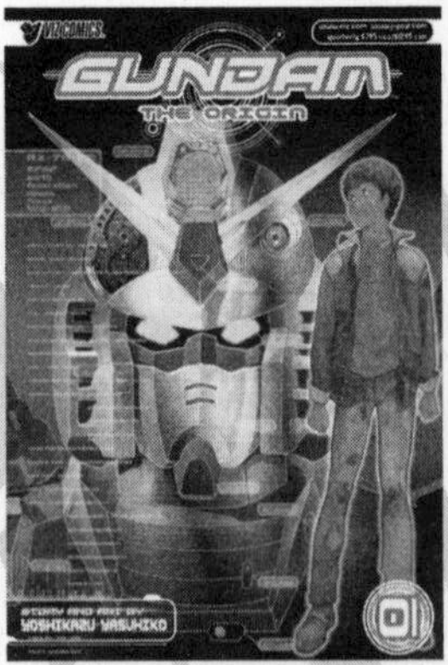

VIZ COMICS
GUNDAM
THE ORIGIN
YOSHIKAZU YASUHIKO
01

Gundam: The Origin vol. 1

Every genre has its forbearers, and where would the world of giant robots be without *Mobile Suit Gundam*? One of the most popular and prolific anime of all time, *Gundam*'s influence can be found in nearly every mecha-infused show of the last thirty years. Yoshikazu Yasuhiko, the original character designer and animation director for that landmark series injects new life into the *Gundam* universe with his breathtaking watercolors and adept storytelling.

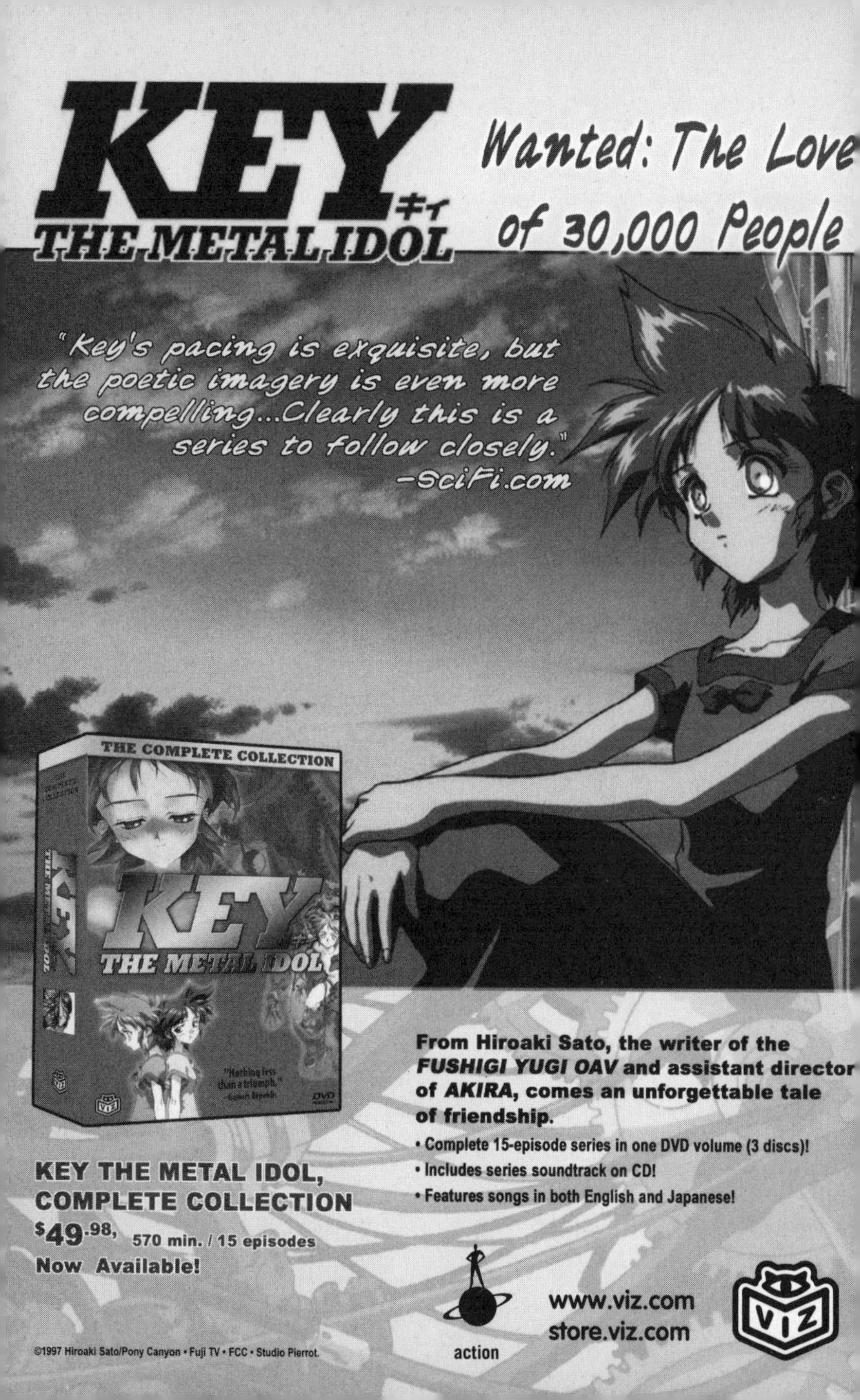
KEY キィ THE METAL IDOL
Wanted: The Love of 30,000 People
"Key's pacing is exquisite, but the poetic imagery is even more compelling...Clearly this is a series to follow closely." —SciFi.com
THE COMPLETE COLLECTION
KEY キィ THE METAL IDOL
From Hiroaki Sato, the writer of the FUSHIGI YUGI OAV and assistant director of AKIRA, comes an unforgettable tale of friendship.
• Complete 15-episode series in one DVD volume (3 discs)!
• Includes series soundtrack on CD!
• Features songs in both English and Japanese!
KEY THE METAL IDOL, COMPLETE COLLECTION
$49.98, 570 min. / 15 episodes
Now Available!
action
www.viz.com
store.viz.com
VIZ
©1997 Hiroaki Sato/Pony Canyon • Fuji TV • FCC • Studio Pierrot.

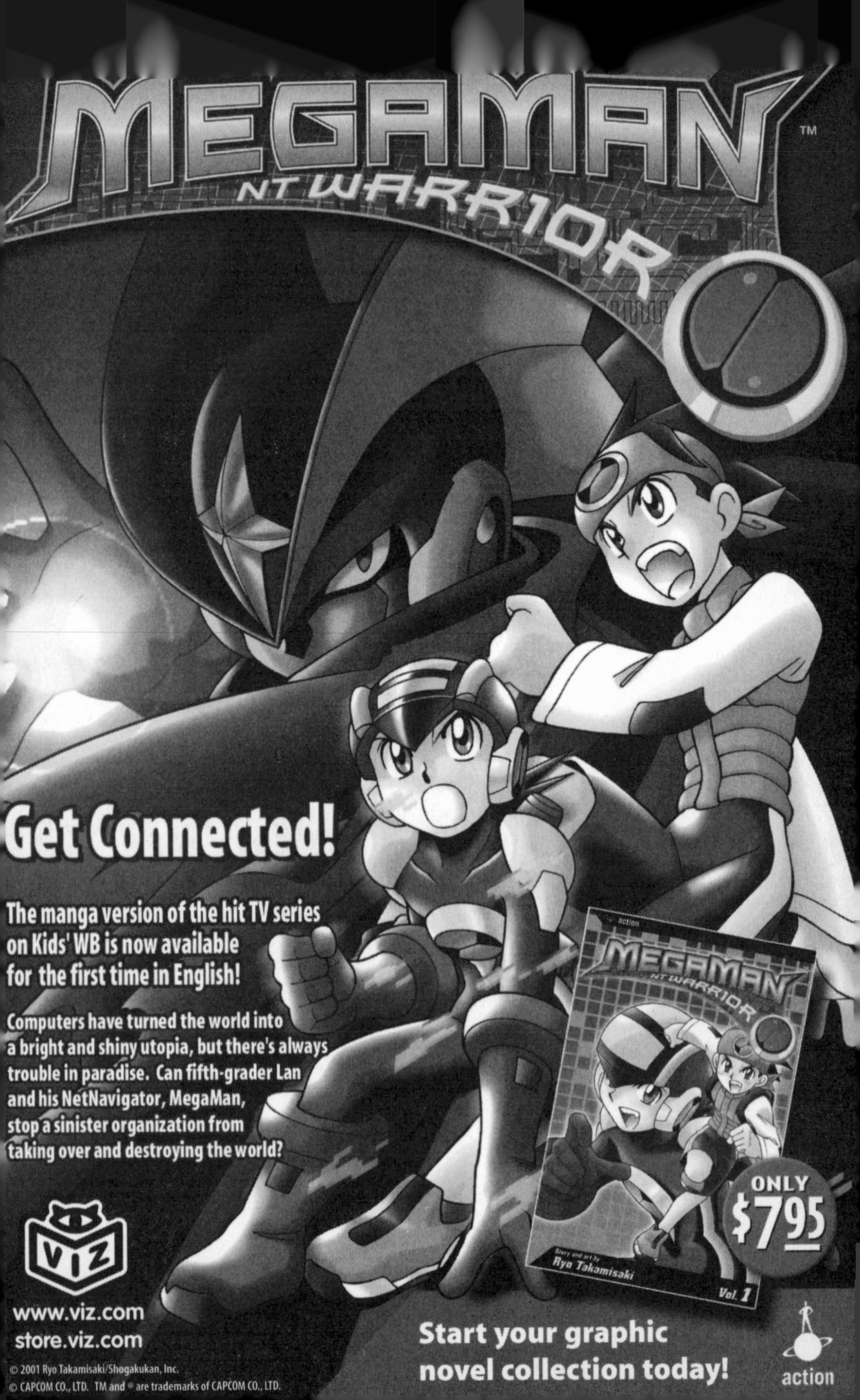
MEGAMAN™
NT WARRIOR
Get Connected!
The manga version of the hit TV series on Kids' WB is now available for the first time in English!
Computers have turned the world into a bright and shiny utopia, but there's always trouble in paradise. Can fifth-grader Lan and his NetNavigator, MegaMan, stop a sinister organization from taking over and destroying the world?
MEGAMAN NT WARRIOR
Ryo Takamisaki
Vol. 1
ONLY $7.95
VIZ
www.viz.com
store.viz.com
Start your graphic novel collection today!
action
© 2001 Ryo Takamisaki/Shogakukan, Inc.
© CAPCOM CO., LTD. TM and ® are trademarks of CAPCOM CO., LTD.

COMPLETE OUR SURVEY AND LET US KNOW WHAT YOU THINK!

☐ Please do NOT send me information about VIZ products, news and events, special offers, or other information.

☐ Please do NOT send me information from VIZ's trusted business partners.

Name: _____

Address: _____

City: _____ **State:** _____ **Zip:** _____

E-mail: _____

☐ Male ☐ Female **Date of Birth** (mm/dd/yyyy): ___ / ___ / ___ (Under 13? Parental consent required)

What race/ethnicity do you consider yourself? (please check one)

☐ Asian/Pacific Islander ☐ Black/African American ☐ Hispanic/Latino

☐ Native American/Alaskan Native ☐ White/Caucasian ☐ Other: _____

What VIZ product did you purchase? (check all that apply and indicate title purchased)

☐ DVD/VHS _____

☐ Graphic Novel _____

☐ Magazines _____

☐ Merchandise _____

Reason for purchase: (check all that apply)

☐ Special offer ☐ Favorite title ☐ Gift

☐ Recommendation ☐ Other _____

Where did you make your purchase? (please check one)

☐ Comic store ☐ Bookstore ☐ Mass/Grocery Store

☐ Newsstand ☐ Video/Video Game Store ☐ Other: _____

☐ Online (site: _____)

What other VIZ properties have you purchased/own? _____

_____

How many anime and/or manga titles have you purchased in the last year? How many were VIZ titles? (please check one from each column)

ANIME
- ☐ None
- ☐ 1-4
- ☐ 5-10
- ☐ 11+

MANGA
- ☐ None
- ☐ 1-4
- ☐ 5-10
- ☐ 11+

VIZ
- ☐ None
- ☐ 1-4
- ☐ 5-10
- ☐ 11+

I find the pricing of VIZ products to be: (please check one)

☐ Cheap ☐ Reasonable ☐ Expensive

What genre of manga and anime would you like to see from VIZ? (please check two)

- ☐ Adventure
- ☐ Comic Strip
- ☐ Science Fiction
- ☐ Fighting
- ☐ Horror
- ☐ Romance
- ☐ Fantasy
- ☐ Sports

What do you think of VIZ's new look?

☐ Love It ☐ It's OK ☐ Hate It ☐ Didn't Notice ☐ No Opinion

Which do you prefer? (please check one)

- ☐ Reading right-to-left
- ☐ Reading left-to-right

Which do you prefer? (please check one)

- ☐ Sound effects in English
- ☐ Sound effects in Japanese with English captions
- ☐ Sound effects in Japanese only with a glossary at the back

THANK YOU! Please send the completed form to:

NJW Research
42 Catharine St.
Poughkeepsie, NY 12601

All information provided will be used for internal purposes only. We promise not to sell or otherwise divulge your information.